Organizing Library Collections

Organizing Library Collections

Theory and Practice

Gretchen L. Hoffman

ROWMAN & LITTLEFIELD
Lanham • Boulder • New York • London

Executive Editor: Charles Harmon
Assistant Editor: Michael Tan
Production Editor: Lara Hahn
Cover Designer: Sarah Marizan

Credits and acknowledgments of sources for material or information used with permission appear on the appropriate page within the text.

Published by Rowman & Littlefield
An imprint of The Rowman & Littlefield Publishing Group, Inc.
4501 Forbes Boulevard, Suite 200, Lanham, Maryland 20706
www.rowman.com

6 Tinworth Street, London, SE11 5AL, United Kingdom

British Library Cataloguing in Publication Information Available

Library of Congress Cataloging-in-Publication Data

Names: Hoffman, Gretchen L., author.
Title: Organizing library collections : theory and practice / Gretchen L. Hoffman.
Description: Lanham : Rowman & Littlefield, [2019] | Includes bibliographical references and index.
Identifiers: LCCN 2019008872 (print) | LCCN 2019019980 (ebook) | ISBN 9781538108529 (Electronic) | ISBN 9781538108505 (cloth) | ISBN 9781538108512 (pbk.)
Subjects: LCSH: Cataloging. | Classification. | Information organization.
Classification: LCC Z693 (ebook) | LCC Z693 .H637 2019 (print) | DDC 025—dc23 LC record available at https://lccn.loc.gov/2019008872

To my parents, whom I lost far too soon.

Contents

Figures and Tables

FIGURES

TABLES

Acronyms

AACR: Anglo-American Cataloguing Rules
AACR1: Anglo-American Cataloguing Rules, First Edition
AACR2: Anglo-American Cataloguing Rules, Second Edition
AAT: Art & Architecture Thesaurus
ALA: American Library Association
ALCTS: Association for Library Collections & Technical Services (ALA)
BIBCO: Monographic Bibliographic Record Cooperative Program
BIBFRAME: Bibliographic Framework Initiative
BISAC: Book Industry Standards and Communications
CaMMS: Cataloging and Metadata Management Section (ALA ALCTS)
CCO: Cataloging Cultural Objects
CONSER: Cooperative Online Serials Program
CSM: Classification and Shelflisting Manual (LCC)
CSS: Cascading Style Sheets
DACS: Describing Archives: A Content Standard
DC: Dublin Core
DCMI: Dublin Core Metadata Initiative
DDC: Dewey Decimal Classification
EAD: Encoded Archival Description
FAST: Faceted Application of Subject Terminology
FDLP: Federal Depository Library Program
FRAD: Functional Requirements for Authority Data
FRBR: Functional Requirements for Bibliographic Records
FRSAD: Functional Requirements for Subject Authority Data
GSAFD: Guidelines on Subject Access to Individual Works of Fiction, Drama, Etc.
HTML: Hypertext Markup Language
HTTP: Hypertext Transfer Protocol
IFLA: International Federation of Library Associations and Institutions
IRI: Internationalized Resource Identifier
ISBD: International Standard Bibliographic Description

ISBN: International Standard Bibliographic Number
ISNI: International Standard Name Identifier
ISO: International Organization for Standardization
ISSN: International Standard Serial Number
LC: Library of Congress
LC-PCC PS: Library of Congress-Program for Cooperative Cataloging Policy Statements
LCC: Library of Congress Classification
LCCN: Library of Congress Control Number
LCDGT: Library of Congress Demographic Group Terms
LCGFT: Library of Congress Genre/Form Terms for Library and Archival Materials
LCMPT: Library of Congress Medium of Performance Thesaurus for Music
LCNAF: Library of Congress National Authority File
LCSH: Library of Congress Subject Headings
LITA: Library and Information Technology Association
LRM: IFLA Library Reference Model
MADS: Metadata Authority Description Schema
MARC: Machine-Readable Cataloging
MeSH: Medical Subject Headings
MODS: Metadata Object Description Schema
NACO: Name Authority Cooperative Program
NAF: National Authority File (Library of Congress)
NASIG: North American Serials Interest Group
NISO: National Information Standards Organization
NLM: National Library of Medicine
OCLC: Company name. Formerly called: Online Computer Library Center
OLAC: Online Audiovisual Catalogers
OPAC: Online Public Access Catalog
PCC: Program for Cooperative Cataloging
RBMS: Rare Books and Manuscripts Section
RDA: Resource Description and Access
RDF: Resource Description Framework
SACO: Subject Authority Cooperative Program
SGML: Standard Generalized Markup Language
SHM: Subject Headings Manual (LCSH)
SSH: Sears List of Subject Headings
SuDocs: Superintendent of Documents Classification
TEI: Text Encoding Initiative
TGM: Thesaurus for Graphic Materials
URI: Uniform Resource Identifier
URL: Uniform Resource Locator
VIAF: Virtual International Authority File
VRA: Visual Resources Association
W3C: World Wide Web Consortium
WEMI: Work—Expression—Manifestation—Item (FRBR)
XML: Extensible Markup Language

Preface

In the not too distant past, libraries had physical collections full of books, serials, and physical media. Today, libraries still hold physical collections, but there has been an explosion of electronic materials collected in libraries, and libraries are collecting large packages of e-books, e-serials, and other e-content. Even the smallest library provides access to a large amount of e-content it would not have collected in the past. There is also much digital content being created in libraries. Academic libraries are building institutional repositories that preserve the intellectual output of colleges and universities. Some academic and public libraries are digitizing items in special collections or archives and making them available as digital collections. Library collections are growing and changing, and library users have access to more library materials than they ever have before.

The organization of library collections is changing, too. Libraries used to have cataloging units full of professional and paraprofessional catalogers who carefully cataloged physical library collections. Today, there is a wide variety of cataloging and metadata practices, and each library has different policies and procedures. Traditional cataloging is still performed in all libraries, but to catalog and manage electronic resources, libraries are purchasing large files of bibliographic records from vendors and just batch loading them "as is" into library catalogs. Some libraries also perform metadata work to describe and provide access to digital collections. In addition to changes in cataloging and metadata practice, it seems as if practice in libraries is continually drifting apart. Larger libraries may have the financial resources to perform metadata projects, create digital collections, participate in cataloging and metadata initiatives, and experiment with new technologies. It is a different story for smaller libraries, which may be struggling to get books on the shelves because they lack the resources to do anything beyond basic cataloging.

There are big changes ahead in cataloging theory and standards as well. There are new models and statements of principles, and cataloging standards seem to be changing constantly. *Resource Description and Access* (RDA), the descriptive cataloging standard, was implemented in libraries starting in 2013, and some libraries have not yet transitioned. However, RDA is already being revised significantly to incorporate the new *IFLA Library Reference Model*, which was published in 2017. A revised RDA may change how cataloging is performed in libraries. Linked open data has the potential to change how libraries make their collections available to users by putting library data on the web. Linked data requires a whole new way of organizing library collections, and the cataloging and metadata field is getting ready. A whirlwind of change seems to be on its way.

The theory and practice of organizing library collections is not as straightforward or as streamlined as it may seem, and I want this book to not only explain theory and practice but also show it in the context of all this change. I wrote this book for beginning library and information science students to help them understand the theory and practice behind organizing library collections. I also wrote this book for anyone interested in learning why and how libraries organize their collections. Instead of a book that focuses just on theory or a book that focuses just on practice, I want this book to show how theory and practice work together.

The first half of this book focuses on cataloging and metadata theory, which can be complex. I try to introduce theory in a clear, straightforward, and understandable way. I want students and readers to walk away knowing why libraries organize their collections and understanding the theory that supports cataloging and metadata practice. I also want students and readers to understand the major standards used to organize library collections in different types of libraries. I hope this book sparks interest and serves as a starting point for deeper explorations in the cataloging and metadata field.

The second half of this book explores cataloging and metadata practice in libraries. I try to show the wide variety of ways libraries organize their collections and how cataloging and metadata work is done in different types of libraries. I want students and readers to walk away with an understanding of how all types of libraries organize their collections. I also try to address many types of work performed to organize library collections, not just cataloging. Cataloging is performed in all libraries, and it is discussed quite a bit in the book. Yet I also discuss metadata work, a newer type of work performed in some libraries to provide access to digital collections, and also serials and government publications. There are many ways to organize library collections, and I hope to open eyes and broaden views about how it is done.

HOW TO USE THIS BOOK

Learning about the organization of library collections can be tough. This is one area of librarianship that is new to most students. There are many models and standards as well as a new vocabulary and a million acronyms. It can be confusing, no doubt about it. If you find yourself lost or overwhelmed, then I suggest you visit a library and walk the stacks, or go online and look at bibliographic records in a library catalog or metadata records in a digital collection. Use them as a touchstone to bring you back to reality. Sometimes it helps to see the end product to understand the theory and practice behind it.

One note about the vocabulary used in the book. I use *digital* or *electronic* to refer to all types of digital materials collected in libraries. Both terms are used in the field. I use the words *items* or *materials* when describing things in library collections. I also use *resources*, but I try to qualify this when I can, for example, *library resources* or *electronic resources*. It is a word used in cataloging to refer to all types of materials collected in libraries, but I have found the word can be confusing for beginning students because it means many things in different contexts. I use the word *users* to refer to the people who use libraries. I use *catalogers* to refer to any type of cataloger, both professional and paraprofessional. I use *metadata specialists* to refer to anyone who works with digital collections, both professional and paraprofessional. I use the word *metadata* in the singular.

In addition, there are many acronyms used in this book because there are many standard acronyms used in the cataloging and metadata field. I know that it can be frustrating to read a bunch of letters, but it was impractical to spell out everything at all times. I tried to be as clear as possible when using acronyms, but sometimes they are unavoidable. To help, I added a list of acronyms on page xv. Please consult this list if you come across an acronym you do not understand. I hope this list is helpful.

I wrote this book to support beginning cataloging and classification courses as well as beginning organization of information courses. I have included several questions at the end of each chapter to spark discussion. They can be used in face-to-face courses or online courses, in small-group or large-group discussions. I also include several class activities that reinforce concepts in each chapter. The activities range from group activities to short assignments to more formal assessments.

I have always found the theory and practice of organizing library collections immensely challenging and fun, like a giant puzzle that does not fit together perfectly. I hope this comes through in the book. If you remember just one thing after reading this book, remember this: Libraries organize their collections to help people.

Acknowledgments

Thanks to my family, friends, and colleagues who supported me as I wrote this book. I could not have finished this book without you. A special thank-you to Travis Schulz. Your love and support made all the difference. You kept me going.

I would like to acknowledge the International Federation of Library Associations and Institutions (IFLA). I used two images from their publications in chapter 3. I contacted them for permission but never received a response.

Part I

THEORY OF ORGANIZING LIBRARY COLLECTIONS

.

1

Purpose and History of Organizing Library Collections

Organization is infused into all aspects of our everyday lives. It helps us make sense of the world and function in the world. The purpose of organization is to create a "functioning whole,"[1] a system whose various parts work together to meet certain goals. Organization is needed everywhere, and systems of organization are created to help us in various ways. A hospital is organized to facilitate the treatment of patients. A retail store is organized to facilitate purchases. A kitchen is organized to facilitate the preparation of food. Individuals and groups organize, too. A person may organize closets, photos, bookshelves, or files to quickly and easily find items. Workplaces organize documents and other items to facilitate work, to make money, and to follow government regulations.

Libraries are organized to help people. The purpose of a library is to serve its community and to provide programs and services that meet the educational, informational, and entertainment needs of the people it serves.[2] According to the American Library Association (ALA), there are almost 117,000 libraries in the United States,[3] each serving a specific community, and each with a specific mission. There are four main types of libraries: academic libraries, which serve students, faculty, and staff in colleges and universities; public libraries, which serve the general public in specific towns, cities, or counties; school libraries, which serve students, teachers, and staff in elementary, middle, and high schools; and special libraries, which serve specialized clientele in a specific environment, such as a law firm, corporation, or government agency.

Libraries have collections. A library offers its community and its users a collection of materials in a variety of formats, and a library is inseparable from its collection. It does not matter if a library collects only physical materials or only electronic materials available online. A library is a library if it has a collection. A library collection, however, is not developed in a vacuum. Materials are purposefully selected for a library to meet the needs of its users and its community, and each library collection is unique. Yet a library cannot collect everything. A library collection is developed carefully through choices made in the collection development process, choices that are informed by users and their needs.[4] A collection serves as a strong foundation that supports a library's mission and meets the needs of its community and its users.

Libraries organize their collections to help people find and use library materials. Organizing library collections is essential to the work of a library. If a library's collection is to be used, then it must be organized well. As an illustration, consider this scenario:

> Imagine walking into your local public library on your lunch break. You are looking for books about starting a business because you want a better life for your family. Like many people, you have no internet access at home, and you do not have a lot of extra money to buy books. You decide to go to the library down the street from your workplace, knowing it will have what you need. The library is a beautiful building filled with books and materials as far as your eye can see. You wander into the library stacks and almost get lost because of the overwhelming number of books in the library. You marvel at the library's collection and know you will be able to find exactly what you need. Upon closer inspection, however, you realize that the books are thrown haphazardly on the shelves. There is no order, there is no signage, there are no call numbers on the books, and there is no library catalog to search. It is chaos. You see book titles on some book spines, but the subjects are thrown together. You realize quickly you will have to flip through each book to find one on starting a business. This is an impossible task.
>
> You ask a reference librarian for help. She is friendly and helpful, but unfortunately, she cannot find where the print books on business are shelved either. She suggests looking in the e-book collection, and she points to a sign above a computer that says, "Search our collection of full-text electronic books." You breathe a sigh of relief because you know you will find an e-book on starting a business. You enter the search words "starting business" in the search box and receive a list of fifty thousand results. This list is unmanageable, but it is similar to any Google search you have done at work. You know the books listed first will be about starting a business. But no such luck. The computer does not give any information about the books. You see only numbers in the results list. You have no idea what each book is titled, who wrote it, or what it is about. Your stomach drops as you realize you must click on each search result individually to determine if it is about starting a business. You check the first ten items on the results list, but none of them are about starting a business. Turns out the computer simply searched the full text of each e-book and retrieved books that had the words *starting* or *business* anywhere in the text. There is no relevance ranking to sort the results for you, so your results include books on all subjects.
>
> You feel defeated, so you leave the library. You wish the library had organized its collection to help you quickly and easily find books on starting a business. Even the reference librarian could not help you. Your lunch break is over. You do not know what you will do next, but perhaps this is a sign you should not start a business after all. You know one thing for sure: You will never go back to that disorganized library.

This is a terrible user experience that illustrates why libraries must organize their collections. Lack of organization in a library can negatively affect library users and library services. A collection must be organized to help people—the library's users—find and use library materials.

Libraries organize their collections for many reasons. Organization is important for retrieval and discovery. Users should be able to find library materials and information quickly and easily. Organization also provides access to items in a library. It helps libraries make their collections available and explains how materials can be accessed. Collectively, libraries work together to preserve the world's knowledge. Library materials that are not organized are essentially lost. Organization also is important for the subject arrangement of a library. Libraries arrange their collections with purpose so users can find what they need, usually by subject, genre, or format. Ultimately, organization helps users. Library collections must be organized if library users are to find and use library materials.

Organizing library collections is crucial, but it is not an easy task. The library profession has a long history of developing standards to organize collections and make library materials accessible to library users. It is a large subject area that includes many standards, models, principles, practices, and policies that make library materials available to library users. This chapter will introduce the organization of library collections. It will discuss library collections and their formats, the factors that influence organization, and the limits of organization, and it will give a brief history of organizing library collections. This chapter will explain why organization is an essential component of library work.

LIBRARY COLLECTIONS

To understand why library collections are organized, it is important to understand the nature of library collections and what formats are collected. A library collection seems like a straightforward concept: all the materials available through a library. However, when one takes a deeper look at a collection, it is anything but simple. A library collection can be quite complex because it is not a singular entity. A library's collection can contain many types of smaller collections, each with different, and sometimes complicated, organizational needs. A collection may include a main collection of physical books, serials, and media available for checkout from the library, or electronic books, electronic serials, and electronic media that are accessed online. A main collection may be broken into smaller collections at various branch libraries, such as individual school libraries in a school district, branch libraries in a public library system, or subject-specific branch libraries in an academic library. All libraries have a main collection that is cataloged and made available to users.

In addition to a main collection, many libraries have other collections, too, such as special collections or archives. These collections contain local, unique, rare, unpublished, and other special types of items that enhance a library's collection and make it unique. A public library could have a collection of local history or genealogical materials. An academic library could have a collection of rare books or photographs, or could be responsible for a university's archives. A school library may have a collection of school yearbooks. Unlike main collections, special collections may or may not be available to users because libraries do not always have the resources to organize them. They may be sitting in boxes in a back room. Many libraries are actively involved in uncovering these collections, digitizing them, and making them available to users online as digital collections. There are other types of digital collections, too, such as institutional repositories and digital archives.

What Libraries Collect

Libraries collect anything needed to help users and to meet their missions: books, serials (e.g., magazines, journals, newspapers), music and other audio recordings, film and video, software, games, objects, images, art, archival materials, and on and on. Everything is fair game for a library's collection. As long as it exists in the world, it can be collected by libraries. A library cannot collect or organize knowledge, ideas, or art in a person's head, no matter how brilliant or creative. However, a library can collect and organize knowledge, ideas, and art that a person has communicated through books, articles, music, video, paintings, objects, and so on. A picture in someone's head cannot be collected or organized. A picture on paper or another medium, or saved in a computer file, *can* be collected and organized. An audio recording of a person describing a picture in their head *can* be collected and organized.

In theory, libraries can collect anything, but in practice, libraries do not collect everything. Choices are made about what to collect and what not to collect; it depends on the needs of each library. Yet library collections overall tend to have similar characteristics, although there are exceptions. One characteristic is that most libraries tend to collect *whole* items. Generally, a library will collect a whole book, not necessarily one chapter from a book, or a whole volume or run of a serial, not necessarily just one issue. Libraries tend to collect mass-published resources, which means libraries tend to own the same materials. Most libraries have open shelves so users can browse and access library resources themselves. Libraries tend to have more general collections with multiple subjects and formats because library users need materials in various subjects and formats. For these reasons, libraries have developed systems of organizing library collections that account for these characteristics, such as standardized bibliographic records and classification schemes that facilitate shelf browsing.

Yet there are always exceptions to each characteristic. Some libraries, like corporate libraries and research libraries, have very specialized collections and very specialized users. They can collect parts of resources (e.g., one chapter from a book), and can collect local, unique, and rare items. It depends on the library. Many libraries have special collections that supplement their main collection or have archival materials. However, keep in mind that although libraries may have special collections, libraries are different from other cultural heritage institutions, such as archives or museums and art galleries. Archives tend to collect unique items of historical, personal, or organizational significance, such as manuscripts, pamphlets, documents, papers, letters, and so on. Two things that are important in the organization of archival collections are provenance and original order. Where the material originated is important, as is keeping the archival materials in its original order, because there is historical value to that order. Those who want to use archival materials usually must make an appointment or request materials. Because of these things, archives organize their materials in ways that meet their own needs, such as using finding aids and registers.

Museums and art galleries tend to collect unique art and objects, either two- or three-dimensional. Usually the public can view the materials, but they cannot touch them, so materials are displayed to the public in purposeful ways. Provenance and condition are very important. It is important to record where each item originated and its current state of preservation. Because of these things, there may be two general types of organization in museums: internal organization, which includes museum records, inventories, and registers; and external organization in the form of displays. However, lines between libraries, archives, and museums may be blurred in practice. An archive or museum may have a library of reference materials, and a library may contain an archive or museum. Libraries may need to work with archivists and curators to organize special collections or archives.

Formats in Libraries

There are many formats collected in libraries, including physical formats available in a library and digital formats (also called electronic formats) available online.

As table 1.1 shows, libraries can collect physical formats that can be touched, like print books, and digital formats that cannot be touched, like e-books. New formats are created all the time, while older formats never really go away. A library may or may not withdraw obsolete formats. An academic library, for instance, could have a large collection of e-books while still holding several old floppy disks for research purposes. This means that the list in table 1.1 is not exhaustive; it is just a starting point to show the wide variety of formats available in libraries. Each format has its own organizational needs, which makes providing access to library collections complex.

Adding to this complexity is that all physical formats can become digital formats, and all digital formats can become physical formats. Many books and serials are published in both print and electronic versions. A library user could print out an e-book or an article from an e-serial. Many libraries are digitizing their print archives and special collections and making the digital copies available online. There are many items that are created on the computer, called born digital, such as digital photographs. A librarian could print out digital items or copy them to a disk or a flash drive. Libraries can copy analog music or film into digital files on the computer. Many libraries have 3-D printers or book printers, and objects or books can be printed on demand. The ability to make physical materials digital and digital materials physical means there can be infinite copies of everything in the world. This makes the organization of library collections even more complicated and challenging because users must know the specific format of each item in a library and whether something is a facsimile or not.

Table 1.1.   **Physical and Digital Formats Collected in Libraries**

Physical Formats *Formats that can be touched.* *Some formats require special equipment.*	Digital Formats *Formats that cannot be touched.* *A computer with specific hardware,* *software, and/or web access is* *required to use them.*
Books	E-books
Serials (e.g., magazines and journals)	E-serials (e.g., magazines and journals)
Films/filmstrips	Websites/Web pages
Blu-ray discs	Databases
Videotapes	PDF files
DVDs	Documents (e.g., Word documents)
Laserdiscs	Spreadsheets (e.g., Excel files)
LP Records (78s, 331/3s, 45s)	Presentations (e.g., PowerPoint)
Cassette tapes	Audio files
8-track tapes	Video files
Compact discs (CDs)	Streaming audio
Photographs	Streaming video
Slides	Blogs
Objects (e.g., rocks, bones, baking utensils)	Wikis
Posters	Digital maps
Art	Digital photographs/images
Pamphlets	Digital art
Scores	Infographics
Kits/manipulatives	Apps
Games	*And more*
Maps/charts	
Floppy disks (large and small)	
Flash drives	
DVD-ROMs	
CD-ROMs	
Microfiche/microfilm/microcards	
And more	

HOW LIBRARY COLLECTIONS ARE ORGANIZED: THEORY

The most robust library collection is useless if it is not organized well. Library collections must be organized so users can find, identify, select, and obtain library resources.[5] Otherwise, library users would be left on their own to hunt for items in a library. There are two main ways that libraries organize their collections: (1) cataloging, done to organize a library's main collection, and (2) metadata work, done to organize items in digital collections.

Cataloging

All libraries catalog their collections. Cataloging is the process of creating bibliographic records that represent materials in a library's main collection and sometimes physical items in special collections. Bibliographic records describe each item in the collection and include access points, subject headings, and a classification or other call number. Bibliographic records are housed in a library catalog that users can search. Collectively, a library catalog represents a library's entire main collection. Cataloging has a long history that is discussed later in this chapter. Cataloging standards were originally created to help catalogers create catalog cards filed in a card catalog. Today, almost every library uses electronic bibliographic records available in an online public access catalog (OPAC). Bibliographic records are encoded in the MARC 21 format, which allows a computer to read and display bibliographic information. See figures 1.1–1.3.[6]

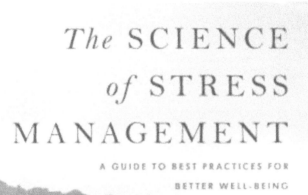

Figure 1.1. *The Science of Stress Management*

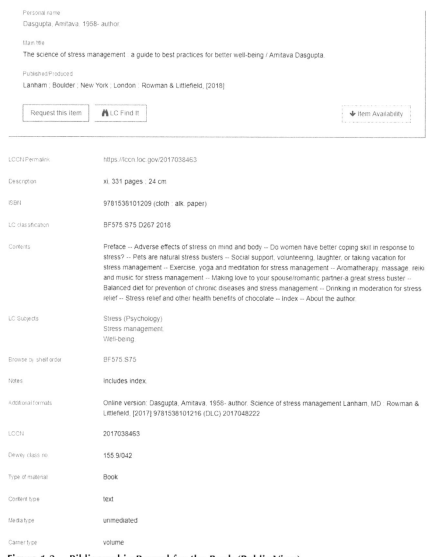

Personal name
Dasgupta, Amitava, 1958- author.

Main title
The science of stress management : a guide to best practices for better well-being / Amitava Dasgupta.

Published/Produced
Lanham ; Boulder ; New York ; London : Rowman & Littlefield, [2018]

Request this item   ♠ LC Find It   ↓ Item Availability

LCCN Permalink   https://lccn.loc.gov/2017038463

Description   xi, 331 pages ; 24 cm

ISBN   9781538101209 (cloth : alk. paper)

LC classification   BF575.S75 D267 2018

Contents   Preface -- Adverse effects of stress on mind and body -- Do women have better coping skill in response to
                        stress? -- Pets are natural stress busters -- Social support, volunteering, laughter, or taking vacation for
                        stress management -- Exercise, yoga and meditation for stress management -- Aromatherapy, massage, reiki
                        and music for stress management -- Making love to your spouse/romantic partner-a great stress buster --
                        Balanced diet for prevention of chronic diseases and stress management -- Drinking in moderation for stress
                        relief -- Stress relief and other health benefits of chocolate -- Index -- About the author.

LC Subjects   Stress (Psychology)
                        Stress management.
                        Well-being.

Browse by shelf order   BF575.S75

Notes   Includes index.

Additional formats   Online version: Dasgupta, Amitava, 1958- author. Science of stress management Lanham, MD : Rowman &
                        Littlefield, [2017] 9781538101216 (DLC) 2017048222

LCCN   2017038463

Dewey class no.   155.9/042

Type of material   Book

Content type   text

Media type   unmediated

Carrier type   volume

Figure 1.2.   Bibliographic Record for the Book (Public View)

Figure 1.1 shows a book called *The Science of Stress Management* by Amitava
Dasgupta. After a library purchases the book, it must be cataloged. A bibliographic
record is created that represents the book, and the information that the public sees is
shown in figure 1.2. The bibliographic record includes a description, provides access
points that link it to other items in the library catalog, and explains what the book
is about. Library users can look at the bibliographic record to determine whether the
book meets their needs. Figure 1.3 shows what catalogers create during the cataloging process, the actual bibliographic record encoded in the MARC 21 format.

000		01980cam a2200325 i 4500
001		20044040
005		20181105081035.0
008		171002s2018 mdu 001 0 eng
906	__	|a 7 |b cbc |c orignew |d 1 |e ecip |f 20 |g y-gencatlg
925	0_	|a acquire |b 1 shelf copy |x policy default
955	__	|b rm13 2017-10-02 |i rm13 2017-10-02 (telework) |w xm09 2017-10-04 |a xn13 2018-08-01 1 copy rec'd., to CIP ver. |a rk20 2018-08-04 |f rf10 2018-08-09 CIP ver. to CALM
010	__	|a 2017038463
020	__	|a 9781538101209 (cloth : alk. paper)
040	__	|a DLC |b eng |c DLC |e rda |d DLC
042	__	|a pcc
050	00	|a BF575.S75 |b D267 2018
082	00	|a 155.9/042 |2 23
100	1_	|a Dasgupta, Amitava, |d 1958- |e author.
245	14	|a The science of stress management : |b a guide to best practices for better well-being / |c Amitava Dasgupta.
264	_1	|a Lanham ; |a Boulder ; |a New York ; |a London : |b Rowman & Littlefield, |c [2018]
300	__	|a xi, 331 pages ; |c 24 cm
336	__	|a text |b txt |2 rdacontent
337	__	|a unmediated |b n |2 rdamedia
338	__	|a volume |b nc |2 rdacarrier
500	__	|a Includes index.
505	0_	|a Preface -- Adverse effects of stress on mind and body -- Do women have better coping skill in response to stress? -- Pets are natural stress busters -- Social support, volunteering, laughter, or taking vacation for stress management -- Exercise, yoga and meditation for stress management -- Aromatherapy, massage, reiki and music for stress management -- Making love to your spouse/romantic partner-a great stress buster -- Balanced diet for prevention of chronic diseases and stress management -- Drinking in moderation for stress relief -- Stress relief and other health benefits of chocolate -- Index -- About the author.
650	_0	|a Stress (Psychology)
650	_0	|a Stress management.
650	_0	|a Well-being.
776	08	|i Online version: |a Dasgupta, Amitava, 1958- author. |t Science of stress management |d Lanham, MD : Rowman & Littlefield, [2017] |z 9781538101216 |w (DLC) 2017048222

Figure 1.3.   Bibliographic Record for the Book (MARC View)

Parts of the Cataloging Process

There are two parts of the cataloging process: (1) descriptive cataloging and (2) subject analysis (also called subject cataloging). Descriptive cataloging is concerned with *description*, which describes things that do not change over time (e.g., title, author, format, publisher, date), and *access*, which directs the creation of name and title access points that bring together materials in the library catalog. Subject analysis includes assigning subject headings and a classification number that give subject access to library resources and organize a library's collection by subject. Subject analysis describes what an item is about (its subject), and sometimes what it is (its genre or form). See figure 1.4 for an illustration. Descriptive cataloging is shown on the left, and subject analysis is shown on the right. Together, they are used to catalog library materials, and along with the MARC 21 encoding standard, they form bibliographic records.

Each part of the cataloging process is guided by several cataloging standards developed by the library profession. This includes the current standard for descriptive

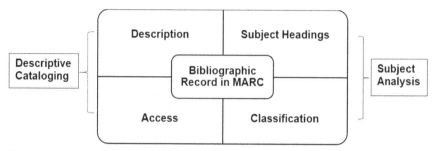

Figure 1.4. Parts of the Cataloging Process

cataloging, called *Resource Description and Access*; subject headings lists, such as the *Library of Congress Subject Headings* and the *Sears List of Subject Headings*; classification schemes, such as the *Dewey Decimal Classification* and the *Library of Congress Classification*; and the MARC 21 format. These standards guide catalogers in the creation of bibliographic records that represent materials available in libraries. Each individual library also can create local cataloging policies that supplement cataloging standards and direct the organization of collections in an individual library. The MARC 21 format will be discussed in chapter 2, descriptive cataloging in chapter 3, subject headings in chapter 4, and classification in chapter 5.

Purpose of Cataloging

The library catalog is the primary information retrieval system in a library and it has a long history. Most people have used library catalogs, either the OPAC in today's library or the card catalog in yesterday's library. A library catalog includes bibliographic records that describe and provide access to each item in a library's main collection. Users can search a library catalog to find relevant items. In one way, a library catalog is an inventory of a library's collection; however, it is much more than an inventory. It uses linked access points to *collocate*, or bring together, related materials by title, author, or subject. It includes lots of bibliographic information to help users *differentiate* like materials. In addition, it *shows relationships* between related materials. Collocation, differentiation, and showing relationships have been purposes of library catalogs and library cataloging for a long time. In 1841 Anthony Panizzi was the first librarian to envision that a library catalog (then in book form) could be more than an inventory, that it could bring together works for users.[7] In 1876 Charles Cutter made one of the most influential statements on the purpose of a library catalog, which he called the "objects" of a library catalog.[8] See "Cutter's Objects of a Library Catalog (1876)."

To Cutter, there are three primary objectives of a library catalog, and cataloging standards and practice have developed to meet these objectives. The first objective expresses the finding purpose of a catalog: Users should be able to find library materials by author, title, or subject. The second objective expresses the collocation purpose of a catalog: A library catalog should bring together like items. The third

---

CUTTER'S OBJECTS OF A LIBRARY CATALOG (1876)

1. To enable a person to find a book of which either
   (A) the author is known.
   (B) the title is known.
   (C) the subject is known.
2. To show what the library has
   (D) by a given author.
   (E) on a given subject.
   (F) in a given kind of literature.
3. To assist in the choice of a book
   (G) as to its edition (bibliographically).
   (H) as to its character (literary or topical).

---

objective expresses the differentiation purpose of a catalog: A library catalog should show the differences between library materials so users can select what they need.

Cutter's objectives shaped the construction of catalogs and the development of cataloging standards and practice. There are newer statements, but they still reflect Cutter's original objectives. One list comes from the 2016 *Statement of International Cataloguing Principles* from the International Federation of Library Associations and Institutions. See the "Objectives and Functions of the Catalogue" below.

OBJECTIVES AND FUNCTIONS OF THE CATALOGUE

The catalogue should be an effective and efficient instrument that enables a user:

6.1 *to find* bibliographic resources in a collection as the result of a search using attributes or relationships of the entities:
   to find a single resource or sets of resources representing:

   all resources realizing the same work
   all resources embodying the same expression
   all resources exemplifying the same manifestation
   all resources associated with a given person, family, or corporate body
   all resources on a given thema
   all resources defined by other criteria (language, place of publication, publication date, content form, media type, carrier type, etc.), usually as a secondary limiting of a search result;

6.2 *to identify* a bibliographic resource or agent (that is, to confirm that the described entity corresponds to the entity sought or to distinguish between two or more entities with similar characteristics);

6.3 *to select* a bibliographic resource that is appropriate to the user's needs (that is, to choose a resource that meets the user's requirements with respect to medium, content, carrier, etc., or to reject a resource as being inappropriate to the user's needs);

6.4 *to acquire or obtain access* to an item described (that is, to provide information that will enable the user to acquire an item through purchase, loan, etc., or to access an item electronically through an online connection to a remote source); or to access, acquire, or obtain authority data or bibliographic data;

6.5 *to navigate and explore* within a catalogue, through the logical arrangement of bibliographic and authority data and the clear presentation of relationships among entities beyond the catalogue, to other catalogues and in non-library contexts.

According to the *Statement of International Cataloguing Principles*, the catalog has five objectives: to find, to identify, to select, to acquire or obtain access, and to navigate and explore. Although "to acquire or obtain access" and "to navigate and explore" are new objectives, the list still reflects Cutter's original objectives of finding, collocating, and differentiating.[9] The newest list comes from the 2017 *IFLA Library Reference Model*. It lists *user tasks*, or what users should be able to do on a library catalog.[10] See the "User Tasks from the *IFLA Library Reference Model*" below.

These user tasks are very similar to those in the *Statement of International Cataloguing Principles*—users should be able to find, identify, select, obtain, and explore on a library catalog—and they still reflect Cutter's original objectives. Each item in

USER TASKS FROM THE *IFLA LIBRARY REFERENCE MODEL*

Find: To bring together information about one or more resources of interest by searching on any relevant criteria;

Identify: To clearly understand the nature of the resources found and to distinguish between similar resources;

Select: To determine the suitability of the resources found, and to be enabled to either accept or reject specific resources;

Obtain: To access the content of the resource;

Explore: To discover resources using the relationships between them and thus place the resources in a context.

a library is described to provide an accurate representation of it. Access points are added to bibliographic records that bring together like resources and show relationships between materials. Bibliographic records show the uniqueness of everything in a library's collection and show the differences between library items. If a user is looking for *Gone Girl*, for example, he or she can understand whether the bibliographic record is for the book, the audiobook, or the movie. A catalog also should allow a user to acquire or obtain library materials. A library catalog should tell a user where an item is located, whether it is in a particular library, branch, or online, and how a user can obtain the item. A user should be able to explore a library catalog to discover relationships. This is done through access points and links in the catalog.

Metadata Work

Cataloging is performed in all libraries, and modern cataloging has been performed in libraries for well over 150 years. However, there is a newer form of work, performed in libraries for the last 25 years or so, called metadata work or metadata projects. Metadata records describe and provide access to a library's digital collections. Digital collections usually contain digital files that a library has created and can include special collections materials that have been digitized, institutional repositories, digital archives, and the like. Unlike library cataloging, metadata records are created only for digital materials in digital collections, and not all libraries have digital collections. Metadata work is performed primarily by academic libraries and larger public libraries. The purpose of metadata records is the same as bibliographic records—to describe and provide access to materials in a library—but how they are created is much different. Unlike library cataloging, metadata work is not standardized across libraries. Libraries that perform metadata work can create their own local policies for their particular digital collections. An individual library has more control over record creation decisions than it does in library cataloging.

Digital collections tend to include special, unique, or local items that are not collected at other libraries, and each separate collection may have different needs. Therefore, metadata work and practice can be quite different among libraries. Instead of creating bibliographic records in the MARC 21 format following cataloging standards, metadata records are created using a metadata schema that has been marked up using XML or another markup language. Metadata schemas are much more flexible than cataloging standards, and libraries can modify metadata schemas to create metadata records that are tailored toward a particular collection. Metadata records created for a digital collection of images, for example, can be quite different from metadata records created for a digital collection of university curriculum materials. In addition to metadata schemas, a library could choose to add subject headings, thesaurus descriptors, or nothing at all. A library may add a classification number or other identifying number, or not. It all depends on the needs of the collection. For an example, see figures 1.5–1.7.[11]

Figure 1.5.   Digital Photograph Created by a Library. *University of North Texas Librar-*
ies, The Portal to Texas History, https://texashistory.unt.edu / *Austin History Center,*
Austin Public Library (https://texashistory.unt.edu/ark:/67531/metapth33391)

title: Birthday Party
creator: Douglass, Neal
date: 1959-03-07
language: No Language
description: Smiling McDonald toddler girl sitting on table with her birthday
  cakes
subject: People - Family Groups
coverage: United States - Texas - Travis County - Austin
coverage: Into Modern Times, 1939-Present
coverage: 1959-03-07
rights: Public
type: Photograph
format: 1 photograph : negative, b&w ; 4 x 5 in.
format: Image
identifier: local-cont-no: ND-59-223-03
identifier: https://texashistory.unt.edu/ark:/67531/metapth33391/
identifier: ark: ark:/67531/metapth33391

Figure 1.6.   Metadata Record for the Digital Photograph (Labels)

```
- <oai_dc:dc xsi:schemaLocation="http://www.openarchives.org/OAI/2.0/oai_dc/
    <dc:title>Birthday Party</dc:title>
    <dc:creator>Douglass, Neal</dc:creator>
    <dc:date>1959-03-07</dc:date>
    <dc:language>No Language</dc:language>
  - <dc:description>
      Smiling McDonald toddler girl sitting on table with her birthday cakes
    </dc:description>
    <dc:subject>People - Family Groups</dc:subject>
    <dc:coverage>United States - Texas - Travis County - Austin</dc:coverage>
    <dc:coverage>Into Modern Times, 1939-Present</dc:coverage>
    <dc:coverage>1959-03-07</dc:coverage>
    <dc:rights>Public</dc:rights>
    <dc:type>Photograph</dc:type>
    <dc:format>1 photograph : negative, b&w ; 4 x 5 in.</dc:format>
    <dc:format>Image</dc:format>
    <dc:identifier>local-cont-no: ND-59-223-03</dc:identifier>
  - <dc:identifier>
      https://texashistory.unt.edu/ark:/67531/metapth33391/
    </dc:identifier>
    <dc:identifier>ark: ark:/67531/metapth33391</dc:identifier>
  </oai_dc:dc>
```

Figure 1.7. Metadata Record for the Digital Photograph (*Dublin Core* and XML)

Figure 1.5 shows a digital photograph created by a library. Figures 1.6 and 1.7 show a metadata record created for the digital photograph using the *Dublin Core* metadata schema in XML. Figure 1.6 shows the labels and figure 1.7 shows the XML coding. The metadata record uses descriptive metadata to describe the photograph, including title, creator, date, subject, and much more. In addition to the descriptive metadata that is shown in figures 1.6 and 1.7, there are more types of metadata used to create the digital photograph in figure 1.5, such as metadata used to preserve it, to provide technical details about the files, and so on. Types of metadata will be discussed in chapter 2 and metadata schemas in chapter 3.

Cataloging and Metadata Standards

The library profession has created many standards, tools, and guidelines used to organize library materials in a standard way across libraries. The standards and the theory behind them will be discussed in more detail in chapters 3–5. Cataloging and metadata standards are not developed at a single library. The library profession works together, nationally and internationally, to develop standards and tools that libraries across the United States (and increasingly, the world) use to organize their materials. Standards help ensure consistency not only within a single library but also across libraries. A public library user in Connecticut will find similar systems of organization as an academic library user in New Mexico. Using the same standards also ensures that library organization is similar as people grow from children to adults. Although standards are used across libraries, individual libraries can customize standards and choose local policies that meet their needs. Standardization and the system of standards development are discussed in chapter 6.

HOW LIBRARY COLLECTIONS ARE ORGANIZED: PRACTICE

All libraries have the same goal of organizing and providing access to their collections. However, cataloging and metadata practice differs among libraries. Cataloging and metadata practice is a part of what has historically been called technical services. Technical services is responsible for library collections, including acquiring, organizing, and managing them. Typically, technical services include four main functions: acquisitions, cataloging/metadata, serials, and preservation, but in some libraries technical services also may include collection development, interlibrary loan, or circulation. Acquisitions is responsible for ordering, paying, and receiving library resources selected through the collection development process. Cataloging/metadata is responsible for describing and providing access to library resources. Serials is responsible for the acquisition, cataloging, and processing of serial publications. Preservation is responsible for maintaining and preserving library collections. See figure 1.8 for an illustration.

All libraries perform acquisitions, cataloging/metadata, serials, and preservation, but each library organizes the work differently, depending on the size of the library and its collection. In a small library there may be no separate "Technical Services Department"; instead, one or two people may perform all technical services work. In a larger library, hundreds of people may be devoted to various aspects of technical

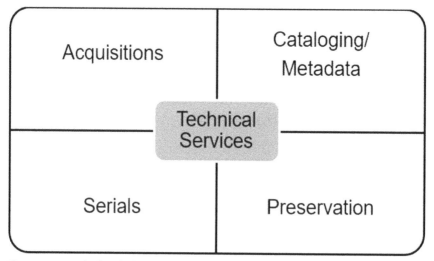

Figure 1.8.   Typical Technical Services Processes

services, each focused on a small part of the work. Technical services work also may be performed at one central location or split among different library branches.

Cataloging is a part of technical services, and it is performed by catalogers and librarians in all libraries. It also can be performed by vendors and contract catalogers. Every library performs cataloging differently depending on the size of its collection and its needs. A large library may have a large cataloging unit with many professional and paraprofessional catalogers who perform cataloging work in-house. A small library may not have a formal cataloging unit, but rather one person who is responsible for all cataloging work in the library. It does not matter who performs cataloging; it is performed to some extent in all libraries, even if a library purchases all bibliographic records from vendors.

Metadata work is performed by metadata specialists and librarians, but this work is not performed in all libraries. A metadata unit may be part of a cataloging unit or it may be located in another area of a library, such as special collections. In libraries that perform metadata work, technical services departments may be called something broader, like "Metadata and Access Services" or "Discovery and Access," to reflect different types of work performed by the department.[12] Cataloging and metadata practice in general will be discussed further in chapter 7.

FACTORS THAT INFLUENCE ORGANIZATION IN LIBRARIES

There are many similarities in how cataloging and metadata work is performed in libraries as a whole, but practices can differ among academic, public, school, and special libraries. Each type of library has different missions, serves different communities, and performs cataloging and metadata work differently. How library collections are organized in different types of libraries will be discussed in more detail in chapter 8. Each individual library is different as well. Each library has its own local cataloging and metadata policies, procedures, practices, and workflow. There are several factors that affect how library collections are organized.

Library Mission and Users

One factor that influences how library collections are organized is the mission of the library and the users it serves. A school library has a different mission and serves a different community (students and teachers in elementary, middle, and high schools) than a public library (residents in a town, city, or county) or an academic library (higher education students and faculty). Different organizational systems are needed to meet different library missions and to serve different users. For example, how children search and find information is different from adults, so an elementary school library will use subject headings for children, not those for adults. A public library serving English- and Spanish-speaking communities can use English and Spanish subject headings. A medical library will use the *Medical Subject Headings*.

Size of Collection

The size of a collection is an important factor in organizational decisions. As the size of a collection goes up, the need for organization goes up. A small collection of 100 books used by a few people needs to be organized for use, but because there are so few books, a formal classification system is probably not needed. The books could be arranged in alphabetical order by genre, title, or author, and users could scan the titles or flip through each book to find what they need. The items need to be cataloged, but the bibliographic records could have minimal information and the subject analysis could be broad. Compare this to a large collection of 20 million books serving 25,000 people. Much more organization is needed for this collection because it would be impossible for users to scan the collection and flip through each book. A description of each book would be helpful for searching purposes. Bibliographic records must describe the books well, and there must be access points so users can search the collection without having to look through each book. A classification scheme would be helpful to organize the books by subject on shelves. Subject headings would be helpful so users know what each book is about.

Complexity of Content

Content affects organization, especially the extent or level to which library collections are organized. Like with size, as the complexity of content goes up, so does the need for organization. For example, there are easy chemistry books written for children, general chemistry books written for the general public, introductory chemistry textbooks for undergraduate students, and very detailed chemistry journal articles for expert faculty and researchers. Language and content get more complicated as an audience gets more specialized. This means that organization becomes more complicated as language, content, and audience become more specialized. A general chemistry collection in a public library serving a small rural community does not need as much subject analysis as a specialized chemistry collection in a research library serving expert researchers. The public library collects general materials, so the subject headings assigned can be broader. The research library collects more complex materials and will need more complex subject analysis to meet the needs of researchers.

Format

Format is an important consideration when developing systems of organization. Providing access to the printed word (e.g., a book) is different from providing access to recorded sound (e.g., music) or moving images (e.g., films). A music library with many music scores and audio recordings will use systems of organization that give users access to notated and recorded music. The collection could contain scores and parts, sheet music, and miniature scores, and users want to know things like instrumentation, genres, and composers. A children's library will use systems of organization that give users access to children's materials. The collection could contain board books, chapter books, pop-up books, and games, and parents and teachers want to know authors, illustrators, topic, reading level, and intended age. Each format has its own needs. Oversized books could be shelved by subject in an oversized section because they will not fit on the regular shelves. CDs could be organized by genre in bins so users can access them easily. Maps could be organized by region and filed flat in large map cases.

Budgets and Other Institutional Factors

Every library has specific needs that affect organizational decisions. For example, a library's budget drives what types of organization are possible. Some libraries have more time, staff, and money than other libraries, which can greatly affect how a library organizes its materials and what types of work can be done. A public library may want to perform a metadata project to digitize a genealogy collection, for example, but it will not be able to perform the project if the budget is not there. Some libraries can afford more organization than others. A library with a healthy budget has the financial resources to hire many catalogers and metadata specialists to perform full and complete cataloging for each item in the library and to create digital collections. A small library with a small budget may have a few overworked catalogers with little time to do much except basic cataloging.

There are other institutional factors as well. For example, a library with closed stacks (materials not open to the public) does not need to use a formal classification scheme to organize materials by subject. An accession number or other number may be all that is needed to retrieve materials. Some libraries are concerned about theft and keep some items behind the counter. Some libraries are concerned with preserving rare items and keep them in locked cases or rooms. Space is another concern. If a library is low on space, some materials may be housed in an off-site storage facility or arranged in a way to maximize space needs. Libraries may want to make room for additional study spaces or student centers, and materials may be moved to other places. A building may have poor environmental conditions, and materials may need to be moved to preserve them. Organization is important to make sure materials are not lost in a remote storage facility and that they are cataloged and easily retrievable.

LIMITS TO ORGANIZING LIBRARY COLLECTIONS

Libraries organize their collections for several important reasons, but there are limitations. Organization does not always help users, and users need to understand organizational systems to use them effectively. The ethical issues surrounding cataloging and metadata theory and practice will be discussed in chapter 9.

No System Can Meet All Needs

Developing systems of organization that help every person is not easy. The library user can be problematic. Chu states when discussing information retrieval, "The essential problem . . . remains how to obtain the right information for the right user at the right time despite the existence of other variables (e.g., user characteristics or database coverage)."[13] The same essential problem exists when trying to *organize* information, too. Systems of organization in libraries want to help users find information, but there is no one "right" user, there is no one "right" kind of information, and there is no one "right" time. There are many users, there are many types of information, and there are many times in users' lives. It is all relative and changes depending on users' needs. There is no one "right" way to organize library collections. The organizational systems developed for libraries tend to be universal in that they try to help as many people as possible; however, they cannot help every user in every situation. There will always exist the challenge of making systems of organization flexible enough to meet everyone's needs. This is a fundamental challenge in library organization and makes the organization of library collections interesting and challenging. An organizational system is only as good as the information put into it. However, every organizational system should reflect what is organized and who will use the system.

Users Must Understand the System

Organization and retrieval are two sides of the same coin, but often they are at odds. An understanding of how library materials are organized is helpful when trying to retrieve them. Understanding when and how to use a controlled vocabulary, understanding a classification system, and knowing what types of bibliographic information can be searched in a library catalog can help users better find library materials. Yet users who are trying to find library materials do not always understand systems of library organization. Organization can be a powerful tool for those who understand the system. At the same time, systems of organization should be created with an understanding of how people search for information. Yet current systems of organization have not necessarily been developed with an understanding of users, their needs, or their information-searching behavior. Most of the systems of organization used in libraries were created in the late nineteenth and early twentieth centuries, before computers. They have been maintained and updated to reflect today's world, but they were not originally developed with an understanding of what users really need from them.

Libraries Must Maintain the System

Systems of organization in libraries are constantly changing as knowledge changes and as better methods and models of organization are developed. A library must keep up with changes, such as an author who changes his or her name, or a classification number that changes meaning. This takes a commitment of library resources, including encouraging staff to keep up with professional development. In addition, a library must have trained librarians and staff who can appropriately use and apply an organizational system. If a system is not followed, then it breaks down and users may not find everything they need.

HISTORY OF ORGANIZING LIBRARY COLLECTIONS

Libraries have a long history of organizing their collections,[14] and developments in the organization of library collections are tied closely to developments in libraries as a whole. How libraries organize their collections has changed over the years as libraries have grown and as new technologies have been adopted. The growth of library collections and the adoption of new technologies lead to new ways to organize collections and to perform cataloging and metadata work. In addition to technological change, there has always been a strong push for efficiency, standardization, and sharing of cataloging work among libraries. Major developments in the history of organizing library collections can be seen through the lenses of growth in libraries, technological developments, and the push for standardization. This section will take a brief look at the history of organizing library collections in the United States starting in 1800. Although this section focuses on organizing library collections in the United States, the standards and theory discussed are applicable to many countries. As library collections grow and as new technologies are adopted, no matter the country, new ways to organize library collections are developed.

1800–1875: Setting the Stage

There were several libraries in the United States before 1800, but library collections were small and access to books was limited. Things began to change in the 1800s as more libraries were founded, and librarians started to think about the best ways to organize collections. Between 1800 and 1875, libraries were starting to be established in the United States. As the United States expanded, so did its libraries. Important government libraries were established during this time, particularly the Library of Congress, created in 1800 with a mission to serve the United States Congress. Its collection was destroyed in 1814, when the British burned Washington during the War of 1812. To replace the collection, Thomas Jefferson sold his personal collection of 6,487 books to Congress for $23,950.[15] Other government libraries were established as well. The Smithsonian Institution was established by the United States Senate in 1846, using a $500,000 gift from James Smithson, with a museum and a library.[16] The precursor to the National Library of Medicine was founded in 1836, as a collection of books and journals that served the surgeon general of the United States Army.[17]

Other types of libraries were expanding across the United States and its territories. Academic libraries were established at many colleges and universities. Public colleges were opening, such as the University of Virginia in 1819, the first public university in the United States. The Morrill Act of 1862 expanded public higher education by giving land to states to establish land-grant schools: colleges or universities that focus on science and agriculture. Public libraries began to appear during this time as well. The first tax-funded public library, the Peterborough Town Library in New Hampshire, was opened in 1833, and the first large public library was the Boston Public Library, founded in 1848 and opened in 1854. School libraries and various special libraries (e.g., theological, societies, law, medical) were established as well.

Libraries and their collections were growing. Libraries primarily collected books and serials, and library catalogs were primarily book catalogs, with printed or hand-written entries listing items in a library. The organization of collections was relatively simple. Library materials were assigned fixed places on shelves, usually in a broad subject area by book number. New books were just added at the end of a row, so although broad subjects were shelved together, specific subtopics could be scattered on the shelves.

As libraries and their collections grew, librarians turned their attention toward cataloging them. One of the most important developments in library cataloging happened in 1841, when Anthony Panizzi published his *Rules for the Compilation of the Catalogue*, considered to be the first list of descriptive cataloging rules. Known as the "91 Rules," it was developed to catalog the collection at the British Museum. The *Rules* were important because Panizzi believed that a library catalog could do more than just serve as an inventory of items; it could help users by bringing together works in the catalog.[18]

After Panizzi, Charles Coffin Jewett added to the cataloging discussion in 1852. Hired in 1846 as the first librarian at the Smithsonian Institution, he had an idea that the Smithsonian should create a "universal catalogue" that would list all the books published in the United States.[19] He wanted to help scholars find books so they would not duplicate work. He also wanted libraries to share standard cataloging information, and he developed detailed rules for library cataloging that would ensure "uniformity" across libraries.[20] Ultimately, Jewett's grand vision was not adopted because it was deemed too expensive, and the Smithsonian Institution wanted to focus on funding scientific research. Jewett was fired in 1855.

1876–Late 1890s: The Beginning of Librarianship and Standardized Cataloging

The time period from 1876 through the late 1890s saw continued growth in libraries and library collections of all types across the United States. Andrew Carnegie, for example, donated money to build public libraries, and many "Carnegie libraries" were built during this time. Colleges and universities continued to be founded, too, with accompanying libraries. In 1876 Johns Hopkins University opened, which adopted a German model of higher education in which faculty also perform research. This model was adopted by colleges and universities across the United States and led to expanding collections in academic libraries.[21] School libraries and special libraries also continued to be established.

Library collections were still primarily books and serials, but collections started to grow. Libraries started adopting a new technology: the card catalog, in which bibliographic information was recorded on 3x5 cards and shelved in drawers in a wooden case. Libraries moved their catalogs from books to card catalogs during this time. Catalog cards were handwritten using a form of writing called library hand. This was a uniform style of writing, taught in library schools, with the purpose of creating legible cards that were easy to understand. Depending on a library and its needs, cards could be arranged in alphabetical order by subject, then subdivided by category (an alphabetico-classed catalog) or arranged by classification number (a classified catalog). Libraries started to move toward dictionary catalogs in the late nineteenth century in which titles, authors, and subjects are interfiled in alphabetical order.

The year 1876 was momentous for library cataloging. Melvil Dewey published the first edition of his *Dewey Decimal Classification* (DDC), Charles Cutter published the first edition of his *Rules for a Dictionary Catalog*, and the American Library Association (ALA) was founded, regarded as the beginning of librarianship, at least in the United States. In the DDC, considered the first formal classification system used in libraries, Dewey tried to represent all knowledge in a numerical decimal classification scheme.[22] The DDC revolutionized library organization because not only did it represent subjects, it also arranged library materials using a relative location. No longer did books need to be shelved in a fixed order. Instead, a book's location was relative; it changed depending on other books at a classification number. Library collections could be arranged by classification numbers that hierarchically represented subjects and their subtopics. Specific subjects were no longer scattered at a broad number; they were brought together on the shelves, and new books could be shelved among existing books on the same topic. The DDC was incredibly influential, and all types of libraries switched to Dewey during this time. It also inspired the creation of many other classification schemes, such as the *Universal Decimal Classification*, created by Paul Otlet and Henri LaFontaine in 1895. It is a popular classification scheme used around the world, but not in the United States.

In addition to the DDC, Cutter's first edition of *Rules for a Dictionary Catalog* was an important milestone in cataloging.[23] It was an influential set of cataloging rules that built on Panizzi's *Rules* and has been influential in the development of cataloging. It was published in four editions between 1876 and 1904 and included rules for description, entry (i.e., access points), and subject headings. In it, Cutter stated the purpose of the library catalog (and cataloging), explained how subject headings should be created, and devised cataloging principles, such as common usage and specific entry. Cutter was a cataloging pioneer. Not only did he first state the purpose of a catalog and create rules for descriptive and subject cataloging, in 1891 he published his own classification scheme called the *Expansive Classification*, which used alphanumeric notations to represent subjects in library collections. He was on the committee that created the first standard subject headings list. He also created the Cutter Table, a tool that helps catalogers assign Cutter Numbers, an alphanumeric notation used to alphabetically arrange library materials within a classification number.

In addition to Dewey's and Cutter's achievements, the founding of the ALA in 1876 has been influential not only on librarianship as a whole but on library cataloging as well. The ALA was quite active in developing cataloging standards during this time. In 1883 it published its *Condensed Rules for an Author and Title Catalog* to help libraries organize their collections.[24] Unlike Cutter's *Rules*, the ALA *Rules* separated descriptive cataloging from subject cataloging, a division that still exists in cataloging today. In 1895 the ALA developed one of the first lists of subject headings used in libraries, called *List of Subject Headings for use in Dictionary Catalogs*. It was developed by an ALA committee that included Charles Cutter, and was based on subject indexes from several academic libraries, such as at the Boston Athenaeum, the Peabody Institute, and Harvard. The first edition calls itself an "Appendix" to the third edition of Cutter's *Rules*, published in 1891.[25] The ALA's subject headings *List* was published in three editions between 1895 and 1914.

Late 1890s–Mid-1940s: Expanding Collections; Typewriters; Cataloging Standards

The late 1890s through the 1940s saw continued growth in libraries, library collections, and the development of more cataloging standards. More public libraries and academic libraries were being established across the United States. Carnegie libraries continued to be built through 1929, and non-Carnegie public libraries and branches were founded. Colleges and universities continued to be founded. The first community college (called a junior college) was founded in 1901, and they expanded rapidly. Special libraries grew as well, particularly corporate libraries,[26] and the Special Libraries Association was founded in 1909. School libraries continued to be established, too, although more slowly than other types of libraries, and the first professional school librarian was appointed in 1900.[27] Library collections grew, particularly in academic and research libraries. The Library of Congress, for instance, grew from 25,000 books in 1814 to well over one million books by the late 1890s. During this time, libraries also started to collect new formats, such as film and music, which required different types of organization.

Most libraries used card catalogs during this time, and a new technology, the typewriter, started to be adopted in libraries at turn of the twentieth century. Instead of cards written in library hand, bibliographic information was typed on cards. Shared cataloging began when the Library of Congress started selling copies of its catalog cards to libraries, which could use the cards in their catalogs instead of typing cards from scratch. The Library of Congress's card program was very influential because it began to standardize cataloging across libraries, and interest in Library of Congress standards and policies started to grow. Cataloging practice at this time was labor intensive. Although cards could be purchased for some library materials, cards were not available for everything. Every library had materials that needed to be cataloged in-house, so libraries were filled with professional catalogers and clerks who typed and filed catalog cards. When access points (called headings) changed, cards had to be manually altered to reflect changes. Librarians also routinely customized cards, adding specific information and guidance to help users. This information could be typed on cards, but often it was handwritten in the margins or on the back of cards. Library users, too, wrote things on cards to provide assistance to others.

More libraries and larger collections called for the development of even more standardized cataloging practices to help libraries organize and manage their collections, and libraries needed help and support. This need was reflected in the ALA's decision to start a separate Cataloging Section in 1900, the third subject-specific group created by the ALA.[28] In addition, the International Federation of Library Associations and Institutions (IFLA) was founded in 1927 (originally called the International Federation of Library Associations), and the Library of Congress started to assume its role as the authority for cataloging in the United States. For descriptive cataloging, the ALA's *Condensed Rules for an Author and Title Catalog* was revised and published in 1908 as a joint publication of the ALA and the Library Association (UK) called *Catalog Rules: Author and Title Entries*, with separate American and English editions.[29] It focused on both description and entry (i.e., author and title access points) on catalog cards. In 1941 the ALA released the preliminary American second edition of its rules in two parts: "Part I: Entry and Headings" and "Part II: Description of Book." This explicitly divided descriptive cataloging into two parts: (1) description and (2) access, a division that remains in descriptive cataloging standards today.[30]

For subject analysis, two of the most influential standards, the *Library of Congress Classification* (LCC) and the *Library of Congress Subject Headings* (LCSH), were developed during this time to deal with the monumental growth of collections at the Library of Congress. Instead of the lofty goal of organizing all knowledge like the *Dewey Decimal Classification*, the LCC was developed as a practical solution to organize the growing collections at the Library of Congress. Since acquiring Jefferson's collection, the Library of Congress had used a modified form of Jefferson's own classification system, but it was no longer working for such a large collection. In 1897 the Library of Congress started work on a new classification scheme, based on Cutter's *Expansive Classification*, that used alphanumeric notations to represent academic disciplines. This large classification was originally published in separate parts between 1901 and 1948.

Following the LCC, in 1898 the Library of Congress started work on its own list of subject headings to provide subject access to its catalog. It was based primarily on the American Library Association's *List of Subject Headings for use in Dictionary Catalogs*, with additional subject headings used at the library. The Library of Congress's list, called *Subject Headings Used in the Dictionary Catalogues of the Library of Congress*, was first published in separate parts between 1909 and 1914. The title was changed to *Library of Congress Subject Headings* in 1975. LCSH became a popular subject headings list in libraries because Library of Congress subject headings were printed on catalog cards purchased by libraries. Therefore, libraries around the country started using the *Library of Congress Subject Headings*, too.

Other library standards were developed during this time. In 1923 Minnie Earl Sears published the first edition of the *Sears List of Subject Headings*, a small general subject headings list still used in some small school and public libraries. In the late 1890s Adelaide R. Hasse created the *Superintendent of Documents Classification* (Su-Docs) to organize publications produced by the US government. It influenced the creation of many US state government classification schemes used to organize state government publications. In the 1930s S. R. Ranganathan developed the *Colon Classification*, a faceted classification scheme used primarily in India, and first published in 1933. Henry Bliss created the *Bliss Bibliographic Classification* in the early part of the twentieth century, but it was published later, between 1940 and 1953. It is used primarily in the United Kingdom.

Mid-1940s–Late 1960s: Development of Computers; Cataloging Principles

For libraries, the time period after World War II and into the late 1960s is marked by a growing body of scientific information, developments in information science, and advancements in computer indexing. After World War II, there was an information explosion as the United States started to focus on science and technology.[31] Libraries—particularly academic, research, and special libraries—started to collect a significant amount of scientific material. There was a massive amount of information being generated, too much for any one human to handle, and there was a need to quickly search and retrieve this information. Computers were ready to take on this task. In the 1950s, researchers such as Mortimer Taube at Documentation, Inc., Hans Peter Luhn at IBM, and others developed automatic indexing using keywords assigned to documents. Computers could search through this massive amount of scientific data much more quickly and efficiently than humans.[32]

Libraries during this time primarily collected print materials—books and serials—but they were increasingly collecting nonprint formats, too. Libraries were still using card catalogs and still had many professional catalogers and clerks typing and filing catalog cards. However, because library collections were growing, particularly in academic and research libraries, card catalogs that interfiled titles, authors, and subjects were becoming impractical for larger libraries. Card catalogs started to be split up by access point into what are called divided catalogs. A library could have one card catalog filed alphabetically by author and title, and another card catalog filed alphabetically by subject. Or a library could have separate card catalogs for authors, titles, and subjects.

During this time, library cataloging entered a crisis period with two camps: (1) catalogers who advocated for detailed rules that covered every cataloging situation, and (2) catalogers who advocated for general rules based on principles. This debate resulted in the development of a statement of cataloging principles and a new descriptive cataloging code. The ALA's 1941 revision of its descriptive cataloging rules was controversial, especially "Part II: Description of Book." It was criticized because the rules were considered too complex, and administrators believed the new edition would make cataloging too expensive.[33] The ALA's cataloging rules needed to change. Enter the Library of Congress. By the 1940s the Library of Congress was the largest research library in the United States. It had developed its own set of descriptive cataloging rules that it used for printing catalog cards. The Library of Congress's rules were based on the ALA *Rules*, but there were specific policies and exceptions for the Library of Congress. Many libraries in the United States purchased catalog cards from the Library of Congress, so libraries wanted to know the Library of Congress's rules for description. In 1949 the Library of Congress published its rules, called *Rules for Descriptive Cataloging in the Library of Congress*.[34] The Library of Congress's rules were much simpler than the ALA's rules, and more importantly, they were based on principles, specifically the "Principles of Descriptive Cataloging" first articulated by Seymour Lubetzky in 1946.[35] The ALA adopted the Library of Congress's rules as a replacement for its own rules of description. The ALA then modified the first part of its descriptive cataloging rules, called "Part I: Entry and Headings," and published the revised rules for name and title access points in 1949.

However, libraries still complained that the ALA rules were too detailed and wanted simplified rules for author and title access points as well. It was clear to many that a more substantive change in descriptive cataloging rules was needed.[36] In 1954, representatives from the ALA and the Library of Congress began work on a new cataloging code. The effort to revise cataloging rules became international when the Library Association (UK) joined the effort (it was working on its own revision of the rules), and the Canadian Library Association, too. All three countries worked together to develop shared cataloging rules. Lubetzky, working at the Library of Congress at the time, served as the first editor from 1956–1962.[37] Lubetzky believed that cataloging should be based on principles rather than on specific rules. He was the first person to articulate cataloging principles, in his 1946 statement "Principles of Descriptive Cataloging" at the Library of Congress. Lubetzky's statement of principles was quite influential because in 1961, IFLA used his ideas to develop an international *Statement of Principles* for cataloging, informally called the Paris Principles.[38] This was the first international statement of cataloging principles, and it was incorporated, in part, into the new set of cataloging rules.[39] The new rules, incorporating some Paris Principles, were published in 1967 as the *Anglo-American Cataloguing Rules* (AACR or AACR1), and it was published in separate North American and British texts. AACR1 was adopted by libraries, and soon after catalogers used the new rules to create catalog cards.

In addition to descriptive cataloging, there were developments in subject analysis. In 1951 David Judson Haykin, chief of the Subject Cataloging Division at the Library of Congress, articulated the principles underlying the *Library of Congress Subject Headings*, stating "the fundamental principle that the reader is the focus in all cataloging principles and practice" and that "convenience" and "logical order" are secondary considerations.[40] In addition, academic libraries started to reclassify their collections from the DDC to the LCC because it better represented academic subjects. There were also developments in how materials were organized in medical libraries. The National Library of Medicine developed the *National Library of Medicine Classification* in the 1940s as a subject specific extension to the LCC (it uses classes that LCC will never develop). It was first published in 1951. In 1960 the *Medical Subject Headings* was published by the National Library of Medicine as both a subject headings list for cataloging and a thesaurus for indexing biomedical journal articles. Both standards are used today to provide subject access to medical library collections. In 1965 the Library of Congress created the Annotated Card Program and the *Children's Subject Headings* to provide better subject access to children's materials.

Late 1960s–Late 1990s: Computers; MARC Format; AACR2

The late 1960s through the late 1990s was a time of much technological change in libraries. Advances in computer technology led to changes in how library collections were organized. The *MAchine-Readable Cataloging* (MARC) format was developed to encode cataloging information in bibliographic records, the online public access catalog (OPAC) was developed, OCLC was founded, and libraries began to share electronic bibliographic records over computer networks.

Up to this time, libraries were still using card catalogs, and there were lots of professional catalogers and clerks that did the typing and filing. Cataloging began to change in the late 1960s when Henriette Avram developed the MARC format, which made bibliographic information on catalog cards machine readable. The information on cards was marked up using the MARC format and entered into bibliographic records that a computer could read and manipulate. OPACs were developed to house bibliographic records. This was a revolutionary change in how libraries provided access to their collections. Instead of cards filed in a card catalog, libraries could describe their collections using bibliographic records housed in an OPAC. Library users did not have to flip through cards or wait their turn to look through a file drawer; they could simply use computers in a library to search the library's collection.

MARC also led to advances in shared cataloging and changed how cataloging is performed in libraries. MARC led to the development of bibliographic utilities, which are databases of bibliographic records that libraries use to share bibliographic records. OCLC was founded in 1967 to serve libraries in Ohio. It developed a bibliographic utility that was originally used by libraries in Ohio, but it proved to be so successful that OCLC opened it up to libraries across the United States in 1978. Because bibliographic information was now automated, libraries could share bibliographic records with one another much more easily. Shared cataloging (also called cooperative cataloging), completely changed the cataloging process. Catalogers did not have to laboriously type and file cards, but instead could create electronic bibliographic records that could be shared among libraries. Cataloging became quicker and more efficient, and library materials were available to users much more quickly than in the past.

Libraries began to move their bibliographic information from cards housed in card catalogs to electronic bibliographic records housed in OPACs accessed through a computer. This led to mass retrospective conversion (or recon) projects in libraries to move cataloging information from cards to bibliographic records. Libraries performed this work in-house or sent cards to outsourcers, like OCLC. By the end of the 1990s most libraries had switched to OPACs. This led to the closing of card catalogs and the destruction of catalog cards.[41] Yet some libraries still worked on retrospective conversion projects through the 2000s, and some libraries still may have pockets of library materials that are available only on catalog cards. Some smaller libraries, such as rural public libraries or church libraries, may still use card catalogs or are in the process of moving to an OPAC.

For cataloging practice, there were consequences of these technological advancements. The MARC format, bibliographic records, and shared cataloging meant that cataloging work became quicker and easier, and the work could be performed by copy catalogers. Professional catalogers were no longer needed to perform the bulk of cataloging work in cataloging departments, and professional cataloger positions were eliminated or turned into supervisory positions. In addition to advances in technology, library budgets started to be cut in the mid-1970s, and libraries were affected by budget cuts through this time and beyond. The rise of shared cataloging gave libraries an opportunity to reorganize and shift budgets elsewhere.

There were also changes to cataloging standards at this time and a push for more international cataloging standards. IFLA developed the *International Standard Bibliographic Description* (ISBD) suite of publications, a sort of international cataloging rules that were incorporated into cataloging codes around the world. First editions of the ISBDs focused on particular formats, such as monographs (1974), serials (1974), nonbook materials (1977), and cartographic materials (1977). However, one particular ISBD, *ISBD(G): General International Standard Bibliographic Description* (1977), was very influential because it standardized the framework for describing library materials, including standard punctuation that should be used to describe cataloging information.[42]

AACR1 was revised during this time as well. There were several reasons, such as incorporating the ISBD(G) framework, bringing together the North American and British editions into one shared volume, adding all amendments and changes since 1967, getting closer to the Paris Principles, and creating a more standardized code that accounted for the needs of computerized cataloging.[43] The editors were Paul W. Winkler from the Library of Congress and Michael Gorman from the British Library. The second edition of the *Anglo-American Cataloguing Rules* (AACR2) was published in 1978 and was adopted by the United States, Canada, United Kingdom, and Australia in 1981. AACR2 was revised in 1988, 1998, and 2002.

For subject analysis, specialized subject thesauri started to be developed. For example, the *Art & Architecture Thesaurus* was developed by the Getty Trust and first published in 1990. The *Thesaurus for Graphic Materials* was developed by the Prints and Photographs Division of the Library of Congress, and first published in 1987.

Librarians also started questioning standards for subject analysis, particularly the *Library of Congress Subject Headings*. Sanford Berman, Joan K. Marshall, and others called on the Library of Congress to change offensive and biased subject headings and classification terms, particularly words and phrases used to describe people.

Late 1990s to the present: The World Wide Web; RDA; Linked Data

Starting the late 1990s, libraries and their collections started to change significantly due to the creation of the World Wide Web by Tim Berners-Lee in 1989. Berners-Lee created three technologies that support the web: Hypertext Markup Language (HTML), the markup language for the web; Uniform Resource Identifiers/Uniform Resource Locators (URI/URL), which are unique web identifiers and web addresses; and Hypertext Transfer Protocol (HTTP), which is used to link and retrieve items on the web. Berners-Lee founded the World Wide Web Consortium (W3C) in 1994 to standardize web technologies so people around the world could share and have access to web content. The web grew quickly as people and organizations stared to create web pages and put content and information online. This growth was aided by several digital formats made available to the public in the early 1990s, such as the JPEG, PDF, and MP3 file formats.

Libraries were quick to realize that the web could be a valuable source of information for users and began to give users access to the web. Publishers started to produce electronic content, including e-books, e-serials, and e-media, that is accessible online or through a separate device. Libraries started to collect increasingly more electronic formats, especially large packages of electronic resources available from library vendors. There has been an unprecedented growth of electronic materials available in libraries, almost too much for some libraries handle. At the same time, some libraries started to purchase fewer physical materials. Library budgets continued to be cut during this time, particularly because of the Great Recession that began in 2007. In addition, library vendors began to sell bibliographic records to libraries. Libraries started to purchase "shelf-ready" materials, which are physical items already processed with call number labels and barcodes, along with bibliographic records that are downloaded into the library catalog. Libraries also started to purchase large files of bibliographic records for electronic resources from vendors, particularly for e-books and e-serials in large databases. This shift toward collecting more electronic and fewer physical resources and purchasing bibliographic records has led to changes in cataloging practice. Instead of copy cataloging bibliographic records and fixing errors before they are added to library catalogs, large files of bibliographic records are added to library catalogs as is through a process called batch processing. Errors are fixed later, if they are found at all.

Libraries also made their library catalogs available online, which changed how library collections are made available to users. Users did not have to go to a library to search a collection. Users with internet access could search a library catalog from the comfort of their homes at any time of the day or night. In the mid-2000s, library catalogs started to improve discovery by incorporating next-generation catalog features and discovery products that enhance bibliographic records with book cover images, summaries, reviews, recommendations, tagging features, links to social media websites, and expanded searching capabilities.

There were several developments in library cataloging during this time. Several models and a revised statement of cataloging principles were published in the 1990s and 2000s. IFLA started work on several conceptual models in the late 1990s. IFLA published the *Functional Requirements for Bibliographic Records* (FRBR), which modeled bibliographic data (description), in 1998; the *Functional Requirements for Authority Data* (FRAD), which modeled authority data (name and title access points), in 2009; and the *Functional Requirements for Subject Authority Data* (FRSAD), which modeled subject authority data, in 2010. IFLA also published the *Statement of International Cataloguing Principles*, a set of cataloging principles that updated the 1961 Paris Principles, in 2009.

In 2004, work began on revising AACR2. Originally referred to as AACR3, the focus of the new cataloging code shifted away quickly from AACR2.[44] Instead, it was renamed *Resource Description and Access* (RDA) to break away from AACR2's focus on cataloging "rules" and move toward a broader and more inclusive set of "instructions." In addition, RDA focuses more on authority control and showing relationships, is better suited for the digital environment, and moves cataloging codes toward the future. RDA incorporates the FRBR model, the FRAD model, and the 2009 *Statement of International Cataloguing Principles*. RDA was first published in 2010 and was tested in libraries between 2010 and 2013; implementation began in libraries in 2013. Implementation is still ongoing in some libraries.

Although RDA implementation is not yet complete in all libraries, RDA is already being revised. In 2016 IFLA published a revised version of the *Statement of International Cataloguing Principles*. In 2017 it published a new model, the *IFLA Library Reference Model* (LRM), which integrates the models on bibliographic data (FRBR), authority data (FRAD), and subject authority data (FRSAD) into one cohesive model. It also reflects linked data approaches to bibliographic information. RDA is being revised to incorporate the LRM model and the new statement of principles in a project called *3R Project: RDA Toolkit Restructure and Redesign*.[45] A beta version of the revised RDA was released in June 2018, and it is significantly different from the original RDA. If approved and implemented, the revised RDA has the potential to change how cataloging and metadata work is performed in libraries.

For subject headings, OCLC developed *Faceted Application of Subject Terminology* (FAST), as simplified LC subject headings based on facets, in 1998. In 2016 the Library of Congress published a new list of genre terms called *Library of Congress Genre/ Form Terms for Library and Archival Materials* (LCGFT). It includes genre terms for multiple subject areas, including fiction. In addition, some public libraries and school libraries explored alternative ways to classify their collections. For example, instead of using strict *Dewey*, some public libraries are using bookstore models to arrange their collections into broad subjects, and some school libraries are arranging their children's collections by genre.

In addition to changes in cataloging, metadata work began during this time as libraries started to create digital libraries and other digital collections. Starting in the late 1990s, libraries began to provide access to their digital collections using non-MARC metadata schemas. Most metadata schemas have been developed outside of libraries in collaboration with other professional communities, such as archives, museums, information technology, and government agencies—any community with an interest in providing access to information on the web. Several metadata schemas—such as *Dublin Core* (1995) for digital resources, *Categories for the Description of Works of Art* (CDWA, 1996) for art works, and *VRA Core* (1996) for visual resources—were developed to describe various types of digital resources available online. The Library of Congress developed the *Metadata Object Description Schema* (MODS), in 2002, and the *Metadata Authority Description Schema* (MADS), as simplified versions of the MARC 21 formats for bibliographic data and authority data, in 2005.

Today, academic and some public libraries use non-MARC metadata schemas to describe their digital collections, and metadata schemas are being used by libraries around the world. The use of non-MARC metadata schemas had led to metadata work, a new form of work in libraries to organize and provide access to digital collections. This work is done to digitize and make special collections or archival materials available as online digital collections. It is also performed for digital institutional repositories that collect the intellectual output of colleges and universities. Libraries have created new metadata positions or have reassigned staff to work on metadata projects. Some technical services departments and cataloging units have been restructured to perform this work.

There is one more development that has the potential to change how library collections are organized: linked open data, an idea first mentioned by Berners-Lee in 2006. Linked data is part of the Semantic Web movement, which wants to make computers understand the meaning of data on the web. For libraries, linked data has been discussed since 2010, and it has the potential to make library data available on the web. Currently, there are many projects and initiatives underway in libraries to publish bibliographic information and cataloging and metadata standards as linked data. One initiative currently under development is the *Bibliographic Framework Initiative* (BIBFRAME), a linked data replacement for MARC that was originally developed in 2012. Linked data in libraries will be discussed in more detail in chapter 10, along with other current developments that may affect how libraries organize their collections in the future.

SUMMARY

This chapter introduced why and how libraries organize their collections, and it presented a brief history of organizing library collections. Libraries organize their collections so library users can find what they need. Organization is essential because it supports the work of libraries and helps libraries meet the needs of their communities. Libraries collect a wide variety of physical and digital/electronic formats that influence how library collections are organized. There are two types of organization work performed in libraries: (1) cataloging, performed in all libraries to organize a library's main collection, and (2) metadata work, performed in some academic and public libraries to digitize and provide access to digital collections. Library cataloging has a long history of developing standards and tools that direct catalogers in their work. Catalogers use standards to create bibliographic records that are shared among libraries. Metadata work is a much newer form of work that is not standardized like cataloging. Metadata records describe unique materials in digital collections, and the work resists standardization. As library collections grow and change, the way they are organized grows and changes. The theory and practice of organizing library collections is always changing to meet the needs of libraries and to help users.

DISCUSSION QUESTIONS

1. Think about things you organize in your everyday life, like your kitchen, bookshelves, closets, filing cabinets, and so on. What do you organize and why? Describe your organizational system. Do you think your system would work for other people?
2. Why do libraries organize their collections? What are the factors that influence organization in libraries? What limits organization?
3. Discuss the history of organizing library collections. How does the growth of libraries and library collections affect how they are organized?

CLASS ACTIVITIES

1. *Library Collection.* The purpose of this assignment is to understand the various collections offered by a library. Visit a library and look at its website to determine the collections that are in the library. What is each collection and what formats are in it? Are there separate sections for particular formats or subjects (e.g., children's, new books, oversized, e-books, databases)? Briefly describe each collection in the library and what is in it.
2. *Library Catalog Critique.* The purpose of this assignment is to better understand online public access catalogs. Pick an online public access catalog available on a library's website. Perform multiple searches, such as keyword, author, subject, or title. Try searching for common words and phrases that an everyday person would use. Then write a short essay that critiques the catalog. Explain the searches that were performed, the results, and whether they were successful. Evaluate what was helpful, what was not helpful, and why.

NOTES

1. Merriam-Webster Online, "Organize," accessed January 9, 2019, https://www.merriam-webster.com/dictionary/organizing.

2. George M. Eberhart, ed., *The Librarian's Book of Lists* (Chicago: American Library Association, 2010), 1; Richard E. Rubin, *Foundations of Library and Information Science*, 4th ed. (Chicago: ALA Neal-Schuman, 2016).

3. American Library Association, "Number of Libraries in the United States: Home," last updated December 26, 2018, https://libguides.ala.org/numberoflibraries.

4. For more information about collection development, see Peggy Johnson, *Fundamentals of Collection Development and Management*, 4th ed. (Chicago: ALA Editions, 2018); Vicki L. Gregory, *Collection Development and Management for 21st-Century Library Collections: An Introduction*, 2nd ed. (Chicago: ALA Neal-Schuman: 2018).

5. International Federation of Library Associations and Institutions, *IFLA Library Reference Model: A Conceptual Model for Bibliographic Information.* (The Hague: IFLA, 2017), https://www.ifla.org/files/assets/cataloguing/frbr-lrm/ifla-lrm-august-2017_rev201712.pdf, 15–16.

6. Library of Congress Catalog, accessed January 9, 2019, https://catalog.loc.gov.

7. Antonio Panizzi, "Rules for the Compilation of the Catalog," in *Catalogue of Printed Books in the British Museum* (London: British Museum, 1841), 1:v–ix.

8. Charles A. Cutter, "Rules for a Printed Dictionary Catalogue," as *Public Libraries in the United States of America: Their History, Condition, and Management: Special Report, Part II.* (Washington, DC: US Government Printing Office, 1876), 10.

9. International Federation of Library Associations and Institutions, *Statement of International Cataloguing Principles (ICP)*, 2016 ed. (The Hague: IFLA, 2017), https://www.ifla.org/publications/node/11015, 10–11.

10. IFLA, *IFLA Library Reference Model*, 15–16.

11. Neal Douglass, "Birthday Party," photograph, March 7, 1959, University of North Texas Libraries, The Portal to Texas History, crediting Austin History Center, Austin Public Library, accessed January 9, 2019, https://texashistory.unt.edu/ark:/67531/metapth33391.

12. For more information about technical services, see, e.g., G. Edward Evans, Sheila S. Intner, and Jean Weihs, *Introduction to Technical Services*, 8th ed. (Santa Barbara, CA: Libraries Unlimited, 2011); John Sandstrom and Liz Miller, *Fundamentals of Technical Services* (Chicago: Neal-Schuman, 2015); Mary Beth Weber, "Introduction: What Is Technical Services?" in *Rethinking Library Technical Services: Redefining our Professional for the Future*, ed. Mary Beth Weber (Lanham, MD: Rowman & Littlefield, 2015), ix–xviii.

13. Heting Chu, *Information Representation and Retrieval in the Digital Age*, 2nd ed. (Medford, NJ: Information Today for the American Society for Information Science and Technology, 2010), 18.

14. For more information about the history of organizing library collections, see Lois Mai Chan and Athena Salaba, *Cataloging and Classification: An Introduction*, 4th ed. (Lanham, MD: Rowman & Littlefield, 2016); Daniel N. Joudrey and Arlene G. Taylor, *The Organization of Information*, 4th ed. (Santa Barbara, CA: Libraries Unlimited, 2018); Daniel N. Joudrey, Arlene G. Taylor, and David P. Miller, *Introduction to Cataloging and Classification*, 11th ed. (Santa Barbara, CA: Libraries Unlimited, 2015); and the work of Francis Miksa and Wayne Wiegand.

15. Library of Congress, "History of the Library of Congress," accessed January 9, 2019, https://www.loc.gov/about/history-of-the-library.

16. Nancy E. Gwinn, "History," Smithsonian Libraries, accessed January 9, 2019, https://library.si.edu/about/history.

17. National Library of Medicine, "A Brief History of NLM," last updated September 26, 2018, https://www.nlm.nih.gov/about/briefhistory.html.

18. Panizzi, *Rules for the Compilation of the Catalog.*

19. Charles A. Jewett, *Smithsonian Report on the Construction of Catalogues of Libraries and of a General Catalog, and Their Publication by Means of Separate, Stereotyped Titles* (Washington, DC: Smithsonian Institution, 1852), 7.

20. Ibid., 6.

21. G. Edward Evans and Stacey Greenwell, *Academic Librarianship*, 2nd ed. (Chicago: ALA Neal-Schuman: 2018).

22. The first edition was titled *A Classification and Subject Index for Cataloguing and Arranging the Books and Pamphlets of a library.*

23. The first edition was titled *Rules for a Printed Dictionary Catalogue.*

24. American Library Association. Cooperation Committee, "Condensed Rules for an Author and Title Catalog," *Library Journal* 8, no. 9–10 (September–October 1883): 251–54.

25. American Library Association, *List of Subject Headings for Use in Dictionary Catalogs* (Boston, MA: Published for the ALA Publishing Section by the Library Bureau, 1895).

26. Alistair Black, "From Reference Desk to Desk Set: The History of the Corporate Library in the United States and the UK before the Adoption of the Computer," in *Best Practices for Corporate Libraries*, ed. Sigrid E. Kelsey and Marjorie J. Porter (Santa Barbara, CA: Libraries Unlimited, 2011), 3–24.

27. Blanche Woolls and Sharon Coatney, *The School Library Manager: Surviving and Thriving* (Santa Barbara, CA: Libraries Unlimited, 2018), 22.

28. After College and Reference Librarians (1889) and Trustees (1890), see "ALA Divisions," accessed January 9, 2019, http://www.ala.org/aboutala/divs.

29. American Library Association, *A.L.A. Catalog Rules: Author and Title Entries*, American ed. (Chicago: American Library Association, 1908).

30. American Library Association, *A.L.A. Catalog Rules: Author and Title Entries*, Preliminary American 2nd ed. (Chicago: American Library Association, 1941).

31. In 1945 Vannevar Bush foreshadowed advancements in computers and technology, calling for the scientific community to focus on organizing, recording, and preserving the world's knowledge. See Vannevar Bush, "As We May Think," *Atlantic*, July 1945, accessed January 9, 2019, http://www.theatlantic.com/magazine/archive/1945/07/as-we-may-think/3881.

32. For more information about the history of keyword searching, see, e.g., Chu, *Information Representation and Retrieval in the Digital Age.*

33. Andrew D. Osborn, "The Crisis in Cataloging," *Library Quarterly* 11 (1941): 393–411.

34. Library of Congress, Descriptive Cataloging Division. *Rules for Descriptive Cataloging in the Library of Congress* (Washington, DC: US Government Printing Office, 1949).

35. Library of Congress, Processing Department. "Principles of Descriptive Cataloging," in *Studies of Descriptive Cataloging: A Report to the Librarian of Congress by the Director of the Processing Department* (Washington, DC: US Government Printing Office, 1946), 25–33.

36. *Anglo-American Cataloging Rules*, North American Text (Chicago: American Library Association, 1967), v–vii.

37. Ibid.

38. International Federation of Library Associations, *Statement of Principles Adopted at the International Conference on Cataloguing Principles, Paris, October, 1961*, annotated ed. with commentary and examples by Eva Verona (London: IFLA Committee on Cataloguing, 1971).

39. Ibid.; *Anglo-American Cataloging Rules*.

40. David Judson Haykin, *Subject Headings: A Practical Guide* (Washington, DC: US Government Printing Office, 1951), 7.

41. The destruction of card catalogs was criticized by some who felt that libraries were destroying their history. See, e.g., Nicolson Baker, "Discards," *New Yorker*, April 4, 1994, 64–70.

42. IFLA, "Superseded ISBDs," last updated January 20, 2015, https://www.ifla.org/isbd -rg/superseded-isbd-s.

43. *Anglo-American Cataloguing Rules*, 2nd ed. (Chicago: American Library Association, 1978), v–xii.

44. Joint Steering Committee for the Development of RDA, "RDA: Resource Description and Access; Background," last updated April 13, 2015, http://www.rda-jsc.org/archivedsite/ rda.html#background.

45. RDA Toolkit, "3R Project," accessed January 9, 2019, https://www.rdatoolkit .org/3RProject.

SELECTED BIBLIOGRAPHY WITH ADDITIONAL READING

American Library Association. *A.L.A. Catalog Rules: Author and Title Entries*. American Edition. Chicago: American Library Association, 1908.

———. *A.L.A. Catalog Rules: Author and Title Entries*. Preliminary American Second Edition. Chicago: American Library Association, 1941.

———. *List of Subject Headings for Use in Dictionary Catalogs*. Boston: Published for the ALA Publishing Section by the Library Bureau, 1895.

American Library Association. Cooperation Committee. "Condensed Rules for an Author and Title Catalog." *Library Journal* 8, no. 9–10 (September–October 1883): 251–54.

A.L.A. Cataloging Rules for Author and Title Entries. Second Edition. Chicago: American Library Association, 1949.

Anglo-American Cataloging Rules. North American Text. Chicago: American Library Association, 1967.

Anglo-American Cataloguing Rules. Second Edition. Chicago: American Library Association, 1978.

Baker, Nicholson. "Discards." *New Yorker*, April 4, 1994, 64–70.

Black, Alistair. "From Reference Desk to Desk Set: The History of the Corporate Library in the United States and the UK before the Adoption of the Computer." In *Best Practices for Corporate Libraries*, edited by Sigrid E. Kelsey and Marjorie J. Porter, 3–24. Santa Barbara, CA: Libraries Unlimited, 2011.

Black, Alistair, and Henry Gabb. "The Value Proposition of the Corporate Library, Past and Present." *Information & Culture* 51 (2016): 192–225.

Buckland, Michael K. "Information as Thing." *Journal of the American Society for Information Science* 42 (1991): 351–60.

Bush, Vannevar. "As We May Think." *Atlantic*, July 1945. http://www.theatlantic.com/maga zine/archive/1945/07/as-we-may-think/3881.

Chan, Lois Mai, and Athena Salaba. *Cataloging and Classification: An Introduction*. Fourth Edition. Lanham, MD: Lowman & Littlefield, 2016.

Chu, Heting. *Information Representation and Retrieval in the Digital Age*. Second Edition. Medford, NJ: Information Today for the American Society for Information Science and Technology, 2010.

Cutter, Charles A. "Rules for a Printed Dictionary Catalogue." Published as *Public Libraries in the United States of America: Their History, Condition, and Management: Special Report, Part II*. Washington, DC: US Government Printing Office, 1876.

Eberhart, George M., ed. *The Librarian's Book of Lists*. Chicago: American Library Association, 2010.

Evans, G. Edward, and Stacey Greenwell. *Academic Librarianship*. Second Edition. Chicago: ALA Neal-Schuman, 2018.

Evans, G. Edward, Sheila S. Intner, and Jean Weihs. *Introduction to Technical Services*. Eighth Edition. Santa Barbara, CA: Libraries Unlimited, 2011.

Gregory, Vicki L. *Collection Development and Management for 21st-Century Library Collections: An Introduction*. Second Edition. Chicago: ALA Neal-Schuman, 2018.

Haykin, David Judson. *Subject Headings: A Practical Guide*. Washington, DC: US Government Printing Office, 1951.

International Federation of Library Associations. *Statement of Principles Adopted at the International Conference on Cataloguing Principles, Paris, October, 1961*. Annotated Edition with commentary and examples by Eva Verona. London: IFLA Committee on Cataloguing, 1971.

International Federation of Library Associations and Institutions. *IFLA Library Reference Model: A Conceptual Model for Bibliographic Information*. The Hague: IFLA, 2017. https://www.ifla.org/files/assets/cataloguing/frbr-lrm/ifla-lrm-august-2017_rev201712.pdf.

———. *Statement of International Cataloguing Principles (ICP)*. 2016 Edition, with minor revisions. The Hague: IFLA, 2017. https://www.ifla.org/publications/node/11015.

Jewett, Charles. A. *Smithsonian Report on the Construction of Catalogues of Libraries and of a General Catalogue; and Their Publication by Means of Separate, Stereotyped Titles*. Washington, DC: Smithsonian Institution, 1852.

Johnson, Peggy. *Fundamentals of Collection Development and Management*. Fourth Edition. Chicago: ALA Editions, 2018.

Joudrey, Daniel N., and Arlene G. Taylor. *The Organization of Information*. Fourth Edition. Santa Barbara, CA: Libraries Unlimited, 2018.

Joudrey, Daniel N., Arlene G. Taylor, and David P. Miller. *Introduction to Cataloging and Classification*. Eleventh Edition. Santa Barbara, CA: Libraries Unlimited, 2015.

Kevane, Michael, and William A. Sundstrom. "The Development of Public Libraries in the United States, 1870–1930: A Quantitative Assessment." *Information & Culture* 49, no. 2 (2014): 117–44.

Library of Congress, Descriptive Cataloging Division. *Rules for Descriptive Cataloging in the Library of Congress*. Washington, DC: US Government Printing Office, 1949.

Library of Congress, Processing Department. "Principles of Descriptive Cataloging." In *Studies of Descriptive Cataloging: A Report to the Librarian of Congress by the Director of the Processing Department*, 25–33. Washington, DC: US Government Printing Office, 1946.

Miksa, Francis L., ed. *Charles Ammi Cutter: Library Systematizer*. Littleton, CO: Libraries Unlimited, 1977.

Miksa, Francis. *The DDC, the Universe of Knowledge, and the Postmodern Library*. Albany, NY: Forest Press, 1998.

———. *The Development of Classification at the Library of Congress*. Occasional papers, University of Illinois at Urbana-Champaign. Graduate School of Library and Information Science 164. Champaign-Urbana: University of Illinois, Graduate School of Library and Information Science, 1984.

———. *The Subject in the Dictionary Catalog from Cutter to the Present*. Chicago: American Library Association, 1983.

Osborn, Andrew D. "The Crisis in Cataloging." *Library Quarterly* 11 (1941): 393–411.

Panizzi, Antonio. "Rules for the Compilation of the Catalogue." In *Catalogue of Printed Books in the British Museum. London*, 1:v–ix. London: British Museum, 1841.

Rubin, Richard E. *Foundations of Library and Information Science*. Fourth Edition. Chicago: ALA Neal-Schuman, 2016.

Sandstrom, John, and Liz Miller. *Fundamentals of Technical Services*. Chicago: Neal-Schuman, 2015.

Tillett, Barbara B. "Catalog It Once for All: A History of Cooperative Cataloging in the United States Prior to 1967 (before MARC)." *Cataloging & Classification Quarterly* 17, no. 3/4 (1993): 3–38.

Weber, Mary Beth. "Introduction: What Is Technical Services?" In *Rethinking Library Technical Services: Redefining our Professional for the Future*, edited by Mary Beth Weber, ix–xviii. Lanham, MD: Rowman & Littlefield, 2015.

Wiegand, Wayne A. "The 'Amherst Method': The Origins of the Dewey Decimal Classification Scheme." *Libraries & Culture* 33 (1998): 175–94.

———. *Irrepressible Reformer: A Biography of Melvil Dewey*. Chicago: American Library Association, 1996.

———. *Part of Our Lives: A People's History of the American Public Library*. Oxford: Oxford University Press, 2015.

Woolls, Blanche, and Sharon Coatney. *The School Library Manager: Surviving and Thriving*. Santa Barbara, CA: Libraries Unlimited, 2018.

2

Metadata and Encoding: Fundamental to Organizing Library Collections

The previous chapter provided an introduction to the organization of library collections. It explained the formats in a library collection and how libraries organize their collections through cataloging and metadata work, and it gave a brief history of organizing library collections. This chapter will start to dig deeper into cataloging and metadata theory, specifically addressing metadata and encoding, fundamental concepts in the organization of library collections. It will describe metadata and discuss the different types of metadata created in libraries. It also will discuss encoding standards, which are used to encode metadata so computers can read and display it to users.

METADATA

Metadata. It may seem like a confusing word, but broadly speaking, metadata just means data about data, or information about information. Metadata is something that describes something else, but in a structured way. And metadata is an essential part of how we function in the world. Think about shopping online on Wayfair, Amazon, or another online site. Each product is described using metadata, such as its color, size, weight, dimensions, and manufacturer. When you shop online, you are actually searching and viewing metadata, the information that describes each product. The more metadata is added, the better you can determine whether you want to purchase the product. Although you may see a picture or a video of a product, you cannot touch or see the real thing. You rely on the metadata to give you an accurate picture of a product. For example, imagine you want to buy a sofa like the one in figure 2.1.[1] It shows a picture of a sofa and a list of metadata about the sofa. Although the picture can help you determine if you like the color and style, the picture alone cannot explain what type of sofa it is, the material used to make it, or where it was made. The metadata is essential to help you determine if you want to purchase the sofa or not.

Product Type	Loveseat
Design	Standard
Seating Capacity	2
Upholstery Material	100% Polyester
Leg Color	Black
Pattern	Solid
Frame Material	Solid Wood
Wood Construction Details	Espresso
Seat Fill Material	Foam
Back Fill Material	Foam
Seat Construction	Pocket Spring
Seat Style	Multiple cushion seat
Back Type	Pillow back
Toss Pillows Included	Yes
Country of Origin	China
Wood Species	Eucalyptus
Weight Capacity	450 Pounds

Figure 2.1.   Metadata for a Sofa on Wayfair.com

Metadata is *everywhere*. Want to rent a car? Metadata that describes each car helps you choose one. Want to order a pizza? Metadata that describes each pizza helps you order one. Want to buy an airline ticket? Metadata about each flight helps you book one. Think about the files you create, like when you take a digital photo or video, or create a Word document or PowerPoint presentation. You create metadata when you name your files or add keywords that describe each file. There is metadata embedded in your files, too, that is automatically added by the software. Word files and PowerPoint presentations, for example, have embedded metadata in the "Properties," such as the file's size, author, and the date it was created. Your digital photos include embedded metadata, too, such as size, dimensions, date, and so on. For example, look at figure 2.2.[2] It shows a digital photograph and some metadata about the digital photograph. There is metadata someone created, such as the file name "Winter Tree." There also is metadata that the software created embedded in the photograph, such as date taken and size.

Although metadata is usually associated with computers, it is not limited to computers or the web. There is lots of metadata in the world that exists outside of computers. Every print sales catalog, such as an L.L.Bean catalog, includes metadata that describes each item for sale. A person cannot touch items in the catalog, but the metadata that describes each item helps consumers choose what to buy. A restaurant menu includes metadata that describes each dish. Diners do not see the food and choose what they want; they rely on the menu to help them choose what to order. Metadata is essential to help us live our lives.

Metadata in Libraries

Metadata is essential for libraries, too. Metadata is used to describe and provide access to library collections. Title, author, subject: they are all examples of metadata that describe something in a library, like a book or a video. Everything in a library should be described so people can find and select library materials. Yet metadata can be a fuzzy concept with many definitions. Daniel N. Joudrey and Arlene G. Taylor sum up the multiple definitions: "What [the definitions] all have in common is the notion that metadata is structured information that describes the important attributes of information resources for the purposes of identification, discovery, selection, use, access, and management."[3] From this definition, it is important to understand that metadata is structured information (e.g., title, author, subject) that describes information resources (e.g., books, serials, music). Metadata is used to identify, discover, select, use, access, and manage a library's collection. It helps people find, choose, and use library materials. Without metadata, people would not be able to use library catalogs or databases. People would not be able to find and view things in digital collections. People would not be able to find and view web pages. Metadata is very important in searching and retrieval.

Steven J. Miller has another definition focused on the functions of metadata. He says, "Metadata is data or information that enables people to perform certain functions

File name

Winter Tree

Date taken
Thursday, February 3, 2011 9:27 PM

Size
3.1 MB

Dimensions
3072 x 2304

Shot
1/250 sec. f/2.8 4.6mm

ISO
--

Device
Canon PowerShot SD800 IS

Folder path
C:\Users\Gretchen\Desktop\Pictures
\2011_02_03

Figure 2.2. Metadata for a Digital Photograph

in relation to the information resources that the metadata is about. Metadata is information that is distinct from the resource which it is about, even when the metadata is embedded in a digital resource."[4] From this definition, it is important to understand that metadata is separate from information resources, like items in a library collection, but metadata can be located *inside or outside* of them. Metadata such as title, author, date, or subject can be located in a library catalog or database and exist outside of the items they represent. Metadata also can be embedded within digital resources—such as within a web page, a digital file, or a digital photograph—to identify the resource and to help computers search for it.

For example, see figures 2.3 and 2.4. Figure 2.3 shows an example of metadata existing outside of a library item, in this case a bibliographic record from a public

Figure 2.3.   Bibliographic Record for a Book (Book Cover)

Authors:	Dean, Kim, 1969-
Title:	Pete the cat and the cool cat boogie
Publisher:	New York, NY : Harper, an imprint of HarperCollinsPublishers, [2017]
Edition:	First edition
Characteristics:	32 unnumbered pages : color illustrations ; 28 cm
Content Type:	text still image
Media Type:	unmediated
Carrier Type:	volume
Series:	Pete the cat
Summary:	Pete the Cat is learning a new dance -- the Cool Cat Boogie! When he hears a groovy beat, he's full of happy feet. But when Grumpy toad tells him, "Pete, you dance all wrong!" Pete is determined to become a better dancer. With the help of his friends and some wise words from Owl, Pete learns that he's the grooviest when he's being himself.
Audience:	Ages 4-8
Additional Contributors:	Dean, James 1957-
ISBN:	9780062404343 0062404342 9780062409096 0062409093
Branch Call Number:	E PET
Reading Level:	480L

Figure 2.3.   Bibliographic Record for a Book (the Record)

library catalog.[5] The metadata, such as title, author, and publisher, represents the children's book *Pete the Cat and the Cool Cat Boogie*, but it exists outside of the book. Library users see the metadata, and it can be manipulated by computers to help search and retrieve on a library's catalog. Figure 2.4 shows selected metadata embedded within the National Library of Medicine's main website.[6] Notice the title, keywords, and description embedded in the source code. The website's metadata is running behind the scenes. A person cannot see the metadata without viewing the source code. The metadata can be manipulated by computers and helps in searching and retrieval on the web.

Metadata may seem like a simple concept, but it means different things to different communities. The word *metadata* is usually associated with computers, because metadata is needed to describe and provide access to information available through a computer, especially online. Therefore, some people assume that metadata is available only on computers. Metadata is vital for searching and retrieval on computers, but going by the definition, libraries have been "providing information" about their collections for centuries with "metadata" that describes and provides access to them. Computers are not necessary to create metadata, and metadata in libraries is known by many terms and phrases, such as bibliographic information, cataloging information, and indexing. It is helpful to take a broader view of metadata in the library and information context. Metadata encompasses all types of information organization, including library cataloging, metadata work, and indexing. Librarianship has always dealt with metadata; it is just the terminology that has changed.

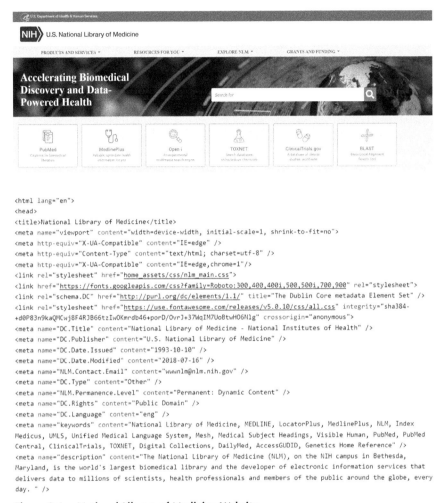

```
<html lang="en">
<head>
<title>National Library of Medicine</title>
<meta name="viewport" content="width=device-width, initial-scale=1, shrink-to-fit=no">
<meta http-equiv="X-UA-Compatible" content="IE=edge" />
<meta http-equiv="Content-Type" content="text/html; charset=utf-8" />
<meta http-equiv="X-UA-Compatible" content="IE=edge,chrome=1"/>
<link rel="stylesheet" href="home_assets/css/nlm_main.css">
<link href="https://fonts.googleapis.com/css?family=Roboto:300,400,400i,500,500i,700,900" rel="stylesheet">
<link rel="schema.DC" href="http://purl.org/dc/elements/1.1/" title="The Dublin Core metadata Element Set" />
<link rel="stylesheet" href="https://use.fontawesome.com/releases/v5.0.10/css/all.css" integrity="sha384-
+d0P83n9kaQMCwj8F4RJB66tzIwOKmrdb46+porD/OvrJ+37WqIM7UoBtwHO6Nlg" crossorigin="anonymous">
<meta name="DC.Title" content="National Library of Medicine - National Institutes of Health" />
<meta name="DC.Publisher" content="U.S. National Library of Medicine" />
<meta name="DC.Date.Issued" content="1993-10-10" />
<meta name="DC.Date.Modified" content="2018-07-16" />
<meta name="NLM.Contact.Email" content="wwwnlm@nlm.nih.gov" />
<meta name="DC.Type" content="Other" />
<meta name="NLM.Permanence.Level" content="Permanent: Dynamic Content" />
<meta name="DC.Rights" content="Public Domain" />
<meta name="DC.Language" content="eng" />
<meta name="keywords" content="National Library of Medicine, MEDLINE, LocatorPlus, MedlinePlus, NLM, Index
Medicus, UMLS, Unified Medical Language System, Mesh, Medical Subject Headings, Visible Human, PubMed, PubMed
Central, ClinicalTrials, TOXNET, Digital Collections, DailyMed, AccessGUDID, Genetics Home Reference" />
<meta name="description" content="The National Library of Medicine (NLM), on the NIH campus in Bethesda,
Maryland, is the world's largest biomedical library and the developer of electronic information services that
delivers data to millions of scientists, health professionals and members of the public around the globe, every
day. " />
```

Figure 2.4.   National Library of Medicine Website

TYPES OF METADATA

Libraries have always created metadata to describe their collections and to help people find library materials. However, libraries primarily create what is called descriptive metadata. The most common type of metadata created in libraries, it describes all physical and digital materials in a library's collection. Yet there are other types of metadata that are important in the management, preservation, and use of digital collections. Broadly speaking, there are three main types of metadata: descriptive metadata, administrative metadata, and structural metadata. It is important to note that the three types of metadata are common across the literature, but some researchers include different categories.[7]

Descriptive Metadata

Descriptive metadata is the primary type of metadata created in libraries. It is used to describe and provide access to each item in a library's collection. It is important because descriptive metadata "provides intellectual access" to library collections.[8] It helps people find and access library materials. Library users search for descriptive metadata when they search library catalogs. Descriptive metadata exists outside of library materials and can include elements like titles, authors, publishers, dates, subject headings, series, and much more—anything that describes and provides access to library materials. Descriptive metadata can be created by anyone, but in libraries, catalogers and metadata specialists usually create it. Unlike other types of metadata, descriptive metadata can be used to describe all types of library materials, physical or digital, and it is the most common type of metadata created in libraries. Descriptive metadata will be discussed in more detail in chapter 3.

Administrative Metadata

Administrative metadata is created only for digital resources in digital collections. It is concerned with things like acquisitions information, ownership and rights, legal access, preservation, and so on. It is important for the management, preservation, and use of digital resources. Administrative metadata can include subcategories of *technical metadata* (information about files), *preservation metadata* (information about preservation activities), and *rights metadata* (information about copyright and rights). *Use metadata* is another subcategory that focuses on things like tracking use and search logs. Administrative metadata is created by metadata specialists and anyone else who creates digital items.

Structural Metadata

Structural metadata is created only for digital resources in digital collections. Structural metadata is concerned with the structural components of digital resources. It includes information about where files are located and how they fit together. Structural metadata is created by metadata specialists and anyone else who creates digital items.

PURPOSE OF METADATA

Metadata is a fundamental aspect of organizing library collections. It is important for several reasons.

Discovery (Searching and Retrieval)

Metadata is important for discovery so users can search and retrieve on library catalogs, databases, and other systems. Metadata helps users find library materials quickly and easily. Metadata supports discovery by describing each item in the library, providing access points, and showing relationships among items in the library. Links in a catalog or database allow users to explore relationships among library items to find exactly what they need. As Marcia Lei Zeng and Jian Qin say, "Whether for everyday life or for scientific endeavors, the search for information depends on two basic questions: 'What is this "thing"? and 'How does this thing relate to other things?'"[9] Searching and retrieval using computers relies on good metadata. It can be much easier and more efficient to search the metadata than to search full-text materials. Bad metadata (i.e., incorrect, misleading, missing, or incomplete) entered into a library catalog or database means bad metadata coming out of a library catalog or database (i.e., few or irrelevant search results). Ultimately, people do not find what they need. Searching for library materials and information relies on good metadata. A user cannot find something if the metadata does not exist.

Good metadata is necessary because computers are limited. They are electronic machines that take data and instructions (input), work with data (processing), and present data (output). That is it. Computers are not human. They cannot act on their own. Computers use programs and algorithms created by humans that tell them what to do, and humans must tell computers how to do *everything*. Computers are getting more intelligent and sophisticated every day because the programs and algorithms being developed by humans are getting more intelligent and sophisticated every day. Humans are smart; computers need help. A library catalog or database could have the most sensitive and sophisticated algorithms to find information, but good searching and retrieval depends on good metadata. An algorithm cannot find anything if the metadata is not there. Garbage in, garbage out, so to speak. Discovery, searching, and retrieval in libraries would not be possible without good metadata.

Representation

Another reason metadata is important is representation.[10] It is through metadata, particularly descriptive metadata, that catalogers and metadata specialists create representations of library materials. Bibliographic records and metadata records represent items in a library's collection. Collectively, a library catalog represents a library's main collection, and a content management database represents items in a digital collection. The creation of representations is important because it is easier and more efficient to search the representations (the descriptive metadata in bibliographic and metadata records) than it is to search each item in a library individually. By representing library materials, metadata allows users to search for library items away from the actual library collection. It would be impossible for a library user to look through every single item in a library. Bibliographic and metadata records represent library materials so a user can look at them to find what they need. Heting Chu explains the importance of representation: "Retrieval performance suffers when information representation is not properly done. The importance of having quality information representation cannot be overemphasized. We should therefore aim for quality information representation so that we can find what we are looking for in the world of digital information."[11]

Organization and Display

Metadata is also important for organizing resources. Classification, for example, represents subjects and allows a library to organize its collection by subject. Materials on the same subject are near each other on the shelves: Cookbooks are shelved with other cookbooks, not with books about electrical engineering or dog training. Bringing together materials on the same subject facilitates browsing of library shelves as well as browsing on library catalogs. Metadata also helps computers display information in specific ways that helps users. Search results can be listed in alphabetical or numerical order, or by relevance or date. Information in bibliographic and metadata records can be displayed to users so it is easily understood.

Interoperability

Interoperability is another reason to use metadata. Interoperability refers to the ability of computer systems to share information with one another. Online information is located on many servers around the world. Everyone's personal computer or device needs to talk to these servers in order to search, retrieve, display, and interact with information online. Computers need to speak the same language, and metadata helps computers communicate with one another.

Preservation

Metadata also helps with the preservation of physical and digital materials. When physical materials are cataloged, a record is made of them and they are made available to users. Instead of uncataloged items deteriorating in a box in the backroom, or digital files buried in a computer folder, library materials are cataloged and made available to users. For materials in digital collections, preservation metadata is added that helps preserve each digital file for any future migration or potential use.

METADATA STANDARDS

There are many metadata standards in the world. Metadata standards need to be flexible and extensible to be used in any context, both inside and outside of libraries. Libraries have been creating metadata for many years, but librarianship and the computer science field talk about metadata standards in different ways, using different vocabularies. For example, what librarianship would call a controlled vocabulary, computer science would call a value vocabulary. Essentially, the phrases mean the same thing, but the concept is viewed with different lenses. When discussing metadata, it is important to understand computer science vocabulary. Marcia Lei Zeng and Jian Qin, for example, discuss four types of metadata standards that reflect a computer science focus:[12]

1. *Standards for data structures:* These types of standards are known by many names, such as metadata schemas, element sets, data dictionaries, or metadata vocabularies. They include a set of elements that describe library resources (e.g., title, author, date), with definitions for each element. However, data structure standards do not dictate content or how particular elements should be described. In libraries, they are used to describe digital collections. *Dublin Core* and *Metadata Object Description Schema* are examples.

2. *Standards for data content:* These are content standards used to describe resources in cultural heritage communities, such as libraries, museums, and archives. Content standards provide detailed explanations about how to describe materials. Content standards provide content only; they do not specify how the metadata is encoded. Examples include *Resource Description and Access*, used primarily in the library community; *Cataloging Cultural Objects*, used primarily in the museum community; and *Describing Archives: A Content Standard*, used primarily in the archival community.

3. *Standards for data values:* These are authorized lists of standard information to be used when describing resources. In the library community, they are called authority files, controlled vocabularies (subject headings lists and thesauri), and classification schemes. One consistent form of a name, subject heading, classification number, and so on is used to link works in a library catalog or database. In libraries, these standards are used to create bibliographic records for the library catalog and metadata records for digital collections. Examples include authorized names and titles from the Library of Congress's National Authority File, the *Library of Congress Subject Headings*, *Sears List of Subject Headings*, *Dewey Decimal Classification*, *Library of Congress Classification*, and many others.

4. *Standards for data exchange:* These are standards used simply to exchange data. They are called encoding standards, encoding languages, or markup languages. They are simply a vehicle to transmit information through a computer. They have nothing to do with content and do not explain how library materials should be described. They simply encode metadata so a computer can read and exchange it. MARC and XML are two examples used in libraries.

It is important to understand that these metadata standards overlap; there is no clean division. Each type of metadata standard functions differently and has a different purpose.

METADATA CREATED IN LIBRARIES

All types of metadata standards are used in libraries in various ways. They are used to create metadata that is housed in records used in libraries. Records describe something in a library's collection, such as a book or a digital photograph. There are four main types of records used in libraries: bibliographic records, authority records, metadata records, and database records.

Bibliographic Records

As discussed in chapter 1, bibliographic records (also called bib records) are the most common form of metadata created in libraries. They describe and provide access to each item in a library's collection. Bibliographic records are housed in a library's catalog, which users can search to find library materials. Bibliographic records are created through the cataloging process. Catalogers create descriptive metadata that describes and provides access to a library's main collection, both physical and digital formats. In some libraries, bibliographic records may be created for physical items in special collections.

Bibliographic records contain primarily descriptive metadata, and the library profession has developed many cataloging standards, tools, and guidelines that guide the creation of bibliographic records in libraries, such as *Resource Description and Access* (RDA), *Library of Congress Subject Headings* (LCSH), and *Dewey Decimal Classification* (DDC), just to name a few. Catalogers use these standards to create consistent bibliographic records.

All libraries catalog their materials, and cataloging work is standardized across libraries. Libraries tend to collect the same mass-published items, so libraries can share bibliographic records. Sharing bibliographic records makes bibliographic information consistent for users. No matter the library catalog system, users search and retrieve the same descriptive metadata in any library. The creation of bibliographic records is discussed in more detail in chapter 3. See figure 2.5 for an example of a bibliographic record.[13] There is lots of descriptive metadata that describes and provides access to the book *Pete the Cat and the Cool Cat Boogie*.

```
001    ocn973762545
003    OCoLC
005    20170505025601.0
008    161205t20172017nyua  b    000 1 eng d
020      |a 9780062404343
020      |a 0062404342
049      |a TNNA
099      |a E |a Dean
100    1  |a Dean, Kim, |d 1969- |e author, |e illustrator.
245    1 0 |a Pete the cat and the cool cat boogie / |c Kimberly and James Dean.
250      |a First edition.
264    1 |a New York, NY : |b Harper, an imprint of HarperCollinsPublishers, |c [2017]
264    4 |c ◆2017.
300      |a 1 volume (unpaged) : |b color illustrations ; |c 28 cm.
336      |a text |b txt |2 rdacontent.
337      |a unmediated |b n |2 rdamedia.
338      |a volume |b nc |2 rdacarrier.
490    1  |a Pete the cat book.
520      |a Pete the Cat is learning a new dance--the Cool Cat Boogie! When he hears a groovy beat, he's full of happy feet. But when
         Grumpy Toad tells him, "Pete, you dance all wrong!" Pete is determined to become a better dancer. With the help of his friends
         and some wise words from Owl, Pete learns that he's the grooviest when he's being himself.
521    1  |a Ages 4-8.
600    0 0 |a Pete, |c the Cat (Fictitious character) |v Juvenile fiction.
650      0 |a Cats |v Juvenile fiction.
650      0 |a Dance |v Juvenile fiction.
650      0 |a Friendship |v Juvenile fiction.
650      0 |a Self-acceptance |v Juvenile fiction.
700    1  |a Dean, James, |d 1957- |e author, |e illustrator.
830      0 |a Pete the cat.
```

Figure 2.5. Example of a Bibliographic Record

Authority Records

Authority records are created by catalogers as part of the cataloging process. They hold metadata about access points, such as names, titles, and subject headings. One consistent form of names, titles, and subject headings must be used on bibliographic records, and authority records include authorized access points, approved cross-references, variant forms, broader terms, narrower terms, related terms, and other information. Authority records are separate from bibliographic records and are never shown to the public. They work with bibliographic records to give users access to the library catalog and to show relationships between items. Authority records will be discussed further in chapter 3. See figure 2.6 for an example of an authority record. It shows an authority record for Kim Dean, one of the authors of *Pete the Cat and the Cool Cat Boogie*.[14] The authority record includes metadata that describes her bibliographic identity.

000 00636cz a2200169n 450
001 9296376
005 20131003073747.0
008 130625n| azannaabn |a aaa
010 __ |a n 2013037135
035 __ |a (OCoLC)oca09505535
040 __ |a DLC |b eng |c DLC |e rda |d TnLvILS
100 1_ |a Dean, Kim, |d 1969-
400 1_ |a Dean, Kimberly, |d 1969-
670 __ |a Pete the cat and his magic sunglasses, 2013: |b ECIP title page (Kim Dean)
670 __ |a Pete the cat and his magic sunglasses, 2013: |b email from publisher 6/24/13 (Kim Dean's bday October 18 1969)
670 __ |a Pete the cat, the first Thanksgiving. c2013: |b cover (Kimberly & James Dean)

Figure 2.6.   Example of an Authority Record

Metadata Records

In addition to bibliographic and authority records, libraries also create metadata records that describe and provide access to digital items in digital collections. This includes creating metadata for items in institutional repositories (collections of materials created by faculty, staff, and students at a college or university) and making digital copies of items in special collections or archives. Digital materials and their metadata records are available in institutional repositories or content management systems, separate databases that house digital items. They are not usually available in a library catalog. Metadata specialists create metadata records, and metadata work is a newer form of work in some libraries that is usually performed separately from cataloging. Although cataloging and metadata work share similarities—they both describe and provide access to library materials—how the work is performed and the types of metadata needed are different.

Creating digital collections is more complex and requires more types of metadata. Metadata specialists do not just create metadata records; they create digital content, too. They make digital copies of physical items and make those digital files available to library users, along with metadata records that describe the digital files. Quite simply, digital files require more than just descriptive metadata. For example, imagine a physical book. Everyone knows how to open a physical book and use it. Libraries do not have to describe things like the glue that was used to secure the binding, how the binder cut the pages, or the type of paper that was used. However, understanding details about digital files is important when it comes to digital collections. Digital resources are much more complex than physical resources. They can include more than one file, and more types of metadata are needed for people to use them and for libraries to manage them. Along with descriptive metadata that describes the content, structural metadata and administrative metadata are needed as well. For example: Who created the digital resource? Who holds the rights? What is the file type and size? How do the files fit together? Digital objects fall apart and are unusable if the administrative and structural metadata are not there to support their use.

Creating digital content can be quite complicated. Flexible metadata schemas and other types of metadata are needed that work across multiple platforms. Imagine a metadata specialist digitizes a photograph and creates a digital file. Structural metadata is added to tell the computer where it is housed, how many files are involved, and how to put the metadata together so users can see the photograph and read its metadata. Administrative metadata is important to explain who owns or has rights to the photograph. Preservation data is added to make sure digital resources can be used for years to come. The Library of Congress maintains several standards used for administrative and structural metadata, such as the *PREMIS Data Dictionary for Preservation Metadata*, a data dictionary used just for preservation metadata; the *Metadata Encoding & Transmission Standard* (METS), which is used to connect all types of metadata and bring together all files associated with a digital resource; *Analyzed Layout and Text Object* (ALTO), used for technical metadata for optical character recognition; *AudioMD* and *VideoMD*, used for technical metadata for audio- and video-based digital objects; *NISO Metadata for Images in XML* (MIX), used for technical metadata for digital image collections; and, *Technical Metadata for Text* (TextMD), used for technical metadata for text-based digital objects.[15]

For descriptive metadata, metadata specialists use various metadata schemas to describe and provide access to items in digital collections. Libraries can choose from a variety of metadata schemas (e.g., *Dublin Core*), and they can tailor the schemas to fit the library's needs. Metadata schemas are much broader and much more flexible than cataloging standards. They usually provide a list of elements—like title, author, or rights—that can be used to describe digital resources, but nothing is prescribed. A library can choose from a wide variety of different metadata schemas, and it can choose to take an existing schema and expand it or make it smaller. A library can even pick and choose from different types of metadata schemas and create an application profile, which is essentially a profile of how the library has applied one or more metadata schemas. That is a nice thing about metadata schemas; a library can modify them to meet its own needs. Specific descriptive metadata schemas will be discussed in chapter 3.

Creation of metadata records for digital collections is not performed in all libraries. It is performed primarily in academic libraries and larger public libraries that have institutional repositories or digital collections. In addition, metadata work is not standardized across libraries. The lack of standardization in metadata work means libraries do not share metadata records for digital collections. Each digital collection usually contains unique and special materials, so it resists standardization and sharing. See figure 2.7 for an example of a metadata record for a digital photograph.[16]

```
<dc:title>Oil Rig</dc:title>
<dc:date>1920~</dc:date>
<dc:language>No Language</dc:language>
-<dc:description>
    Wooden oil rig, the first in Shannon, TX around 1928.
</dc:description>
-<dc:subject>
    Business, Economics and Finance - Oil and Gas - Oil Wells
</dc:subject>
<dc:subject>People</dc:subject>
<dc:coverage>United States - Texas - Clay County - Shannon</dc:coverage>
<dc:coverage>Oil and Gas, 1901-Present</dc:coverage>
<dc:rights>Public</dc:rights>
<dc:type>Photograph</dc:type>
<dc:format>1 photographic print : b&w : 5 x 3 1/2 in.</dc:format>
<dc:format>Image</dc:format>
<dc:identifier>local-cont-no: 06.030.59</dc:identifier>
-<dc:identifier>
    https://texashistory.unt.edu/ark:/67531/metapth16449/
</dc:identifier>
<dc:identifier>ark: ark:/67531/metapth16449</dc:identifier>
```

Figure 2.7.   Example of a Metadata Record

Database Records in Reference Databases

Bibliographic records and metadata records are created by libraries. However, there is another type of metadata used in libraries that is not created by libraries. Database records are created by publishers, organizations, or database vendors to describe items in reference databases (e.g., Academic Search Complete, ScienceDirect, Education Resources Information Center [ERIC]). Libraries do not index individual articles published in journals, magazines, newspapers, or other similar serial publications. Database vendors and publishers are responsible for indexing articles and providing access to them in reference databases. Databases index various materials, like articles in journals, magazines, and newspapers, chapters in edited books, technical reports, videos, and more. Each item in a database is described in a database record, sometimes with the full-text version attached. Databases are important because they help users find journal articles and other items that are not usually cataloged by libraries. However, this work is not standardized across databases. Each database vendor or publisher determines what metadata to describe and how to describe it.

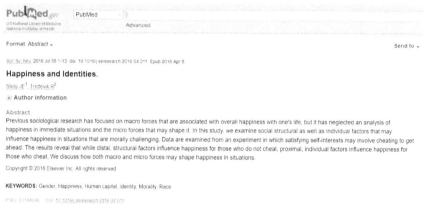

Figure 2.8.   Example of a Database Record

Libraries have no control over the metadata in databases; libraries simply pay for the privilege of accessing the databases. The only control libraries have over information in databases is picking the best databases for their users within their budgets. See figure 2.8 for an example of a database record from PubMed. [17]

ENCODING STANDARDS AND MARKUP LANGUAGES

So far, this chapter has discussed different types of metadata and the types of metadata created by libraries to describe and provide access to their collections. Bibliographic records are created through the library cataloging process and provide access to a library's main collection. Metadata records are created through metadata work and provide access to a library's digital collections. Descriptive metadata will be discussed in chapter 3, subject analysis in chapter 4, and classification in chapter 5. To provide a foundation for these chapters, it is important to first discuss encoding standards and markup languages. In today's digital environment, encoding standards and markup languages are an essential part of how libraries make their collections available to users. Computers have to be told what to do, and bibliographic information and metadata must be encoded for a computer to display, search, navigate, and use it. Encoding standards and markup languages are what enable a computer to read and manipulate bibliographic information. Encoding standards and markup languages have been revolutionary in libraries. They were not needed when library information was recorded on cards filed in card catalogs. For years, libraries developed systems of organization that had nothing to do with computers. It was not until the late 1960s and early 1970s that libraries started using computers for cataloging purposes and developed encoding standards that made bibliographic information machine readable. This led to the development of electronic bibliographic records, online public access catalogs to house these records, and shared cataloging that allows libraries to share bibliographic records.

Encoding and Its Purpose

When thinking of encoding, think computers. In order for metadata, especially descriptive metadata, to be displayed and manipulated by a computer, it needs to be encoded. An encoding standard is a system of letters, numbers, or symbols that contains metadata. It wraps the metadata and transmits it, like a bag, a box, or a container. Encoding standards do not provide the "intellectual access" to library materials, such as title, author, or subject.[18] That information comes from following descriptive metadata standards. Encoding standards do not care what metadata goes in them or what language is used to create the metadata. Encoding allows computers to talk to one another so information can be shared. Computers can read metadata, sort it out, and display it to users. Encoding also gives access to records by searching parts of a record separately. For example, when a user searches for a "title" on a library catalog, the encoding allows the user to search for titles only.

Here is an example: Imagine a dad needs to bring a batch of cookies to a bake sale. He cannot safely get the cookies to the bake sale without putting the cookies into a container and bringing them to the bake sale. Loose cookies would crumble and get all over the car. The container, though, is not the cookies. It has nothing to do with the recipe and ingredients used to make the cookies. The container is just a way for the dad to transport the cookies from his house to the bake sale. That is similar to how encoding standards help computers transport metadata. Encoding standards having nothing to do with the metadata; they just transport the metadata.

Look back at figures 2.5 and 2.6. They include the bibliographic record for *Pete the Cat and the Cool Cat Boogie* and the authority record for Kim Dean, encoded in the MARC 21 format. The encoding is the three-digit numbers (called tags), two-digit numbers (called indicators), and the |a, |b, |2, etc. symbols (called subfields). They wrap the metadata, the bibliographic and authority information, so a computer can read it. Figure 2.7 shows another example of an encoding standard used in libraries, in this case XML. This is a metadata record for a digital photograph. It was described using the *Dublin Core* metadata schema, which dictates broadly what needs to be described, like the title, date, and subject. The markup language, XML, wraps the metadata using tags created just for *Dublin Core* like <dc:title> </dc:title>. Each element is wrapped by tags so a computer can read the metadata and display it to users.

There are several encoding standards used in libraries, but the most widely used are MARC 21, for bibliographic and authority records, and XML, for metadata records.

ENCODING STANDARDS IN LIBRARIES: MARC

MAchine-Readable Cataloging (MARC) is an encoding standard used primarily in library cataloging. It allows a computer to read and display bibliographic and authority information. In the library cataloging context, MARC is an encoding standard for computers. It does not explain how to describe library materials; it simply takes bibliographic information and makes it machine readable.

MARC has been around a relatively short time in the history of cataloging, but its impact has been immense. MARC was created in the late 1960s by Henriette Avram at the Library of Congress. It was one of the first encoding schemes ever created for computers. At the time, bibliographic information was typed on 3x5 catalog cards filed in card catalogs. Computers were starting to be used at the Library of Congress and other libraries during this time, and the Library of Congress wanted to find a way to computerize cataloging information so users could search for library materials with a computer. Avram came up with an encoding system that essentially matched the *Anglo-American Cataloguing Rules*, the descriptive cataloging rules in force at the time. Each "area of description" in the *Rules* (e.g., title and statement of responsibility, edition, publication information), as well as name and title access points, were contained in a separate field represented by a three-number tag. Each field was broken down hierarchically into subfields that matched specific parts of each area of description. Fields for subject headings and classification numbers were added as well.

MARC was originally adopted in libraries in 1971, and there have been several versions used in various countries over the years. The current version, MARC 21, was published between 1999 and 2000 and is used in many countries, including the United States, Canada, the United Kingdom, and Germany. MARC 21 is maintained by the Network Development and MARC Standards Office of the Library of Congress, and there are five types of MARC 21 formats that can be used in libraries: *MARC 21 Format for Bibliographic Data*, used by all libraries to create bibliographic records; *MARC 21 Format for Authority Data*, used by all libraries to create authority records; *MARC 21 Format for Holdings Data*, used by some libraries to display serial and nonserial holdings; *MARC 21 Format for Classification Data*, used by the developers of classification schemes to create classification records; and *MARC 21 Format for Community Information*, used by some libraries for nonbibliographic information.[19] There is also a separate MARC format called *Universal MARC Format* (UNIMARC) that is maintained by IFLA. It is different from MARC 21 and is used in some countries around the world.[20]

MARC Structure and Characteristics

MARC is standardized across libraries in the United States. All libraries use it to encode their bibliographic records and authority records. MARC includes several parts such as a fixed field, variable fields, tags, indicators, and subfields. The fixed field (008) is just for computers. It includes specific pieces of information about a record, and computers use it to display information, limit searches, and so forth. The rest of the bibliographic record contains variable fields, which include bibliographic or authority information. A field is an entire line that contains specific pieces of cataloging information directed by cataloging standards. For instance, the 245 field includes the title and statement of responsibility elements. Catalogers use the instructions in RDA to create the 245. The 650 field is for subject headings. Catalogers add subject headings from whatever subject headings list is used in a library, such as LCSH.

Figure 2.9 shows the bibliographic record for the book *The Art of the Fold.*[21] Reading the bibliographic record from left to right, the three-digit numbers are the tags: for example, the 245 tag. Next are the indicators. They are one or two numbers that appear after the tag. The indicators tell the computer something about the data and are used in indexing and displaying the information. The fields are then divided into subfields, which break down the bibliographic information into separate subelements. For example, in the 245 field, the subfield a (|a) contains the title, which is "The art of the fold." The subfield b (|b) contains other title information, which in this case is the subtitle, "how to make innovative books and paper structures." The subfield c (|c) contains the statement of responsibility—the people responsible for creating the book—which are "Hedi Kyle and Ulla Warchol."

The information in the different fields, such as title, publisher, and author, is added following separate cataloging standards. MARC does not tell catalogers how to describe library materials; it just allows a computer to read and display the information. It works together with cataloging standards to create bibliographic records. Encoding each part of a bibliographic record makes MARC rich and detailed, much more so than other encoding standards or markup languages. For bibliographic records, there are more than 200 separate MARC fields that can be used to create

001	on1023492081	
003	OCoLC	
005	20181003092359.0	
008	180926t20182018enka b 000 0 eng d	
020	|a 1786272938 |q hardcover	
020	|a 9781786272935 |q hardcover	
035	|a (OCoLC)1023492081	
040	|a YDX |b eng |e rda |c YDX |d ORX |d YDX	
092	|a 736.98 |a K994a	
100	1 |a Kyle, Hedi, |e author.	
245	14 |a The art of the fold : |b how to make innovative books and paper structures / |c Hedi Kyle and Ulla Warchol.	
264	1 |a London : |b Laurence King Publishing Ltd, |c 2018.	
264	4 |c ©2018	
300	|a 192 pages : |b illustrations ; |c 26 cm	
336	|a text |b txt |2 rdacontent	
336	|a still image |b sti |2 rdacontent	
337	|a unmediated |b n |2 rdamedia	
338	|a volume |b nc |2 rdacarrier	
504	|a Includes bibliographical references.	
650	0 |a Paper folding (Graphic design).	
650	0 |a Paper folding (Graphic design) |x Technique.	
700	1 |a Warchol, Ulla, |e author.	

Figure 2.9.   Bibliographic Record Encoded in MARC 21

detailed bibliographic records. Plus, there are several local MARC fields so libraries can add their own local library information. For authority records, there are almost 150 fields that can be used to create authorized access points for names, titles, and subjects. It is important to note that catalogers must know MARC in order to create bibliographic and authority records.[22]

MARC Advantages and Disadvantages

MARC changed the way that libraries made their collections available to users. No longer did users need to flip through endless cards in a card catalog. They could use a computer to quickly search for bibliographic records housed in an online public access catalog. MARC makes the cataloging process more efficient. Because bibliographic records are electronic, libraries can quickly and easily share bibliographic records with one another. Library materials are available to users much faster. In addition, MARC is a rich encoding standard. Everything on a bibliographic record is broken down and encoded, so each piece of information can be searched separately. Bibliographic information encoded in MARC can be more detailed than other types of encoding standards.

However, MARC is used almost exclusively to create bibliographic and authority records in libraries. It does not translate well to nonlibrary contexts. Today's digital environment is all about linking and sharing data across communities online. MARC has a hard time playing nice with other data communities, and it has been criticized strongly for its inflexibility.[23] In addition, MARC does not work that well with RDA, the new descriptive cataloging standard. MARC was developed to work with the old *Anglo-American Cataloguing Rules*, and it works very well with that standard. However, RDA is different from the old *Rules*; it is based on different models, focuses on showing relationships, and is generally more flexible. MARC is not flexible enough to accommodate the elements and relationships that can be shown through RDA. Basically, MARC cannot do what RDA needs it to do. Currently, the Library of Congress is working on an initiative to replace the MARC format, called the *Bibliographic Framework Initiative* (BIBFRAME). It is a linked data model that uses RDF. It is currently being tested in some libraries with no firm date for implementation across libraries. BIBFRAME will be discussed in chapter 10.

Still, MARC is a survivor. Many people have called for its death, but it keeps on going.[24] There are billions of bibliographic and authority records in MARC in library catalogs around the world. Although BIBFRAME is supposed to replace MARC, it will take libraries years to transition. MARC will used in libraries for many years to come.

ENCODING STANDARDS IN LIBRARIES: DIGITAL COLLECTIONS

MARC is used to encode bibliographic and authority records created through the library cataloging process. It is the primary encoding standard for library cataloging. Metadata records that are created for digital collections, however, do not typically use MARC. Instead, libraries can choose from a wide variety of metadata schemas, and this metadata is encoded primarily using the Extensible Markup Language. Unlike catalogers who need to know the MARC format to create bibliographic records, metadata specialists do not need to necessarily know XML or other markup languages. They can use templates to create metadata records.

Extensible Markup Language (XML)

XML is one of the most popular markup languages used by data communities around the world. It allows for the sharing of structured information online. In libraries, XML is used to encode metadata records in digital collections. XML takes all sorts of metadata and codes it so computers can exchange, use, and display digital resources online. Users can search and retrieve digital resources and see the metadata.

XML is a relatively recent markup language, first released in 1998. However, the history of XML actually starts with Standard Generalized Markup Language (SGML), which was developed at IBM in the 1970s and became an international standard in 1986 (ISO 8879). Essentially, SGML is a master standard that explains how to create other markup languages. SGML is very powerful and quite complicated. It has many uses and has been applied in many industries and organizations that need to manage information. One important SGML application is Hypertext Markup Language (HTML), used to create web pages. Tim Berners-Lee invented the World Wide Web in 1989, and he created HTML to encode web pages so a computer can display them. HTML uses fixed, predefined tags (e.g., <title> </title>) and can be used only to display web pages. However, the web was expanding rapidly in the 1990s, and there was a need for a more flexible and simpler SGML that could do more than just display web pages. XML was the solution. It is a simpler and more flexible subset of SGML that can be used in many contexts. Because it is a subset of SGML, XML operates as a master standard, too, and it explains how to create other markup languages for the web. It is maintained by the World Wide Web Consortium. Figure 2.10 shows how SGML, HTML, and XML are related.

XML uses tags to encode metadata, like HTML. However, unlike HTML, XML tags are not fixed or predefined. XML tags can be modified to meet the needs of any

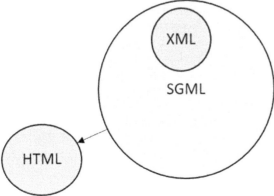

Figure 2.10. How SGML, HTML, and XML Are Related

community in any web environment. For example, in HTML, <title> </title> must be used to encode the title of a web page. Using XML, tags can be created for any needed element, and a tag can be called anything like <main title> </main title>, <book title> </book title>, <formal title> </formal title>, and so on. There are a few rules that must be followed, but as long as they are followed, XML tags can be modified for any purpose.

The ability to apply XML in different contexts gives XML its flexibility. As long as the opening tag uses <> and a closing tag uses </>, anything can go on the tag, and XML can be combined with any metadata schema or standard to create a set of tags for a particular purpose. Here is an example: Imagine a child has a collection of candy bars he or she wants to describe online. He or she could create a descriptive metadata schema with four elements: brand, chocolate type, size, and type of nut. He or she could use XML to create tags just for this candy bar metadata schema, shown in table 2.1.

Table 2.1.   XML Example

Candy Bar Metadata Schema in XML	Example: Hershey's With Almonds
<brand> </brand>	<brand>Hershey's</brand>
<chocolate type> </chocolate type>	<chocolate type>Milk chocolate </chocolate type>
<size> </size>	<size>King size</size>
<type of nut> </type of nut>	<type of nut>Almonds</type of nut>

The left-hand column shows tags that were created using XML. The right-hand column shows the metadata about one candy bar, a King Size Hershey's Milk Chocolate Bar with Almonds, encoded in XML. This very simple example illustrates that XML can be used to create tags for any collection and for any purpose. Yet XML is more than just the tags. Computers need rules and structure to be able to read, search, display, and use XML tags. A document type definition (DTD) or XML schema must be created that defines everything needed for the particular XML "document" or separate markup language, such as the rules to follow, the hierarchy, and where to put information.[25]

In libraries, XML has been used as the markup language for several metadata schemas used to describe and provide access to digital collections, such as *Dublin Core*, *Metadata Object Description Schema*, *Metadata Authority Description Schema*, and many others. Each metadata schema uses XML to encode their elements, and each one is expressed in different ways, depending upon what tags are needed for each schema. An example is shown in figure 2.11. It shows a digitized postcard and a *Dublin Core* metadata record that describes this postcard.[26]

Now look at figure 2.12, which shows the same *Dublin Core* metadata record with the XML tags.[27] The *Dublin Core* metadata has been encoded using XML. *Dublin Core* is the metadata schema. The *Dublin Core* elements (e.g., dc:title, dc:date) have been combined with XML (<> . . . </>) to create tags just for use with *Dublin Core* (<dc:title> </dc:title>).

Figure 2.11. Metadata Record for a Postcard (Postcard). *University of North Texas Libraries, The Portal to Texas History,* https://texashistory.unt.edu / *Private Collection of Joe E. Haynes* (https://texashistory.unt.edu/ark:/67531/metapth35839)

title: ["Red Riding Hood" Cat]
creator: Barnes, G.L.
language: English
description: Color postcard of a cat in a Red Riding Hood costume.
 Correspondence on the back reads, " Hello! Rosa Louise Your Baboo Dorothy
 K." It is addressed to Miss Rosa Louise Dill, 527 S. 18th St., Paris, Texas.
 It is postmarked Oklahoma, Okla on Jan 13, 1908.
subject: postcards
subject: Social Life and Customs - Pets - Cats
subject: costumes
coverage: New South, Populism, Progressivism, and the Great Depression,
 1877-1939
coverage: 1908~
type: Postcard
format: 1 postcard: color; 3 1/2 x 5 1/2 in.
format: Image
identifier: local-cont-no: 056
identifier: https://texashistory.unt.edu/ark:/67531/metapth35839/
identifier: ark: ark:/67531/metapth35839

Figure 2.11.   *Continued*

```
<dc:title>["Red Riding Hood" Cat]</dc:title>
<dc:creator>Barnes, G.L.</dc:creator>
<dc:language>English</dc:language>
<dc:description>
    Color postcard of a cat in a Red Riding Hood costume. Correspondence on the back reads, "
    Hello! Rosa Louise Your Baboo Dorothy K." It is addressed to Miss Rosa Louise Dill, 527 S.
    18th St., Paris, Texas. It is postmarked Oklahoma, Okla on Jan 13, 1908.
</dc:description>
<dc:subject>postcards</dc:subject>
<dc:subject>Social Life and Customs - Pets - Cats</dc:subject>
<dc:subject>costumes</dc:subject>
<dc:coverage>
    New South, Populism, Progressivism, and the Great Depression, 1877-1939
</dc:coverage>
<dc:coverage>1908~</dc:coverage>
<dc:type>Postcard</dc:type>
<dc:format>1 postcard: color; 3 1/2 x 5 1/2 in.</dc:format>
<dc:format>Image</dc:format>
<dc:identifier>local-cont-no: 056</dc:identifier>
<dc:identifier>
    https://texashistory.unt.edu/ark:/67531/metapth35839/
</dc:identifier>
<dc:identifier>ark: ark:/67531/metapth35839</dc:identifier>
```

Figure 2.12.   Metadata Record for a Postcard (the Record)

MARCXML

MARCXML is another markup language used to encode metadata records. MAR-CXML uses existing bibliographic records encoded in MARC and wraps them in XML so they can be used in an XML environment. MARC is pretty inflexible, so an XML shell is added that allows MARC to interact with other metadata encoded in XML. MARCXML is maintained by the Network Development and MARC Standards Office at the Library of Congress.

Text Encoding Initiative (TEI) Guidelines

The *TEI Guidelines for Electronic Text Encoding and Interchange* is used to encode literary texts, such as books, poems, manuscripts, speeches, scripts, and plays. It was developed originally as a separate encoding standard, but now it uses XML. Work on the *Guidelines* began in 1988, drafts were released in the early 1990s, and a final first edition was released in 1994. The latest edition is P5, released in 2007. It is maintained by the TEI Consortium. Some digital libraries may use TEI to encode digital texts.

Markup Languages Advantages and Disadvantages

Advantages of markup languages such as XML are their flexibility and interoperability. XML can be used in many contexts and can be used to create markup languages that describe any collection for any purpose. XML can be as simple or as complex as needed. In addition, unlike MARC, which is used primarily in libraries, XML is used by many data communities across the web, and it is standardized across the web. Metadata coded using XML can be used in different environments. It is easier for computer systems to talk to each other because they are using the same XML language. However, markup languages tend not to be as detailed as MARC. Although it is possible to create a very rich and complex markup language using XML, there would have to be hundreds of tags to match the complexity of MARC. This would hinder the flexibility and simple construction of XML. In addition, because markup languages are coming from the computer science community, librarianship has had to learn the vocabulary of computer science, which is not necessarily a bad thing. It is just that although librarianship was the first profession to develop systems and standards for describing metadata, computer science seems to be creating all the rules for metadata on the web. It sometimes feels like librarianship has no voice in the discussion and is running to catch up.

SUMMARY

This chapter discussed metadata, a fundamental part of organizing library collections that is important for many reasons, including discovery, representation, and interoperability. There are three broad types of metadata: descriptive, administrative, and structural. Catalogers primarily create descriptive metadata when creating bibliographic records, but metadata specialists create all types of metadata when creating digital collections. This chapter also introduced encoding standards used in libraries, such as MARC 21 and XML, that encode metadata so computers can read, display, and manipulate it. The next chapter will focus exclusively on descriptive metadata. It will discuss descriptive cataloging standards and metadata schemas, and how libraries use them to provide access to their collections.

DISCUSSION QUESTIONS

1. What is metadata and why is it important?
2. What types of metadata do you use in your everyday life? Where do you find it? Provide examples of when metadata helped you and when it did not help you. What worked? What was frustrating and why?
3. Discuss cataloging and metadata work. What is the purpose of each one and what are their similarities and differences? If you are currently working in a library, talk about the cataloging and metadata work performed in your library.
4. What are encoding standards? How do they help libraries provide access to collections?

CLASS ACTIVITIES

1. *Compare and Contrast Bibliographic and Metadata Records.* Pick a library catalog, such as the Library of Congress catalog, that shows bibliographic records in MARC. For metadata records, use the Portal to Texas History or another database that shows XML coding. Pick three bibliographic records and three metadata records for a variety of formats and compare and contrast them. What are the similarities and differences? Are the records easy to read and understand? Add screen captures of the records, including the public side and the coding side, to illustrate what you find.
2. *Compare and Contrast Bibliographic and Database Records.* Pick three bibliographic records from a library catalog and a three database records from a reference database (e.g., Library & Information Science Source), and compare and contrast the records. What are the similarities and differences? Are the records easy to read and understand? Add screen captures of the records (the public side only) to illustrate what you find.

NOTES

1. Wayfair.com, accessed January 10, 2019, https://www.wayfair.com.
2. Photograph taken by the author.

3. Daniel N. Joudrey and Arlene G. Taylor, *The Organization of Information*, 4th ed. (Santa Barbara, CA: Libraries Unlimited, 2018), 181.

4. Steven J. Miller, *Metadata for Digital Collections: A How-To-Do-It Manual* (New York: Neal-Schuman, 2011), 1.

5. Denton Public Library Catalog, accessed January 10, 2019, https://library.cityofden ton.com.

6. National Library of Medicine, accessed January 10, 2019, https://www.nlm.nih.gov.

7. There are various categories of metadata in the literature. See, e.g., Anne J. Gilliland, "Setting the Stage," in *Introduction to Metadata*, 3rd ed., ed. Murtha Baca (Los Angeles: Getty Publications, 2008), 1–19; Joudrey and Taylor. *The Organization of Information*; Miller, *Metadata for Digital Collections*; Jenn Riley, *Understanding Metadata: What Is Metadata, and What Is It For?* (Baltimore, MD: National Information Standards Organization, 2017), accessed January 10, 2019, https://www.niso.org/publications/understanding-metadata-2017; Marcia Lei Zeng and Jian Qin, *Metadata*, 2nd ed. (Chicago: Neal-Schuman, 2016).

8. Miller, *Metadata for Digital Collections*, 10.

9. Zeng and Qin, *Metadata*, 3.

10. For more information about representation, see, e.g., Brian O'Connor, *Explorations in Indexing and Abstracting: Pointing, Virtue, and Power* (Englewood, CO: Libraries Unlimited, 1996).

11. Heting Chu, *Information Representation and Retrieval in the Digital Age*, 2nd ed. (Medford, NJ: Information Today for the American Society for Information Science and Technology, 2010), 51.

12. Zeng and Qin, *Metadata*, 23; see also Miller, *Metadata for Digital Collections*, 23.

13. Nashville Public Library Catalog, accessed January 10, 2019, https://library.nashville.org.

14. Library of Congress Authorities, accessed January 10, 2019, https://authorities.loc.gov.

15. Library of Congress, "Standards," accessed January 10, 2019, https://www.loc.gov/ librarians/standards.

16. "Oil Rig, Photograph, 1920," University of North Texas Libraries, The Portal to Texas History, crediting Clay County Historical Society, accessed January 10, 2019, https://texashis tory.unt.edu/ark:/67531/metapth16449.

17. PubMed, US National Library of Medicine, National Institutes of Health, accessed January 10, 2019, https://www.ncbi.nlm.nih.gov/pubmed.

18. Miller, *Metadata for Digital Collections*, 10.

19. Library of Congress, Network Development and MARC Standards Office, "MARC Standards," accessed January 10, 2019, https://www.loc.gov/marc.

20. IFLA, "UNIMARC Strategic Programme," accessed January 10, 2019, https://www .ifla.org/unimarc.

21. Nashville Public Library Catalog.

22. For more information about MARC 21 for bibliographic data, see, Library of Congress, Network Development and MARC Standards Office, "MARC 21 Format for Bibliographic Data," accessed January 10, 2019, https://www.loc.gov/marc/bibliographic; for more information about MARC 21 for authority data see, Library of Congress, Network Development and MARC Standards Office, "MARC 21 Format for Authority Data," accessed January 10, 2019, https://www.loc.gov/marc/authority.

23. See, e.g., David J. Flander, "Applying XML to the Bibliographic Description," *Cataloging & Classification Quarterly* 33, no. 2 (2001): 17–28; Roy Tennant, "MARC Must Die," *Library Journal* 127, no. 17 (October 15, 2002): 26–28.

24. Tennant, "MARC Must Die."

25. There are many resources available if you are interested in learning more about XML. For an introduction, see e.g., Joe Fawcett, Liam R. E. Quin, and Danny Ayers, *Beginning XML*, 5th ed. (Indianapolis: Wiley, 2012).

26. G. L. Barnes, ["Red Riding Hood" Cat], postcard, undated, University of North Texas Libraries, The Portal to Texas History, crediting Private Collection of Joe E. Haynes, https://texashistory.unt.edu/ark:/67531/metapth35839.

27. Ibid.

SELECTED BIBLIOGRAPHY WITH ADDITIONAL READING

Chu, Heting. *Information Representation and Retrieval in the Digital Age*. Second Edition. Medford, NJ: Information Today for the American Society for Information Science and Technology, 2010.

Coyle, Karen. "Understanding Metadata and Its Purpose." *Journal of Academic Librarianship* 31 (2005):160–63.

Fawcett, Joe, Liam R. E. Quin, and Danny Ayers. *Beginning XML*. Fifth Edition. Indianapolis: Wiley, 2012.

Flander, David J. "Applying XML to the Bibliographic Description." *Cataloging & Classification Quarterly* 33, no. 2 (2001): 17–28.

Gilliland, Anne J. "Setting the Stage." In *Introduction to Metadata, third edition,* edited by Murtha Baca, 1–19. Los Angeles: Getty Publications, 2008. http://www.getty.edu/publications/intrometadata/setting-the-stage.

Greenberg, Jane. "Understanding Metadata and Metadata Schemes." *Cataloging & Classification Quarterly* 40, no. 3/4 (2005):17–36.

Intner, Sheila S., and Jean Weihs. *Standard Cataloging for School and Public Libraries*. Fifth Edition. Santa Barbara, CA: Libraries Unlimited, 2015.

Joudrey, Daniel N., and Arlene G. Taylor. *The Organization of Information*. Fourth Edition. Santa Barbara, CA: Libraries Unlimited, 2018.

Joudrey, Daniel N., Arlene G. Taylor, and David P. Miller. *Introduction to Cataloging and Classification*. Eleventh Edition. Santa Barbara, CA: Libraries Unlimited, 2015.

Liu, Jia. *Metadata and Its Applications in the Digital Library: Approaches and Practices*. Westport, CT: Libraries Unlimited, 2007.

Miller, Steven J. *Metadata for Digital Collections: A How-To-Do-It Manual*. New York: Neal-Schuman, 2011.

O'Connor, Brian C. *Explorations in Indexing and Abstracting: Pointing, Virtue, and Power*. Englewood, CO: Libraries Unlimited, 1996.

Riley, Jenn. *Understanding Metadata: What Is Metadata, and What Is It For?* Baltimore, MD: National Information Standards Organization, 2017. https://www.niso.org/publications/understanding-metadata-2017.

Tennant, Roy. "MARC Must Die." *Library Journal* 127, no. 17 (October 15, 2002): 26–28.

Yott, Patrick. "Introduction to XML." *Cataloging & Classification Quarterly* 40, no. 3/4 (2005): 213–35.

Zeng, Marcia Lei, and Jian Qin. *Metadata*. Second Edition. Chicago: Neal-Schuman, 2016.

3

Describing and Providing Access to Library Collections

The last chapter introduced the concept of metadata. It discussed why metadata is important and how it is used to organize library collections. There are three broad types of metadata: descriptive metadata, administrative metadata, and structural metadata. Bibliographic and authority records contain descriptive metadata, while all types of metadata are used to create digital collections. The last chapter also discussed encoding standards, which are used to encode metadata so computers can read, display, and use it. This chapter will focus specifically on descriptive metadata and how it is used to describe and provide access to library collections. It will introduce descriptive metadata and then discuss specific descriptive cataloging standards and metadata schemas used to create descriptive metadata in libraries.

DESCRIPTIVE METADATA AND ITS PURPOSE

Descriptive metadata is the primary type of metadata created in libraries. Marcia Lei Zeng and Jian Qin define descriptive metadata as "[m]etadata used to identify and describe collections and related information resources (examples include cataloging records, finding aids, specialized indexes, and curatorial information)."[1] Descriptive metadata "provides intellectual access" to library materials, describing things like title, format, publisher, date, people associated with a resource, and so on.[2] Descriptive metadata allows users to know what items are available through a library, to find and access library materials, and to choose items that meet their information needs. Specific standards, guidelines, and schemas are used to ensure consistent descriptive metadata across libraries.

There are two broad types of descriptive metadata that will be discussed in this chapter: (1) content standards and (2) metadata schemas. Content standards, such as descriptive cataloging standards, and metadata schemas are used to describe and provide access to library collections. Think about these standards and schemas as rules, instructions, or guidelines for creating descriptive metadata. They are created with a specific purpose, such as describing items in a library, archive, or museum; describing a particular format; or describing digital resources. Each standard or schema chooses specific elements: the attributes, properties, or characteristics used to describe library materials. Each standard or schema includes a different set of elements to be used when describing a particular collection. Each standard or schema has a different purpose and determines *what* elements to describe (e.g., format, title, author, page numbers). Each standard or schema also decides *how* information should be described (e.g., capitalization, punctuation, word order, fullness of description), and some standards or schemas even explain *where* to take the information (e.g., take the title from the title page). In addition, all standards or schemas explain how to show relationships among elements and among items in a collection.

Descriptive metadata can be simple or complex, depending on the standard or schema, its audience, and the format(s) it describes. Content standards can describe any format collected in libraries, and they include specific guidelines for each format. For example, how one describes the content of a book (e.g., book title, author, illustrator) is different from how one describes the content of a music album (e.g., album title, performer, record label, songs) or a motion picture (e.g., film title, producers, actors). Metadata schemas are used to describe digital materials, digital images, digital art works, and so forth.

Each standard or schema makes choices about the elements that should be described. These decisions may seem objective, but they are not. Standards and schemas are created by many people with different ideas, viewpoints, backgrounds, and cultures. Although people work together to make the best decisions for all users, something is always missing, and standards and schemas cannot meet the needs of all users at all times. All standards and schemas leave things out, which can affect access to library materials. As Elaine Svenonius says, "Access to records in an online catalog is limited only by what is not described."[3] Users cannot search for things that are not described in a record. If an element is not included in a record, it cannot be found on a library catalog or other retrieval system. For example, if a user wants to look up the color of a book on a library catalog, they cannot do it because color is not described. Even if a database searches a full-text collection of electronic books, users cannot find things searching for words that are not used in the books.

General Descriptive Metadata Example: Car Collection

As an example, imagine you have a collection of cars and you want to create a database with information about each car in your collection. You want to describe the elements of each car (e.g., make, model, size) and provide access points to search your database. First, you pick the elements that are important to you: for example, the make (e.g., Ford, Chevrolet, BMW), model (e.g., Fusion, Focus, Explorer), year of manufacture, color, seat fabric, radio features, and anything else that is important to you. If you have a general interest in cars, the elements you may choose are make, model, year, and color. If you are a car expert, then you also may want to describe the engine, wheels, and transmission. It really depends on you and your needs. You also can create the specific instructions to describe each element: for example, for the color element, you may want to use only generic color names and capitalize each color, like "Blue," "Red," or "White." Alternately, you could choose to use the carmaker's colors and use all lowercase letters, like "cobalt," "crimson," or "pearl." Or you could choose not to have any specific instructions about how to record color. It is up to you and the purpose of your system. You also can decide how you want to retrieve information in your database: Do you want to search by make? Model? Color?

Everything in your system is up to you because the collection is just for you. You get to create the database with your needs in mind. Things get complicated, however, when other people try to search your collection. Because you have described your collection just for you, it would be difficult for someone else who had different needs to find cars in your collection. If a person wanted to search for a particular engine but you did not describe engines in your database, then the person will not be able to find the information. Helping users is the end goal of any organizational system, but creating standards and schemas to meet everyone's needs is very difficult. It is the fundamental challenge of organizing library collections in general, and descriptive metadata in particular.

DESCRIPTIVE METADATA IN LIBRARIES: DESCRIPTIVE CATALOGING

The primary form of descriptive metadata created in libraries are bibliographic records that describe and provide access to a library's main collection (e.g., books, serials, maps, music, video). Descriptive cataloging standards are the rules, guidelines, or instructions that guide the creation of bibliographic records, and they are developed by the library profession. Library cataloging has typically been divided into two broad types of cataloging: descriptive cataloging (description and access) and subject analysis, also called subject cataloging (subject headings and classification). This chapter will focus on descriptive cataloging; subject analysis will be discussed in chapters 4 and 5. Descriptive cataloging is the part of the cataloging process that describes the objective elements of items in the collection and provides name and title access into the collection. Descriptive cataloging also shows relationships, explaining such things as how people are related to an item, how items are related to other items, and how items are related to each other across the library catalog. The current descriptive cataloging standard used in libraries is *Resource Description and Access* (RDA). There are two parts of descriptive cataloging: description and access.

Descriptive Cataloging: Description

Description is concerned with describing each item in a library's collection. It answers questions like: What is it? What is the title? Who created it? What does it look like? Description is concerned with how to describe the elements that do not change over time, like the title, publisher, page numbers, and so on. Description helps to create a representation of an item so a user can search for items away from the actual collection. Description also differentiates each item from all other items in the collection. Users should understand how items differ so they can choose which items they want. Description is more objective than subject analysis. Catalogers describe what they see. Description does not include subject analysis, which is a subjective process to explain what an item is about.

As noted above, description describes elements that do not change over time, such as the title, format, page numbers, publisher, and so on. For example, see figure 3.1 for an example of a bibliographic record for the second edition of the print

Figure 3.1.   Bibliographic Record for a Book (Book Cover)

book *How to Teach: A Practical Guide for Librarians* by Beverley E. Crane, published in 2017 by Rowman & Littlefield.[4] The descriptive elements of this particular book include title (How to teach : a practical guide for librarians), edition (Second edition), author (Beverley E. Crane), publisher (Rowman & Littlefield), series and series number (Practical guides for librarians, 35), and page numbers (xix pages of front matter; 253 pages of text), among others. These elements do not change over time. This bibliographic record will always describe the second edition of the print book *How to Teach: A Practical Guide for Librarians* by Beverley E. Crane, published in 2017 by Rowman & Littlefield. If a third edition is published, then the third edition will be cataloged separately. The descriptive elements of this edition, or manifestation, will not change.

000		01847cam a2200397 i 4500
001		19609832
005		20180702181429.0
008		170425s2017 mdua bf 001 0 eng
906	__	|a 7 |b cbc |c orignew |d 1 |e ecip |f 20 |g y-gencatlg
925	0_	|a acquire |b 2 shelf copies |x policy default (ex.)
955	__	|b xk14 2017-04-25 |i xk14 2017-04-25 |w xk14 2017-04-25 to CIP |a xn11 2017-12-28 1 copy rec'd., to CIP ver. |f xk06 2018-07-02 copy 1 to BCCD, copy 2 to CALM
010	__	|a 2017020370
020	__	|a 9781538104149 (pbk. : alk. paper)
040	__	|a DLC |b eng |c DLC |e rda |d DLC
042	__	|a pcc
050	00	|a ZA3075 |b .C73 2017
082	00	|a 028.7071 |2 23
100	1_	|a Crane, Beverley E., |e author.
245	10	|a How to teach : |b a practical guide for librarians / |c Beverley E. Crane.
250	__	|a Second edition.
264	_1	|a Lanham, Maryland : |b Rowman & Littlefield, |c [2017]
300	__	|a xix, 253 pages : |b illustrations ; |c 29 cm.
336	__	|a text |b txt |2 rdacontent
337	__	|a unmediated |b n |2 rdamedia
338	__	|a volume |b nc |2 rdacarrier
490	0_	|a Practical guides for librarians ; |v 35
504	__	|a Includes bibliographical references and index.
650	_0	|a Information literacy |x Study and teaching |v Handbooks, manuals, etc.
650	_0	|a Information literacy |x Web-based instruction |v Handbooks, manuals, etc.
650	_0	|a Library orientation |v Handbooks, manuals, etc.
650	_0	|a Library orientation |x Web-based instruction |v Handbooks, manuals, etc.
650	_0	|a Web-based instruction |x Design |v Handbooks, manuals, etc.
650	_0	|a Teaching |v Handbooks, manuals, etc.
650	_0	|a Lesson planning |v Handbooks, manuals, etc.
650	_0	|a Libraries and education.
776	08	|i Online version: |a Crane, Beverley E., author. |t How to teach |b Second edition. |d Lanham, Maryland : Rowman & Littlefield, 2017 |z 9781538104156 |w (DLC) 2017020380

Figure 3.1. Bibliographic Record for a Book (the Record)

Description may seem pretty straightforward. A cataloger just describes what he or she sees on the book or other item. Done and done. Yet description can be complicated. Multiple formats are collected in libraries, each with specific cataloging instructions and best practices. How a cataloger describes books (e.g., title, author, publisher) is different from how a cataloger describes serial publications (e.g., title, corporate body, volume numbering), music (e.g., title, composer, songs), videos (e.g., title, production company, director, actors), and on and on for each format. Each format must be handled on its own cataloging terms, so to speak. In addition to special descriptive needs for each format, different user groups and libraries need different things. For example, think of a classical music album containing Beethoven symphonies. A casual listener in a public library may want to know the specific format (CD, record, tape, streaming), which symphonies are on the album, the orchestra, the conductor, the publisher, and the date the album was released. An expert listener in an academic music library might want to know all of those things and also where and when the music was recorded, how the music was recorded, if there are program notes that explain the symphonies, and so on.

Description can get complicated quickly. Not only do catalogers need to account for different formats and the needs of users and libraries, they need to deal with each separate item on its own terms. Publishers can be very inconsistent about where they put descriptive information on items, if they add information at all. A descriptive cataloging standard includes instructions and guidelines for handling specific cataloging situations, but library materials do not always fall neatly within descriptive cataloging standards. This makes cataloging challenging, frustrating, and fun. Catalogers often have to use what is called cataloger's judgment to make decisions about the best way to provide access to library materials. There can be some tricky situations, and cataloging has long history of working out descriptive cataloging problems so users know important information about each item in a library, what differentiates each item from other library resources, and how each item is related to other items in a library.

Descriptive Cataloging: Access

In addition to description, descriptive cataloging guides name and title access into a library collection. It guides the creation of consistent access points that govern how users will access, or retrieve, items in the collection. Descriptive cataloging is concerned with providing users with consistent access into a library's collection. A user should be able to perform a search on a library catalog and receive a list of all items in the collection by a particular name or title (and also subject). Providing access to library collections is vital so users can find and select library materials, both bibliographic records in a library catalog and metadata records in a digital collection. Access points allow users to search a collection for known elements, and the most common elements used to search library collections are name, title, and subject. These elements come from Charles Cutter's "Objects" for a catalog and have been the primary access points in library catalogs (card and online) since that time.[5] This access goes beyond simple keyword searching that just searches for specific words in the catalog. Keyword searching is beneficial, but it alone cannot bring together all items in a library. Keyword searching is limited to the words in a search query. To help users use and explore library catalogs and to bring together items in the library catalog, consistent and controlled names, titles, and subjects must be used on bibliographic records.

Yet providing consistent and controlled access points is complicated. These complications arise because people and publishers are inconsistent with names, titles, and subjects on library items. For example, an illustrator named Bette Beth Evans could use a number of various names on her works: Bette B. Evans, Bette Beth Evans, B. B. Evans, B. Beth Evans, or even just Bette. She could change her name to Bette Beth Evans-Garza, Bette Beth Evans Garza (no hyphen), or Bette Beth Garza. She could assume a pseudonym and publish works under a different name, like Ivan Garza. How can libraries bring together works under all forms of the same name while also differentiating works by pseudonyms? The same issue happens with titles. A classic work can be known by many titles. An example is *Alice in Wonderland*. Lewis Carroll's work is known by that title, and versions of it have been published under the title. However, the actual title of the book is *Alice's Adventures in Wonderland*. How can the library bring together books under both titles so users retrieve both forms of the title in a search—not to mention different language versions, abridged versions, adaptations, and so on? The same thing applies to subject headings. For example, think about the subject "automobiles." Books and other items could use the word "automobiles" in the text, but they could also use synonyms such as cars, motorcars, or autos. How can the library catalog bring together all forms of a subject? Bringing together all forms of a name, title, or subject in the library catalog is important so that library users do not have to perform multiple searches to chase down library materials.

Authority Control

Access points in bibliographic records must be consistent and controlled to bring together materials in the catalog. *Authority control* is the name given to the process of providing consistent access points on bibliographic records. By assigning one "authorized" form of a name, title, or subject heading to bibliographic records, a cataloger "controls" the access points. Access points under authority control are names (e.g., personal names, corporate names, family names), some titles (e.g., preferred titles, collective titles, series titles), and subject headings (e.g., *Library of Congress Subject Headings*, *Sears List of Subject Headings*). However, descriptive cataloging focuses only on name and title access points. Subject headings are access points, too, but each list of subject headings or thesaurus guides subject authorities work, which will be discussed in chapter 4.

Access points are added to bibliographic records to bring together and differentiate works in the catalog. There are three main purposes of authority control.

It collocates, or brings together, materials in the library catalog. One consistent form of a name, title, or subject is assigned so all works in the catalog are brought together during a search. Authority control is also important because it differentiates like materials. Through authority control, cataloging differentiates people with the same name, works with the same title, and so on. Authority control also shows relationships. It shows how people, subjects, and works are related to one another. Bibliographic records can show that a work is an adaptation of another work or that a work is a translation of another work. Authority control makes it easier for users to find materials in the library.

Authorized access points are kept in authority records. Each authorized name, title, and subject has its own authority record. Information in authority records is considered authority data, and authority records are created separately from bibliographic records. Authority records are created following instructions in RDA, the current descriptive cataloging standard, and the *MARC 21 Format for Authority Data* to encode the information. Just like with bibliographic records, RDA explains what content to add to authority records, and MARC 21 encodes the authority information so a computer can read and display it. Authority records are kept in an authority file, which is a separate file that works with a library's online public access catalog. Users cannot access or see the authority file. It is running behind the scenes helping them in their searches. Most libraries have their own local authority file with access points just for items in their collections, but some libraries (e.g., some school libraries) may not use one. Instead, they rely on access points for names, titles, and subjects to match up in the catalog, which does not always happen. There is also a National Authority File maintained by the Library of Congress. It is the master authority file that every library uses. Individual libraries will update their own local authority files to keep up with the many changes and additions that are continually being made in the Library of Congress National Authority File.[6]

Access Points for Names

It is important to add access points for names, which include people, corporate bodies, and families. Authorized access points for names are added to bibliographic records when they create a work: for example, if a person writes a book or composes a piece of music. Names also are added when they contribute to something, like if a person illustrates a children's book, translates something, edits something, and so on. Authority control differentiates people with the same name: Is a user looking for Bette B. Evans the illustrator or Bette B. Evans the mechanical engineer? Or for John Smith the farmer born in 1962 or John Smith the farmer born in 1862? Cataloging tries to have one unique access point, a bibliographic identity for every name used in bibliographic records, including authors, composers, actors, musicians, illustrators, artists, editors, and on and on—anyone who creates or contributes to something. RDA governs the creation of access points and directs catalogers how to make each name unique by adding elements such as middle names, birth and/or death years, occupation, and so on. For example, there are twelve people in the Library of Congress National Authority File with the name Jason Jones. (See the list below.)[7] To differentiate each person named Jason Jones, birth years, occupations, or middle initials and/or names are added to make each access point unique.

AUTHORIZED NAME ACCESS POINTS FOR "JASON JONES"

Jones, Jason
Jones, Jason, 1973–
Jones, Jason, 1977–
Jones, Jason, 1978–
Jones, Jason, 1980–
Jones, Jason, 1981–
Jones, Jason B., 1971–
Jones, Jason (Businessman)
Jones, Jason (Jason Scott), 1971–
Jones, Jason L. (Jason Leon)
Jones, Jason Robert
Jones, Jason Scott

Cataloging also brings together variations of the same name, as in the Bette B. Evans example. People may use different forms of their name, and it is the job of authority control to pull together all variations. Catalogers assign one authorized form of a name to be used as an access point on bibliographic records. An example is Walter Dean Myers. To bring together all items associated with Walter Dean Myers in the library catalog, he has been assigned one authorized access point, which is "Myers, Walter Dean, 1937–2014." This is the only access point that should be used on bibliographic records that include his name as a creator or a contributor. See figure 3.2 for the authority record for Walter Dean Myers from the Library of Congress's National Authority File.[8]

Figure 3.2 shows two versions of the authority record, one with labels and one coded in the *MARC 21 Format for Authority Data*. The authority record lists lots of information about Walter Dean Myers, such as his authorized access point, "Myers, Walter Dean, 1937–2014," and his birth year, death year, field of activity, location, and so on. There also are two variant names added as cross-references so if users search for an unauthorized variant name, a library catalog will direct them to the authorized form of the name, as shown below.

Myers, Walter Milton, 1937–2014
    See: Myers, Walter Dean, 1937–2014

LC control no.: n 79047598
LCCN Permalink: https://lccn.loc.gov/n79047598
Descriptive conventions: rda
LC classification: PS3563.Y48
Personal name heading: Myers, Walter Dean, 1937-2014
Variant(s): Myers, Walter M. (Walter Milton), 1937-2014
Myers, Walter Milton, 1937-2014
Located: Harlem (New York, N.Y.)
Birth date: 19370812
Death date: 20140701
Place of birth: Martinsburg (W. Va.)
Place of death: Manhattan (New York, N.Y.)
Field of activity: Young adult literature Children's literature Poetry
Profession or occupation: Authors
Found in: Where does the day go? 1969: t.p. (Walter M. Myers)
Contemp. auth., 1978: v. 33-36 (Myers, Walter Dean, 1937-; auth. of: Where does the day go?)
The righteous revenge of Artemis Bonner, 1992: CIP t.p. (Walter Dean Myers)
New York times (online), viewed July 3, 2014 (in obituary published July 2: Walter Dean Myers; b. Walter Milton Myers, 1937, Martinsburg, W. Va.; raised in Harlem by Florence and Herbert Dean; took the pen name Walter Dean Myers in honor of his foster parents; d. Tuesday [July 1, 2014], Manhattan, aged 76; his realistic portrayal of the struggles of youths in the city made him a best-selling children's book author; was an evangelist for literacy and education)
Gale biography in context website, viewed July 3, 2014 (Walter Dean Myers; b. Walter Milton Myers, Aug. 12, 1937, Martinsburg, W. Va.)
Wikipedia, July 17, 2014 (Walter Dean Myers (birth name: Walter Milton Myers) born August 12, 1937; July 1, 2014; writer of children's books best known for young adult literature. He has written over one hundred books including picture books and nonfiction. He has won the Coretta Scott King Award for African-American authors five times. As of January 2012, Myers was the Library of Congress National Ambassador for Young People's Literature, a two-year position created to raise national awareness of the importance of lifelong literacy and education)

LC control no.: n 79047598
LCCN Permalink: https://lccn.loc.gov/n79047598
HEADING: Myers, Walter Dean, 1937-2014

000 02226cz a2200301n 450
001 27539
005 20140718104923.0
008 790611n| azannaabn |a aaa
010 __ |a n 79047598 |z n 85230332 |z n 91112477
035 __ |a (OCoLC)oca00280946
040 __ |a DLC |b eng |e rda |c DLC |d DLC |d OCoLC |d DLC
046 __ |f 19370812 |g 20140701
053 _0 |a PS3563.Y48
100 1_ |a Myers, Walter Dean, |d 1937-2014
370 __ |a Martinsburg (W. Va.) |b Manhattan (New York, N.Y.) |e Harlem (New York, N.Y.)
372 __ |a Young adult literature |a Children's literature |a Poetry |2 lcsh
374 __ |a Authors |2 lcsh
375 __ |a male
377 __ |a eng
400 1_ |a Myers, Walter M. |q (Walter Milton), |d 1937-2014
400 1_ |a Myers, Walter Milton, |d 1937-2014
670 __ |a Where does the day go? 1969: t.p. (Walter M. Myers)
670 __ |a Contemp. auth., 1978: |b v. 33-36 (Myers, Walter Dean, 1937-; auth. of: Where does the day go?)
670 __ |a The righteous revenge of Artemis Bonner, 1992: |b CIP t.p. (Walter Dean Myers)
670 __ |a New York times (online), viewed July 3, 2014 |b (in obituary published July 2: Walter Dean Myers; b. Walter Milton Myers, 1937, Martinsburg, W. Va.; raised in Harlem by Florence and Herbert Dean; took the pen name Walter Dean Myers in honor of his foster parents; d. Tuesday [July 1, 2014], Manhattan, aged 76; his realistic portrayal of the struggles of youths in the city made him a best-selling children's book author; was an evangelist for literacy and education)
670 __ |a Gale biography in context website, viewed July 3, 2014 |b (Walter Dean Myers; b. Walter Milton Myers, Aug. 12, 1937, Martinsburg, W. Va.)
670 __ |a Wikipedia, July 17, 2014 |b (Walter Dean Myers (birth name: Walter Milton Myers) born August 12, 1937; July 1, 2014; writer of children's books best known for young adult literature. He has written over one hundred books including picture books and nonfiction. He has won the Coretta Scott King Award for African-American authors five times. As of January 2012, Myers was the Library of Congress National Ambassador for Young People's Literature, a two-year position created to raise national awareness of the importance of lifelong literacy and education)

Figure 3.2. Authority Record for Walter Dean Myers

Authority control also helps users navigate pseudonyms. RDA instructs catalogers to create separate bibliographic identities for pseudonyms. The pseudonym and the real name are linked through the authority record. Users searching for J. K. Rowling, for instance, are directed to books by her pseudonyms through the use of "see also" references, as shown below.

Rowling, J. K.
 Search Also Under: For works of this author written under other names, search also under: Galbraith, Robert; Scamander, Newt; Whisp, Kennilworthy
  See Also: Galbraith, Robert
  See Also: Scamander, Newt
  See Also: Whisp, Kennilworthy

Authority control can also show users how corporate body names have changed. Corporate bodies such as professional associations, universities, or organizations may issue materials under different forms of their name. For example, Texas Woman's University and its earlier name, Texas State College for Women, are linked together through the authority file, as shown below. Users can find materials that were issued under both names.

Texas Woman's University
 Earlier Heading: Texas State College for Women

Access Points for Titles

Titles are access points on bibliographic records. Usually the cataloger adds the title of the item being cataloged to the bibliographic record, and nothing else needs to be done. However, there are some instances in which authority control is performed for titles. Although most editions of books and other items are published one time only, there are some situations that require an additional access point for a title to be added to a bibliographic record. These access points are called preferred titles in RDA (previously called uniform titles in older cataloging rules) and are added to bibliographic records under certain situations to bring together works published under more than one title, to bring together different language versions of a title, and to differentiate works with the same title. They also are added to bibliographic records for some collections, religious works, some conferences, and some legal documents and treaties.

Authorized access points for titles are added to bibliographic records to bring together works that are published under more than one title. See below for an example that shows part of a bibliographic record for J. K. Rowling's *Harry Potter and the Sorcerer's Stone*, including both labels and MARC.

Personal Name:	100 1_ |a	Rowling, J. K.
Preferred Title:	240 10 |a	Harry Potter and the philosopher's stone
Main Title:	245 10 |a	Harry Potter and the sorcerer's stone / |c by J.K. Rowling ; illustrations by Mary GrandPré.

The first Harry Potter book was originally published in the United Kingdom as *Harry Potter and the Philosopher's Stone*, and in the United States as *Harry Potter and the Sorcerer's Stone*. Because *Harry Potter and the Philosopher's Stone* is the original title, RDA directs catalogers to use it as the preferred access point for the work. This brings together all versions of the work in the catalog, no matter what is printed on the actual books. This is especially important for classic works that may have been published numerous times using various titles. Using one consistent authorized access point allows the catalog to bring together all versions for the user.

Preferred titles also are added to bring together all language versions of a work in the catalog. For an example, see below.

Personal Name:	100 1_ |a	Allende, Isabel.
Preferred Title:	240 10 |a	Casa de los espíritus. |l English
Main Title:	245 14 |a	The house of the spirits : |b a novel / |c Isabel Allende ; translated from the Spanish by Magda Bogin.

"Allende, Isabel. Casa de los espíritus. English" is the preferred title access point for the English-language version of *The House of the Spirits* by Isabel Allende. "Casa de los espíritus" is the title in its original language, and "English" is the language of the translation.

Authorized access points for titles are used in many other cases as well. Access points for titles are added to differentiate works with the same title. There are lots of periodicals called "Bulletin," for example, and many films and television shows are remakes. For music scores and audio recordings, access points are used to differentiate musical works with the same title. Musical works, particularly for classical music, often have generic titles based on musical form, like symphony. Many composers have written a "Symphony no. 5," for example. Creating an access point for each "Symphony no. 5" differentiates them from one another and also brings together each work in the library catalog. Series titles are also under authority control, and many libraries provide access to series titles.

Authority Control for Subjects

Authority records also are created for subjects, but keep in mind that subject analysis is separate from descriptive cataloging. Libraries use controlled vocabularies to provide subject access to library materials, including subject headings lists and thesauri. There is an authorized access point for each subject heading or thesaurus descriptor used in a library catalog. When consistently assigned to bibliographic records, they bring together all works on a subject. If a user searches for an unauthorized form of a subject, they will be directed to an authorized form, as shown below.

Moving-pictures and music
    See: Motion pictures and music

Authority control is important to help users search library catalogs and find library materials. Authority control is a unique aspect of cataloging and organizing library collections. Libraries do not throw users in the catalog and let them wander around aimlessly until they find what they need. Libraries structure information to help users find what they need. Authority control has become even more important as libraries perform linked data projects, which will be discussed in chapter 10.

RESOURCE DESCRIPTION AND ACCESS

Libraries in the United States (and increasingly around the world) use the same standard for descriptive cataloging, although local cataloging policies may differ in individual libraries. The current descriptive cataloging standard used in libraries is *Resource Description and Access* (RDA), which replaced the *Anglo-American Cataloguing Rules*, second edition, revised (AACR2), and implementation in libraries began in 2013. RDA is a large set of instructions that directs descriptive cataloging in libraries. RDA is considered a content standard because it explains how to describe content. It does not dictate the encoding standard to be used. Yet RDA is primarily used with the MARC 21 format to create bibliographic and authority records.

RDA is an international descriptive cataloging standard. RDA was originally developed by the Joint Steering Committee, with representation from national libraries and library associations in the United States, Australia, the United Kingdom, Canada, and Germany. However, RDA has become a global standard and the Joint Steering Committee has been reorganized and renamed to include representation from all parts of the world. Since 2015, RDA has been maintained by the RDA Steering Committee, which has representation from six geographic areas around the world (Africa, Asia, Europe, Latin America and the Caribbean, North America, and Oceania).[9] RDA is available in multiple languages, including English, Catalan,

Finnish, French, German, Italian, and Spanish, and more translations are planned. RDA is published jointly by the American Library Association, the Canadian Federation of Library Associations, and the Chartered Institute of Library and Information Professionals (CILIP) in the UK. A print version is available for purchase, but RDA is available primarily in an online subscription database called the RDA Toolkit.[10]

RDA was first published in 2010, tested between 2010 and 2013, and implementation began in libraries in the United States starting in March 2013. However, implementation is not yet complete. Some libraries, particularly smaller libraries, have not implemented RDA and are still using the old AACR2 cataloging rules. Although every library in the United States will need to switch to RDA (cataloging is standardized and AACR2 is no longer being updated), it may take some time for all libraries to use it exclusively. Some libraries are still using AACR2 to some extent due to budget issues, time and staff issues, library catalog issues, or technology issues.[11] Libraries used AACR2 for more than thirty years, and there are billions of bibliographic records in library catalogs that were created using the old rules. RDA instructions are different enough that records created in RDA and records created using AACR2 do not always play nicely together in some library catalogs. Some libraries have upgraded their old AACR2 records to RDA, but some libraries have not done that. Some libraries are using hybrid AACR2 and RDA records, and some libraries have AACR2 records and RDA records in the same catalog.

3R Project: RDA Toolkit Restructure and Redesign

RDA has not yet been implemented in all libraries, but RDA is already being revised. The revision is called the *3R Project: RDA Toolkit Restructure and Redesign*. The project began in 2017,[12] and parts of Revised RDA and the RDA Toolkit were released in a beta format in June 2018.[13] A final decision is supposed to be made in 2020. When and if it is approved, there will be a one-year countdown clock for transitioning to Revised RDA. After the one-year is over, Revised RDA will be the only version available. Because RDA is changing quite dramatically during the writing and publishing of this book, it would be helpful to know the models and principles underlying the first edition of RDA (which will be referred to as "Original RDA") as well as the proposed revision of RDA (which will be referred to as "Revised RDA"). In the next section, I will try to discuss both versions in a clear way, but please understand that changes are dynamic, and by the time this book is published RDA may or may not have changed. It is important to stay on top of RDA developments.

Characteristics of RDA

RDA is a set of instructions for descriptive cataloging. It explains how to describe library materials and how to provide access to them. The characteristics of Original RDA and Revised RDA will be discussed.

Original RDA

Original RDA is different from descriptive cataloging standards that came before it, such as AACR2. Like AACR2, it explains what cataloging information to add to bibliographic records and how to provide access, but RDA is much less prescriptive. Instead of cataloging "rules," RDA is a set of cataloging "instructions." Libraries have more options and catalogers can use more judgment. Original RDA also focuses exclusively on content. It does not dictate how bibliographic information should be displayed or what encoding standard should be used. AACR2 was used to create catalog cards, so it dictated how those cards should be formatted. Even after libraries automated and began using bibliographic records, AACR2 could be used only with the MARC format to create bibliographic and authority records. Like AACR2, Original RDA is based on cataloging principles, specifically *International Federation of Library Associations and Institutions* (IFLA)'s 2009 *Statement of International Cataloguing Principles*. Unlike AACR2, Original RDA is based on models. It incorporates models for bibliographic and authority data including IFLA's *Functional Requirements for Bibliographic Records* (FRBR) and *Functional Requirements for Authority Data* (FRAD) models. Original RDA also mentions the *Functional Requirements for Subject Authority Data* (FRSAD), but it was not really incorporated into Original RDA. Original RDA focuses more on authority control and showing relationships than AACR2. It also works better than AACR2 to account for new digital formats and cataloging in a networked environment. AACR2 was developed to describe primarily physical resources and did not handle digital resources well. Original RDA can handle new digital formats and new content, and can use library data in new ways. As Chris Oliver says, "RDA is a standard designed for the digital environment."[14] Unlike AACR2, RDA has been linked data ready since it was published.

Revised RDA

Revised RDA builds on the characteristics of Original RDA. There are several objectives of the 3R Project and Revised RDA. Revised RDA will incorporate the *IFLA Library Reference Model* (LRM), a new model that combines the IFLA models discussed previously: FRBR, FRAD, and FRSAD. Revised RDA also incorporates the 2016 edition of the *Statement of International Cataloguing Principles*. Revised RDA also will focus more on relationships than Original RDA,[15] and it will broaden Original RDA so it can be used by communities outside of libraries. Although RDA has always been linked data ready, it needs to be even more flexible and extensible to move libraries toward a linked data environment.

RDA Elements

RDA is a set of instructions that guide the work of catalogers. There are hundreds of elements that can be used to create bibliographic records and authority records. RDA includes many options, but it cannot cover every possible cataloging situation. Catalogers often use cataloger's judgment in the application of RDA.

There are quite a few differences between Original RDA and Revised RDA that may change how cataloging is performed.

Original RDA

Original RDA includes ten core elements that should be added to bibliographic records, when present, on an item.[16] Table 3.1 shows the ten core elements. This is just the minimum; a library can always add more information.

Table 3.1. Original RDA Core Elements for Bibliographic Records

RDA Core Element	Explanation	Instructions
Title	Describes the title proper, which is the title of the resource excluding any subtitles, parallel titles, or part titles	Required element
Statement of Responsibility	Statement of the names and corporate bodies responsible for the intellectual content of a resource	Required element, if present on resource
Edition Statement	Statement of edition and its designation: Second edition, Revised edition, etc.	Required element, if present on resource
Numbering of Serials	Statement that explains the numeric, alphabetic, and/or chronological designation of first issue/part and last issue/part of a serial *Current serial:* Volume 3, number 5 (June 2019)– *Inactive serial:* Number 1 (1910)– number 100 (2010).	Required element for serial publications
Production Statement	Date of production for an unpublished resource	Required element for an unpublished resource
Publication Statement	Includes the place of publication, publisher's name, and date of publication for published resources	Required element for published resources
Series Statement	Includes the series title proper, its numbering, if present, and the subseries, if present	Required element, if present on resource
Identifier for Manifestation	Standard numbers such as ISBN, ISSN, publisher's numbers, etc.	Required element, if present on resource
Carrier Type	Information about format and housing, e.g., audio disc, film cassette, volume	Required element
Extent	Number of units in a resource, such as 1 audio disc, 3 volumes, 1 online resource, etc. For single books, page numbers are recorded instead	Required element

In addition to the ten core elements, there are hundreds of other elements and detailed instructions that explain how to catalog particular formats (e.g., serials, moving images, audio recordings), how to handle difficult cataloging situations, how to format each element, and where to take information. Original RDA also governs access points, including the creation of authorized access points for names and titles, and when to add them to bibliographic records. It ensures consistency of bibliographic and authority data across libraries and the standardization of data in bibliographic records. With all libraries using the same code, it is easier to share cataloging and easier for users to understand library data.

Original RDA is standardized, but each library creates specific policies for its users and materials. The most widely used policies are the Library of Congress-Program for Cooperative Cataloging Policy Statements (LC-PCC PS), which explain how the Library of Congress and its Program for Cooperative Cataloging has interpreted RDA.[17] Think of the policy statements as the case law for RDA: there are the RDA instructions, and the policy statements explain how the instructions are applied in practice. Because the Library of Congress and the PCC create many bibliographic and authority records used by libraries around the country, their policy statements are extremely important. The policy statements have been added to Original RDA, and many libraries choose to follow them. However, not *all* libraries use them. It is up to each individual library to determine its own cataloging policies.

Revised RDA

Revised RDA does not include required core elements, like Original RDA. Instead, there are about 1,700 individual elements that can be used. In addition, Revised RDA may become less of a set of instructions catalogers can use for descriptive cataloging and more like a metadata schema or data dictionary that can be used by many communities. This makes Revised RDA a little more than just "revised." Original RDA is a content standard becoming more like a metadata schema, and this is not an easy transition. Revised RDA defines entities, elements, and relationships, but does not necessarily provide explicit instructions about how library catalogers should create bibliographic records. Instead, Revised RDA is intended to be used with an application profile, which is a description of how a community uses a metadata schema in practice. Application profiles would explain how to create bibliographic records based on Revised RDA. Instead of following the instructions in Revised RDA directly, library catalogers would follow the instructions and guidance in one or more application profiles. Potentially, application profiles could be created for any format, subject, or library. Currently, there are no application profiles created for library cataloging, but they will need to be created if Revised RDA is approved. Perhaps the Library of Congress and the PCC will create the main application profile.

In addition, Revised RDA wants to be more extensible and flexible for use in multiple environments and by multiple communities. However, having a flexible standard means providing more options for use; explicit cataloging instructions are not included in Revised RDA. This may be extremely problematic for library catalogers who need specific cataloging instructions and for libraries who rely on them. Although Revised RDA is trying to be looser and more flexible to be used by more communities, cataloging is left with the old conundrum of how to best embody cataloging experience in rules. There has always been a tension between simplified cataloging rules based on principles and detailed cataloging rules based on experience. Revised RDA seems to be moving cataloging more toward the principles side of the debate, to include very few explicit instructions at all. Cataloging is complex, and there is a large body of experience to draw on. A flexible cataloging standard based on principles and models is needed, but so are specific instructions that help catalogers perform their jobs.

RDA Principles

RDA is based on principles. Original RDA incorporates the 2009 edition of the *Statement of International Cataloguing Principles*, and Revised RDA incorporates the 2016 edition. The *Statement* includes a list of thirteen "General Principles" that should be used when creating cataloging codes. They are shown below.[18]

---

2 GENERAL PRINCIPLES

The following principles direct the construction and development of cataloguing codes, the decisions that cataloguers make and policies on access to and exchange of data. Of these, the convenience of the user is the most important, while principles 2.2 through 2.13 are in no particular order. If there is a conflict among principles 2.2–2.13, the principle of interoperability should be rated higher than others.

  2.1. *Convenience of the user.* Convenience means that all efforts should be made to keep all data comprehensible and suitable for the users. The word "user" embraces anyone who searches the catalogue and uses the bibliographic and/or authority data. Decisions taken in the making of descriptions and controlled forms of names for access should be made with the user in mind.

  2.2. *Common usage.* Vocabulary used in descriptions and access points should be in accordance with that of the majority of users.

  2.3. *Representation.* A description should represent a resource as it appears. Controlled forms of names of persons, corporate bodies and families should be based on the way an entity describes itself. Controlled forms of work titles should be based on the form appearing on the first manifestation of the original expression. If this is not feasible, the form commonly used in reference sources should be used.

  2.4. *Accuracy.* Bibliographic and authority data should be an accurate portrayal of the entity described.

2.5. *Sufficiency and necessity*. Those data elements that are required to: facilitate access for all types of users, including those with specific needs; fulfil the objectives and functions of the catalogue; and describe or identify entities, should be included.

2.6. *Significance*. Data elements should be relevant to the description, noteworthy, and allow for distinctions among entities.

2.7. *Economy*. When alternative ways exist to achieve a goal, preference should be given to the way that best furthers overall expediency and practicality (i.e., the least cost or the simplest approach).

2.8. *Consistency and standardization*. Descriptions and construction of access points should be standardized as far as possible to enable consistency.

2.9. *Integration*. The descriptions for all types of resources and controlled forms of names of all types of entities should be based on a common set of rules to the extent possible.

2.10. *Interoperability*. All efforts should be made to ensure the sharing and reuse of bibliographic and authority data within and outside the library community. For the exchange of data and discovery tools, the use of vocabularies facilitating automatic translation and disambiguation is highly recommended.

2.11. *Openness*. Restrictions on data should be minimal in order to foster transparency and conform to Open Access principles, as declared also in the IFLA Statement on Open Access. Any restriction on data access should be fully stated.

2.12. *Accessibility*. The access to bibliographic and authority data, as well as searching device functionalities, should comply with international standards for accessibility as recommended in the IFLA Code of Ethics for Librarians and other Information Workers.

2.13. *Rationality*. The rules in a cataloguing code should be defensible and not arbitrary. If, in specific situations, it is not possible to respect all the principles, then defensible, practical solutions should be found and the rationale should be explained.

RDA Models

Both Original RDA and Revised RDA incorporate an entity-relationship model, a type of model used in the computer science field to model data. An entity-relationship model chooses and describes *entities*, or the things that are the focus of the model. It shows the *attributes* of those entities, which are the elements that make up the entities. It also shows relationships among the entities and explains how they are related. The *IFLA Library Reference Model* defines entities, attributes, and relationships this way:

Entities: the classes which are the focus of interest;
Attributes: the data which characterizes instances of entities;
Relationships: the properties which link instances of entities.[19]

Using the classic car collection example from the beginning of the chapter, the model would focus on cars. There are many ways to model the collection, but perhaps the entities could be sedans, coupes, and roadsters, and the attributes could be the elements picked to describe the cars, such make, model, and year. The model would also show how the entities of sedans, coupes, and roadsters are related.

The models that have been developed for libraries are not data models. They are *conceptual models* used to provide a picture of the "bibliographic universe,"[20] which includes everything that is collected in libraries and other cultural heritage institutions, both physical and digital, published and unpublished, mass-produced and unique. The entities include things like works, persons, corporate bodies, and so on. They do not describe specific formats or the carriers of content. Attributes describe each entity, what was referred to as *elements* at the beginning of the chapter. For example, for a work, attributes (elements) can include title and author. For a person, attributes can include preferred form of name and year of birth.

Relationships are important because they show how entities are related in library collections. For example: How is a person related to a work? Is that person an author? An illustrator? A composer? How are works related to other works? Is something an adaptation? A translation? A copy? There are lots of relationships in library collections, but bibliographic relationships, especially, can be very complicated. Works are related to other things, in many ways. For example, take a well-known work such as *The Great Gatsby*. It was originally published in 1925, and it has been republished again and again in different editions, both print and digital. There are several translations into other languages, several audiobooks, a graphic novel, literary criticism, commentaries, reviews written about it, study guides, and summaries. There are four motion pictures based on the book, released in 1926, 1949, 1974, and 2013, and there is a television movie and other programs. There are several plays and an opera based on *The Great Gatsby* as well. Cataloging tries to sort out these bibliographic relationships and make them transparent and easy for users to understand.[21]

FRBR Model

Perhaps the most influential model has been IFLA's *Functional Requirements for Bibliographic Records* (FRBR), published in 1998, which was developed as a conceptual model that showed "a 'generalized' view of the bibliographic universe."[22] It wanted to show the "universe" of what is collected in libraries, what defines them, and how they are related to each other. It is an entity-relationship model that modeled the entities, attributes, and relationships of library materials and mapped them to *user tasks*, or what users do on library catalogs.[23]

There are many parts to the FRBR model, but the group 1 entities that focus on Work—Expression—Manifestation—Item (WEMI) have been the most influential. Original RDA incorporated this model, and Revised RDA keeps this model, too. Figure 3.3 shows the basic WEMI model,[24] and definitions follow.

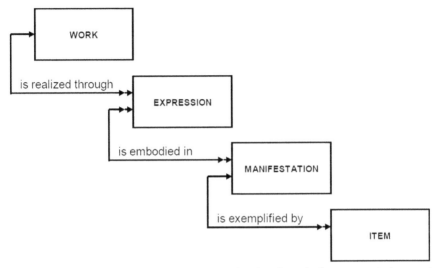

Figure 3.3.   FRBR WEMI Model. *International Federation of Library Associations and Institutions (IFLA)*

Work: "A distinct intellectual or artistic creation." This is an abstract idea only; it does not exist in an actual format in libraries yet. It is not embodied in any format or carrier.

Expression: "The intellectual or artistic realization of a work." This is also an abstract idea. It does not exist in an actual format in libraries yet. It is not embodied in any format or carrier.

Manifestation: "The physical embodiment of an expression of a work." This is a real thing; it exists in an actual format in libraries, like a book, a PDF file, a map, etc. It is a carrier of the expression.

Item: "A single exemplar of a manifestation." This is a real thing, too, but it is a specific item that is in a library. [25]

This model can be confusing even for experienced catalogers. To give an example, look at *The Great Gatsby* in the FRBR model:

The Work: The Great Gatsby by F. Scott Fitzgerald. This work (*The Great Gatsby*) is "a distinct intellectual or artistic creation." It is abstract idea only; it does not exist in an actual form in libraries yet.

The Expression: The Great Gatsby by F. Scott Fitzgerald, edited by Ruth Prigozy. This expression (the "Prigozy" version) is "the intellectual or artistic realization of a work." However, this expression is also an abstract idea; it does not exist in an actual form in libraries yet.

The Manifestation: The Great Gatsby by F. Scott Fitzgerald, edited by Ruth Prigozy published by Oxford University Press in 2008. The manifestation (the 2008 Oxford University Press publication) is "the physical embodiment of an expression of a work." This is the real thing. It exists as an actual book in libraries. The book is a carrier of the expression.

The Item: A library's copy of *The Great Gatsby* by F. Scott Fitzgerald edited by Ruth Prigozy published by Oxford University Press in 2008. This item is "a single exemplar of a manifestation." This is the real thing, too, but it is a specific copy that is housed in a library.

A work is a distinct intellectual product; it is not embodied in a carrier, like a book. For example, *The Great Gatsby* is a work. The next level down is the expression, which is a realization of a work. *The Great Gatsby* edited by Ruth Prigozy is one expression. This is still an intellectual concept; it is not embodied in a carrier like a book. A user may ask, "I want to read the Prigozy *The Great Gatsby*," but they do not care which version they read. The next level down is the manifestation. This level is the actual carrier of the work, the specific publication and format. The Oxford University Press version of the book published in 2008 is a manifestation. The last level down is the item, which is a specific item or copy. A copy of the book housed in a library is an item.

The FRBR model and its language are important because it was incorporated into Original RDA. Instead of focusing only on formats (such as books, serials, or maps) or focusing on just elements (such as title, author, or notes), RDA is based on a conceptual model and focuses on how entities, attributes, and relationships work together at a higher level. In addition to FRBR, which deals with bibliographic data, Original RDA also incorporated IFLA's *Functional Requirements for Authority Data* (FRAD), published in 2009, which modeled authority data. There was also the *Functional Requirements for Subject Authority Data* (FRSAD), published in 2010, which modeled subject authority data, but it was not really incorporated in Original RDA.

IFLA Library Reference Model

Revised RDA is incorporating a new model, the *IFLA Library Reference Model* (LRM), which is the new model of the "bibliographic universe" approved in August 2017. It calls itself "a high-level conceptual reference model developed within an enhanced entity-relationship modelling framework."[26] The LRM consolidates the three IFLA functional models—FRBR, FRAD, and FRSAD—into one super entity-relationship model. The models were combined because each "Functional Requirements" model was created by a separate committee, had different definitions for terms, and looked at bibliographic, authority, and subject data problems and solutions in different ways. They did not match each other well. There was a need to combine the models to have a streamlined and cohesive model that addressed all types of data.[27] The LRM describes its purpose this way: "The model considers bibliographic information pertinent to all types of resources generally of interest to libraries; however, the model seeks to reveal the commonalities and underlying structure of bibliographic resources. The model selected terms and created definitions so that they may be applicable in a generic way to all types of resources, or to all relevant entities."[28]

LRM also includes a model of *aggregates*, first proposed by the IFLA Working Group on Aggregates.[29] An aggregate pulls together different things into one manifestation, or one published thing. For example, an issue of a journal or other serial publication can include different articles. A music album can be a compilation of different songs by many people, like a soundtrack. A book may be a collection of short stories, poems or novels by one person or many people. There are many other examples of aggregates, and the concept of aggregates is being incorporated into Revised RDA.[30] LRM also addresses the modeling of serial works, a topic not handled well by the FRBR models.

IFLA Library Reference Model Entities

There are eleven entities in the LRM. These entities include the WEMI model from FRBR, but there are several new entities as well. Please see the LRM entities and their definitions below.[31]

Res: Res ("thing" in Latin) is the top entity in the model. Res includes both material or physical things and concepts. Everything considered relevant to the bibliographic universe, which is the universe of discourse in this case, is included. Res is a superclass of all the other entities that are explicitly defined, as well as of any other entities not specifically labeled.

Work: The intellectual or artistic content of a distinct creation

Expression: A distinct combination of signs conveying intellectual or artistic content

Manifestation: A set of all carriers that are assumed to share the same characteristics as to intellectual or artistic content and aspects of physical form (defined by both the overall content and the production plan for its carrier or carriers)

Item: An object or objects carrying signs intended to convey intellectual or artistic content

Agent: An entity capable of deliberate actions, of being granted rights, and of being held accountable for its actions (includes the entities *person* and *collective agent*)

Person: An individual human being

Collective Agent: A gathering or organization of persons bearing a particular name and capable of acting as a unit (includes corporate bodies and families)

Nomen: An association between an entity and a designation that refers to it

Place: A given extent of space

Time-span: A temporal extent having a beginning, an end and a duration

In addition to new LRM entities, the LRM includes a new model of relationships, shown in figure 3.4.[32] The LRM entities are in capital letters in the boxes, and arrows show the relationships. The original FRBR model of Work—Expression—Manifestation—Item is a part of the LRM model. Each WEMI entity is related to the Agent entity, which contains the entities of Person and Collective Agent. They create a Work or Expression, create, manufacture or distribute a Manifestation, or own or modify an Item. The Work entity is related to the entity Res, a new entity that means "thing" in Latin. Res is the top entity in LRM and includes all other entities. Res is associated with the entities of Time-span and Place. Nomen is a controlled something, such as an authorized access point for a name or a subject. It is related to Res and Agent.

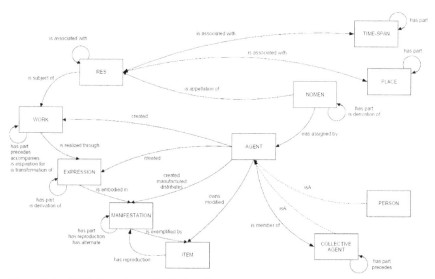

Figure 3.4. LRM Overview of Relationships. (Now that's a model!) *International Federation of Library Associations and Institutions (IFLA)*

Revised RDA Entities

The LRM can be an imposing model. It combines FRBR, FRAD, and FRSAD into one super-model, and many of the words, like Res and Nomen, are new to most catalogers. It is a broad picture of the "bibliographic universe" that covers all resources typically collected by libraries and shows the "underlying structure of bibliographic resources."[33] This structure has always been there—libraries have been cataloging their collections for a long time—but the LRM model makes the structure explicit. It names the entities, identifies the attributes, and shows the relationships. Revised RDA is incorporating LRM, but Revised RDA is different. There are thirteen entities that are slightly different from LRM. The Revised RDA entities and their definitions are shown below.[34]

RDA Entity: An abstract class of key conceptual objects in the universe of human discourse that is a focus of interest to users of RDA metadata in a system for resource discovery. An RDA entity includes an agent, collective agent, corporate body, expression, family, item, manifestation, nomen, person, place, time-span, and work.

Work: A distinct intellectual or artistic creation, that is, the intellectual or artistic content

Expression: An intellectual or artistic realization of a work in the form of alpha-numeric, musical or choreographic notation, sound, image, object, movement, etc., or any combination of such forms

Manifestation: A physical embodiment of an expression of a work

Item: A single exemplar or instance of a manifestation

Agent: A person or two or more persons capable of acting as a unit

Person: An individual human being who lives or is assumed to have lived

Collective Agent: A gathering or organization of persons bearing a particular name and capable of acting as a unit; a collective agent includes a *corporate body* and a *family*

Corporate Body: An organization or group of persons or organizations that is identified by a name and is capable of acting as a unit

Family: Two or more persons related by birth, marriage, adoption, civil union, or similar legal status, or who otherwise present themselves as a family

Nomen: A designation that refers to an RDA entity; a designation includes a name, title, access point, identifier, and subject classification codes and headings

Place: A given extent of space

Time-span: A temporal extent having a beginning, an end and a duration

RDA keeps many of the same entities as LRM, such as Work, Expression, Manifestation, Item, Agent, Collective Agent, Nomen, Time-span, and Place. It does not use the term Res, but instead uses RDA Entity as a superclass entity that refers to other entities. In addition, Revised RDA combines the LRM entity Person into the RDA entity Agent. An agent can be a person, family, or corporate body in RDA, while a Collective Agent is a family or a corporate body. The elements of Time-span and Collective Agent are new to Revised RDA. Original RDA included several of these entities, but Revised RDA is arranged around these entities. Unlike Original RDA, a cataloger will need to know the entities in order to use Revised RDA.

OTHER CONTENT STANDARDS

Original RDA is considered a content standard for libraries. It is used to describe and provide access to library collections. In addition to RDA, there are content standards used primarily in archives and museums. Libraries that have archival collections or art and architecture collections may use these content standards, too.

Describing Archives: A Content Standard

Just as RDA is for libraries, *Describing Archives: A Content Standard* (DACS) is a content standard used to describe and provide access to materials in archives (e.g., personal papers, diaries, lists, notes, photographs, drawings, manuscripts). It was developed by the Society of American Archivists and first published in 2004. DACS was adopted in 2005 as "the official content standard of the U.S. archival community."[35] The second edition was published in 2013. It can be used to create finding aids and bibliographic records, and can be used with various encoding standards and metadata schemas, such as MARC 21 and *Encoded Archival Description* (EAD).

Cataloging Cultural Objects

Cataloging Cultural Objects (CCO) is a content standard used to describe and provide access to cultural works and their images, "including architecture, paintings, sculpture, prints, manuscripts, photographs and other visual media, performance art, archaeological sites and artifacts, and various functional objects from the realm of material culture."[36] CCO was developed by professionals in cultural heritage institutions (e.g., libraries, archives, and museums), and it is maintained by the Visual Resources Association. It was published by the American Library Association in 2006 and intended for use by cultural heritage institutions that have art and architecture collections.

DESCRIPTIVE METADATA IN LIBRARIES: METADATA SCHEMAS

RDA is the descriptive cataloging standard that guides the creation of bibliographic and authority records. Libraries also use metadata schemas (also called metadata element sets) to create metadata records that describe and provide access to digital collections. There are many metadata schemas in the world that provide descriptive metadata. Some are general metadata schemas (e.g., *Dublin Core*) that are used by many communities that organize data. Some are used primarily in cultural heritage institutions, such as libraries, museums, and archives (e.g., *Encoded Archival Description*, *Metadata Object Description Schema*, *Metadata Authority Description Schema*). There also are metadata schemas for specific communities, such as art (e.g., *VRA Core*). Each metadata schema has been created with a specific purpose, and each one defines the elements used to describe various types of digital resources. Some metadata schemas are very broad and have basic elements only. Other metadata schemas have very specific elements. Unlike content standards like RDA, metadata schemas do not concern themselves with transcribing content. They are considered data *structure* standards only. They do not dictate content; they are simply a set of elements that can be used to describe digital resources. As discussed in chapter 2, most metadata schemas are expressed using XML, but other encoding standards can be used.

Metadata records are not standardized across libraries, like bibliographic records. Unlike mass-published items in a library's main collection, items in a digital collection tend to be unique and special, and usually not found at many libraries. Collections can vary widely and may have different needs. A digital collection of rare cookbooks needs to be described differently than a digital collection of photos by local newspaper photographers, and differently than a digital collection of local family genealogical materials. A library can use any metadata schema and can modify a schema to meet its needs. It is up to each individual library. Authority control in digital collections (assigning consistent names, titles, and subjects) is not standardized either. Each library can decide if it wants to provide authority control in its metadata records, and if so, what controlled lists or vocabularies to use. Some libraries may add names to the local authority file so that names are consistent in a digital collection and in a library catalog; other libraries may not do that. Some libraries may use a subject headings list or thesaurus to provide consistent subject access; other libraries do not. It depends on the library and its needs. Each library handles access and authority control for digital collections in its own way.

Although resources in digital collections may be unique and may resist standardization, metadata records can be easier to create than bibliographic records. There are no strict instructions when using a metadata schema, like there is when using Original RDA. Libraries can make metadata records as simple or as complex as needed. In addition, when creating metadata records, metadata librarians do not have to understand how to code using XML. They use templates to do the work and usually need to focus on entering content only. This is different from library cataloging, in which catalogers need to know RDA and MARC 21 to create bibliographic records.

METADATA SCHEMAS USED IN LIBRARIES

There are several metadata schemas used in libraries. Each library chooses which schema works best for its digital collections.

Dublin Core

The most widely used metadata schema in libraries is *Dublin Core. Dublin Core* is a general metadata schema. It is a set of elements used to describe digital resources available online. *Dublin Core* is used by many communities around the world, both library and nonlibrary. In libraries, it is used to describe and provide access to digital collections. It is maintained by the Dublin Core Metadata Initiative (DCMI), and because *Dublin Core* is used by many metadata communities (not just libraries), DCMI takes a much broader focus. It is governed by professionals from around the world who work in various fields, including information technology, librarianship, and education.[37] Decisions made by DCMI affect how *Dublin Core* is used by libraries and other organizations.

Dublin Core began at a 1995 conference in Dublin, Ohio, hosted by OCLC, which is how it got its name. The goal was to create a simple set of elements that would be easy for anyone, not just library catalogers, to use. It began as a way to catalog web pages and information on the web. *Dublin Core* started to be used by libraries and nonlibraries in the late 1990s to create digital libraries, and today it is used to describe all types of digital collections.

Dublin Core originally had a list of fifteen elements called "Simple Dublin Core," which included Creator, Contributor, Publisher, Title, Date, Language, Format, Subject, Description, Identifier, Relation, Source, Type, Coverage, and Rights. There also was a "Qualified Dublin Core," in which different communities could modify the simple elements and add other things appropriate for them. It allowed a community to expand or reduce the elements to meet its needs. For example, because *Dublin Core* was so simple, it did not include things that are helpful for libraries, like edition and audience. A library could choose to use the library application profile and add edition and audience and other elements specifically for library materials.

In 2012 *Dublin Core* replaced "Simple Dublin Core" and "Qualified Dublin Core" with the *DCMI Metadata Terms*. It is a list of fifty-five properties that can be used to describe resources. See the list below.[38]

DCMI METADATA TERMS

abstract	date	isPartOf	relation
accessRights	dateAccepted	isReferencedBy	replaces
accrualMethod	dateCopyrighted	isReplacedBy	requires
accrualPeriodicity	dateSubmitted	isRequiredBy	rights
accrualPolicy	description	issued	rightsHolder
alternative	educationLevel	isVersionOf	source
audience	extent	language	spatial
available	format	license	subject
bibliographicCitation	hasFormat	mediator	tableOfContents
conformsTo	hasPart	medium	temporal
contributor	hasVersion	modified	title
coverage	identifier	provenance	type
created	instructionalMethod	publisher	valid
creator	isFormatOf	references	

However, Simple Dublin Core did not go away. Of these fifty-five properties, fifteen of them are considered the "Classic Dublin Core," called the *Dublin Core Metadata Element Set*. The list is shown below.[39]

CLASSIC DUBLIN CORE METADATA ELEMENT SET

contributor	publisher
coverage	relation
creator	rights
date	source
description	subject
format	title
identifier	type
language	

These elements can be expanded by using the properties from the *DCMI Metadata Terms* to create new elements. In addition, XML is the markup language usually used to create *Dublin Core* tags and transmit *Dublin Core* data. Figure 3.5 shows an example of a *Dublin Core* metadata record, including the record with labels and the record coded in XML.[40]

title: Birthday Party
creator: Douglass, Neal
date: 1959-03-07
language: No Language
description: Smiling McDonald toddler girl sitting on table with her birthday
 cakes
subject: People - Family Groups
coverage: United States - Texas - Travis County - Austin
coverage: Into Modern Times, 1939-Present
coverage: 1959-03-07
rights: Public
type: Photograph
format: 1 photograph : negative, b&w ; 4 x 5 in.
format: Image
identifier: local-cont-no: ND-59-223-03
identifier: https://texashistory.unt.edu/ark:/67531/metapth33391/
identifier: ark: ark:/67531/metapth33391

```
- <oai_dc:dc xsi:schemaLocation="http://www.openarchives.org/OAI/2.0/oai_dc/
    <dc:title>Birthday Party</dc:title>
    <dc:creator>Douglass, Neal</dc:creator>
    <dc:date>1959-03-07</dc:date>
    <dc:language>No Language</dc:language>
  - <dc:description>
      Smiling McDonald toddler girl sitting on table with her birthday cakes
    </dc:description>
    <dc:subject>People - Family Groups</dc:subject>
    <dc:coverage>United States - Texas - Travis County - Austin</dc:coverage>
    <dc:coverage>Into Modern Times, 1939-Present</dc:coverage>
    <dc:coverage>1959-03-07</dc:coverage>
    <dc:rights>Public</dc:rights>
    <dc:type>Photograph</dc:type>
    <dc:format>1 photograph : negative, b&w ; 4 x 5 in.</dc:format>
    <dc:format>Image</dc:format>
    <dc:identifier>local-cont-no: ND-59-223-03</dc:identifier>
  - <dc:identifier>
      https://texashistory.unt.edu/ark:/67531/metapth33391/
    </dc:identifier>
    <dc:identifier>ark: ark:/67531/metapth33391</dc:identifier>
  </oai_dc:dc>
```

Figure 3.5.   Example of a Dublin Core Metadata Record

Metadata Object Description Schema

Metadata Object Description Schema (MODS) is an XML metadata schema focused on bibliographic data in libraries. It was developed at the Library of Congress in 2002 for use by libraries performing digital projects. The latest version is MODS 3.7, released in January 2018. The Network Development and MARC Standards Office of the Library of Congress is responsible for maintaining the schema. It is based on the *MARC 21 Format for Bibliographic Data*, which is used to create bibliographic records along with cataloging standards. MODS includes a small element set based on the most common elements used to create bibliographic records. MODS splits the difference between MARC/RDA and *Dublin Core*. It is simpler than MARC/RDA, but more specific than the Classic Dublin Core. There are twenty "top elements," shown below.[41]

MODS 20 TOP ELEMENTS

titleInfo	abstract	identifier
name	tableOfContents	location
typeOfResource	targetAudience	accessCondition
genre	note	part
originInfo	subject	extension
language	classification	recordInfo
physicalDescription	relatedItem	

In MODS, at least one element must be used. Some top elements have optional subelements. For example, the element *language* has subelements *languageTerm* and *scriptTerm*. As with *Dublin Core*, there are no specific instructions for how to enter data into each element. MODS is particularly useful for digital collections that want to use a simpler element set than MARC. RDA has been mapped to MODS, so libraries can use the instructions in RDA to create MODS records.

Metadata Authority Description Schema

Metadata Authority Description Schema is an XML metadata schema just for authority data that is used in conjunction with MODS. It was originally released in 2005, and the latest version is MADS 2.1, released in 2016. It is maintained by the Network Development and MARC Standards Office of the Library of Congress. MADS is based on the *MARC 21 Format for Authority Data*, which is used to create authority records using RDA and other cataloging standards. Like MODS, MADS includes a small element set based on the most common elements used to create authority records. There are twelve primary elements, shown below, and more than fifty subelements that can be used to create MADS records.[42]

```
┌─────────────────────────────────────────────────────────────────┐
│                    MADS 12 PRIMARY ELEMENTS                       │
│                                                                   │
│          authority      classification      note                 │
│          related        fieldOfEndeavor     url                  │
│          variant        identifier          extension            │
│          affiliation    language            recordInfo           │
└─────────────────────────────────────────────────────────────────┘
```

Some primary elements have several subelements. For example, the element *affiliation* has subelements of *position, organization, address, email, phone,* and more.

Other Metadata Schemas

There are several other metadata schemas used in libraries and other cultural heritage institutions. Here is a short list.

Categories for the Description of Works of Art

Categories for the Description of Works of Art (CDWA) is a metadata schema used to describe artworks. It calls itself "a set of guidelines for best practice in cataloging and describing works of art, architecture, other material culture, groups and collections of works, and related images, arranged in a conceptual framework that may be used for designing databases and accessing information."[43] There are about 540 elements, and about 50 elements are considered core. It uses an XML schema called *CDWA Lite* to encode and transmit the data. CDWA was originally released in 1996, and the most recent revision was in 2016. The Getty Vocabulary Program of the Getty Research Institute maintains CDWA.

Encoded Archival Description

Encoded Archival Description (EAD) is used to describe and encode archival finding aids, which list the items in an individual archival collection (e.g., the archives of a person, the archives of an organization). It was first published in 1998, and the latest version is EAD3, version 1.1.0, published in 2018. EAD was created originally as an encoding standard only, but now it is an XML metadata schema as well. There are 165 elements in the tag library. It is used primarily in archives, but libraries with archival collections may use EAD to create electronic finding aids. EAD can be used with DACS. It is maintained by the Society of American Archivists and the Library of Congress.[44]

VRA Core *(Visual Resources Association)*

VRA Core is an XML metadata schema used to describe works of visual culture and their images (e.g., paintings, sculptures, photographs). The first version was released in 1996, and the current version is 4.0, released in 2007. It is used by cultural heritage institutions and other communities that "need to manage information about and provide access to cultural heritage works and their images."[45] The Library of Congress's Network Development and MARC Standards Office partners with the Visual Resources Association to host *VRA Core.*[46]

ONIX for Books *(Online Information Exchange)*

ONIX for Books is an XML metadata schema used to create records in the publishing industry. Publishers use it to share book information with booksellers and wholesalers. It was developed by the Association of American Publishers and was first released in 2000. Today, it is maintained jointly by EDItEUR, Book Industry Communication in the UK, and the Book Industry Study Group (BISG) in the United States. The latest version is 3.0.1, released in 2012.[47] ONIX is important for libraries because the publishing industry shares its information with libraries. ONIX is mapped to MARC 21, and the publishing industry and library profession worked together to create the *RDA/ONIX Framework for Resource Categorization* in 2006. This is a shared set of elements that facilitate interoperability between data from the publishing industry (ONIX) and libraries (RDA).

SUMMARY

This chapter discussed descriptive metadata and how it is used to describe and provide access to library collections. To create bibliographic and authority records, most libraries use the current descriptive cataloging standard, *Resource Description and Access.* It provides instructions for description (describing what library materials look like) and access, which provides name and title access into a library's collection. To create metadata records, libraries use a metadata schema, such as *Dublin Core.* Libraries can choose from multiple standards and metadata schemas if they have a need for them. For example, an academic library with a main library collection, a digital collection, and an archive, can use RDA to describe materials in the main collection, *Dublin Core* to describe materials in a digital collection, and *Describing Archives: A Content Standard* to describe its archival materials.

DISCUSSION QUESTIONS

1. Imagine you are organizing your personal music collection, either physical or digital (e.g., CD, record, tape, iTunes). How would you organize your collection and why? What are the elements would you pick to describe your collection and why?
2. What is descriptive metadata? What types of descriptive metadata are created in libraries, and how are they created?

3. Describe the characteristics, similarities, and differences of Original RDA and Revised RDA.
4. Compare and contrast *Resource Description and Access* and *Dublin Core*. What are the similarities and differences?

CLASS ACTIVITIES

1. *Catalog Your Closet.* Pretend you are creating a database that stores information about the clothes in your closet. You will create a short descriptive cataloging system (descriptive metadata schema), catalog five items of your clothing, and answer several questions. In this exercise, you are the user, so you need to create a database for you. You will:

   A. Pick five of the most important elements to describe your clothes collection (e.g., type, designer, etc.) and explain why you picked them. Think about the elements that are most meaningful for you.
   B. Create guidelines for each element. For example, where will you take the information about each element? How will you enter information so it is consistent? How will you differentiate each item? Describe the guidelines for each element and explain why you devised them.
   C. Pick two access points to be used when searching the database. Which specific elements would you like to search? Explain your choices.
   D. Describe (catalog) five items of clothing from your closet using the elements you chose and your guidelines for description.
   E. Evaluate your system. What worked? What would you change about your system and why? If you were to expand your system, what other elements would you add and why?

   Activity Questions. Answer the following questions:

   A. Pretend your clothes are part of a fashion designer's latest collection. You are creating a database to hold information about the designer's collection. The designer will manufacture and sell these items to customers. What elements would you pick and why?
   B. Pretend your clothes are part of a museum's collection of "Twenty-first-Century Fashion." You are creating a database to hold information about the museum's collection. The museum will keep this collection permanently. Sometimes the collection will be on display and sometimes it will be in storage. What elements would you pick and why?

2. *Cataloging Assignment.* If this textbook is used in a cataloging course, then you should create bibliographic records for books (and/or other items) focusing on descriptive cataloging only (description and access points). Look for authorized name and title access points in the Library of Congress National Author-

ity File. Practice tests that reinforce descriptive cataloging guidelines, and in which you find authorized access points for names and titles, also are helpful.

3. *Metadata Assignment.* If this textbook is used in a metadata course, then you should create metadata records for digital items using a specific metadata schema, like *Dublin Core.* Focus on descriptive elements only; add subject headings later. Practice tests in which you find authorized access points for names also are helpful.

NOTES

1. Marcia Lei Zeng and Jian Qin, *Metadata*, 2nd ed. (Chicago: Neal-Schuman, 2016), 19.

2. Steven J. Miller, *Metadata for Digital Collections: A How-To-Do-It Manual* (New York: Neal-Schuman, 2011), 10.

3. Elaine Svenonius, *The Intellectual Foundation of Information Organization* (Cambridge, MA: MIT Press, 2000), 23.

4. Library of Congress Catalog, accessed January 11, 2019, https://catalog.loc.gov.

5. Charles A. Cutter, "Rules for a Printed Dictionary Catalog," as *Public Libraries in the United States of America: Their History, Condition, and Management: Special Report, Part II* (Washington, DC: US Government Printing Office, 1876), 10.

6. Library of Congress Authorities, accessed January 11, 2019, https://authorities.loc.gov.

7. Ibid.

8. Ibid.

9. RDA Steering Committee, "RDA Regions." accessed January 11, 2019, http://www .rda-rsc.org/regions.

10. RDA Toolkit, accessed January 11, 2019, https://www.rdatoolkit.org.

11. See, e.g., Chris Evin Long, "RDA Implementation in Large US Public Libraries," *Library Resources & Technical Services* 62, no. 3 (2018): 98–113.

12. RDA Toolkit, "3R Project: Kickoff Announcement," October 12, 2016, accessed January 11, 2019, https://www.rdatoolkit.org/3Rproject/announcement.

13. RDA Toolkit Beta Site, accessed January 11, 2019, https://beta.rdatoolkit.org/rda.web.

14. Chris Oliver, *Introducing RDA: A Guide to the Basics* (Chicago: American Library Association, 2010), 2.

15. See, e.g., Kate James, "Basics of Attributes and Relationships," presentation at the American Library Association Annual Conference, New Orleans, LA, June 22, 2018.

16. RDA Toolkit, "0.6.5. Section 1: Recording Attributes of Manifestation and Item," 2015, accessed January 11, 2019, http://access.rdatoolkit.org.

17. Library of Congress-Program for Cooperative Cataloging Policy Statements (LC-PCC PS) are available in the *RDA Toolkit* at http://access.rdatoolkit.org.

18. International Federation of Library Associations and Institutions, *Statement of International Cataloguing Principles (ICP)*, 2016 ed. (The Hague: IFLA, 2017), accessed January 11, 2019, https://www.ifla.org/publications/node/11015.

19. International Federation of Library Associations and Institutions, *IFLA Library Reference Model: A Conceptual Model for Bibliographic Information* (The Hague: IFLA, 2017), https:// www.ifla.org/files/assets/cataloguing/frbr-lrm/ifla-lrm-august-2017_rev201712.pdf, 17.

20. Phrase used by Patrick Wilson in "The Catalog as Access Mechanism: Background and Concepts," *Library Resources & Technical Services* 27, no. 1 (1983): 4; also stated in

International Federation of Library Associations and Institutions, *Functional Requirements for Bibliographic Records: Final Report* (The Hague: IFLA, 1998), 6.

21. Barbara B. Tillett, "Bibliographic Relationships," in *Relationships in the Organization of Knowledge*, ed. Carol A. Bean and Rebecca Green (Dordrecht: Kluwer Academic, 2001), 19–35.

22. IFLA, *Functional Requirements for Bibliographic Records*, 6.

23. Ibid., 3.

24. Ibid., 13. I contacted IFLA for permission to use this image but did not receive a response.

25. Ibid., 12–13.

26. IFLA, *IFLA Library Reference Model*, 9.

27. Chris Oliver, "IFLA Library Reference Model: What and Why?" presentation at the American Library Association Annual Conference, New Orleans, LA, June 25, 2018.

28. IFLA, *IFLA Library Reference Model*, 9.

29. International Federation of Library Associations and Institutions, *Final Report of the Working Group on Aggregates*, September 12, 2011, accessed January 11, 2019, https://www.ifla.org/files/assets/cataloguing/frbrrg/AggregatesFinalReport.pdf.

30. IFLA, *IFLA Library Reference Model*, 93–96.

31. Ibid., 20–36.

32. Ibid., 86. I contacted IFLA for permission to use this image but did not receive a response.

33. Ibid., 9.

34. "Entities," RDA Toolkit Beta Site, accessed May 15, 2019, https://beta.rdatoolkit.org/rda.web.

35. Society of American Archivists, "Preface," in *Describing Archives: A Content Standard (DACS)*, 2nd ed. (Chicago: Society of American Archivists, 2013), accessed January 11, 2019, https://www2.archivists.org/standards/DACS/preface.

36. Visual Resources Association, *Cataloging Cultural Objects: A Guide to Describing Cultural Works and Their Images* (Chicago: American Library Association, 2006), xiii.

37. Dublin Core Metadata Initiative, accessed January 11, 2019, http://dublincore.org.

38. Dublin Core Metadata Initiative, "DCMI Metadata Terms," accessed January 11, 2019, http://dublincore.org/documents/dcmi-terms.

39. Dublin Core Metadata Initiative, "Dublin Core Metadata Element Set," accessed January 11, 2019, http://dublincore.org/documents/dces.

40. Metadata records for the image in chapter 1: Neal Douglass, "Birthday Party," photograph, March 7, 1959, University of North Texas Libraries, The Portal to Texas History, crediting Austin History Center, Austin Public Library, accessed January 9, 2019, https://texashistory.unt.edu/ark:/67531/metapth33391.

41. Metadata Object Description Schema (MODS), "MODS Elements and Attributes," last updated August 2, 2018, accessed January 11, 2019, https://www.loc.gov/standards/mods/userguide/generalapp.html.

42. Metadata Authority Description Schema (MADS), "Outline of Elements and Attributes in MADS 2.1," last updated April 13, 2017, accessed January 11, 2019, https://www.loc.gov/standards/mads/mads-outline.html.

43. "Introduction," in *Categories for the Description of Works of Art (CDWA)*, last updated October 23, 2017, accessed January 11, 2019, http://www.getty.edu/research/publications/electronic_publications/cdwa/introduction.html.

44. Library of Congress, "Encoded Archival Description (EAD)," last updated January 4, 2019, accessed January 11, 2019, http://www.loc.gov/ead.

45. Library of Congress, "An Introduction to VRA Core," October 28, 2014, accessed January 11, 2019, https://www.loc.gov/standards/vracore/VRA_Core4_Intro.pdf.

46. Library of Congress, "VRA Core: Official Website," last updated February 15, 2018, accessed January 11, 2019, https://www.loc.gov/standards/vracore.

47. Book Industry Study Group (BISG), "ONIX for Books," accessed January 11, 2019, https://bisg.org/page/ONIXforBooks.

SELECTED BIBLIOGRAPHY AND ADDITIONAL READING

Adamich, Tom. "FRBR Models and RDA Updates." *Technicalities* 37, no. 5 (2017): 14–17.

Brenndorfer, Thomas. *RDA Essentials*. Chicago: ALA Editions, 2016.

Carlyle, Allyson, and Lisa M. Fusco. "Understanding FRBR as a Conceptual Model: FRBR and the Bibliographic Universe." *Bulletin of the American Society for Information Science and Technology* 33, no. 6 (2007): 12–16.

Coleman, Anita S. "From Cataloging to Metadata: Dublin Core Records for the Library Catalog." *Cataloging & Classification Quarterly* 40 (2005): 153–81.

Coyle, Karen. *FRBR, Before and After: A Look at Our Bibliographic Models*. Chicago: ALA Editions, 2016.

Cutter, Charles A. "Rules for a Printed Dictionary Catalogue." Published as *Public Libraries in the United States of America: Their History, Condition, and Management: Special Report, Part II*. Washington, DC: US Government Printing Office, 1876.

Dunshire, Gordon. Outcomes of the RDA Toolkit Restructure and Redesign Project (RSC/Chair/19), June 8, 2018. http://rda-rsc.org/node/575.

———. "RDA Linked Data and the New RDA Toolkit." Presentation at the American Library Association Annual Conference, New Orleans, LA, June 25, 2018.

Elings, Mary W., and Gunter Waibel. "Metadata for All: Descriptive Standards and Metadata Sharing Across Libraries, Museums, and Archives." *First Monday* 12 no. 3–5 (2007).

Glennan, Kathy. "Instantiating LRM in RDA." Presentation at the American Library Association Midwinter Conference, Denver, CO, February 9, 2018.

———. "RDA, Linked Data, & the 3R Project." Presentation at the American Library Association Midwinter Conference, Denver, CO, February 11, 2018.

Goliff, Nancy A. "Authority Control in a School Library." *Arkansas Libraries* 66, no. 3 (2009): 13–16.

Gorman, Michael. "Authority Control in the Context of Bibliographic Control in the Electronic Environment." *Cataloging & Classification Quarterly* 38 (2004): 11–21.

International Federation of Library Associations and Institutions. *Final Report of the Working Group on Aggregates*, September 12, 2011. https://www.ifla.org/files/assets/cataloguing/frbrrg/AggregatesFinalReport.pdf.

———. *Functional Requirements for Bibliographic Records: Final Report*. The Hague: IFLA, 1998.

———. *IFLA Library Reference Model: A Conceptual Model for Bibliographic Information*. The Hague: IFLA, 2017. https://www.ifla.org/files/assets/cataloguing/frbr-lrm/ifla-lrm-august-2017_rev201712.pdf.

———. *Statement of International Cataloguing Principles (ICP)*. 2016 Edition, with minor revisions. The Hague, IFLA: 2017. https://www.ifla.org/publications/node/11015.

James, Kate. "Basics of Attributes and Relationships." Presentation at the American Library Association Annual Conference, New Orleans, LA, June 22, 2018.

Joudrey, Daniel N., and Arlene G. Taylor. *The Organization of Information*. Fourth Edition. Santa Barbara, CA: Libraries Unlimited, 2018.

Long, Chris Evin. "RDA Implementation in Large US Public Libraries." *Library Resources & Technical Services* 62, no. 3 (2018): 98–113.

Maxwell, Robert L. *Maxwell's Handbook for RDA: Resource Description & Access: Explaining and Illustrating RDA: Resource Description and Access Using MARC 21*. Chicago: ALA Editions, 2013.

Miller, Liz. "Resource Description and Access (RDA): An Introduction for Reference Librarians. *Reference & User Services Quarterly* 50 (2011): 216–22.

Miller, Steven J. *Metadata for Digital Collections: A How-To-Do-It Manual*. New York: Neal-Schuman, 2011.

Oliver, Chris. "IFLA Library Reference Model: What and Why?" Presentation at the American Library Association Annual Conference, New Orleans, LA, June 25, 2018.

———. *Introducing RDA: A Guide to the Basics*. Chicago: American Library Association, 2010.

Society of American Archivists. "Preface." In *Describing Archives: A Content Standard (DACS)*, second edition. Chicago: Society of American Archivists, 2013. https://www2.archivists.org/standards/DACS/preface.

Svenonius, Elaine. *The Intellectual Foundation of Information Organization*. Cambridge, MA: MIT Press, 2000.

Tillett, Barbara B. "Bibliographic Relationships." In *Relationships in the Organization of Knowledge*, edited by Carol A. Bean and Rebecca Green, 19–35. Dordrecht: Kluwer Academic, 2001.

———. *What Is FRBR? A Conceptual Model for the Bibliographic Universe*. Washington, DC: Library of Congress Cataloging Distribution Service, 2004. http://www.loc.gov/cds/downloads/FRBR.PDF.

Visual Resources Association. *Cataloging Cultural Objects: A Guide to Describing Cultural Works and Their Images*. Chicago: American Library Association, 2006.

Wilson, Patrick. "The Catalog as Access Mechanism. Background and Concepts." *Library Resources & Technical Services* 27, no. 1 (1983): 4–17.

Zeng, Marcia Lei, and Jian Qin. *Metadata*. Second Edition. Chicago: Neal-Schuman, 2016.

Žumer, Maja. "IFLA Library Reference Model (IFLA LRM): Harmonisation of the FRBR Family." *Knowledge Organization* 45, no. 4 (2018): 310–18.

4

Providing Subject Access to Library Collections

The last chapter focused on descriptive metadata and its role in creating bibliographic, authority, and metadata records. This chapter will discuss how libraries provide subject access to their collections. Subject access is important because it allows users to find library materials by subject, topic, genre, and form. It meets the objectives and functions of a catalog from the *Statement of International Cataloguing Principles*: "[T]he catalogue should be an effective and efficient instrument that enables a user . . . to find a single resource or sets of resources representing . . . all resources on a given thema."[1] Subject analysis is the process concerned with determining subjects, and sometimes genres or forms, and providing access to them through a controlled vocabulary. Catalogers and metadata specialists provide controlled access to subjects on bibliographic and metadata records by adding subject headings or thesaurus descriptors from a controlled vocabulary and classification numbers from a classification scheme. Catalogers and metadata specialists provide a bridge between users and those responsible for creating or contributing to library materials. Users also have uncontrolled subject access to library collections through natural language (keyword) searching and tagging. The first part of the chapter discusses subject analysis is general, including determining subjects, language, and controlled and uncontrolled vocabularies. The second part of the chapter discusses specific controlled vocabularies used to provide subject access to library collections. Classification will be discussed in chapter 5.

SUBJECT ANALYSIS

Subject analysis, in general, is the process of determining what something is *about*. Subject analysis also can be used to determine the form or genre of something, or what it *is*. For example, the television program *Seinfeld* is *about* four friends living in New York City, but it *is* a situation comedy. There are four main types of subject analysis.

1. *Cataloging: Subject headings and thesaurus descriptors.* In the cataloging process, subject headings and/or thesaurus descriptors from a controlled vocabulary are added to bibliographic or metadata records to describe, broadly, what each item in a library is about and sometimes its genre or form.
2. *Cataloging: Classification.* In the cataloging process, one classification number is assigned that describes what library materials are about and organizes library collections by subject. Libraries may use formal library classification schemes, such as the *Dewey Decimal Classification*, and/or may use more informal systems, such as accession numbers or homegrown schemes.
3. *Indexing.* Indexing is the process of providing in-depth subject access to books, journal articles, and other publications. There are various types of indexing at various levels. One type is back-of-the-book indexing, in which an indexer creates an index that provides subject access to almost every page of a book. Another type of indexing is performed for reference databases. Indexers use a thesaurus to assign descriptors to articles and other items in a database. Indexes may be available in print, but online databases have replaced many print indexes. Indexing is usually performed outside of libraries by authors, professional indexers, or computers. Assigning subject headings is a type of indexing, too, but subject headings are much broader than indexing descriptors.
4. *Abstracting.* Abstracting is a form of subject analysis that summarizes something in a short form. Abstracts are created for journal articles, chapters in edited books, conference presentations, speeches, items in databases, and so on. It gives the reader an idea of what something is about to help them determine if they want to read it, listen to it, or watch it. Abstracts are created outside of libraries by authors, professional indexers and abstractors, and others.

Of the four types of subject analysis, adding subject headings and classification numbers to bibliographic and metadata records is performed most often in libraries, which will be the focus of this chapter. There are two parts to subject analysis: (1) determining the subject and/or the genre or form, and (2) assigning appropriate subject headings or thesaurus descriptors from a controlled vocabulary. This process may seem straightforward, but it can be quite complex, messy, and subjective. Everyone uses language differently; there can be many interpretations of the subject; and knowledge, meaning, and language change over time. Keeping up with changes is difficult for controlled vocabularies and the catalogers and metadata specialists who apply them. How can a person really know what something is about? There are different approaches to determining subjects.

Determining Subjects

In 1968 Patrick Wilson asked a fundamental question: "What is it about?"[2] This question is at the heart of subject analysis. "What is it about?" is asked all the time about books, movies, television shows, and many other things. It is a simple question that can be quite complex to answer. Ask fifty people what the movie *The Godfather* is about and there will be multiple answers: Italian Americans, the mafia, power, revenge, family, Don Corleone, Michael Corleone, and on and on. How does a cataloger sort through all these options to determine what something is about? At first thought, it may seem easy to describe what something is about. A book about rabbits is a book about rabbits, after all. You would assign "Rabbits" as the subject heading, right? Well, wait a minute. Does the book discuss all rabbits or just domesticated rabbits? Is it a scientific book about *Leporidae*, the family that includes rabbits and hares? Does it focus on preventing wild rabbits from eating a garden? Is it a children's book about taking care of rabbits as pets? Or is it really an exploration of how rabbits are portrayed in art works? What if an author uses the word *bunnies*, instead of *rabbits*, in the text? You can go down the rabbit hole trying to determine what something is about. Yet subject analysis must be performed to help users find materials in libraries by subject and to help users determine whether library materials meet their needs.

Subject analysis has been performed in libraries for a long time, and there have been several theories about how to determine subjects. In 1876 Charles Cutter was the first librarian to discuss subject analysis, in the first edition of his *Rules for a Dictionary Catalog*. In his "Objects" for a catalog, Cutter said that a library catalog should "enable a person to find a book of which . . . the subject is known" and "show what the library has on a given subject."[3] This means that (1) the library catalog should provide subject access so users can search for subjects, and (2) the library catalog should bring together all books on the same subject. Cutter also explained principles and rules for creating subject headings, which he called subject entry. He first stated the principle of common usage, which says subject headings should follow the form the public uses. He also first stated the principle of specific entry, which says a cataloger should be as specific as possible when choosing subject headings.[4] In the fourth edition of his *Rules*, published in 1904, Cutter told catalogers to always think about the user: "The convenience of the public is always to be set before the ease of the cataloger. In most cases they coincide."[5]

To Cutter, subject headings assigned by catalogers will, in most cases, coincide with what users would want. That makes the subject analysis process straightforward. All subject headings a cataloger assigns to items in a library will be helpful to users. The cataloger just needs to look at the item being cataloged to find subject headings. This is called document-centered indexing. This approach makes sense because a cataloger needs to look carefully at the item being cataloged. This is an important part of the subject analysis process. When cataloging a book, a cataloger should read the title, contents, back cover, jacket, inside flaps, and even the introduction, preface, or first chapter to understand what the book is about and what the author is trying to convey. Then the cataloger needs to find appropriate subject headings and/or thesaurus descriptors that best describe what the book is about.

Subject analysis as document-centered indexing was not questioned for almost seventy years. Catalogers found subject headings in the items being cataloged.

Things changed, however, in 1968 when Wilson asked, "What is it about?" Wilson, a library and information science philosopher, was one of the first people to question if subjects can actually be determined. In the chapter "Subjects and the Sense of Position" in his *Two Kinds of Power*, Wilson talks about four ways to determine the subject: (1) the purposive way, (2) the figure-ground way, (3) the objective way, and (4) the appeal to unity, or to rules of selection and rejection.[6] The purposive way means that subjects are found by understanding an author's purpose in writing a document. If catalogers understand why an author wrote something, then that is where they will find subjects. However, this way does not take users into consideration; an author's purpose may not match how a user interprets an author's words or uses the item. The figure-ground way means that catalogers should determine the most important "character" of an item. Whatever the document is predominantly about is the subject. However, this way ignores everything else an item is about, which may be of interest to users. The objective way means that catalogers should use words that occur most often. Count up the words, and those words with the highest number are the subjects. However, do the most common words really represent a document well or always explain what an item is about? The appeal to unity, or to rules of selection and rejection, means that when an author writes something, he or she rejects ideas and accepts ideas. The subject forms as an author writes the document. Catalogers can find the subject by understanding what has been accepted and rejected by the author, and what holds the document together. Yet it would be very difficult for anyone but a subject expert to use this method. A cataloger without special knowledge could not effectively find the subject.

What was Wilson's conclusion? That subjects are indeterminate. All four ways to determine subjects have their advantages and disadvantages, and there is no way to determine subjects conclusively and objectively. Finding subjects is inherently a subjective process. Two people using the same method would arrive at two different subjects. There are no "right" subjects that describe everything a document is about. Wilson's question is the basis of a concept in subject analysis called aboutness. Determining the aboutness of an item can be quite difficult, and the concept of aboutness was debated in the 1960s and 1970s by various scholars who had different ideas about where to find subjects. Some argued that the subject is found in documents,[7] and others argued that the subject is found in documents and users.[8]

Because of Wilson's question and the debate about aboutness, subject analysis theory moved past document-centered indexing and the idea that subjects are exclusively found in documents. Although catalogers certainly find subjects by looking at library items, subject analysis theorists started to look to users as sources of aboutness and advocated for more user-centered approaches to cataloging and indexing. There are two broad approaches to users: the cognitive viewpoint and social construction.

The cognitive viewpoint focuses on an individual user's mind.[9] An understanding of users' information behavior and needs (e.g., how users solve problems, how users approach searching, what terms and phrases are used to search for information) can help build better organization and retrieval systems. The cognitive viewpoint acknowledges that social context is important, but ultimately, searching is performed by individual users. For subject analysis, this means that subjects are found in users' minds.

As opposed to the cognitive viewpoint, social construction says subjects are socially constructed, or developed for users by society. Users do not exist in a vacuum. Users were born and raised in certain places and have certain backgrounds, values, cultures, beliefs, and education. Users' lives and realities have been constructed, often without them realizing it. Users bring all of this socially constructed reality to a search. For example, two people searching for information in rural Minnesota probably will search for information in similar ways because they share a similar culture. They would approach a search differently from a person in Chile, who was raised in an entirely different culture. For subject analysis, instead of focusing on individual users, subjects are found in subject domains, or groups of individuals. Understanding the domain of speech pathology (e.g., research methods, terminology, subtopics), for example, means the cataloger creates and assigns subject headings that meet the domain's specific needs. A cataloger should focus on domains and their unique information needs to find subjects.

One of the first people to discuss domains was Dogbert Soergel. In 1985 he introduced the idea of request-oriented indexing. Instead of focusing on what a document is about, he suggests that an indexer should start with the question, "Under what descriptors should this entity, be it a book or other resource, be found?"[10] Soergel says subjects are found in anticipated questions and users' needs, not what documents are about. He rejects the notion of a single user. Instead, subjects are found in groups, and indexes and other tools should be created for a specific clientele. Another person to discuss domains in subject analysis is Birger Hjørland. Influenced by Soergel's request-oriented indexing, he argues that subject analysis should focus on domains. Hjørland rejects Wilson's argument of subject indeterminacy. Hjørland argues that subjects *can* be found, but they are not found in the minds of users or authors. Understanding a domain and how it uses knowledge can be used as a source to find subjects, and he advocates domain analysis as a way to study domains.[11] Jens-Erik Mai also advocates taking a domain-centered approach in indexing: Instead of finding the subject in documents, subjects and their meaning can only come from users in their domains.[12]

Where are subjects found? Subject analysis is a subjective and complicated process, and there are advantages and disadvantages to all approaches. There is no one right way to determine a subject. Perhaps all three approaches (documents, users, domains) are beneficial and should be used together when determining subjects.

Language

Determining subjects can be complex, and language adds to this complexity. Language is used to convey complex thoughts, feelings, and ideas, and language can be extremely problematic in subject analysis. Authors, users, and catalogers all use language differently, and language evolves over time. Subject headings assigned to library materials in 1920, for example, will be different from those assigned in 2020. If catalogers are supposed to provide a bridge between authors and users, is each group served well? Can catalogers reflect an author's intent as well as account for how users actually search for items in libraries?

Authors and users are very inconsistent with language because, well, everyone is different. Everyone has different backgrounds and uses language differently. One person's "sofa" is another person's "couch" is another person's "settee," and everyone searches for information in different ways. Marcia J. Bates says, "In study after study across a wide range of environments, it has been found that for any target topic, people will use a very wide range of different terms, and no one of those terms will occur very frequently."[13] Bates mentions three main linguistic differences that arise when people search for information:

1. *Morphological.* This refers to word form, for example, "automobile" or "automobiles." This can be a problem because if the information retrieval system does not account for plurals, a user must use exact search terms or a truncation device.
2. *Syntactic.* This refers to word order, for example, "automobile repair" or "repair of automobiles." Humans know both phrases mean the same thing, but they are not the same thing to computers and information retrieval systems. A user must search for a subject in multiple ways.
3. *Semantic.* This refers to meaning, for example, "automobiles" or "cars." Information retrieval systems have difficulty accounting for semantic differences. Users often must search for many synonymous words and phrases to find everything about a certain topic.[14]

Catalogers are very inconsistent with language, too. Interindexer consistency refers to how consistent catalogers are when they assign subjects to the same item. It has been found that interindexer consistency is pretty low. For example, in a classic study, 340 library students were asked to assign subject headings to six books, and students assigned an average of sixty-two different subject headings to each book.[15] People just do not assign the same subject headings, and subject analysis can be a very subjective process. Consistently applying subject headings is a concern for catalogers because in order to bring together items on the same subject in a library catalog, they must be assigned the same subject headings. If every cataloger assigns different subject headings to items, how is it possible that catalogers can help users find anything?

Images and Objects

Determining subjects is difficult. It becomes even more difficult for library materials that cannot explain in words what they are about, like images and objects. Books and serials tell you what they are about, but images and objects cannot always do that. A cataloger can describe them, measure them, and note the color, distinguishing features, age, and so forth, but it is hard to know what they are about without a caption. Images have unique indexing problems because they have unique qualities and attributes. There is a difference between what an image is *of*, or a description of what is seen in an image, and what it is *about*, or what an image means or represents.[16] For example, a painting *of* two women sitting on a bench can be *about* religious devotion. An image *of* a cat and a dog can be *about* friendship. A picture *of* a yellow daffodil can be *about* spring. Objects can be difficult to index as well, because the significance of an object is very important. A quill pen is just an old feather unless it was used to write the Declaration of Independence; then it has significance and represents freedom, liberty, and independence. Problems arise because catalogers and metadata specialists do not always know the intent or context of an image or object.

The first part of the subject analysis process may seem disappointing. Everything seems subjective, aboutness is difficult to determine, there are different theories about where to find subjects, language is complicated, and images and objects do not always explain what they are about. How can catalogers and metadata specialists actually perform subject analysis that will help users? All is not lost. Libraries help users by providing subject access to their collections. There are two types of vocabularies that help users find materials by subject in libraries: controlled vocabularies and uncontrolled vocabularies.

CONTROLLED VOCABULARIES

The first part of the subject analysis process is determining subjects. The second part of the subject analysis process is finding appropriate subject headings in a controlled vocabulary. As discussed in chapter 1, libraries have a long history of using controlled vocabularies to provide subject access to their collections. The first standardized subject headings list used in libraries was the *List of Subject Headings for Use in Dictionary Catalogs* first published by the American Library Association in 1895. Lists of subject headings, thesauri, and genre terms have continued to be developed ever since. A controlled vocabulary is a list of approved words and phrases used to represent subjects. A controlled vocabulary can be a list of subject headings, a thesaurus, or any other controlled list of terms. A controlled vocabulary controls language by using *one* authorized form of words and phrases for each subject or concept in the vocabulary. It uses cross-references to direct users from unauthorized subjects to authorized subjects and to show relationships between subjects (e.g., broader terms, narrower terms, related terms). For example, imagine a user searches a library catalog for the Library of Congress subject heading "Trousers." The user may see something like this:

Trousers
    See: *Pants*

If a user searches the unauthorized term "Trousers," on a library catalog, he or she should be directed to the authorized subject heading "Pants." If a user clicks on the link "Pants," he or she may see something like this:

> *Pants* (22)
>   Narrower Term: *Cuffs (Clothing)*
>   Narrower Term: *Jeans (Clothing)*

There are twenty-two bibliographic records that have been assigned the subject heading "Pants." There also are two narrower terms, "Cuffs (Clothing)" and "Jeans (Clothing)," in case one of those narrower subject headings better meets the user's needs.

In this way, a controlled vocabulary helps users find what they need on library catalogs. Controlled vocabularies are considered *pre-coordinated indexing* because the responsibility is on the cataloger to assign subject headings or indexing terms before a user performs a search. The cataloger puts the terms or phrases together for the user before searching. There are two primary types of controlled vocabularies: subject headings lists and thesauri.

Types of Controlled Vocabularies: Subject Headings Lists

One type of controlled vocabulary is a subject headings list, which is a list of authorized words and phrases used as subject headings on bibliographic records. Subject headings tell users what library materials are about, and they give subject access to a library's collection. For example, here are the Library of Congress subject headings assigned to the book *100 Questions Every First-Time Home Buyer Should Ask* by Ilyce R. Glink:

1. House buying.
2. Residential real estate—Purchasing.
3. House buying—United States.
4. Residential real estate—Purchasing—United States.

The subject headings explain what the book is about, and each subject heading is a link that collocates all items in a library catalog assigned that same subject heading. For the most part, subject headings lists tend to be broad in coverage to cover all subjects collected in libraries.

One authorized form of a subject is assigned to bibliographic records. Using one consistent subject heading on bibliographic records brings together items in the catalog. This allows users to search for specific subject headings or click on a subject heading within a bibliographic record to get a list of library materials. Most subject headings are under authority control, as discussed in chapter 3, so authority records

LC control no.: sh 85062539

LCCN Permalink: https://lccn.loc.gov/sh85062539

HEADING: House buying

000 00558cz a2200229n 450

001 4713768

005 20120326095839.0

008 860211i| anannbabn |b ana

010 __ |a sh 85062539

035 __ |a (DLC)sh 85062539

035 __ |a (DLC)60453

040 __ |a DLC |c DLC |d DLC

053 _0 |a HD1361 |b HD1395.5

150 __ |a House buying

450 __ |a Home buying

450 __ |a Home purchase

450 __ |a House purchasing

550 __ |w g |a Real estate business

550 __ |a Home ownership

550 __ |a House selling

906 __ |t 7749 |u ---- |v 0

953 __ |a xx00 |b se01

LC control no.: sh 85062539

LCCN Permalink: https://lccn.loc.gov/sh85062539

LC classification: HD1361 HD1395.5

Topical subject heading: House buying

Variant(s): Home buying

Home purchase

House purchasing

See also: Real estate business

Home ownership

House selling

Figure 4.1. Authority Record for LC Subject Heading "House buying"

are created for them. See figure 4.1 for an example. It shows the authority record for the Library of Congress subject heading "House buying," both with the labels and the record coded in MARC 21. The record includes the authorized form of the subject heading, "House buying," three variants of the subject (unauthorized subject headings), and three related subject headings (see also).

Several subject headings lists have been developed by the library profession, such as the *Library of Congress Subject Headings*, a general subject headings list used in many libraries. The *Children's Subject Headings* is a list of Library of Congress subject headings that have been modified for children. They are used in libraries with children's collections. The *Sears List of Subject Headings* is a small list of general subject headings used in some small school and public libraries. The *Medical Subject Headings* is a subject headings list used by medical libraries, some academic libraries, and in the PubMed database. Libraries can use multiple subject headings lists in their library catalogs depending on their needs. Lists of subject headings used most often in libraries will be discussed later in the chapter.

Types of Controlled Vocabularies: Thesauri

A second type of controlled vocabulary is a thesaurus. A thesaurus is a list of authorized words and phrases, called descriptors, used for indexing a specialized subject area or collection. There are many thesauri available in many fields and subject areas, usually developed and maintained by professional associations, governmental bodies, libraries, and other institutions. For example, the *Art & Architecture Thesaurus* represents the art and architecture fields, the *Thesaurus of ERIC Descriptors* represents the education field, and the *UNBIS Thesaurus* (United Nations Bibliographic Information System) represents United Nations documents. The *Medical Subject Headings* perform double duty as a subject headings list and a thesaurus because it is used to index biomedical journal articles for the PubMed database. Like subject headings lists, thesauri are built to show relationships between descriptors through broader terms, narrower terms, and related terms. They show how the subject is mapped, and some thesauri show an explicit hierarchy of terms. For an example, see figure 4.2.[17] It shows information about the ERIC descriptor "Visual Perception." The relationships are shown with broader terms, narrower terms, and related terms, and the descriptor is a part of the larger category "Learning and Perception." It also shows two terms not used in the thesaurus (unauthorized terms).

Thesauri are used for many purposes. Catalogers and metadata specialists add thesaurus descriptors to bibliographic and metadata records. Many libraries use thesauri to give better subject access to specialized collections. A library could even create its own thesaurus for a specialized collection. For example, a corporate librarian at a candy factory could create a thesaurus of terms and concepts used in the library's collection, with particular candy-making techniques, ingredients, tools, types of candy, and whatever else was needed. Thesauri are also used to index journal articles and other items in research databases, but this work is usually performed by database vendors, not by libraries.

Controlled vocabularies such as subject headings lists and thesauri are used to provide subject access to library collections. There are several issues involved in the construction and application of controlled vocabularies that affect how users search for subjects in libraries. Understanding how a controlled vocabulary works can help

Visual Perception

Scope Note: Ability to interpret what is seen

Category: Learning and Perception

🔍 Search collection using this descriptor

Broader Terms

Perception

Narrower Terms

Depth Perception

Visual Acuity

Visual Discrimination

Use this term instead of

Contrast (2004)

Contrast Ratios (2004)

Related Terms

Color

Dimensional Preference

Language Processing

Perception Tests

Perceptual Impairments

Sensory Experience

Sensory Training

Vision

Vision Tests

Visual Learning

Visual Literacy

Visual Stimuli

Visualization

Figure 4.2.   ERIC Descriptor for Visual Perception

users better utilize subject headings and descriptors in their searches. Catalogers must understand how a controlled vocabulary works in order to assign appropriate subject headings.

Controlled Vocabulary Construction Issues

Each controlled vocabulary is constructed differently. There are several construction issues involved in creating a cohesive and coherent vocabulary that controls language. Controlling language is complex because language is used to represent complex things and ideas, it changes over time, and people use it differently. Adequately representing subjects can be problematic for controlled vocabularies and the catalogers who apply them. These construction issues must be dealt with by a controlled vocabulary and can have implications for users and catalogers.

Scope and Audience

One issue for controlled vocabularies is its scope and audience. What does the controlled vocabulary cover? What are its boundaries? What does it focus on? Is the controlled vocabulary a general subject headings list representing all subjects? Is it a specialized thesaurus for a certain subject area or discipline? Who is the primary audience of the controlled vocabulary? General library users? Researchers in a specialized field? Each controlled vocabulary has a different scope and serves a different audience, which drive what is included in, and excluded from, a controlled vocabulary.

Terminology and Word Choice

Another issue is terminology and choice of words in the controlled vocabulary. Which words will the controlled vocabulary choose—popular or technical terms? How does the vocabulary choose which words and phrases will be authorized and which will be unauthorized? How does it determine which words and phrases will be used as cross-references? How does it handle synonyms (automobiles or cars; dirt or soil; pants or trousers)? Each controlled vocabulary must determine how it chooses words.

Warrant

Warrant refers to when terms in a controlled vocabulary can be added or changed. What gives a controlled vocabulary the authority to add or change subject headings or thesaurus descriptors? Elaine Svenonius discusses three types of warrant.[18] The main type of warrant is called literary warrant, a principle in many controlled vocabularies that means subject headings or descriptors are not added or changed until something has been published about a topic. Some controlled vocabularies may utilize use warrant, which means that users' vocabulary and their subjects warrant inclusion in a controlled vocabulary. There is also structural warrant, in which words and phrases are added for structural reasons only. Each controlled vocabulary handles warrant differently.

Word Forms

The form of words is something a controlled vocabulary needs to consider. How does a controlled vocabulary choose the form of words? Does it use the singular or plural form of nouns? How does it handle abbreviations? Acronyms? Which spelling conventions will it use? How will the controlled vocabulary handle hyphenated words? What about homonyms? How does the vocabulary differentiate between terms that are spelled the same but have different meanings? Each controlled vocabulary handles word forms differently.

Word Order/Direct Entry

Another issue is how the controlled vocabulary orders words and phrases. What order is used? In controlled vocabularies, phrases can be ordered in many ways. An example is shown below.

    Direct entry/order: Herbal medicine
    Indirect order: Medicine from herbs
    Inverted order: Medicine, Herbal
    Subdivided: Medicine—Herbs

Each controlled vocabulary determines which order to use, and some controlled vocabularies utilize all forms. Direct entry is a principle of subject analysis that says controlled vocabularies should be as direct as possible when naming subject headings. In the example above, direct entry would be "Herbal medicine." Today, direct entry is preferred in most subject headings lists, because it is how users usually search for library materials. When one wants to look for a book about herbal medicine, "Herbal medicine" makes sense as a subject heading, rather than "Medicine—Herbs." Direct entry also is preferred over indirect order and inverted order because computers have made it possible to perform keyword searches using any word order.

Structure

Each controlled vocabulary is structured in different ways. A thesaurus may use main terms only, while a subject headings list may include a main heading and several subdivisions. Are all possible subjects listed in the controlled vocabulary? Do catalogers have to put together subject headings for themselves? How are words and phrases arranged in the controlled vocabulary? Does the controlled vocabulary use cross-references to show relationships between broader terms, narrower terms, and related terms? If so, which ones? Does it give scope notes about certain terms? Is it tied to a certain classification scheme? All of these questions are answered by controlled vocabularies, and each one is structured differently.

Controlled Vocabulary Application Issues

In addition to issues involved in controlled vocabulary construction, there are issues when applying a controlled vocabulary in practice. As discussed earlier in the chapter, it can be difficult to determine subjects and adequately represent what something is about. Catalogers not only must analyze an item to determine the subject(s), which is difficult enough, they must then know how to translate those subjects into the language of a controlled vocabulary. To apply subject headings and thesaurus descriptors in a consistent and effective way, catalogers need to understand the system of each controlled vocabulary they use.

Aboutness

Determining the aboutness of an item can be the most difficult part of subject analysis. Not only are there differing theories of determining subjects, but everyone uses language differently, and aboutness can be very subjective. In addition, catalogers often must catalog in all subject areas. A lack of subject knowledge is a hindrance when applying subject headings if aboutness is difficult to determine. A cataloger may have to research a subject to determine what something is about, and then find corresponding controlled vocabulary terms.

Choosing the Predominant Subject

Catalogers have to determine which subject is "predominant,"[19] or the one subject that captures what something is about. This is important for libraries that tie classification to subject headings. The first subject heading on a bibliographic record often determines the classification number. In most cases, it is considered the most important subject heading. Sometimes it is difficult to pick the predominant subject because library materials can be about multiple subjects. Catalogers must use judgment, and what they determine to be the predominant subject may not match what users or authors would say it is.

Specificity (Specific Entry)

Specificity, which refers to how specific a cataloger needs to be while cataloging, is an issue when applying a controlled vocabulary. Specificity, or specific entry, is a principle in library cataloging first stated by Charles Cutter in 1876. He said that catalogers should be as specific as possible when assigning subject headings. If a book is about beagles, a cataloger should assign the subject heading for beagles, not the subject heading for the broader category of dogs.[20] Specificity can be difficult to achieve in practice because books can be about multiple specific topics, and sometimes assigning a broader category is necessary.

Exhaustivity

Exhaustivity is another application issue. It refers to how deep a cataloger or indexer should go when cataloging or indexing. For back-of-the-book indexes, for example, exhaustivity is quite high. An indexer will be exhaustive while indexing and provide access to every concept in the book. An indexer takes a deep dive. However, in library cataloging, exhaustivity is quite low because catalogers assign only a few subject headings that represent broadly what a library item is about. Cataloging is fairly shallow; it does not describe subjects too deeply. Each controlled vocabulary has instructions about how exhaustive to be when assigning terms.

Interindexer Consistency

As discussed earlier in the chapter, interindexer consistency refers to how consistent catalogers are when applying terms to the same item. It has been found that interindexer consistency is low. Two catalogers do not apply the same subject headings to library materials. The subjective nature of subject analysis means that applying subject headings or thesaurus descriptors consistently is a concern for catalogers. Library materials on the same topic are not always assigned the same subject headings or thesaurus descriptors, which means they may not always be brought together for users in a library catalog.

Rules/Guidelines

Controlled vocabularies have guidelines about assigning subject headings or thesaurus descriptors. There may be numerous instruction sheets and scope notes about how to assign subject headings and descriptors. Learning the rules of a controlled vocabulary can be challenging for catalogers. It takes much training and experience to learn to assign subject headings properly. In a large controlled vocabulary, for example, catalogers may not be aware of all the subject headings available for use. A cataloger could catalog for years without touching certain subject areas.

Advantages and Disadvantages of Controlled Vocabularies

There are advantages and disadvantages of controlled vocabularies. The main advantage is that it brings together everything in a library's collection on a certain subject. Using one authorized subject heading or thesaurus descriptor controls language and helps users find everything in a library catalog or a database on a certain topic. There is a better chance users will retrieve relevant material using a controlled vocabulary because all results should be relevant to their search. A controlled vocabulary has *low recall* and *high precision* when searching on library catalogs and other systems. This means that a user may not receive many results in a search (low recall), but those results should be relevant and more precise than a keyword search (high precision). For example, imagine a user searches for "Fixing Fords" on a public library catalog because he or she wants to fix a Ford automobile. The search retrieves zero books about fixing Fords. The user may feel discouraged and think the library has nothing on the topic. However, if the user searches for a Library of Congress subject heading, such as, "Ford automobile—Maintenance and repair—Handbooks, manuals, etc.," he or she will find that the library actually has numerous repair manuals for Ford automobiles.[21]

Another advantage is that controlled vocabularies use cross-references to point users to authorized subject headings and to show relationships. "Use" or "see" references direct users from unauthorized subject headings and descriptors to authorized subject headings and descriptors. If a user searches for the Library of Congress subject heading "Garden egg" in a library catalog, then the user will be taken to the authorized subject heading of "Eggplant." Broader terms and narrower terms show the hierarchical arrangement of subjects in a controlled vocabulary, and related terms show nonhierarchical relationships. For example, a user looking for information about Labrador retrievers would see that the Library of Congress subject heading "Labrador retriever" falls in the broader subject categories of "Retrievers" and "Dog breeds." To perform a wider search, users could be directed to search for those subject headings as well.

Pre-coordinated indexing is also an advantage. The cataloger assigns and puts together subject headings before the user searches for them. This takes the responsibility off users and puts it on the cataloger. Users do not have to use the best terms or search for multiple variations of words. Users just have to find the authorized subject heading or descriptor to find relevant materials. Users are able to narrow down searches and pinpoint exactly what is most relevant to them.

There are many problems with controlled vocabularies, too. One problem is that it is impossible to create a controlled vocabulary that controls all ways language is used. Controlled vocabularies can never include all words and phrases, provide all possible cross-references, or show all relationships. Choices are made about what subjects to include in a vocabulary, the approved forms, and how words and phrases are arranged. Authors, users, and catalogers use language in different ways. There will never be a perfect system that accounts for all ways that people use language.

Another problem is that users must use the language of the controlled vocabulary, and they need to find a subject heading before a search. This is problematic because language in a controlled vocabulary is artificial and unnatural. It is a *controlled* vocabulary with a separate *approved* language. Users cannot use their own natural language. They must use the language of the controlled vocabulary when searching, which can be frustrating. For example, imagine a user wants to find a book at the Library of Congress about women in film, and he or she performs a browse search for the presumed subject heading "Women in film" in the Library of Congress catalog. "Women in film," however, is not an authorized Library of Congress subject heading (the list the library uses), and there is no cross-reference to the authorized subject heading. The user then performs a keyword search for "women in film," which retrieves more than 9,000 results. Some results are relevant to the search but most are not. It turns out the authorized subject heading is "Women in motion pictures," but the user would not necessarily think of that.[22]

Another problem with controlled vocabularies is that subject headings need to be changed often to make room for new concepts and subjects and to reflect current language. It can take a long time for subject headings and descriptors to be changed, especially in large controlled vocabularies such as the *Library of Congress Subject Headings*. Language and society change quickly, but controlled vocabularies may change slowly. A library also must have a good system of authority file maintenance to keep up with controlled vocabulary changes. If subject headings are added or changed in the Library of Congress National Authority File, then each library has to update authority records in its local authority file and update subject headings on bibliographic records. If additions and changes are not reflected in a library catalog, then collocation is lost. Bibliographic records that are assigned a new subject heading and bibliographic records that still have the old form of the subject heading are not brought together in the catalog. As a result, users will not find everything a library has on a certain subject.

UNCONTROLLED VOCABULARIES

Uncontrolled vocabularies are the other type of vocabulary used to provide subject access to library collections. Unlike controlled vocabularies, uncontrolled vocabularies do not control language at all, and they apply only to searching on computers. As discussed in chapter 1, there was an information explosion after World War II as the United States started to focus on science and technology. A massive amount of information was being generated, and automatic indexing, also called keyword searching or natural-language searching, was developed to search through the data quickly and efficiently. Mortimer Taube came up with the idea of searching for keywords, which he called uniterms, and the term *keywords* started to be used in the 1950s with developments in automatic indexing by Hans Peter Luhn.[23] As technology progressed, new ways to store and retrieve information were developed. The development of the World Wide Web by Tim Berners-Lee in 1989 led to an even larger explosion of information and new digital formats. The development of social media tools such as Facebook and Twitter has led to social information organization, in which people organize information together. There are two main types of uncontrolled vocabularies: keyword searching and tagging.

Types of Uncontrolled Vocabularies: Keyword Searching

Most people are familiar with keyword searching, such as searching on Google. Basically, people can use their own natural language to search for anything, using any words. There is no control whatsoever. The computer matches words in the search query to the text of items in a computer file, database, or the web using sophisticated algorithms created by humans. For example, a computer can weight for relevance, putting the most relevant results at the top of the results list. A computer can perform proximity searching, searching for two or more terms with a specific distance between words. Stemming happens when a computer cuts off suffixes during a search. A computer also can account for spelling errors if it is programmed to do so. On library catalogs and digital collections, it means the computer is looking in bibliographic records and metadata records. A user's search words must match the words on the records. A computer could use the most sophisticated algorithms, but if words in the search query are not in bibliographic or metadata records, a user will not get relevant results.

Keyword searching is considered *post-coordinated indexing* because the user has responsibility for putting together search terms and phrases. This puts the user, not the cataloger, in control of the search. It also is a search with *high recall* and *low precision*. A user will receive lots of results (high recall), but very few of them may be relevant (low precision).

Advantages and Disadvantages of Keyword Searching

There are many advantages and disadvantages of keyword searching. One big advantage is that users can use their own language. Users do not have to make their language conform to the language of a controlled vocabulary. It frees users from the restraints of a controlled vocabulary. Keyword searching also is fast. A computer can search through large amounts of text very quickly and give users almost instantaneous results, which saves time. Keyword searching is quite effective when a user does not have an exact search focus. If a user is exploring a topic or wants general knowledge, keyword searching is helpful.

Keyword searching is considered post-coordinated indexing, so users have control over how they search for materials. No middleman, like a cataloger, is needed. Users can perform a basic search, like in a Google search, or they can use advanced features to narrow a search. For example, searching specific fields (title, author, subject), using Boolean logic (and, or, not), or using truncations devices to search all forms of a word can help users formulate better search queries and get more precise search results. On some computer systems, users also are allowed to limit searches before or after the search is performed.

Keyword searching does not deal with controlled vocabulary issues like determining aboutness, choosing approved words, creating a structure, exhaustivity, specificity, or problems with application. A computer does not have to figure out categories, hierarchy, specificity, or exhaustivity. A computer simply matches the search terms. Input—processing—output. No thinking involved.

Yet there are disadvantages to keyword searching. The biggest problem is that it assumes that words in the records or text, such as an author's words or cataloger's words, represent what something is about. For example, if a book is about "dogs," but an author or cataloger uses the word "hounds" only, how will a user find the book with a search for "dogs" only? An author or cataloger might say a book is about "marriage," but a user might say the book is about "family." If a user looks for "family" only, he or she will not find the book. Sometimes a user must perform multiple searches using various word combinations to find things. A user may not have the time, inclination, or knowledge to perform multiple searches, and may give up.

Because keyword searching is considered post-coordinated indexing, it does not account for the difficulties of language. All language issues that controlled vocabularies smooth out are not considered in keyword searching. Users are forced to figure out searching on their own. They may have to perform many searches to find what they need. This is problematic because users may not know the best words to use, they may not try searching synonyms, their words may be misspelled, their search could be too broad or too narrow, or there could be problems with language use (plurals, order of words, etc.). This can prevent users from adequately searching for library materials. In addition, users must understand each computer system separately in order to search it effectively. For example, some systems do not account for spelling errors or give alternative choices. There also is no structure or hierarchy in keyword searching. Users cannot see how subjects are related. There are no helpful suggestions to search broader or narrower terms. Users must figure out the hierarchy and relationships themselves, or ask for help.

In addition, language is ambiguous. Humans can work with ambiguous language, but computers cannot. Computers are not human. They are getting smarter every day, but they cannot perform intellectual work like a human. They do not deal well with ambiguity. They cannot search for meaning, tone, flavor, and so on. They cannot account for things like irony and satire. For example, the phrase, "That baby is so cute, I want to eat him up" would be searched very literally—"baby cute eat"—by a computer. Perhaps the computer would attempt to search for library materials about eating babies, which is disturbing and not at all what is meant by the phrase. Computers also do not understand context, nor can they get at what a user really needs. A person may search for "History of Motown" but may be looking for Diana Ross's birthday. A human librarian can determine what a user really needs by performing a reference interview, but computers cannot do that on their own.

In addition, there are disadvantages with search results. Keyword searching gives users many search results, but sometimes those results are imprecise and few may be relevant. Users do not want to sift through thousands of results. In addition, a user's search words may not match words on bibliographic or metadata records. For example, imagine a user needs information about growing houseplants. "Houseplants" seems like a reasonable keyword search, and a keyword search for "Houseplants" on a public library catalog results in nineteen bibliographic records that include the word "houseplants." The computer simply retrieved books with the word "houseplants" anywhere on the bibliographic records. However, the Library of Congress subject heading is "House plants," and there are actually thirty-two bibliographic records in the public library catalog about houseplants, almost double what the user's keyword search retrieved.[24]

Types of Uncontrolled Vocabularies: Social Tagging

In addition to keyword searching, another type of uncontrolled vocabulary is social tagging. Social tagging, or collaborative tagging, is a very popular activity online. This is when someone adds a subject descriptor to describe online resources like a website, a tweet, a blog, and even library bibliographic records. Instead of a cataloger's subject headings or an author's words, users describe what something is about. Tags can be anything: words, phrases, numbers, punctuation marks, and even emojis. Users are free to tag using whatever they want, and when users use the same tag, it collectively builds uncontrolled access to online resources. Tagging is social; people organize things on the web collaboratively with other people. Social tagging became popular with the adoption of social networking tools, such as social cataloging websites like LibraryThing, social bookmarking websites like Diigo, and social networking sites like Twitter. People from all walks of life perform tagging online. Collectively, social tagging is a folksonomy, which is a categorization of many tags. It is the "taxonomy" of the "folk," or a people's classification.

Social tagging is beneficial for many of the same reasons as keyword searching. It is an uncontrolled vocabulary. People assign their own words as tags and tell other people what something is about. Tags do not have to be approved, and there are no complicated rules for constructing them. Users can bypass controlled vocabularies (cataloger's language), the words in the text (author's language), and even the problems of keyword searching. Tags do not even need to explain what an item is about. Tags like "good book," "omg," "kshdfh23," or "mom" are just as valid as tags that describe what an item is about, like "care of babies," "feeding babies," and "bonding with babies." That is the power of tags; people decide what tags to add. Tags also can describe things not always added to bibliographic records, such as mood, themes, reading programs, or book club suggestions. These types of tags can help people understand if a certain item meets their needs.

However, like keyword searching, social tagging lacks all the advantages of a controlled vocabulary. People do not have to be consistent or accurate. People can tag however they want. One user's interpretation of an item may be wrong or misleading. Adding the tags "Chick Lit" and "Romance" to the movie *The Hurt Locker* would be terribly misleading. Tags may be deeply personal and have meaning only to one user. For example, "Peggy's favorite" means nothing except to one person. Misspelled words, offensive language, offensive viewpoints, and more can be included in tags. In addition, tags do not necessarily reflect everyone's viewpoint; they represent only what a few taggers decided to add. It may be difficult to know what something is really about.

Using Controlled and Uncontrolled Vocabularies Together

On library catalogs, controlled vocabularies and uncontrolled vocabularies have their advantages and disadvantages. In practice, using keyword searching *in combination with* a controlled vocabulary can help users find relevant materials. When a user performs a keyword search, he or she is casting a wide net. The results may be imprecise, but the user can explore a topic. When a user performs a search using a controlled vocabulary, however, it is a narrower search. It is effective when the user knows exactly what he or she is looking for. The user will receive fewer results than a keyword search, but the results will be pretty precise. Working together, a user can perform a keyword search, find library materials that are relevant, and then click a subject heading or thesaurus link on a bibliographic record to find other library materials on that subject. Many studies have shown that subject headings and keyword searching can work together to help users find library materials.[25]

In addition to keyword searching and subject headings, tags and subject headings can be beneficial for library users. Some library catalogs give users the ability to tag bibliographic records, so that both subject headings and tags are assigned to some items in a library catalog. Using subject headings and tags may help users find library materials. Several studies have shown that tagging can enhance, but not replace, subject headings on bibliographic records. Tags and subject headings work together to improve subject access to library materials,[26] and may be especially helpful for classic literature and popular fiction.[27] For an example, see figure 4.3.[28]

Figure 4.3 shows subject headings and tags assigned to the book *Jane Eyre* by Charlotte Brontë. There are several subject headings that describe broadly what *Jane Eyre* is about or its genres. The subject headings are fairly broad and describe more objective elements of the book. They do not really touch on specific themes. The subject headings are much different from the tags. There are many more tags, with

SUBJECT HEADINGS

› Governesses — Fiction.
› Fathers and Daughters — Fiction.
› Mentally Ill Women — Fiction.
› Charity-schools — Fiction.
› Married People — Fiction.
› Country Homes — Fiction.
› Young Women — Fiction.
› Orphans — Fiction.
› England — Fiction.
› Bildungsromans.
› Romance Fiction.
› Love Stories.

Explore further by tag...

romance (8)
premier's reading... (5)
classics (3)
fiction (3)
love (3)
classic (2)
dark (2)
feminism (2)
gothic (2)
governesses (2)
1001 books you mu... (1)
100 swoon-worthy ... (1)
5th grade (1)
6th grade (1)
7th grade (1)
8th grade (1)
9th grade (1)
adult (1)
appendix b (1)
ar 7.0-7.9 (1)
ar 7.9 (1)
bildungsroman (1)
character-driven (1)

child abuse (1)
classic literature (1)
classics by women (1)
common core (1)
debut novels (1)
desire (1)
development (1)
early feminist wo... (1)
endearing charact... (1)
exemplar (1)
faith (1)
fictional-biograp... (1)
gr. 11-12 (1)
great american re... (1)
happy (1)
historical (1)
historical fiction (1)
historical novel (1)
institutions (1)
integrity (1)
light (1)
literary fiction (1)
may-december roma... (1)

mental illness (1)
miss sara recomme... (1)
miss sara's top p... (1)
moody (1)
morals (1)
mysterious (1)
new york state (1)
nypl staff pick (1)
orphans (1)
pbs great america... (1)
perseverance (1)
reading level z (1)
roman (1)
satsifying ending (1)
second chances (1)
teens (1)
tgar2018 (1)
tragedy (1)
tween reads (1)
tweens reading te... (1)
victorian (1)
victorian era (1)
young adult (1)

young adults (1)
young teens (1)

Figure 4.3. Subject Headings and Tags for *Jane Eyre*

the most commonly assigned tags listed at the top. There are some tags that describe subjects of the book, such as governesses, orphans, and mental illness, and some that touch on themes in the book, such as perseverance, love, and faith. There are tags for grades, reading levels, recommended book lists, and book club reading lists, which may be helpful to users. There also are some misleading tags that do not belong on the list. For example, "historical fiction" is not appropriate because *Jane Eyre* is not historical fiction. It was published in 1847 and takes place as Jane grows up in the late 1700s/early 1800s. It may seem like history to twenty-first-century readers, but *Jane Eyre* was a contemporary story when it was published. In addition, "New York State" is misleading because the book takes place in the north of England. Tags like "happy" and "light" do not reflect the mood of the book. Despite the problems and issues with tags, they can work together with subject headings to help users better understand what library materials are about.

CONTROLLED VOCABULARIES USED IN LIBRARIES

So far, this chapter has discussed the subject analysis process, including theories of how subjects are determined, issues with language, and how controlled and uncontrolled vocabularies provide subject access to library collections. The last half of the chapter will discuss specific controlled vocabularies used in libraries. Libraries can choose from a variety of subject headings lists and thesauri that fit their collections and meet the needs of their users. There are broad subject headings lists used in all types of libraries, children's subject headings used in public and elementary school libraries, and very specialized thesauri used in academic, research, and special libraries. In addition, libraries can use multiple subject headings or thesauri. For example, a library may use the *Library of Congress Subject Headings* for its main collection but the *Thesaurus for Graphic Materials* for a special photograph collection. It depends on the library, its collections, and its needs.

LIBRARY OF CONGRESS SUBJECT HEADINGS

The *Library of Congress Subject Headings* (LCSH) is the most widely used subject headings list in the world, and it has a long history. In 1898 James C. M. Hanson, chief of the Catalogue Division at the Library of Congress, wanted the library to create a list of subject headings just for its collection. The library was moving from a classed catalog (one arranged by classification number) to a dictionary catalog (one arranged in alphabetical order by name, title, and subject access points), and he wanted the library to have subject headings that matched the *Library of Congress Classification*, a new classification scheme being developed at the library around the same time. Work began on the new subject headings list, using the American Library Association's *List of Subject Headings for Use in Dictionary Catalogs* as its primary source of subject headings, along with other subject headings lists and reference books.[29]

Titled *Subject Headings used in the Dictionary Catalogues of the Library of Congress*, the first edition was published between 1909 and 1914 in separate parts. The title was changed to *Library of Congress Subject Headings* with the publication of the eighth edition in 1975. LCSH has been published annually since the eleventh edition (1988). Bound volumes were published on paper through the thirty-fifth edition (2013), after which editions became available online only. It is nicknamed the "Red Books" because the paper volumes were bound in red. LCSH was developed originally to provide access to the Library of Congress's collection, but libraries began to adopt LCSH when subject headings were printed on catalog cards the Library of Congress sold to libraries. Today, LCSH has been adopted by many libraries in the United States, especially academic and public libraries. Libraries around the world use versions of the LCSH modified for specific countries and languages. LCSH works with the *Library of Congress Classification*, a classification scheme used in most academic libraries. There is a corresponding LC classification number for almost every subject heading in LCSH. However, libraries do not have to use the *Library of Congress Classification* to use LCSH. They are connected but independent. Public libraries that use LCSH primarily use the *Dewey Decimal Classification*, for example.

LCSH is a very large list of subject headings. There are more than 342,000 subject headings listed in LCSH, and around 5,000 new subject headings are added every year.[30] The Library of Congress updates LCSH monthly, and additions and changes are made primarily by librarians at the Library of Congress and libraries that participate in the Subject Authority Cooperative Program (SACO). Others can submit suggestions through a web form.

LC subject headings are added to bibliographic records to facilitate subject access to library materials. Subject headings describe what library materials are *about*. They bring together similar materials in the library catalog to help users find materials a library has on a subject. Subject headings are broad in nature. The Library of Congress instructs catalogers to add around one to three LC subject headings to a bibliographic record. A subject heading should be added if a topic is covered in at least 20 percent of a book or other item. The Library of Congress has a limit of six subject headings, but catalogers can add up to ten subject headings.[31] LCSH includes subject headings for subjects, concepts, and groups of people, but it also includes subject headings for some geographic names, some corporate and family names, and some preferred titles. Examples of LC subject headings are shown below.

Household appliances	Electric Meratus Mountains (Indonesia)
Renters insurance	Three Sisters Wilderness (Or.)
Fame	Rothschild family
Security (Psychology)	Kennedy family
Church musicians	Beowulf
Interior decorators	Bible. English (Middle English)

In addition to subject headings included in LCSH, personal names, corporate names, geographic names, and preferred titles not already in LCSH also can be used as subject headings on bibliographic records. Authorized forms are taken from the Library of Congress National Authority File and are added to bibliographic records. Examples are shown below.

> King, Martin Luther, Jr., 1929–1968
> Rowling, J. K.
> Denton (Tex.)
> Microsoft Corporation
> Chicago Mass Choir
> Tokyo (Japan)
> Austen, Jane, 1775–1817. Pride and prejudice

LCSH Structure and Characteristics

LCSH is a controlled vocabulary. LCSH controls language by using *one* authorized form of a subject heading and providing cross-references from other possible forms of the subject. LC subject headings are constructed in a specific way. There are two parts: (1) main headings, which are added to every subject heading, and (2) subdivisions, which are added after main headings when needed.

Main Headings

The first part of a subject heading is a main heading. This is the main subject or concept. It answers the question, What is it about? Every subject heading assigned to bibliographic records includes a main subject heading. Main subject headings can be topical subject headings, personal names, family names, geographic names, corporate body names, meetings/conferences, or preferred titles of works. There are several types of topical subject headings in LCSH. LCSH is more than one hundred years old and has been continually updated, so it reflects many differing policies about subject headings, and subject headings are not always consistent. According to the *Subject Headings Manual*, there are eight types of subject headings.[32]

Simple nouns. Simple nouns are used often in LCSH, and the plural form of nouns is used when appropriate. Examples include: Tables; Furniture; Elephants; Appetizers; Economists; Basketball; Knitting; Love. Names of specific animal breeds are singular: Bloodhound; Lion; Giraffe.

Compound nouns. These nouns include two words or concepts. Examples include: Hydrogeology; Handlebodies; Newsprint. LCSH also includes several hyphenated words: On-line; Audio-visual aids.

Nouns with parenthetical qualifiers. This type of subject heading uses a qualifier in parentheses to limit or explain the subject heading. Examples include: Cooking

(Pears); Insanity (Law); Jig (Dance); Growlers (Electrical Engineering). Qualified headings also distinguish words with the same spelling but different meanings: Screens (Plants); Screens (Mining); Screens (Church decoration).

Nouns with adjectives. These subject headings use adjectives to describe the noun. LCSH favors direct entry today. Examples include: Traditional medicine; Baked products; Frozen broccoli; Legal ethics.

Inverted headings. These subject headings are nouns with adjectives, too, but inverted headings move the noun to the beginning of the subject heading, such as Art, Medieval. Inverted headings were used often in LCSH when libraries had card catalogs. This allowed subject headings to be filed in alphabetical order by the main noun instead of the adjective. It assisted users in card catalog searches by gathering together all subject headings on a topic: Cooking, American; Cooking, Korean; Cooking, Mexican; and so on. Today, inverted headings are not necessarily needed to search online catalogs, but they still exist in LCSH. The policy is to use direct entry or "normal word order" whenever possible, except in certain circumstances, such as for subject headings that include languages, ethnicities, and nationalities, and in a few other cases.[33]

Phrases with prepositions. There are several subject headings with prepositions in LCSH. One common preposition is *in*. It implies representation, use, or time. An example is "Love in art." This subject heading is assigned to materials that discuss how love is represented or portrayed *in* art works. Another example is "Music in the workplace." It would be assigned to materials that describe how music is used *in* workplaces. Other common prepositions include *of, with, from, for, to, by,* and *against*. Examples include: Otitis media with effusion; Leaflets dropped from aircraft; Music by child composers; Claims against decedents' estates; Education of princesses; Grooming for men.

Compound phrases. Compound phrases are used to bring together two or more things in a subject heading. Sometimes they are simply descriptive: Library food and beverage policies; Lease or buy decisions; Chalk mines and mining. A compound phrase also can imply a relationship between two concepts or things: for instance, "Astrology and agriculture." This subject heading is used for library materials about the relationship between astrology *and* agriculture. Another example is "Politics and literature." This subject heading would be used for library materials about the relationship between politics *and* literature.

Complex phrases. These are subject headings that include many words in a phrase. They may or may not include prepositions. Examples include: Snails as carriers of disease; Polar bear watching industry; Mammals on postage stamps; Ground source heat pump systems.

During cataloging, a main subject heading is added with no subdivisions for an introduction or general look at a topic. It may not be about any one aspect of a subject, or it may be about all aspects of a subject. For example, a general book about Amish furniture would be assigned the subject heading "Amish furniture." An introduction to the field of geology would be assigned the subject heading "Geology." A book discussing the relationship between crime and weather would be assigned the subject heading "Crime and weather."

Subdivisions

The second part of an LC subject heading is a subdivision. Subdivisions bring out aspects of the main topic, making a subject heading more specific to better describe what something is about. Subdivisions answer questions like: Does the item's main subject focus on a particular aspect of the topic? Does the item's main subject take place during a specific chronological time period? Does the item's main subject focus on a particular geographic place? Is the item being cataloged a particular form, like a dictionary or a periodical? Table 4.1 shows examples of the main subject heading "Library science" with different subdivisions after it.

Table 4.1.   LCSH Main Headings and Subdivisions

LCSH Main Heading and Subdivisions	What the Item Is About
Library science—Moral and ethical aspects	Ethics in librarianship
Library science—History—20th century	History of librarianship in the twentieth century
Library science—United States	Librarianship in the United States
Library science—Dictionaries	A dictionary about librarianship

Subdivisions are added after main headings to provide more information about the main subject heading. Subdivisions allow catalogers to be more specific with subject headings, and they let users know more about the specific subject of a book or other item. However, catalogers cannot add any words they want as subdivisions. There are many rules governing the use of subdivisions. Subdivisions must be authorized, too. Sometimes main headings and subdivisions are put together as a subject heading and published in LCSH before catalogers use them. Sometimes main headings and subdivisions are not published in LCSH, so catalogers must put them together following the rules.

There are millions of possible main heading and subdivision combinations, more than could ever be published in LCSH. Therefore, another characteristic of LCSH is that it allows catalogers to add main headings and subdivisions as needed in certain circumstances. There are pattern headings that a cataloger can follow to create a subject heading based on an established pattern. There also are free-floating subdivisions, a list of more than 3,600 subdivisions that can be added after main headings, such as History; Social aspects; Fiction; Periodicals; Law and legislation.[34] These subdivisions can "float freely" behind main subject headings, but only under certain circumstances. There are lots of rules for adding them, depending on the main subject heading.

There are four types of subdivisions in LCSH: (1) topical, (2) geographic, (3) chronological, and (4) form. *Topical subdivisions* are added behind main headings when an item is about a particular topical aspect of the main subject. For example, a book about the history of library science: Library science—History; a book about golf clubs: Golf—Equipment and supplies; or a book about religion in film: Motion pictures—Religious aspects. There are many topical subdivisions that can be added.

Geographic subdivisions explain if something focuses on a particular place. They go behind main headings, topical subdivisions, and sometimes chronological subdivisions, too. Places must be authorized and are taken from the Library of Congress National Authority File. For example, a book about rodeos in the United States: Rodeos—United States; or a book about the history of library science in Estonia: Library science—Estonia—History. The trick, however, is that geographic subdivisions cannot be added after every subject heading. Sometimes they are allowed and sometimes they are not allowed. In addition, there is a special way that cities in the United States, Canada, and Great Britain are added as geographic subdivisions, which is called indirect subdivision. If an item is about a city in the United States, Canada, or Great Britain, then the state, province, or constituent country is listed first. For example, a book about women in Denton, Texas: Women—Texas—Denton. If an item is about a city in other parts of the world, then the country comes first. For example, a book about women in Paris: Women—France—Paris.

Chronological subdivisions are added after main subject headings, topical subdivisions, and sometimes geographic subdivisions. They are added when an item is about a certain time period. They are used primarily for items about historical and sociological topics. They are often paired with a topical subdivision, and there are particular ways to use them. For example, a book about modern architecture in the 1900s: Architecture, Modern—20th century; or a book about the history of library science in the 1800s: Library science—History—19th century.

Form subdivisions are added at the very end of subject headings to explain if an item is a particular form or genre. A form subdivision explains what an item is, not what it is about. Is it a dictionary? An encyclopedia? A handbook? A work of fiction? For example, a dictionary of sociology is *about* sociology, but it *is* a dictionary: Sociology—Dictionaries. Form subdivisions are not used at the end of every subject heading, only when the item being cataloged is a particular form. Examples include: Dictionaries, Periodicals, Fiction, Juvenile fiction, Juvenile literature, Biography, and many more.

Cross-References

Another characteristic of LCSH is its use of cross-references. Cross-references are an important part of LCSH. They are used to show several types of relationships among subject headings. However, LCSH does not include all possible cross-references. Cross-references follow literary warrant, too, so there must be a reason to add a cross-reference in LCSH. Cross-references and their types are shown in table 4.2.

Table 4.2. Types of Cross-References in LCSH

Equivalence Relationship	Hierarchical Relationship	Associative Relationship	General References
USE: Use or See UF: Used for	BT: Broader terms NT: Narrower terms	RT: Related terms	SA: See also

One type of relationship is called an equivalence relationship. It references unauthorized forms of the subject heading to authorized forms, and vice versa. "USE" and "UF" are the codes used to link authorized and unauthorized subject headings, and they are reciprocals. There are more than 362,000 equivalence cross-references in LCSH. Here is an example of an equivalence cross-reference:

Software ecosystems   Ecosystems, Software
    UF Ecosystems, Software   USE Software ecosystems

On the left, the authorized subject heading "Software ecosystems" is in bold. It is the authorized form of the subject heading that should be added to bibliographic records. "Software ecosystems" is used for (UF), or used instead of "Ecosystems, Software." Used for (UF) terms are always unauthorized forms of the subject heading. In this way, the language is controlled so unauthorized forms lead to authorized forms. On the right, the see reference "USE" explains which authorized subject heading to use. Use (USE) terms are always authorized forms of the subject heading. "Ecosystems, Software" is not used in LCSH; instead, "Software ecosystems" is used. Catalogers should add "Software ecosystems" to bibliographic records, and users should use "Software ecosystems" when searching for subject headings.

Subject headings also are used to show hierarchical relationships, how subject headings fall within subject categories. This is done through broader terms (BT) and narrower terms (NT). They help catalogers know where the subject heading falls within a hierarchy, in case a broader term or narrower term is more appropriate as a subject heading. It also helps users know the broader and narrower subject headings to search. Here is a hierarchical relationship example:

Corrals
    BT Fences
    NT Cattle pens

"Corrals" is the authorized subject heading. It fits within the broader category/term (BT) "Fences," and it has one narrower category/term (NT) "Cattle pens."

Associative relationships show nonhierarchical relationships between subject headings. Using related terms allows LCSH to show many relationships between subject headings that are not broader or narrower categories. They can show relationships without having to specify categories. Here is an example of an associative relationship:

Nonprescription drug industry
    BT Pharmaceutical industry
    RT Drugs, Nonprescription

The subject heading "Nonprescription drug industry" is related to (RT) the subject heading "Drugs, Nonprescription." Although the nonprescription drug industry manufactures nonprescription drugs, the subject heading "Nonprescription drug industry" is not a broader or narrower category of "Drugs, Nonprescription." They cannot be linked hierarchically, but they are related to one another (RT). The "Nonprescription drug industry," however, is a part of the broader (BT) "Pharmaceutical industry."

A final type of relationship is called general references. This is a see also (SA) reference to a group of subject headings. This type of reference does not explain a relationship but directs catalogers and users to broader categories of subject headings that may be helpful. For an example of a general reference, see below:

Farces
Here are entered collections of farces. Works on the farce as a literary form are entered under Farce.
    BT Drama
    SA *headings for farces qualified by language or nationality,*
        e.g., Hindi farces; Cuban farces
    NT Drolls

For the subject heading "Farces," catalogers and users are directed to see also (SA) subject headings for farces that have a language or nationality in them, such as Hindi farces or Cuban farces.

Literary Warrant

An important characteristic of LCSH is that it is based on the concept of literary warrant. This means that a subject heading is created *only* when something has been published on a subject and the subject heading is needed for cataloging. Concepts, subjects, groups of people, or places do not exist in LCSH until something has been published about them. The Library of Congress does not need to own an item on a new topic for a subject heading to be added to LCSH. The item just needs to be in a library collection somewhere. It is important to understand that LCSH does not reflect the world of knowledge; it reflects only the knowledge that has been published and collected in libraries.

Current American Usage

Another characteristic of LCSH is that it reflects current American usage of language. Because LCSH was developed in the United States, it uses American spelling and forms of words. For example, it uses "Eggplant" instead of "Aubergine," "Information organization" instead of "Information organisation," "Subject cataloging" instead of "Subject cataloguing." Libraries in other countries can adapt LCSH to reflect their own languages and cultures.

Technical Terms

One last characteristic is that LCSH uses technical terms over popular terms. The Library of Congress is a research library, and LCSH was created to provide subject access to the Library of Congress's collection. Therefore, LCSH reflects a more technical language used by researchers and scholars. LCSH is as precise as possible when using language and does not necessarily reflect the everyday language of the public. For example, LCSH uses the technical term "Swine" rather than the more popular term "Pigs." Technically, pigs and swine are not the same thing; pigs are young swine. It uses "Automobiles" instead of the more popular term "Cars." Technically, cars are not just automobiles; there are many types of cars, like railroad cars and trolley cars. It uses "Infants" instead of the more popular term "Babies." Infants is the technical term.

LCSH *Subject Headings Manual*

LCSH is a large subject headings list, and there is a large *Subject Headings Manual* that directs catalogers in the construction and application of LC subject headings. There are currently around three hundred instruction sheets and seven appendices that explain numerous things, such as when to add new subject headings, how subject headings are constructed, how many subject headings to add to bibliographic records, how to add subdivisions, and on and on. Perhaps the most beneficial instruction sheets include instructions about how to add subject headings for different subject areas, audiences, genres, and formats. For example, there are instruction sheets about how to add subject headings for biography, literature, juvenile (children's) materials, cooking and cookbooks, comics and comic characters, archaeology, legal materials, indexes, history, music—you name it. Catalogers must use the *Subject Headings Manual* to apply LCSH properly. LCSH is a large subject headings list with numerous instruction sheets, so it can take years for catalogers to learn how to assign subject headings for different subjects, genres, and formats.[35]

LCSH Advantages and Disadvantages

There are several advantages and disadvantages of LCSH. The main advantage is that it helps users by providing one consistent form of a subject. In this way, LCSH controls language. It also gives the library catalog its "syndetic" structure,[36] because there are cross-references to authorized subjects and to broader, narrower, and related subjects. However, there are not enough cross-references to cover all uses of language. Using LCSH also can help users narrow down their searches. Clicking on a subject heading link in a library catalog can give users a list of relevant library materials assigned that same subject heading. LCSH also works well for libraries with general research collections, because the subject headings do not go too deeply into any one subject area.

There are many disadvantages of LCSH as well. One problem is that it is very large and quite complex. It can be difficult for both users and catalogers to find an appropriate subject heading. Its use of technical terms also can be a disadvantage because users may not use technical terms when searching. Also, LCSH works well for libraries that have general collections, but it may not work well for libraries with specialized collections. Medical libraries, for example, use the *Medical Subject Headings* because LCSH is not specific enough to meet the needs of researchers in the biomedical sciences. In addition, LCSH is large and complex. It is sometimes difficult to find an authorized subject heading because LCSH does not use natural language. It is an artificial language that has been constructed and can be confusing.

Another disadvantage is that LCSH can be slow to change. Because LCSH is a large vocabulary, the Library of Congress can take a long time to add or update subject headings. LCSH may not always reflect current usage, current knowledge, or the most culturally sensitive terms and phrases. It takes a lot of work to keep pace with knowledge. LCSH also has been criticized for having an American, white, male, East Coast, Christian, heterosexual bias. LCSH tends to reflect the dominant culture and majority viewpoints, and can exclude or marginalize subjects, concepts, and groups that do not fit into it. This issue will be discussed in more detail in chapter 9. Finally, it can be difficult for some libraries to keep up with subject heading changes and additions. LCSH is updated monthly, and a library must update its local authority file to reflect changes and additions made to subject headings in the Library of Congress National Authority File. Not only do subject authority records need to be added and updated, bibliographic records must be updated to reflect current subject headings.

CHILDREN'S SUBJECT HEADINGS

Many libraries with children's collections use the *Children's Subject Headings*, a list of more than 900 LC subject headings modified for children. Think of the *Children's Subject Headings* as exceptions to some regular LC subject headings. The *Children's Subject Headings* began in 1965 when the Library of Congress created the Annotated

Card Program "to provide a more appropriate and in-depth subject treatment of juvenile titles and to offer easier subject access to those materials."[37] The Annotated Card Program took existing adult LC subject headings and modified them for children. The first edition, *Subject Headings for Children's Literature*, was published in 1969 and included a list of children's subject headings and instructions for assigning them. The current name of the Annotated Card Program is the Children's and Young Adults' Cataloging Program (CYAC), which maintains the *Children's Subject Headings* today.[38] Any library can choose to use the *Children's Subject Headings*, but they are used most often by libraries with children's collections, such as public and elementary school libraries.

Children's Subject Headings Structure and Characteristics

The *Children's Subject Headings* is structured similarly to the *Library of Congress Subject Headings* with its use of main headings, subdivisions, and cross-references. Like LCSH, the *Children's Subject Headings* is based on literary warrant, and changes to the *Children's Subject Headings* are published in the LCSH monthly lists. There are some differences, however. The biggest difference is that the *Children's Subject Headings* uses popular terms instead of technical terms. For example, it uses "Imaginary playmates" instead of LCSH's "Imaginary companions"; "Babies" instead of "Infants"; "Belly button" instead of "Navel." It also uses subject headings not necessarily in LCSH, such as "Junk," and includes some subject headings that are identical to LCSH, such as "Friendship" and "Theaters—Stage setting and scenery." In addition, some subject headings are pulled from the *Sears List of Subject Headings*.

The *Children's Subject Headings* also differ from LCSH because it does not include words that refer to children, such as *children* or *juvenile*. This is because the subject headings are already for children; it would be redundant to repeat those words in subject headings. For example, fiction is treated differently in each list. In LCSH the form subdivisions "Juvenile fiction" or "Juvenile literature" are added at the end of subject headings to tell users if something is children's fiction or children's nonfiction. In the *Children's Subject Headings*, however, the form subdivision "Fiction" is added at the end of a subject heading to tell users if an item is children's fiction. The subject heading alone is used for children's nonfiction. For example, a *Children's Subject Heading* would be "Dogs—Fiction" as opposed to LCSH's "Dogs—Juvenile fiction." See a comparison of the *Children's Subject Headings* and LCSH in table 4.3, which shows the differences in types of main subject headings as well as how each list treats children's fiction and nonfiction.

The *Children's Subject Headings* are to be used in conjunction with LCSH. Libraries that use the *Children's Subject Headings* cannot use the subject headings list alone because it does not cover all children's subjects. For example, "Holidays" is in LCSH but not in the *Children's Subject Headings*. Yet "Holidays" still can be added as a subject heading to bibliographic records for children's materials because it is in LCSH.

Table 4.3.   Comparison of *Children's Subject Headings* and LCSH

Children's Subject Headings	Library of Congress Subject Headings
Babies	Infants—Juvenile literature
Water moccasin	Agkistrodon piscivorus—Juvenile literature
Roller skating	Roller-skating—Juvenile literature
Pigs—Fiction	Swine—Juvenile fiction
Dogs—Fiction	Dogs—Juvenile fiction
Cheating—Fiction	Cheating (Education)—Juvenile fiction

Children's Subject Headings Advantages and Disadvantages

The *Children's Subject Headings* are helpful because they provide better access to children's materials. The subject headings use popular terms and phrases that children would use and that are used in children's literature. This helps children and parents find appropriate materials. However, libraries that use both subject headings lists may need to be careful. Both adult LCSH and *Children's Subject Headings* may be added to bibliographic records. A library that uses both lists of subject headings may show all subject headings in its library catalog, which can be confusing for users if there are no labels to distinguish the subject headings. For example, figure 4.4 shows subject headings assigned to the children's book *Amelia Bedelia Helps Out* from a public library catalog.[39]

The subject headings are similar, but subject headings that end with "Fiction" are *Children's Subject Headings*, and subject headings that end with "Juvenile fiction" are LCSH. Showing both sets of subject headings can be confusing for users who do not know that separate subject headings lists are being used in the library. There are

SUBJECT HEADINGS

› Amelia-Bedelia (Fictitious Character) — Juvenile Fiction.

› Helping Behavior — Juvenile Fiction.

› Household Employees — Juvenile Fiction.

› Amelia-Bedelia (Fictitious Character) — Fiction.

› Helpfulness — Fiction.

› Household Employees — Fiction.

› Humorous Stories.

Figure 4.4.   Subject Headings for *Amelia Bedelia Helps Out*

no labels to help users distinguish between the two lists. Users may think the subject headings ending in "Fiction" are incorrect because "Juvenile fiction" would be appropriate for a children's book.

LIBRARY OF CONGRESS GENRE/FORM TERMS FOR LIBRARY AND ARCHIVAL MATERIALS

The *Library of Congress Genre/Form Terms for Library and Archival Materials* (LCGFT) is a list of genre terms, also called genre headings, that can be used on bibliographic records. Genre terms are not subject headings. A genre term describes what an item *is*, such as its form or genre, not what an item is *about*. For example, a book may be *about* mythical creatures, but it *is* fantasy fiction. A television program may be *about* geography, but it *is* an educational television program. A reference work may define sociological terms and phrases, but it *is* a dictionary. Genre terms are helpful for users searching for specific types of materials in libraries. Users may want to read a particular genre of fiction, such as romance fiction, sports fiction, or historical fiction. Users may want to watch a particular genre of film or television, such as horror films, thrillers, or situation comedies (sitcoms). Users may want to listen to a particular type of music, such as rock music, country music, or rhythm and blues music.

Genre terms have an interesting history. Although some subject headings lists add form subdivisions at the end of some subject headings, adding separate genre terms to bibliographic records is a relatively new practice. One of the first lists of genre terms, *Guidelines on Subject Access to Individual Works of Fiction, Drama, Etc.* (GSAFD), was published by the American Library Association in 1990. It was created primarily for public libraries to give users better access to specific genres, particularly fiction. Many public libraries adopted this list and started adding genres to their bibliographic records. The second edition of GSAFD was published in 2000, and the Library of Congress adopted it in 2001 as part of its instructions to give "increased subject access to fiction."[40] However, the GSAFD list focuses on fiction only, and there was a need to include genre terms for other subject areas. In 2007 the Library of Congress started a project to create a separate list of genre terms for multiple subject areas, including fiction, and in 2016 it published a new list called *Library of Congress Genre/Form Terms for Library and Archival Materials*. It includes more than 2,100 genre terms for literature, film and television programs (moving images), radio programs, cartographic materials, law materials, general library materials, music, religion, and artistic and visual works. See below for examples.

Architectural drawings	Essays
Apocalyptic comics	Fantasy films
Databases	Fight songs
Demographic surveys	Indexes

Karaoke	Romance television programs
Latin jazz	Thanksgiving Day sermons
Reference works	Thematic maps
Relief prints	Travelogues (Radio programs)
Rock concert films	Treaties

LCGFT Structure and Characteristics

LCGFT has a similar structure to the *Library of Congress Subject Headings*. It includes main genre terms and uses cross-references to direct users from unauthorized genre terms to authorized genre terms (UF and USE). It also shows relationships with broader terms (BT), narrower terms (NT), and related terms (RT). Scope notes are added to some genre terms to explain when the genre term can be used, and there is a separate manual with more than twenty instruction sheets and four appendices to help catalogers construct and apply genre terms correctly. In addition, LCGFT is based on literary warrant, updates are published on LCSH's monthly lists, and authority records for each genre term have been added to the Library of Congress National Authority File.[41]

LCGFT is a separate list from LCSH. Library of Congress catalogers are instructed to add genre/form terms to bibliographic records,[42] but individual libraries do not have to use it. Libraries can choose to add genre terms, and a library can choose to use LCGFT or GSAFD. It is up to an individual library to pick the list that best meets its needs. In addition, LCGFT records are in the Library of Congress National Authority File, but GSAFD genre terms are not. A library will need to buy a copy of the book or a library can get GSAFD authority records from the American Library Association that can be downloaded into a library's local authority file.

LCGFT Advantages and Disadvantages

The primary advantage of using LCGFT is that it provides access to genres in libraries. Users looking for a specific genre can find all materials in a library collection in that genre. LCGFT also provides access to multiple genres in many subject areas. It is helpful for many users, from a teenager looking for dystopian fiction to a lawyer looking for treaties. Adding genre terms and subject headings to bibliographic records provides more subject access to a library's collection. Not only will library users know what library materials are about (subject headings), they will know what they are (genre terms).

A disadvantage is that LCGFT is a new list, and adding genre terms is a relatively new Library of Congress policy. Although genre terms for fiction have been added to bibliographic records since 2001, genre terms for other subject areas are just starting to be added to bibliographic records. Genre terms will not be added retroactively to older bibliographic records, so users may not retrieve everything a library has in a certain genre. Another disadvantage is that libraries that adopt LCGFT or switch from GSAFD will have to update their local authority files and bibliographic records with current genre terms, which can be time-consuming and expensive.

SEARS LIST OF SUBJECT HEADINGS

The *Sears List of Subject Headings* is a controlled vocabulary created specifically for small libraries, such as public, school, and church libraries. It is a smaller list of subject headings intended for both adults and children. The preface to the twenty-second edition states, "What Sears hopes to offer . . . is a basic list that includes many of the headings most likely to be needed in small libraries together with patterns and examples that will guide the cataloger in creating additional headings as needed."[43] The language is less technical and more direct than the *Library of Congress Subject Headings*, which makes it a good option for school and public libraries. *Sears* was created by Minnie Earl Sears, who recognized a need for subject headings that could be used by small libraries. Library users at small libraries needed simplified subject headings that were easy to understand and were not as technical or complicated as LCSH. *Sears* was first published in 1923 under the title *List of Subject Headings for Small Libraries*. The title was changed to *Sears List of Subject Headings* with the publication of the sixth edition in 1950. This was done to honor Minnie, who passed away in 1933. *Abridged Dewey Decimal Classification* numbers were added to *Sears* starting with the fourth edition (1939), and the *Children's Subject Headings* were added starting with the thirteenth edition (1986). With the twenty-second edition (2018), *Sears* incorporated the *Library of Congress Genre/Form Terms* for literature and music, as well as the *Canadian Companion*, a version of *Sears* for Canadian libraries published since 1978. *Sears* is maintained by an advisory board and published every four years or so, currently by Grey House Publishing. *Sears* is also available in an online subscription database.[44]

Sears Structure and Characteristics

The structure of the *Sears List of Subject Headings* is almost identical to LCSH. Minnie based *Sears* on subject headings from nine small libraries that had the reputation for good cataloging, but she followed the form and structure of LCSH.[45] The main differences between the two subject headings lists are that *Sears* uses more popular language than LCSH and *Sears* is much smaller in size. *Sears*, perhaps, can be thought of as simplified LCSH. Instead of a subject headings list that describes every subject, it includes only those subject headings that would be used in small libraries. See table 4.4 for a comparison.

There are four types of *Sears* subject headings that can be used on bibliographic records. Topical headings represent subjects, and describe what an item is about. Form headings represent genres and forms, and describe what an item is, not what it is about. Topical headings and form headings are published in *Sears*. Not published in *Sears* are geographic headings, which describe places and political jurisdictions,

Table 4.4. Comparison of *Sears* Subject Headings and LCSH

Sears Subject Headings	Library of Congress Subject Headings
Bedspreads	Coverlets
Pigs	Swine
At risk students	Problem youth—Education
Audiovisual education	Audio-visual education
Preschool education	Education, Preschool
Cooking—Vegetables	Cooking (Vegetables)

and names, including personal names, corporate names, and preferred titles of works. Geographic headings and names can be used as subject headings on bibliographic records but they are not published in Sears. Instead, geographic headings and names come from a library's local authority file.

Similar to LCSH, *Sears* subject headings are constructed using main headings and subdivisions. There are several types of main headings. Single nouns, both in the plural and singular form, are used for a single concept: Skyscrapers; Technology; Personality; Animals. Compound headings are used to describe a single concept or show a relationship: Children and war; Gold mines and mining; Labor laws and legislation. Adjectives with nouns puts an adjective before the noun, usually in direct order: Guide dogs; Automobile insurance; Environmentally induced diseases; Financial services industry. Phrase headings are used when subject headings are read as a phrase: Children of working parents; Animals as carriers of disease; Animals in police work; Equal pay for equal work. *Sears* also uses qualified headings to explain subject headings, or to distinguish similarly spelled words with different meanings: Showers (Parties); Life support systems (Medical environment); Annuals (Plants); Timesharing (Real estate).

Sears also uses the same subdivisions as LCSH: topical, geographic, chronological, and form. Subdivisions are added after main subject headings to more closely reflect what library items are about. They bring out aspects of the main subject heading. Topical subdivisions are added after main subject headings to bring out aspects of that topic: American literature—Women authors; Clothing and dress—Social aspects; Africa—History; Music—History and criticism. Geographic subdivisions are added to limit subject headings by place, but unlike LCSH, places are not subdivided indirectly: Environmental policy—Canada; Actors—United States; Streets—New York (N.Y). Chronological subdivisions are added primarily to history subject headings to limit subject headings by time period: Architecture—United States—1600–1775, Colonial period; Germany—History—1815–1866. Form subdivisions are added at the end of subject headings to bring out a form or genre: Geography—Dictionaries; Engineering—Periodicals; Automobile travel—Guidebooks.

Sears also is structured similarly to LCSH with its use of cross-references. Cross-references such as use (USE) and use for (UF) direct users from unauthorized forms of subject headings to authorized forms of subject headings, and vice versa. Broader terms (BT), narrower terms (NT), and related terms (RT) are used to show relationships. See also (SA) references show larger categories. In addition, classification numbers from *Abridged Dewey* are added to *Sears*. This is helpful for libraries that use *Abridged Dewey* to classify their collections. *Sears* subject headings and *Abridged Dewey* classification numbers work together to provide subject access to small library collections.

Sears Advantages and Disadvantages

There are some advantages and disadvantages of using the *Sears List of Subject Headings*. The primary advantage is that it works well for small collections with popular subjects. Libraries with small collections do not need a large subject headings list like LCSH. Instead, a smaller list like *Sears* is easier to understand and to use, and *Sears* subject headings are not as complex as LCSH. In addition, *Sears*'s use of popular words and phrases is an advantage for users of small libraries who use everyday language. The users of small public and school libraries do not usually use technical language for research purposes. *Sears* gives the cataloger the freedom to create specific types of subject headings to meet their users' needs. *Sears* also helps the cataloger by linking subject headings to *Abridged Dewey* numbers to assist them when classifying library materials. In addition, *Sears* is smaller and nimbler. Although there are general principles of application, there are no complex instructions, like there is for LCSH. *Sears* can more easily update subject headings to reflect current knowledge and terminology.

A disadvantage of *Sears* is that the responsibility is on the cataloger to create subject headings, and a library should have its own local authority file. *Sears* was created with the assumption that catalogers will be maintaining a local authority file, and this may not necessarily be the case for small libraries that cannot afford to maintain one. In addition, although the content of *Sears* is maintained by library professionals, it is published by a commercial publisher. Unlike LCSH, which is free, *Sears* costs around $200. This may not seem like a lot of money, but some libraries cannot afford to purchase the latest edition or subscribe to the database. Libraries may be using old editions of *Sears*, which can include old, outdated, and insensitive terms, and do not reflect the latest *Abridged Dewey* numbers. In addition, *Sears* is published every four years or so. Language changes very quickly, and although *Sears* updates its headings, it may take some time for subject headings to be changed or added to *Sears*. A final disadvantage is that libraries may need to switch to LCSH to save costs. Libraries are increasingly purchasing bibliographic records from vendors that already have LC subject headings on them. It may be cost-prohibitive to pay library vendors to add *Sears* subject headings. Yet despite its disadvantages, *Sears* still remains a good subject headings list for small libraries.

MEDICAL SUBJECT HEADINGS

The *Medical Subject Headings* (MeSH) is a controlled vocabulary of more than 27,000 terms used to provide subject access to medical library collections and biomedical information.[46] It is maintained by the National Library of Medicine. MeSH is unlike other controlled vocabularies used in libraries because it performs a dual role as a subject headings list to catalog medical library collections *and* as a thesaurus to index biomedical journal articles. MeSH was created by the National Library of Medicine to provide subject access to the library's collection. MeSH is based on the National Library of Medicine's *Subject Heading Authority List*, published in 1954, which was a list of subject headings used by the National Library of Medicine at the time. It included subject headings used in the library's catalog as well as subject headings in older medical indexes such as the *Current List of Medical Literature* and the *Quarterly Cumulative Index Medicus*. MeSH was created after the National Library of Medicine took over the publication of a new version of *Index Medicus* in 1960, which needed a new subject headings list.[47]

Today, National Library of Medicine catalogers use MeSH to catalog the library's collection, and National Library of Medicine indexers use MeSH to index biomedical journal articles on the MEDLINE database, which is available for free through PubMed. It is estimated that more than 850,000 journal articles are indexed for MEDLINE/PubMed each year.[48] The specialized language of the biomedical sciences as well as its large volume of publications require very specific and detailed cataloging and indexing. In addition to the National Library of Medicine, MeSH is used for cataloging by medical libraries and academic libraries with medical collections, and these libraries may use both MeSH and the *Library of Congress Subject Headings*, depending on their needs.

MeSH Structure and Characteristics

The subject headings in MeSH are focused on biomedical sciences, including medicine, nursing, life sciences, veterinary medicine, dentistry, and so on. MeSH also includes some subject headings from other fields, such as information science, agriculture, and music, which are added as needed to reflect the National Library of Medicine's collection. Most MeSH subject headings use current terminology used in the biomedical sciences. Some examples are below.

Alice in Wonderland Syndrome	Integumentary System
Cardiomyopathy, Hypertrophic, Familial	Neonicotinoids
Delayed Graft Function	Polyendocrinopathies, Autoimmune
Electrogalvanism, Intraoral	Transplantation Chimera

MeSH terms and phrases are not used by people in everyday life. They reflect subjects in the biomedical sciences to help researchers and practitioners find biomedical information.

A helpful feature of MeSH is that it is arranged hierarchically into a tree structure, using broader and narrower terms. There are sixteen trees in MeSH that cover broad subject categories, as seen on the following page.

MeSH TREES

Anatomy [A]
Organisms [B]
Diseases [C]
Chemicals and Drugs [D]
Analytical, Diagnostic and Therapeutic Techniques, and Equipment [E]
Psychiatry and Psychology [F]
Phenomena and Processes [G]
Disciplines and Occupations [H]
Anthropology, Education, Sociology, and Social Phenomena [I]
Technology, Industry, and Agriculture [J]
Humanities [K]
Information Science [L]
Named Groups [M]
Health Care [N]
Publication Characteristics [V]
Geographicals [Z]

Each tree is divided hierarchically into subcategories. See a tree structure example in figure 4.5.[49]

Figure 4.5 shows a partial MeSH tree for "Diseases." It shows the hierarchy for "Bacterial Infections and Mycoses." The term falls under the broader term of "Diseases" with five narrower terms under it. The subject heading "Central Nervous System Infections" is further subdivided into two terms, and the term "Brain Abscess" is subdivided again. The classification numbers listed refer to terms in the tree structure only; they are not National Library of Medicine classification numbers. The MeSH tree structure is helpful for catalogers, indexers, and users so they can see the whole hierarchy of broader and narrower terms. It allows catalogers and indexers to assign the most appropriate subject headings and indexing terms. It allows users to search

Diseases [C] ⊖
    Bacterial Infections and Mycoses [C01] ⊖
        Bacterial Infections [C01.252] ⊕
        Central Nervous System Infections [C01.395] ⊖
            Brain Abscess [C01.395.250] ⊖
                Toxoplasmosis, Cerebral [C01.395.250.500]
            Central Nervous System Bacterial Infections [C01.395.500]
        Infection [C01.539] ⊕
        Mycoses [C01.703] ⊕
        Zoonoses [C01.908]

Figure 4.5.   Partial MeSH Tree Example

for biomedical information more effectively because the structure is available to users in the PubMed database.

On the cataloging side, catalogers add MeSH subject headings to bibliographic records. MeSH subject headings are constructed in two parts: descriptors (main headings) and optional qualifiers (subheadings). Descriptors are the main subject headings in MeSH. Descriptors answer the question, What is the item about? Every subject heading will include a main descriptor. Examples are shown below.

Dermatologic Agents
Drug-Related Side Effects and Adverse Reactions
Skin Diseases
Periodontal Diseases

The second part of a subject heading is a qualifier. Qualifiers are added only when needed to be more specific. Qualifiers are similar to those used in LCSH, but only one qualifier can be added after a descriptor. Qualifiers are added after a descriptor to bring out a particular aspect of the main topic, and they always begin with a lowercase letter. Examples of qualifiers include: drug effects; injuries; surgery; growth & development; and many more. Also similar to LCSH, a cataloger or indexer cannot add just any qualifier after a subject heading. Only certain qualifiers may be added after subject headings. Examples are shown below.

Dermatologic Agents—therapeutic use
Drug-Related Side Effects and Adverse Reactions—veterinary
Skin Diseases—drug therapy
Periodontal Diseases—microbiology

In addition to topical subject headings and subdivisions, other things can be used as MeSH main subject headings, such as geographic places, publication types, names, and titles of works, but they are never used as subdivisions.

MeSH is a separate subject headings list from LCSH. It is the only subject headings list not related to LCSH. MeSH is specific to the biomedical sciences. However, MeSH is a source of subject headings for LCSH. LCSH includes many subject headings included in MeSH, but because LCSH is a general subject headings list, it tends to use broader MeSH subject headings. In addition, there are some differences in the formatting of the subject headings. MeSH uses direct entry whenever possible, and it does not often explain subject headings with qualifiers. See table 4.5 for a comparison of MeSH and LCSH.

Table 4.5. Comparison of *Medical Subject Headings* and LCSH

Medical Subject Headings	Library of Congress Subject Headings
Heart Diseases	Heart—Diseases
Medicine, Traditional	Traditional medicine
Transfer Factor	Transfer factor (Immunology)
Adrenocortical Hyperfunction	Hyperadrenocorticism
Pulmonary Alveolar Proteinosis	*Not in LCSH*
Median Arcuate Ligament Syndrome	*Not in LCSH*

MeSH Advantages and Disadvantages

MeSH is an excellent subject headings list for the biomedical sciences. Its dual role as a subject headings list for cataloging medical library collections and a thesaurus for indexing biomedical journals serves researchers and practitioners in the biomedical sciences very well. It ensures consistent terminology when searching for biomedical materials. However, catalogers need specialized training and specialized knowledge to assign subject headings properly. A cataloger must understand the language used in the biomedical sciences or items may be cataloged incorrectly.

FACETED APPLICATION OF SUBJECT TERMINOLOGY

One of the newest developments in subject headings is *Faceted Application of Subject Terminology* (FAST). This is an OCLC project that began in 1998 and was created in collaboration with the Library of Congress. FAST is not a separate list of subject headings that has been created following a set of principles. Instead, FAST takes LC subject headings and separates them into facets so they are easier to apply and use. OCLC wants FAST to be "simple to learn and apply, faceted-navigation-friendly, and modern in its design."[50] Currently, there are more than 1.7 million FAST subject headings and growing, available in the searchFAST database.[51] They are used on library bibliographic records, in some databases, and in linked data projects. FAST subject headings are added to bibliographic records in OCLC's Connexion database, and libraries can choose to use FAST subject headings in their library catalogs or not.

Think of FAST as simplified LCSH. LC subject headings can be quite complicated to construct. There are topical main headings and subdivisions, geographic main headings and subdivisions, chronological main headings and subdivisions, and genre/form headings and form subdivisions. In addition, personal names, family names, corporate names, and titles of works can be used as subject headings. Catalogers follow many complex instructions to construct subject headings, and there are innumerable combinations of possible subject headings in LCSH.

FAST breaks down LC subject headings into facets, or aspects, of subject headings. There are eight facets in FAST that correspond loosely to parts of LC subject headings: Topical, Geographic, Chronological, Form/Genre, Personal names, Corporate names, Uniform (Preferred) titles, and Events. The basic rules of FAST is that facets are listed as separate subject headings, and only headings and subdivisions from the same facet are allowed to be put together. A subject heading like Women—History is allowed in FAST because both of them are from the topical facet. A subject heading like Women—Ohio would not be allowed because "Women" is a topical facet and "Ohio" is a geographic facet. For example, here is an LC subject heading:

Banks and banking—Accounting—Law and legislation—United States.

This subject heading includes a topical main heading (Banks and banking), two topical subdivisions (Accounting; Law and legislation) and a geographic subdivision (United States). FAST separates this subject heading into different facets, in this case the topical facet and the geographic facet. There would be two FAST subject headings:

1. Banks and banking—Accounting—Law and legislation. (Topical facet)
2. United States. (Geographic facet)

FAST Advantages and Disadvantages

An advantage of FAST is that it breaks down complex LC subject headings into facets that can be manipulated by computers. It is also easier for users to understand the subject headings and for catalogers to apply the subject headings. There are no complicated rules for constructing subject headings; catalogers just need to match facets. A disadvantage is that it may add to the workload of libraries who use OCLC's Connexion bibliographic utility. FAST headings are added to bibliographic records in Connexion, so libraries must decide if they want to use them in their library catalog.

OTHER CONTROLLED VOCABULARIES

Libraries use a variety of other subject headings lists and thesauri to provide subject access to their collections. Each controlled vocabulary has been created for a specific purpose and audience, and controls language in certain ways. Here are a few of the more commonly used titles.

BISAC Subject Headings

Created by the Book Industry Study Group, *BISAC Subject Headings* are used by the publishing industry.[52] Some public libraries have rearranged their collections to follow a bookstore model using *BISAC Subject Headings*. They are added to biblio-graphic records and match BISAC codes, which are used as classification numbers. The main BISAC categories are shown below.

BISAC CATEGORIES

ANTIQUES & COLLECTIBLES	LAW
ARCHITECTURE	LITERARY COLLECTIONS
ART	LITERARY CRITICISM
BIBLES	MATHEMATICS
BIOGRAPHY & AUTOBIOGRAPHY	MEDICAL
BODY, MIND & SPIRIT	MUSIC
BUSINESS & ECONOMICS	NATURE
COMICS & GRAPHIC NOVELS	PERFORMING ARTS
COMPUTERS	PETS
COOKING	PHILOSOPHY
CRAFTS & HOBBIES	PHOTOGRAPHY
DESIGN	POETRY
DRAMA	POLITICAL SCIENCE
EDUCATION	PSYCHOLOGY
FAMILY & RELATIONSHIPS	REFERENCE
FICTION	RELIGION
FOREIGN LANGUAGE STUDY	SCIENCE
GAMES & ACTIVITIES	SELF-HELP
GARDENING	SOCIAL SCIENCE
HEALTH & FITNESS	SPORTS & RECREATION
HISTORY	STUDY AIDS
HOUSE & HOME	TECHNOLOGY & ENGINEERING
HUMOR	TRANSPORTATION
JUVENILE FICTION	TRAVEL
JUVENILE NONFICTION	TRUE CRIME
LANGUAGE ARTS & DISCIPLINES	YOUNG ADULT FICTION
	YOUNG ADULT NONFICTION

Each category is further broken down by specific subject, genre, or form to make BISAC subject headings more specific. For example, *The LEGO Architecture Idea Book* by Alice Finch is assigned three BISAC subject headings.

CRAFTS & HOBBIES—Models.
CRAFTS & HOBBIES—General.
ARCHITECTURE—General.

Some public librarians believe that BISAC is easier for users to understand. However, the system was created for the publishing industry and it reflects market demands, not what is necessarily best for users.

Bilindex

Bilindex is a list of Spanish subject headings equivalent to the *Library of Congress Subject Headings*, but it incorporates some of the more practical elements of *Sears*. *Bilindex* subject headings may be added to bibliographic records of libraries that serve Spanish-speaking populations.

Art & Architecture Thesaurus

The *Art & Architecture Thesaurus* (AAT) is a thesaurus just for the art and architecture fields. It was first published in 1990 and it is maintained by the Getty Vocabulary Program of the Getty Research Institute. Some academic and research libraries with art and architecture collections add these thesaurus descriptors to bibliographic records and metadata records.

Thesaurus for Graphic Materials

The *Thesaurus for Graphic Materials* (TGM) includes descriptors for visual materials, such as pictures, photographs, prints, drawings, and so on. It was originally published in 1987 by the Prints and Photographs Division of the Library of Congress, and includes more than 7,000 subject terms and more than 650 genre/form terms. Academic and research libraries with specialized visual materials collections add these thesaurus descriptors to bibliographic records and metadata records.

Rare Books and Manuscripts Section Thesauri

The Rare Books and Manuscripts Section (RBMS) thesauri include six thesauri that focus on terms used in rare books and special collections cataloging. The six thesauri are: (1) *Binding Terms*, (2) *Genre Terms*, (3) *Paper Terms*, (4) *Printing & Publishing Evidence*, (5) *Provenance Evidence*, and (6) *Type Evidence*. The thesauri were originally published between 1986 and 1991, and they are maintained by the Bibliographic Standards Committee of the Rare Books and Manuscripts Section of the Association of College and Research Libraries of the American Library Association (ACRL/ALA). They include descriptors that focus on genre, form, or physical characteristics. Academic and research libraries with rare book and manuscript collections can add these thesaurus descriptors to bibliographic records and metadata records.

Other Thesauri

There are many other thesauri libraries can use to provide subject access to their collections. Many libraries have collections in specialized subject areas that need in-depth subject analysis. A library can use any thesaurus to give more detailed subject access to their materials. For example, a library could use the *NASA Thesaurus* for a collection of NASA technical reports, the *UNBIS Thesaurus* for a collection of United Nations documents, or the *Transportation Research Thesaurus* for a collection of transportation information. There is also the *Library of Congress Medium of Performance Thesaurus for Music* (LCMPT) and the *Library of Congress Demographic Group Terms* (LCDGT).

Homegrown Thesauri

A library could create its own thesaurus to provide subject access to a specialized collection. For example, a public library with a collection of local genealogical materials can create a thesaurus (or an index) to provide better subject access to that collection. Thesauri can be especially helpful for special libraries that need to provide subject access to specialized collections, such as in a corporate library or law firm library.

Ontologies

Ontologies are not necessarily used in libraries but are helpful in professional settings. Ontologies are focused on a domain or subject area. An ontology lists the vocabulary, or the language, of a domain. It is very much like a controlled vocabulary except that ontologies are not necessarily hierarchical. They often use facets to show the language in a domain. For example, in the domain of education, words in an ontology might include *learning*, *assessment*, and *lesson plans*. For the domain of candy making, words in an ontology might include *coating*, *tempering*, and *molds*.

SUMMARY

This chapter began a discussion about how libraries give subject access to their collections. It discussed subject analysis and issues surrounding how to determine subjects. Subject analysis can be a complex and subjective process. Authors, users, and catalogers use language differently, and it can be challenging for catalogers to connect users to library materials. This chapter also discussed controlled vocabularies and uncontrolled vocabularies. Each type of vocabulary has its advantages and disadvantages and helps users in different ways. Finally, the chapter talked about specific controlled vocabularies used in libraries, such as the *Library of Congress Subject Headings*, *Sears List of Subject Headings*, and FAST subject headings. Chapter 5 will continue the discussion of subject access by focusing on classification.

DISCUSSION QUESTIONS

1. What is aboutness and why is it difficult to determine?
2. What are controlled vocabularies and uncontrolled vocabularies? What are the advantages and disadvantages of each one?

3. What are the characteristics, advantages, and disadvantages of the *Library of Congress Subject Headings*?
4. Besides the *Library of Congress Subject Headings*, what other subject headings lists or thesauri are used in libraries? In what type of library are they used, and what are their characteristics, advantages, and disadvantages?

CLASS ACTIVITIES

1. *Group Subject Analysis.* With your classmates, read a short news article and assign two subject headings/descriptors that describe the article. There are no rules. Assign subject headings you think best describe what the article is about. Then the instructor or someone else will collect the responses and make a list of all subject headings/descriptors assigned, with the number of people who assigned each one. Discuss the results with your classmates. Can the class come to consensus?
2. *Tagging Assignment.* The purpose of this exercise is to understand the differences between tags and subject headings. Find bibliographic records for five of your favorite fiction books on a library catalog that has both subject headings and tags, such as the Chicago (IL) Public Library or the Austin (TX) Public Library. The books can be children's or adult fiction. (Fiction is preferred because there is a better chance that bibliographic records will have tags.) Evaluate the subject headings and tags. What are the similarities and differences? How would they be helpful to the end user? What would improve them? Include a screen capture of the subjects and tags assigned to each bibliographic record.
3. *Cataloging Assignment.* If this textbook is used in a cataloging course, then you should assign subject headings, such as the *Library of Congress Subject Headings*, to bibliographic records for books. Perform subject analysis to determine what the books are about. Then look for authorized LC subject headings in the Library of Congress National Authority File. Practice tests in which you find LC subject headings also are very helpful.
4. *Metadata Assignment.* If this textbook is used in a metadata course, then you should add subject headings or thesaurus descriptors to metadata records. Practice tests in which you find subject headings or thesaurus descriptors also are very helpful.

NOTES

1. International Federation of Library Associations and Institutions, *Statement of International Cataloguing Principles (ICP)*, 2016 ed., with minor revisions (The Hague: IFLA, 2017), https://www.ifla.org/publications/node/11015, 10.
2. Patrick Wilson, *Two Kinds of Power: An Essay on Bibliographical Control* (Berkeley: University of California Press, 1968).

3. The first edition was published under the title *Rules for a Printed Dictionary Catalogue*. Charles A. Cutter, "Rules for a Printed Dictionary Catalog," as *Public Libraries in the United States of America: Their History, Condition, and Management: Special Report, Part II* (Washington, DC: US Government Printing Office, 1876), 10.

4. Ibid., 37.

5. Charles A. Cutter, *Rules for a Dictionary Catalog*, 4th ed. (Washington, DC: US Government Printing Office, 1904).

6. Wilson, *Two Kinds of Power*, 69–92.

7. See, e.g., W. J. Hutchins, "The Concept of 'Aboutness' in Subject Indexing," *Aslib Proceedings* 30 (1978): 172–81; M. E. Maron, "On Indexing, Retrieval and the Meaning of About," *Journal of the American Society for Information Science* 28 (1977): 38–43.

8. See, e.g., R. A. Fairthorne, "Content Analysis, Specification, and Control," *Annual Review of Information Science and Technology* 4 (1969): 73–109.

9. See, e.g., Peter Ingwersen, *Information Retrieval Interaction* (London: Taylor Graham, 1992); Peter Ingwersen and Peter Willett, "An Introduction to Algorithmic and Cognitive Approaches for Information Retrieval," *Libri* 45 (1995): 160–77.

10. Dagobert Soergel, *Organizing Information: Principles of Data Base and Retrieval Systems* (Orlando, FL: Academic Press, 1985).

11. Birger Hjørland, "The Concept of 'Subject' in Information Science," *Journal of Documentation* 48 (1992): 172–200.

12. Jens-Erik Mai, "Analysis in Indexing: Document and Domain Entered Approaches," *Information Processing and Management* 41 (2004): 599–611.

13. Marcia J. Bates, "Indexing and Access for Digital Libraries and the Internet: Human, Database, and Domain Factors," *Journal of the American Society for Information Science* 49 (1998): 1185–205.

14. Ibid.

15. Oliver L. Lilley, "Evaluation of the Subject Catalog: Criticisms and a Proposal," *American Documentation* 5 (1954): 41–60.

16. Sara Shatford Layne, "Some Issues in the Indexing of Images," *Journal of the American Society for Information Science* 45 (1994): 583–88.

17. ERIC Thesaurus, accessed January 11, 2019, https://eric.ed.gov.

18. Elaine Svenonius, *The Intellectual Foundation of Information Organization* (Cambridge, MA: MIT Press, 2000), 135–36.

19. "Order of Subject Headings, H80" in *Subject Headings Manual*, last updated June 2013, accessed January 11, 2019, https://www.loc.gov/aba/publications/FreeSHM/H0080 .pdf, 1.

20. Cutter, "Rules for a Printed Dictionary Catalogue," 37.

21. LA County Library Catalog, accessed January 11, 2019, https://lacountylibrary.org.

22. Library of Congress Catalog, accessed January 11, 2019, https://catalog.loc.gov.

23. For more information about the history of keyword searching, see, e.g., Heting Chu, *Information Representation and Retrieval in the Digital Age*, 2nd ed. (Medford, NJ: Information Today for the American Society for Information Science and Technology, 2010).

24. Denton Public Library Catalog, accessed January 11, 2019, https://library.cityofdenton.com.

25. See, e.g., Tina Gross and Arlene G. Taylor, "What Have We Got to Lose? The Effect of Controlled Vocabulary on Keyword Searching Results," *College & Research Libraries* 66 (2005): 212–30; Tina Gross, Arlene G. Taylor, and Daniel N. Joudrey, "Still a Lot to Lose:

The Role of Controlled Vocabulary in Keyword Searching." *Cataloging & Classification Quarterly* 53 (2015): 1–39; Thomas Mann, "Will Google's Keyword Searching Eliminate the Need for LC Cataloging and Classification?" *Journal of Library Metadata* 8, no. 2 (2008): 159–68; Sevim McCutcheon, "Keyword vs Controlled Vocabulary Searching: The One with the Most Tools Wins," *Indexer* 27, no. 2 (2009): 62–65.

26. See, e.g., Peter J. Rolla, "User Tags versus Subject Headings: Can User Supplied Data Improve Subject Access to Library Collections?" *Library Resources & Technical Services* 53 (2009): 174–84; Louise F. Spiteri, "Incorporating Facets into Social Tagging Applications: An Analysis of Current Trends," *Cataloging & Classification Quarterly* 48, no. 1 (2010): 94–109; Kwan Yi and Lois Mai Chan, "Linking Folksonomy to Library of Congress Subject Headings: An Exploratory Study," *Journal of Documentation* 65, no. 6 (2009): 872–900.

27. Christine DeZelar-Tiedman, "Exploring User-Contributed Metadata's Potential to Enhance Access to Literary Works: Social Tagging in Academic Library Catalogs," *Library Resources & Technical Services* 55, no. 4 (2011): 221–33.

28. Chicago Public Library Catalog, accessed January 12, 2019, https://www.chipublib.org.

29. Library of Congress, "Introduction," *Library of Congress Subject Headings*, 40th ed. (2018), https://www.loc.gov/aba/publications/FreeLCSH/freelcsh.html#Introduction, viii.

30. Ibid., vii.

31. Library of Congress, "Assigning and Constructing Subject Headings: H180," *Subject Headings Manual*, last updated February 2016, accessed January 11, 2019, https://www.loc.gov/aba/publications/FreeSHM/H0180.pdf.

32. Ibid.

33. ALA, "Introduction," *Library of Congress Subject Headings*, viii.

34. Library of Congress, "Free-Floating Subdivisions: H1095," *Subject Headings Manual*, last updated August 2018, accessed January 11, 2019, https://www.loc.gov/aba/publications/FreeSHM/H1095.pdf.

35. Library of Congress, *Subject Headings Manual*, accessed January 11, 2019, https://www.loc.gov/aba/publications/FreeSHM/freeshm.html.

36. Cutter, "Rules for a Printed Dictionary Catalog," 15.

37. Library of Congress, *Introduction to Children's Subject Headings* (2018), https://www.loc.gov/aba/publications/FreeLCSH/freelcsh.html#CSH, i.

38. Library of Congress, "About the Program: Children's and Young Adults' Cataloging Program (CYAC)," last updated April 13, 2015, accessed January 11, 2019, https://www.loc.gov/aba/cyac/about.html.

39. Chicago Public Library Catalog.

40. Library of Congress, "Literature: Fiction; H 1790," *Subject Headings Manual*, last updated November 2015, accessed January 11, 2019, https://www.loc.gov/aba/publications/FreeSHM/H1790.pdf.

41. Library of Congress, *Library of Congress Genre/Form Terms for Library and Archival Materials (LCGFT)* (2018), https://www.loc.gov/aba/publications/FreeLCGFT/freelcgft.html.

42. Library of Congress, "Assigning Genre/Form Terms: J1110," *Library of Congress Genre/Form Terms Manual*, last updated January 2016 (draft), accessed January 11, 2019, https://www.loc.gov/aba/publications/FreeLCGFT/J110.pdf.

43. "Preface," in *Sears List of Subject Headings*, 22nd ed. (Amenia, NY: Grey House, 2018), A-8.

44. *Sears List of Subject Headings* website, https://searslistofsubjectheadings.com.

45. "A History of the Sears List," *Sears List of Subject Headings*, 22nd ed. (Amenia, NY: Grey House Publishing, 2018), A-11-13.

46. National Library of Medicine, "Indexing for Medline: Introduction; What Do We Index?" last updated December 5, 2017, accessed January 11, 2019, https://www.nlm.nih.gov/bsd/indexing/training/INT_010.html.

47. National Library of Medicine, "History of MeSH," last updated March 7, 2017, accessed January 11, 2019, https://www.nlm.nih.gov/mesh/intro_hist.html. *Index Medicus* was the print version of MEDLINE. It is no longer being published in print as of 2004, but it still exists as a subset of journals on PubMed.

48. National Library of Medicine, "Indexing for Medline: Introduction; Who Are the Indexers?" last updated January 18, 2017, accessed January 11, 2019, https://www.nlm.nih.gov/bsd/indexing/training/INT_020.html.

49. National Library of Medicine, *Medical Subject Headings* (2019), accessed January 11, 2019, https://meshb.nlm.nih.gov/search.

50. OCLC, "FAST (Faceted Application of Subject Terminology)," accessed January 11, 2019, https://www.oclc.org/research/themes/data-science/fast.html.

51. searchFAST, http://fast.oclc.org/searchfast.

52. Book Industry Study Group, *Complete BISAC Subject Headings List*, 2018 ed., https://bisg.org/page/bisacedition.

SELECTED BIBLIOGRAPHY WITH ADDITIONAL READING

Badke, William. "The Treachery of Keywords." *Online* 35, no. 3 (May/June 2011): 52–54.

Bates, Marcia J. "Indexing and Access for Digital Libraries and the Internet: Human, Database, and Domain Factors." *Journal of the American Society for Information Science* 49 (1998): 1185–205.

Book Industry Study Group. *Complete BISAC Subject Headings List*. 2018 Edition. https://bisg.org/page/bisacedition.

Broughton, Vanda. *Essential Library of Congress Subject Headings*. New York: Neal-Schuman, 2012.

———. *Essential Thesaurus Construction*. London: Facet, 2006.

Chan, Lois Mai. *Library of Congress Subject Headings: Principles and Application*. Fourth Edition. Westport, CT: Libraries Unlimited, 2005.

Chu, Heting. *Information Representation and Retrieval in the Digital Age*. Second Edition. Medford, NJ: Information Today for the American Society for Information Science and Technology, 2010.

Cosentino, Sharon L. "Folksonomies: Path to a Better Way?" *Public Libraries* 47 (2008): 42–47.

Cutter, Charles A. "Rules for a Printed Dictionary Catalogue." Published as *Public Libraries in the United States of America: Their History, Condition, and Management: Special Report, Part II*. Washington, DC: US Government Printing Office, 1876.

———. *Rules for a Dictionary Catalog*. Fourth Edition. Washington, DC: US Government Printing Office, 1904.

DeZelar-Tiedman, Christine. "Exploring User-Contributed Metadata's Potential to Enhance Access to Literary Works: Social Tagging in Academic Library Catalogs." *Library Resources & Technical Services* 55, no. 4 (2011): 221–33.

Fairthorne, R. A. "Content Analysis, Specification, and Control." *Annual Review of Information Science and Technology* 4 (1969): 73–109.

Ferris, Anna M. "Birth of a Subject Heading." *Library Resources & Technical Services* 62, no. 1 (2018): 16–27.

Gross, Tina, and Arlene G. Taylor. "What Have We Got to Lose? The Effect of Controlled Vocabulary on Keyword Searching Results." *College & Research Libraries* 66 (2005): 212–30.

Gross, Tina, Arlene G. Taylor, and Daniel N. Joudrey. "Still a Lot to Lose: The Role of Controlled Vocabulary in Keyword Searching." *Cataloging & Classification Quarterly* 53 (2015): 1–39.

Hjørland, B. "Epistemology and the Socio-cognitive Perspective in Information Science." *Journal of the American Society for Information Science and Technology* 53 (2002): 257–70.

Hjørland, Birger. "The Concept of 'Subject' in Information Science." *Journal of Documentation* 48 (1992): 172–200.

Hjørland, B., and H. Albrechtsen. (1995). "Toward a New Horizon in Information Science: Domain-analysis." *Journal of the American Society for Information Science* 46 (1995): 400–25.

Hutchins, W. J. "The Concept of 'Aboutness' in Subject Indexing." *Aslib Proceedings* 30 (1978): 172–81.

Ingwersen, Peter. *Information Retrieval Interaction.* London: Taylor Graham, 1992.

Ingwersen, Peter, and P. Willett. "An Introduction to Algorithmic and Cognitive Approaches for Information Retrieval." *Libri* 45 (1995): 160–77.

International Federation of Library Associations and Institutions. *Statement of International Cataloguing Principles (ICP).* 2016 Edition, with minor revisions. The Hague: IFLA, 2017. https://www.ifla.org/publications/node/11015.

Layne, Sara Shatford. "Some Issues in the Indexing of Images." *Journal of the American Society for Information Science* 45 (1994): 583–88.

Library of Congress. *Children's Subject Headings.* 2018. https://www.loc.gov/aba/publications/FreeLCSH/freelcsh.html#CSH.

———. *Library of Congress Genre/Form Terms for Library and Archival Materials* (LCGFT). 2018. https://www.loc.gov/aba/publications/FreeLCGFT/freelcgft.html.

———. *Library of Congress Subject Headings* PDF files. 2018. https://www.loc.gov/aba/publications/FreeLCSH/freelcsh.html.

———. *Subject Headings Manual,* Library of Congress, 2016. https://www.loc.gov/aba/publications/FreeSHM/freeshm.html.

Lilley, Oliver L. "Evaluation of the Subject Catalog: Criticisms and a Proposal." *American Documentation* 5 (1954): 41–60.

Mai, Jens-Erik. "Analysis in Indexing: Document and Domain Entered Approaches." *Information Processing and Management* 41 (2004): 599–611.

Mann, Thomas. "Will Google's Keyword Searching Eliminate the Need for LC Cataloging and Classification?" *Journal of Library Metadata* 8, no. 2 (2008): 159–68.

Maron, M. E. "On Indexing, Retrieval and the Meaning of About." *Journal of the American Society for Information Science* 28 (1977): 38–43.

Martel, Charles. "Preface." In *Subject Headings Used in the Dictionary Catalogues of the Library of Congress,* second edition. Washington, DC: US Government Printing Office, 1919.

McCutcheon, Sevim. "Keyword vs Controlled Vocabulary Searching: The One with the Most Tools Wins." *Indexer* 27, no 2 (2009): 62–65.

National Library of Medicine. *Medical Subject Headings*. 2019. https://meshb.nlm.nih.gov/search.

OCLC. "FAST (Faceted Application of Subject Terminology)." https://www.oclc.org/research/themes/data-science/fast.html.

Pirmann, Carrie. "Tags in the Catalogue: Insights from a Usability Study of LibraryThing for Libraries." *Library Trends* 61 (2012): 234–47.

Porter, John. "Folksonomies in the Library: Their Impact on User Experience, and Their Implications for the Work of Librarians." *Australian Library Journal* 60 (2011): 248–55.

Rolla, Peter J. "User Tags versus Subject Headings: Can User Supplied Data Improve Subject Access to Library Collections?" *Library Resources & Technical Services* 53, no. 3 (2009): 174–84.

Sears List of Subject Headings. Twenty-second Edition. Amenia, NY: Grey House, 2018.

Soergel, Dagobert. *Organizing Information: Principles of Data Base and Retrieval Systems*. Orlando, FL: Academic Press, 1985.

Speller, Edith. "Collaborative Tagging, Folksonomies, Distributed Classification or Ethnoclassification: A Literature Review." *Library Student Journal* (2007).

Spiteri, Louise F. "Incorporating Facets into Social Tagging Applications: An Analysis of Current Trends." *Cataloging & Classification Quarterly* 48, no. 1 (2010): 94–109.

Svenonius, Elaine. 2000. *The Intellectual Foundation of Information Organization*. Cambridge, MA: MIT Press, 2000.

Wichowski, Alexis. "Survival of the Fittest Tag: Folksonomies, Findability, and the Evolution of Information Organization. *First Monday* 14, no. 5 (May 2009). https://firstmonday.org/article/viewArticle/2447/2175.

Wilson, Patrick. *Two Kinds of Power: An Essay on Bibliographical Control*. Berkeley: University of California Press, 1968.

Yi, Kwan, and Lois Mai Chan. "Linking Folksonomy to Library of Congress Subject Headings: An Exploratory Study." *Journal of Documentation* 65, no. 6 (2009): 872–900.

5

Classifying Library Collections

The last chapter began a discussion about how libraries provide subject access to their collections. It introduced subject analysis, the process of determining subjects, and it discussed one part of the process, which is assigning subject headings or descriptors from a controlled vocabulary. This chapter extends the discussion of subject access and focuses on the other part of providing access to subjects: classification. In libraries, classification numbers represent subjects and genres or forms, and are used to organize physical library collections. The chapter will discuss classification, formal classification schemes used in libraries, and alternatives to formal classification.

CLASSIFICATION

Classification, in the most general sense, is putting things into classes, groups, or categories in a deliberate way. The "things" could be anything, like objects, subjects, people, industries, professions, knowledge—anything and everything. There are always reasons for classification; it is done with purpose. Humans are very good at categorizing and classifying things. As Geoffrey C. Bowker and Susan Leigh Star say, "To classify is human."[1] It is how we make sense of the world, and categorization and classification happen all the time in everyday life. A child who separates his or her toys into groups is classifying. People group kitchen items, such as silverware, glasses, and dishes, for use and storage. Stores classify merchandise so shoppers can find and purchase it. Record stores classify by musical genre; grocery stores classify by packaging or ingredient; clothing stores classify by age, gender, size, and type of clothing. People are classified, too. Children are classified in schools by age, gender, or ability. How people are classified can affect services that are received, how they perform their jobs, or how they are treated. Think about a hospital emergency room. The doctors and nurses classify patients to determine their level of need. Are the injuries life threatening? If so, then a patient will be admitted immediately. If not, then a patient must wait to be seen. The patient does not decide. Think, too, about a work classification. A library worker may be classified as "Library Technician 2," and this classification determines job duties and how much the worker is paid. The worker does not decide. Sometimes people can buy their way into a classification. Airlines have first class, business class, and economy class, and each classification receives different levels of service depending on the price paid.

Everyone creates categories and classifies. An ugly downside of classification is that people may think their categories reflect an inherent truth about the world and are the only "right" way to see the world. This can be something relatively harmless as the "right" way to load a dishwasher (although this can be a hot button issue in some households). Classification becomes problematic if categories become inflexible or turn into stereotypes. Classification is always deliberatively performed, and it can have consequences.[2] There is no one right way to classify anything. Everyone categorizes and classifies things differently, and things do not always fall neatly into categories. As an illustration, look at figure 5.1. Put the pictures into categories that make sense to you.

Figure 5.1.   Put Pictures into Categories. *This Photo* (https://commons.wikimedia.org/wiki/File:Kingdom_of_animals.png) *by Unknown Author is licensed under CC BY-SA* (https://creativecommons.org/licenses/by-sa/3.0/).

What categories did you pick? Each person reading this book will have different categories and a different idea of how to arrange the pictures. There are only twelve pictures of animals, but there are multiple categories. There could be categories of animals with horns, fur, feathers, or scales; animals that live in water or live on land; animals that are predators or prey; and on and on. There are many possible ways to categorize and classify anything in the world.

In everyday life, categorization and classification are similar. Both involve the process of putting things into categories, groups, or classes in a deliberate way. There are formal classification schemes that take categorization one step further and build a notational scheme (a combination of letters, numbers, symbols, or punctuation) to represent the categories, for example, the World Health Organization's International Classification of Diseases (ICD) publications[3] or the World Intellectual Property Organization's *International Patent Classification.*[4] A special type of classification is a taxonomy, which classifies a specific industry, discipline, group, or subject for a specific purpose, usually without a notation. It uses some sort of hierarchy, or tree structure, to arrange the categories. Think of Carl Linnaeus's taxonomy of biological organisms: kingdom, phylum, class, order, family, genus, species. Organisms are classed into very broad categories (kingdoms) and then arranged hierarchically until very specific categories are reached (species). Taxonomies are commonly used in professional settings such as organizations or businesses to classify resources and to show how they are hierarchically related.

LIBRARY CLASSIFICATION

In everyday life, anything and everything can be categorized and classified, and there are many classification schemes and taxonomies in organizations, industries, disciplines, and other areas of life. In libraries, classification schemes are used to provide subject access to library collections. Library classification is defined as the arranging of knowledge into subject categories, and then building a notational scheme to represent those categories. The library profession has developed several formal library classification schemes, such as the *Library of Congress Classification* and the *Dewey Decimal Classification*, that attempt to organize the knowledge contained in library collections, and each one uses a notational scheme to represent the subjects in it. Notations are like codes or shorthand. They consist of a combination of numbers, letters, symbols, or punctuation marks that represent subjects. For example, the Library of Congress subject heading "Noise pollution" can be represented by a notation, such as "TD892" in the *Library of Congress Classification* or "363.74" in the *Dewey Decimal Classification*. When given the same classification number, all library materials on a subject are brought together for users. Library classification schemes are considered formal because they arrange subjects in a deliberate way and assign specific notations that represent subjects, and much work is done to maintain the scheme regularly.

Libraries classify their collections for two primary reasons. One reason is to provide access to library collections by subject. Classification works together with controlled vocabularies to provide subject access, therefore meeting Charles Cutter's objective of giving subject access through the catalog.[5] They also meet the objectives and functions of a catalog from the *Statement of International Cataloguing Principles*, which states that "the catalogue should be an effective and efficient instrument that enables a user . . . to find a single resource or sets of resources representing . . . all resources on a given thema."[6] The catalog brings together library materials by subject. This allows library users to browse library collections to find similar materials.

Another reason for classification is quite practical. A classification number can be used to organize physical library collections by subject, which is done in the United States. Classification brings subjects and their subtopics together on library shelves. Classification numbers encourage relative book locations, which means that books are not shelved at one fixed location. Newer books are shelved among older books at a classification number, keeping each subject area together. A classification number directs users where to find something in the library. Users do not have to spend hours hunting in the library. Everything is gathered together for the user.

Classification also allows browsing. In open stacks, users can browse the shelves to find what they want. Once a user finds a classification number, they go to that classification number in the library and browse the titles. Browsing can be very effective, because everything has been brought together for users. Users can browse the collection to find what they need.

As the complexity and size of a collection go up, so does the need for classification. A smaller collection may not need to classify as deeply as a very large collection with millions of volumes. A small collection with 1,000 books can classify broadly, or perhaps not even use a formal library classification at all. Users can easily browse the collection. It is a different story for large collections with millions of volumes. It would be impossible to shelve the entire collection alphabetically by author. It would be chaos for the library and for users. Using a formal library classification ensures that the library is organized in a manageable way for users and that users can find materials on specific topics.

Although classification numbers are used to organize libraries, classification numbers are more than just a street address. In fact, classification does not need to be tied to physical shelf organization at all. Libraries in the United States have used classification for shelving purposes, but classification is much more powerful than a shelving scheme. Because classification numbers tend to reflect subjects and forms, classification schemes can exist independently of physical shelf organization. More electronic and digital materials are being collected in libraries, but classification is still useful for these materials. Because classification represents subjects, it can bring together all items in the library on a particular subject, no matter if that item is in a physical or digital format.

LIBRARY CLASSIFICATION: CONSTRUCTION ISSUES

Each classification scheme is constructed differently. Library classification attempts to classify all knowledge, or at least the knowledge that has been published and collected in libraries. This is a big undertaking that leads to many questions, such as: How can a library classification scheme adequately reflect knowledge in a way that will be helpful to all users? How is a classification scheme structured? How does it determine what to name subjects in the classification scheme? How does it deal with issues of language? What type of notational scheme is used? How does a classification scheme incorporate new subjects? The questions for a classification scheme are endless, and there are many construction issues to consider.

Purpose and Structure

Each classification scheme is structured differently and has a different focus. Some classification schemes are general classification schemes that reflect all published knowledge and subjects, such as the *Dewey Decimal Classification* or the *Library of Congress Classification*. Other classification schemes are much more specific and focus on certain subject areas or forms, such as the *National Library of Medicine Classification*'s focus on medicine, and the *Superindentent of Documents Classification*'s focus on US government publications. Classification schemes share similar issues with subject analysis and controlled vocabularies. Each classification scheme has a separate viewpoint, is subjective, and deals with issues of language. A library classification scheme can be thought of as a separate artificial language. Each one is its own system. It develops a vocabulary, chooses subject categories and subcategories, names subjects, and shows specific relationships. A classification scheme may not always reflect a user's categories or subjects.

Notations

All classification schemes use notations. These are numbers, letters, punctuation marks, or symbols that represent the categories in the scheme. Each classification scheme uses different notations. For example, the *Dewey Decimal Classification* uses only Arabic numbers formatted in a certain way, and the *Library of Congress Classification* uses letters and numbers formatted in a certain way. For example, here are two classification numbers for the LC subject heading "Knitting."

Library of Congress Classification: TT820
Dewey Decimal Classification: 746.432

Each notation represents the subject "Knitting," but the notations are very different. It is important to understand how each classification scheme formats its notations and how those notations represent subjects. Some classification schemes try to incorporate mnemonic devices to help users identify certain subjects or forms, as well.

Captions

In addition to notations, each classification scheme includes captions that describe each notation. These are words and phrases that describe each subject or form. Captions for each classification scheme are created independently from any controlled vocabulary. Although classification schemes and controlled vocabularies work together to provide subject access to library collections, captions do not always match. Classification schemes and controlled vocabularies are separate systems that use different words and phrases. For example, take the LC subject heading "Cooking (Vegetables)." In the *Library of Congress Classification*, that subject heading is classified at TX801, but the specific LCC caption is: "Vegetables (Preparation)—General works." The entire hierarchy is "Home economics—Cooking—Vegetables (Preparation)—General works." Both the subject heading and the classification number represent the same thing: cooking vegetables. They are just called by different names.

Hierarchy

Most classification schemes are hierarchical, at least in part, meaning they arrange a classification scheme into categories that logically fit inside one another, showing a hierarchical relationship. A classification starts with very broad categories that are divided into subcategories, which are subdivided again and again until the end of a category is reached. Relationships are hierarchical, focusing on how the categories in each class are related, not necessarily how they relate to other parts of the classification scheme. Notations follow the categories and get more specific further down the hierarchy. Most classification schemes use hierarchy to some degree, and some classification schemes are more hierarchical than others. See below for an example of how the subject "Hounds" is hierarchically classified in the *Dewey Decimal Classification*.

HOUNDS (636.753) IN THE DEWEY DECIMAL CLASSIFICATION

600: Technology
    630: Agriculture
        636: Animal husbandry
            636.1–636.8: Specific kinds of domestic animals
                636.7: Dogs
                    636.72–636.75: Specific breeds and groups of dogs
                        636.75: Sporting dogs, hounds, terriers

636.753: Hounds
636.7532: Gazehounds (Sighthounds)
636.7533: Afghan hound
636.7534: Greyhound
636.7535: Wolfhounds
636.7536: Scent hounds (Tracking hounds)
636.7537: Beagle
636.7538: Dachshund

The top of the hierarchy is "Technology," then "Agriculture," then "Animal husbandry," and then "Dogs" (a specific kind of domestic animal) is subdivided until the category of "Hounds" is reached. Finally, specific hound breeds are listed. The notations follow the hierarchy, becoming more specific and expressive as they go down the hierarchy. The notations start with 600 for "Technology" and end with 636.753 for "Hounds," and there are more specific numbers for each type of hound breed.

Enumerative

Some classification schemes are enumerative. This means a notation (classification number) is assigned to everything in a particular classification scheme, such as subjects, concepts, people, government agencies, and so on. Classification schemes differ in their level of enumeration. For example, the *Library of Congress Classification* is a very enumerative classification scheme because a classification number is added for almost every subject needed in the scheme. It works well with the *Library of Congress Subject Headings*, and there is a corresponding LC classification number for almost every LC subject heading. This is different from the *Dewey Decimal Classification*, which is not quite as enumerative. There are base numbers in the classification for many subjects, but outside tables are used to build numbers that bring out aspects of subjects not already enumerated in the classification scheme.

Faceting

Faceting refers to notations that remain constant across a classification scheme. Facets can represent things like subjects, places, forms, certain aspects of topics—just about anything. Facets are helpful because unlike enumeration, classification numbers do not have to be added for every possible subject. All classification schemes include some sort of faceting, but some schemes use faceting more than others. Tables are usually used to build notations that bring out various facets. For example, the *Dewey Decimal Classification* is not a very enumerative classification scheme, so catalogers use many tables to bring out aspects of subjects. A cataloger classifying a cooking dictionary in *Dewey* would use the base number of 641.5 for "Cooking," and then use a table to add the number "03" meaning "Dictionaries." The built number is 641.503. Building numbers remains relatively constant across *Dewey*, but the instructions at each classification number must allow it.

There is a special type of classification called faceted classification, also known as analytico-synthetic classification, which uses facets to build classification numbers. Instead of having predetermined classification numbers for every subject, faceted notations are put together by the cataloger to reflect or express the subject. S. R. Ranganathan, author of *The Five Laws of Library Science*, developed faceted classification in the 1930s.[7] He created the *Colon Classification*, first published in 1933, which is a faceted classification scheme.[8] There are five facets in the *Colon Classification*: personality, material, energy, space, and time (PMEST), and it uses punctuation marks before the notations to separate the facets. The *Universal Decimal Classification*, published by Paul Otlet and Henri LaFontaine in 1895, is also a faceted classification scheme.

In a faceted classification scheme, each subject, activity, place, and so on in each facet is represented by a notation (e.g., GG6 for "Gardening"). Punctuation marks and symbols separate the facets and are used as indicators or signifiers. Each faceted classification scheme has specific rules about how to put together the notations and punctuation marks. Together, the facets represent each aspect of a subject. Faceted classification is very flexible and can show more things with notations, like relationships and complex subjects. For example, imagine a book is about "the relationship of medicine and art in Medieval Europe." There are several things a cataloger would want to bring out in a classification number. The book is about the *relationship of medicine and art*, it specifically focuses on *Europe*, and the time period is the *Medieval period* (ca. fifth to fifteenth century). See below for the rules in this sample faceted classification scheme.

Notations	Punctuation
Medicine: Y77	To signify a relationship: []
Art: T56	To signify a place: +
Europe: D34	To signify a time period: -
Medieval period: SD11	

Put the notation together following the rules and the classification number is:

Y77 [T56] +D34 -SD11

It reads like this: Medicine's (Y77) relationship to art ([T56]) in Europe (+D34) during the Medieval period (-SD11).

Every faceted classification scheme has specific rules for how to create notations. It would be difficult to bring out all aspects of the subject in the previous example using an enumerative classification system because it is hard to show relationships in such systems. A relationship cannot be brought out in an enumerative scheme unless a classification number for the relationship is already set up in the classification system. In a faceted classification, catalogers would not necessarily have to make that choice; instead, they would follow the rules to create the notation. Faceted classification is helpful because it can show relationships and bring out very complex topics. It is more flexible and can be very expressive with its subjects. Keeping notations constant is helpful so notations are easier to put together and to understand. The classification scheme remains constant no matter the subject. However, the notations can get very long, and it may confuse users who do not understand the system. Faceted classification systems are not used very much in the United States; however, they are popular in other countries.

Hospitality

Hospitality, also called flexibility, refers to how easily a classification scheme welcomes new topics. Knowledge changes constantly, and classification schemes must make room for new subject areas. Some classification schemes handle change better than others.[9] For example, the *Dewey Decimal Classification* uses one thousand base numbers only, not enough to adequately represent all subjects. Sometimes new topics have to be squeezed into the system in artificial ways, and sometimes numbers have to be reassigned. This is different from a large classification scheme like the *Library of Congress Classification*, which can incorporate new subjects much more easily and never has to reuse classification numbers.

Literary Warrant

As discussed in chapter 4, most controlled vocabularies are based on literary warrant, which means that a subject heading is not added or changed until something has been published about it. The creation of a new subject heading is warranted because it has been published in the literature. Literary warrant applies to classification schemes as well. Many classification schemes are based on literary warrant. A classification number will not be created or modified until something has been published on a new topic.

Bias

Like controlled vocabularies, classification schemes also have been accused of bias and may marginalize subjects and people. The major library classification schemes, such as the *Dewey Decimal Classification* and the *Library of Congress Classification*, are general classification schemes created to meet the needs of a wide variety of users, developed in the late 1800s based on nineteenth-century structures of knowledge. They were developed in the United States, are based on Western ways of thinking, and have been criticized for showing an American white, male, East Coast, Christian, heterosexual bias. Decisions have been made about what to include in the classification scheme and what to exclude. If a user does not fit the general user profile, his or her ideas and concepts may be marginalized or left out of the scheme.[10] This issue will be discussed further in chapter 9.

LIBRARY CLASSIFICATION: APPLICATION ISSUES

In addition to construction issues in library classification schemes, there are also application issues. There are different ways to apply each classification scheme and assign classification numbers. It is necessary to learn about the characteristics and construction of classification schemes in order to learn how to assign classification numbers to library materials. Classification schemes include various instructional materials that help catalogers assign classification numbers. However, learning to use a classification scheme can be quite difficult. It may take catalogers much training and experience to understand how to assign classification numbers appropriately.

Predominant Subject

As a part of the subject analysis process, a classification number is usually assigned after subject headings have been added to a bibliographic record. One application issue is that a cataloger needs to assign a classification number that matches the predominant subject of the item. Most libraries use the *Library of Congress Subject Headings*, for example, so a classification number usually needs to match the first LC subject heading assigned to a bibliographic record. Assigning an appropriate classification number is a relatively straightforward process for classification schemes that match subject headings lists. For instance, the *Library of Congress Classification* matches the *Library of Congress Subject Headings*, the *NLM Classification* matches the *Medical Subject Headings*, and the *Dewey Decimal Classification* matches the *Sears List of Subject Headings*. Assigning classification numbers can get complicated if libraries use classification schemes that do not match their subject headings list well, such as using the *Dewey Decimal Classification* and the *Library of Congress Subject Headings*. A cataloger may need to find a classification number that best fits the book but does not necessarily match the first subject heading on the bibliographic record exactly. In addition, because classification is a part of subject analysis, a cataloger may need to go back and forth between subject headings and classification numbers, changing subject headings as needed to best represent the subjects in the book. Subject analysis can be an iterative process, trying to find the best subject headings and classification number for an item.

Choosing One Classification Number

For countries that use classification for shelving, such as the United States, only one classification number can be assigned to books and other library materials. This is problematic because books do not always fit into just one classification number. Library materials could potentially be classified in many areas. There are many books, for example, that discuss multiple topics, relationships, the influence of one subject on another, and so on. Each formal library classification scheme has instructions about how to handle these situations, but catalogers often must exercise cataloger's judgment to determine the best classification number. The classification number picked may not always represent an item well.

Subjectivity

Classification, as a part of the subject analysis process, is subjective. Just like no two catalogers will necessarily choose the same subject headings, no two catalogers will necessarily assign the same classification number. There can be multiple interpretations of the subject, which can make it difficult for catalogers to apply a classification scheme consistently.

Complex Systems

Just like with controlled vocabularies, classification systems can be complex and difficult for users and catalogers to understand. Some classification numbers can get very long and confusing, and a classification scheme may intimidate users. Catalogers must be trained to use the system and understand how the system works. It takes time and experience to apply a classification system appropriately. Users must be familiar with a classification system to find library materials, and catalogers must understand a classification system to assign classification numbers properly.

Instructional Materials

Each classification scheme includes notes, instructions, manuals, or indexes to help catalogers assign classification numbers, and most of them have online databases that include the classification scheme and its instructional materials. Instructions and notes can be built into a classification scheme that direct catalogers about when and how to assign classification numbers or choose among different numbers. Manuals are used to help catalogers in certain situations, to direct them in classifying certain subject areas, how to make a choice between numbers, when and how to apply tables, and so on. Some classification schemes have a separate manual to help catalogers, and some classification schemes also include an index to search captions in the classification scheme. Some classification schemes allow catalogers to search subject headings lists to correlate classification numbers. There may be a separate index or a tool in the classification scheme's online database.

Maintenance

Maintaining classification schemes can be difficult, time consuming, and costly for libraries. To keep up with new knowledge, classifications are updated often, and libraries must keep up with changes. Otherwise, library materials on the same subject are not brought together on library shelves, and they will be scattered at different numbers. This is especially a problem for the *Dewey Decimal Classification* because it reuses numbers. Libraries must reclassify their materials to reflect new numbers, but libraries may not have the time, staff, or money to reclassify materials. This means that items on the same subject could be shelved in different places in the library.

ARRANGING LIBRARY COLLECTIONS

In the United States, classification numbers are used to organize physical library collections, especially book and serial collections. Because of this, catalogers must do more than just add a classification number on an item. A classification number represents a subject or form, but more needs to be done to differentiate each item within a certain classification number. A call number must be added to each physical item in a collection. A call number is the entire notation that is put on an item. It is used to "call" the item. A basic call number consists of:

1. Classification number +
2. Cutter number

Some library classification schemes add work marks or year of publication to call numbers as well. To collocate library materials, a classification number is added that represents the subject. Classification numbers come from a classification scheme, such as the *Dewey Decimal Classification* or the *Library of Congress Classification*. Because many books can be assigned the same classification number, a unique identifier is also assigned to distinguish items from one another. This unique identifier is called a cutter number (also called a book number or suffix), and various tables are used to create them, depending on the classification scheme. The cutter number consists of one letter and one or more numbers that represent the primary access point (formerly called main entry in AACR2), which is usually the author or title of the book; for example, Hoffman = H64. Cutter numbers are named for Charles Cutter, who developed cutter tables in the late nineteenth century to arrange items at each classification number in alphabetical order. Various cutter tables can be used depending on the classification scheme.

In addition to differentiating items within a classification number, books should be shelved alphabetically by author or by title within a classification number. Adding a cutter number keeps alphabetical order within the classes and differentiates items at a classification number. Cutter numbers are not set in stone, however. They can be changed or modified as needed to fit a library's catalog. The cataloger just needs to make sure the items fall in alphabetical order within each classification number. See table 5.1 for an example. Notice how the books are shelved in alphabetical order within the classification number either by the author's last name or by title when there is no author.

Classification is important for electronic/digital library collections, too. Classification numbers represent subjects, and those numbers could be useful to gather materials together in the library catalog and to help users search for subjects. It does not matter if the items are physical or digital. However, although classification numbers are beneficial, cutter numbers are not necessarily needed. Electronic/digital resources

Table 5.1. Call Numbers for LC Subject Heading "Fishing"

Book	DDC Call Number	LCC Call Number
Author: None Title: Gigantic book of fishing stories	799.1 G459	SH441 .G526 2007
Author: Henry Gilbey Title: Adventure fishing	799.1 G466a	SH441 .G53 2003
Author: Henry Gilbey Title: Complete fishing manual	799.1 G466c	SH441 .G535 2011
Author: Sid W. Gordon Title: How to fish from top to bottom	799.1 G6621h	SH441 .G58 1997
Author: Eric Greinke Title: Art of natural fishing	799.1 G8248a	SH441 .G598 2007

do not exist physically, so they do not need cutter numbers to arrange them on library shelves. Some libraries just add classification numbers with no cutter numbers to their electronic book and serial items, because computers can be programmed to sort items alphabetically within classification numbers.

CLASSIFICATION SCHEMES USED IN LIBRARIES

Two of the most widely used classification schemes around the world are the *Dewey Decimal Classification* and the *Universal Decimal Classification*, but not in the United States. In United States libraries, the most-used classification schemes are the *Dewey Decimal Classification*, which is used to classify materials in school, public, and some smaller academic libraries, and the *Library of Congress Classification*, which is used to classify materials in most academic, research, and some public and special libraries. Other classification schemes are used in libraries, too, such as the *Superintendent of Documents Classification*, used to classify federal government documents in some academic, public, and special libraries, and the *NLM Classification*, used in medical libraries. Libraries also use alternatives to formal classification to organize various collections. The major formal classification schemes and some alternatives will be discussed.

DEWEY DECIMAL CLASSIFICATION

The *Dewey Decimal Classification* (DDC) is probably the most well-known and influential classification scheme used in libraries today. It has a wide reach and is used in more than 140 countries and 60 national bibliographies, and there are more than 30 foreign-language translations.[11] In the United States, DDC is used primarily in public libraries, school libraries, and some small academic libraries. It is one of the oldest classification schemes still in use in libraries today, and it is going strong. DDC was created by Melvil Dewey, who started work on the classification in 1873 and published it anonymously in 1876 under the title *A Classification and Subject Index for Cataloguing and Arranging the Books and Pamphlets of a Library*. Dewey's original purpose for the classification was to organize all knowledge, which he divided into ten main classes based on Arabic numbers 0–9. Dewey put his name on the second edition in 1885, and the title was changed to the *Dewey Decimal Classification* with the publication of the fifteenth edition in 1952. *Abridged Dewey Decimal Classification*, an abridged edition meant for libraries under 20,000 volumes, was first published in 1900. A library can choose whether it wants to use the full edition or the abridged edition.

DDC is maintained by the Library of Congress, and the two have a long history together. Even though the Library of Congress does not use DDC to classify its own collection, it recognized that many libraries around the United States use it and that assigning Dewey numbers would help libraries. Dewey's editorial office moved to the Library of Congress in 1923, and in 1930 the Library of Congress started printing Dewey numbers on catalog cards sent to libraries.[12] Today, classifiers in the Dewey Program at the Library of Congress add DDC numbers to bibliographic records and Cataloging in Publication (CIP) information. In the beginning of the twentieth century, Melvil Dewey established his own publishing house, Forest Press, just to publish DDC. In 1988 OCLC purchased Forest Press, and today OCLC publishes the scheme. However, the Library of Congress still has editorial control over the scheme, and Library of Congress and OCLC staff work together at the Dewey Program to maintain the classification. There is also an international Editorial Policy Committee that oversees Dewey and votes on changes suggested by the LC/OCLC editorial team.[13]

The most recent full edition is the twenty-third edition (2011) and the most recent abridged edition is the fifteenth edition (2012), but it has been continually updated since that time on OCLC's WebDewey online subscription database. As of June 2018, OCLC is no longer publishing print versions of either edition in English. Instead, DDC is available primarily through WebDewey, but there is a "Dewey Print-On-Demand option" for libraries that still want a print copy.[14]

DDC Structure and Characteristics

DDC is a general classification scheme based on disciplines, and it covers all subjects within disciplines. It divides knowledge into ten main classes by broad discipline. The ten main classes are broken down hierarchically into a hundred divisions, and then broken down again hierarchically into a thousand sections. Numbers represent subjects in the classification scheme, and captions explain what each number means. See table 5.2 for the ten main classes and examples from the hundred divisions and thousand sections.

Table 5.2.   DDC Main Classes with Examples of Divisions and Sections

Ten Main Classes	Hundred Divisions of 500: Science	Thousand Sections of 520: Astronomy
000 Computer science, information & general works	500 Science	520 Astronomy and allied sciences
100 Philosophy & psychology	510 Mathematics	521 Celestial mechanics
200 Religion	520 Astronomy	522 Techniques, procedures, apparatus, equipment, materials
300 Social sciences	530 Physics	523 Specific celestial bodies and phenomena
400 Language	540 Chemistry	524 [Unassigned]
500 Science	550 Earth sciences & geology	525 Earth (Astronomical geography)
600 Technology	560 Fossils & prehistoric life	526 Mathematical geography
700 Arts & recreation	570 Biology	527 Celestial navigation
800 Literature	580 Plants (Botany)	528 Ephemerides
900 History & geography	590 Animals (Zoology)	529 Chronology

The ten main classes are in the left-hand column. These are then divided into a hundred divisions. The middle column shows the divisions of the main class "Science" (500). The hundred divisions are then broken down into a thousand sections. The right-hand column shows the sections in the division "Astronomy" (520). *Dewey* is limited to a thousand sections. All published knowledge must be made to fit within those sections. Each section is further divided hierarchically, depending on the subject needs of each section. The subjects are broken down hierarchically until the last category is reached. See below for an example of the subject "Chronology."

CHRONOLOGY (529) IN THE DEWEY DECIMAL CLASSIFICATION

500: Science
    520: Astronomy
        529: Chronology
            529.1: Days
            529.2: Intervals of time
            529.3: Calendars
            529.4: Western calendars
            529.5: Calendar reform
            [529.6: Unassigned]
            529.7: Horology

Hierarchy

DDC is a hierarchical system. It starts with very broad categories which are subdivided again and again into very specific categories. The categories fit logically in the system. See below for an example of the subject "Aquarius."

AQUARIUS (133.5276) IN THE DEWEY DECIMAL CLASSIFICATION

100: Philosophy & psychology
    130: Parapsychology & occultism
        133: Specific topics in parapsychology and occultism
            133.5: Astrology
                133.52–133.58: Specific aspects of western
                    astrology
                133.52: Signs of the zodiac
                  133.527: Second six signs
                    133.5276: Aquarius

The classification for "Aquarius" starts with the very broad category "Philosophy & psychology," which is broken down hierarchically again and again until it reaches the specific category "Aquarius." Numbers are added to each category in the hierarchy to show more specificity. The more numbers that are added, the more specific and expressive the classification number.

Broad or Close Classification

A strength of DDC's hierarchy is that it allows for broad or close classification. Broad classification uses only the top numbers of a classification scheme. Close classification goes down to the farthest areas of a classification scheme that are available. Libraries can choose to use the numbers at the top of the hierarchy or go down to the bottom of the classification. This choice depends on the library, its users' needs, and the size of its collection. Please see the previous example, "Aquarius." Depending on the rules of the scheme or the needs of a library, a library could classify broadly and classify a book on "Aquarius" with all other works on "Astrology" at 133.5, or a library could classify very closely and assign 133.5276, which is the most specific number for "Aquarius." Broad classification does not work well for large collections because too many books end up at one broad number. Close classification does not work well for smaller collections because books are shelved near each other but scattered at different classification numbers.

To assist catalogers, the Dewey Program at the Library of Congress uses segmentation marks, such as a forward slash (/) or a prime ('), to tell catalogers where they can cut off numbers. For example, "796.323/63" is the *Dewey* number assigned by the Library of Congress to an item about college basketball. The hierarchy is shown below.

COLLEGE BASKETBALL (796.32363) IN THE DEWEY DECIMAL CLASSIFICATION

700: Arts & recreation
    790: Sports, games & entertainment
        796: Athletic and outdoor sports and games
            796.3: Ball games
                796.32: Inflated ball thrown or hit by hand
                    796.323: Basketball
                        796.3236: Specific types
                            of basketball
                            **796.32363: College
basketball**

The slash tells catalogers that a book on college basketball could be assigned the broader number "796.323" for "Basketball" or "796.32363" for "College basketball," the closest number. Many libraries dictate how many numbers can be added after the decimal point. Some libraries assign the first three numbers only. There is a lot of flexibility when assigning *Dewey* numbers.

Notation

DDC uses Arabic numbers only, and every number is a decimal number. There are no whole numbers in the classification scheme. For example, "Library science" is classified at 020, but it is not the whole number "twenty." The classification is read number by number, so it is "zero two zero." The leading zero is never removed in the 0XX class. A *Dewey* classification number is always formatted with three numbers, and then a decimal point and other numbers are added, if needed. If there are more than three numbers in a classification, there is always a decimal point placed after the third number. Here are some examples:

379.1535	School districts
539.7	Atomic and nuclear physics
641.875	Nonalcoholic beverages

One important thing about DDC is that the decimal point is not really a decimal point. Because every number is a decimal, a decimal point is not needed. Instead, the decimal point is actually a "psychological pause."[15] Take the decimal point out of 379.1535 in the first example above, and the classification number is really 3791535. However, looking at a long string of numbers can be confusing. The decimal point is always added after the third number to help people read and transcribe classification numbers more easily.

Number Building and Tables

Another characteristic of DDC is that classification numbers are built using tables. This is where DDC incorporates some faceting. DDC is not an especially enumerative scheme. It is a rather small classification scheme, in four volumes only, so it does not assign a number to every possible subject that is needed. Instead, external tables are used to expand the scheme, and catalogers use these tables to build numbers when they need them. Specificity is not built into DDC; specificity is added on. Catalogers find a base number and then add numbers from a table to the end of the base number. Dewey uses nine external tables (six main tables and three sub-tables) to add specificity to a classification number.

There are instructions in DDC that explain when and how to add table numbers. The most widely used table is "Table 1: Standard Subdivisions." It includes nine specific subdivisions for specific subjects (e.g., history, education, philosophy) or forms (e.g., dictionaries, encyclopedias) that are common to most subjects across the classification scheme. Each subdivision is divided into more specific numbers. A cataloger can add numbers to make a classification number more specific to the subject of an item. This is especially helpful when an item is about a particular aspect of a subject, a geographic area (called geographic treatment), a specific time period, or a specific form. Here is an example: A book is about all types of fishing in the United States. The LC subject heading is: "Fishing—United States." The DDC base number for "Fishing" is 799.1. Then 09, the number for "History, geographic treatment, biography," is added to indicate that a number will be added for the United States (a geographic treatment). Then 73 is added, which is the number for the United States. The whole DDC number is: 799.10973. There are instructions in the schedules that tell catalogers when they can and cannot add table numbers and how to do it. Catalogers need to follow those directions.

DDC can be used to represent complex subject headings by using tables to add more numbers at the end of a base number. However, those numbers can get outrageously long, especially if the cataloger wants to bring out multiple aspects such as a topical subdivision and a form, or if the base number is already long. As an example, imagine classifying a book about the forest products industry in the United States. The LC subject heading is: "Forest products industry—United States." The DDC base number for "Forest Products" is 338.17498. Then 09 is added to indicate that a number will be added for a geographic area. After that, 73 is added, which is the number for the United States. The whole classification number is: 338.174980973. That is the most specific *Dewey* number for the subject heading, but it is very long. Most libraries would not classify this closely because it may confuse users and would not fit easily on a spine label. Perhaps those libraries would stop at 338.1 for "Agricultural Economics."

Literary Warrant

Today, DDC is based on literary warrant. Classification numbers are not created or changed until something has been published on a subject. Literary warrant was not built into the original classification scheme that Melvil Dewey created, however. Dewey wanted his numbers to remain constant and thought his scheme should not be changed. However, knowledge changes quickly and DDC has had to change the meanings of numbers over the years. For example, the internet and space travel did not exist when Dewey published his system in 1876. Because DDC is based on numbers and has room for only one thousand sections, there is not enough room to keep numbers the same. Therefore, DDC has had to reuse and reassign numbers, and it must use literary warrant to keep up with changes in knowledge.

Assigning DDC Classification Numbers

In the classification process, the DDC number assigned to an item is based on the first subject heading on the bibliographic record. Most libraries use the *Library of Congress Subject Headings*, but DDC does not match LCSH well. A cataloger must assign a DDC number that is as close as possible to the LC subject heading. Sometimes catalogers use the first subject heading and sometimes they have to look at all subject headings to find the best DDC number. Sometimes there may be more than one DDC number that matches a particular subject heading. In these cases, catalogers must determine the appropriate main class and decide where a book should be classified. A book can be classed in different areas depending on the viewpoint. For example, a book about costume jewelry making can take a social customs viewpoint (391.7) or an arts and design viewpoint (739.27). Table 5.3 shows some examples of LC subject headings and DDC numbers. Some LC subject headings and DDC captions match or are pretty close. However, for an LC subject heading like "Identity (Philosophical concept)," the DDC caption matches but the words are not the same. In the case of the LC subject heading "Yoga," there are two places a cataloger could classify a book depending on the content of the book. A cataloger would have to use cataloger's judgment and choose the most appropriate number.

Table 5.3.   Examples of LC Subject Headings Matched to DDC

LC Subject Heading: Fishing	LC Subject Heading: Laundry
DDC number: 799.1 DDC caption: Fishing	DDC number: 648.1 DDC caption: Laundering and related operations
LC Subject Heading: Identity (Philosophical concept)	LC Subject Heading: Yoga
DDC number: 126 DDC caption: The self	DDC number: 204.36 DDC caption: Yoga (under Religious experience, life, practice) OR DDC number: 294.5436 DDC caption: Yoga (under Hinduism)

Manual and Relative Index

DDC includes lots of resources to help catalogers find and assign the best classification numbers. There are many notes listed in the classification schedules and tables that assist catalogers in knowing which classification numbers should be assigned to certain subjects, and when and how table numbers should be added. In addition, DDC includes a manual with instructions about certain numbers and classes. Catalogers must always read the notes and manual to assign appropriate DDC numbers. In addition, there is a relative index that can help catalogers look for certain subjects. The relative index is an index to the captions in DDC. It does not match any existing subject headings list. In addition, the WebDewey online database gives users the ability to search the relative index and DDC captions, as well as the ability to search for specific subject headings from the *Library of Congress Subject Headings*, *Sears List of Subject Headings*, *Medical Subject Headings*, and *BISAC Subject Headings*.

Assigning DDC Call Numbers

There are two parts to a DDC call number: a classification number that brings together items on the same subject and a cutter number (also called a book number) that differentiates each item. Sometimes a work mark is added to the end of a cutter number to represent the title of a book. Work marks are helpful to differentiate items if an author has written more than one book on a subject.

1. DDC classification number
2. Cutter number + work mark

After a cataloger assigns an appropriate DDC number, as previously explained, a cutter number is added to distinguish the book or other item from all other items within that same classification number. This cutter number represents the author or, if there is no author, the title. Libraries can use a wide variety of cutter tables with DDC, such as Cutter's *Two-Figure Author Table*, *Cutter-Sanborn Three-Figure Author Table*, or OCLC's *Dewey Cutter Program*, which expands cutter tables to four figures. Each DDC library uses the list that works best for its collection. A work mark, usually a lowercase letter, may be added at the end of the cutter number to represent the first word of the title. See table 5.4 for examples. Some libraries, however, do not add cutter numbers at all, instead they add the classification number only.

DDC Advantages and Disadvantages

There are many advantages to DDC. The system works best in libraries with very general or popular collections that do not have specialized materials, such as those of public libraries and school libraries. DDC is also very flexible. A library can choose to use the full DDC or the *Abridged Dewey*, and a library can choose to class things broadly or closely. A library can use DDC to meet the needs of the

Table 5.4. Examples of DDC Call Numbers

Author	Title	First LC Subject Heading	DDC Call Number	DDC Call Number Breakdown
Steven Pinker	Enlightenment Now: The Case for Reason, Science, Humanism, and Progress	Progress	303.44 P6553e	303.44 = DDC classification number (Growth and development, under Social change) P6553e = Cutter for Pinker (P6553) + work mark (e) for first word of title (Enlightenment)
Amy Shojai	Complete Kitten Care	Kittens	636.807 S55926c	636.807 = DDC classification number (Kittens) S55926c = Cutter for Shojai (S55926) + work mark (c) for first word of title (Complete)
Richard E. Rubin	Foundations of Library and Information Science	Library science—United States	020.973 R8961f	020.973 = DDC classification number (Information science—United States) R8961f = Cutter for Rubin (R8961) + work mark (f) for first word of title (Foundations)
Daniel Shumski	Will It Skillet?: 53 Irresistible and Unexpected Recipes to Make in a Cast-Iron Skillet	Skillet cooking	641.77 S5626w	641.77 = DDC classification number (Frying and sautéing) S5626w = Cutter for Shumski (S5626) + work mark (w) for first word of title (Will)

library. It is relatively easy to assign DDC numbers, although it can get complicated if a cataloger has to use tables to build numbers. Another advantage of DDC
is that it uses Arabic numbers, so it transcends language. Library users who read
multiple languages and scripts can understand DDC.

DDC also has its disadvantages. It does not work well for libraries with very
large collections or collections that cover many specialized academic disciplines.
DDC does not handle complex subjects easily. Although it is possible to classify
complicated subjects, DDC numbers can become long and unwieldy, which may
be unhelpful for users. Users may find the numbers confusing and have a hard time
finding materials on shelves.

Another disadvantage is that there is little room for growth in DDC, and classification numbers in DDC can change meaning. There are only ten main classes and a
thousand sections, so it has to reuse numbers. There is not enough room to keep pace
with new knowledge and keep numbers the same. In addition, libraries must reclassify their collections if numbers change so that books on the same subject are shelved
together. This can cost libraries time, labor, and money, and a library may not have the
resources to reclassify. Perhaps this is not a major issue for libraries that weed their collections often and do not keep older materials; eventually materials will be withdrawn
from the library. However, it is a problem for those libraries that keep older materials,
like small academic libraries. If an academic library cannot keep up with DDC reclassification, collocation is lost.

Another disadvantage is that DDC does not match the *Library of Congress Subject
Headings* well. LCSH is large and DDC is small, and the language of LCSH does not
match the language of DDC. Finding a DDC classification number based on the first
LC subject heading can be difficult. Often, a cataloger has to find the DDC number
that fits the best, which is not necessarily one that matches the first LC subject heading exactly. In addition, DDC can be confusing for catalogers, especially if numbers
need to be built. DDC is not an especially enumerative scheme, and the system was
designed to be small and flexible. A DDC number can be created to represent complex subject headings, but a cataloger has to use external tables to build numbers.
The responsibility is on the cataloger to build numbers, and it can be difficult to do
this. It takes a lot of time, training, and experience to assign DDC numbers correctly.

One final disadvantage is that like any system of subject analysis, DDC has been
accused of bias and marginalization. It was created based on nineteenth-century
views of knowledge, and although it has been modified over the years to keep up
with new knowledge, it still organizes knowledge in certain ways, and choices are
made about what to include and what to exclude in the system.

LIBRARY OF CONGRESS CLASSIFICATION

Along with the *Dewey Decimal Classification*, the *Library of Congress Classification*
(LCC) scheme is one of the most-used classification schemes in the United States. It
is a general classification scheme based on academic discipline. It is used primarily in

academic, research, and special libraries, but it is used in a few large public libraries, too, such as the Chicago Public Library and the Boston Public Library. LCC is good for general research collections that cover many subject areas. LCC does not work as well for broad or popular collections, such as those found in school and public libraries. LCC also does not work well for very specialized subject collections, such as medicine. LCC is a much larger classification scheme than the *Dewey Decimal Classification*. Instead of ten main classes based on Arabic numbers, LCC is divided into twenty-one disciplines, each represented by a letter of the alphabet (it does not use *I, O, W, X,* or *Y*). Notations of letters and numbers represent subjects in the classification. See table 5.5 for a comparison of the main schedules in LCC and the main classes in DDC.

Table 5.5. Main Schedules in LCC and Main Classes in DDC

Library of Congress Classification *Main Schedules*	Dewey Decimal Classification *Main Classes*
A: General Works	000 Computer Science, Information &
B: Philosophy. Psychology. Religion	General Works
C: Auxiliary Sciences of History	100 Philosophy & Psychology
D: World History and History of Europe,	200 Religion
Asia, Africa, Australia, New Zealand, etc.	300 Social Sciences
E: History of the Americas	400 Language
F: History of the Americas	500 Science
G: Geography. Anthropology. Recreation	600 Technology
H: Social Sciences	700 Arts & Recreation
J: Political Science	800 Literature
K: Law	900 History & Geography
L: Education	
M: Music and Books on Music	
N: Fine Arts	
P: Language and Literature	
Q: Science	
R: Medicine	
S: Agriculture	
T: Technology	
U: Military Science	
V: Naval Science	
Z: Bibliography. Library Science. Information	
Resources (General)	

LCC has a unique history. After Thomas Jefferson sold his personal collection of books to the Library of Congress in 1815, the library used the classification system Jefferson created for his books. The library continued to use Jefferson's classification system, with several modifications, until the late 1890s. By this time the library's collection had grown to more than one million books, and the library needed to move into a new building. Jefferson's classification system was not working well as a classification scheme for the library; the library had simply outgrown it. In 1897 James C. M. Hanson and Charles Martel at the Library of Congress were given the responsibility of creating the new classification scheme for the library. They originally asked Melvil Dewey if they could use the *Dewey Decimal Classification* as the basis for the new scheme, but Dewey said no. He did not want his system modified. Charles Cutter, however, was open to modifications of his *Expansive Classification*, a scheme with alphanumeric notations, so Hanson and Martel based LCC on that, especially borrowing Cutter's use of letters to represent disciplines. In 1899 Hanson created the initial outline for LCC, and he added numbers to the letters to expand the scheme. After two years of debate, the classification scheme began officially in 1901.[16]

LCC is a large classification scheme published in many volumes. Each of the twenty-one main classes is published in one or more separate volumes, each volume called a schedule. LCC was originally published in twenty-eight separate schedules between 1901 ("Classes E–F: America: History and Geography") and 1948 ("Subclass PG: Russian Literature"). An exception is "Class K: Law," which was published in thirteen separate schedules between 1969 ("Subclass KF: Law of the United States") and 2017 ("Subclasses KI–KIL: Law of Indigenous Peoples"). Parts of "Subclass KB: Religious Law" are still under construction.[17] Today, including law, the classification has grown to include forty-one separate schedules, and each schedule is developed and maintained separately by groups of subject experts. Like the *Library of Congress Subject Headings*, the Library of Congress updates LCC monthly, and additions and changes are made primarily by librarians at the Library of Congress and libraries that participate in the Subject Authority Cooperative Program (SACO). Other people can submit suggestions through a proposal form. The Library of Congress is no longer printing the classification on paper, but LCC is available online in free PDF files and through an online subscription database called Classification Web.

Structure and Characteristics

Each schedule in LCC is developed and maintained separately, so there really is no overall structure that is common to all schedules. Each schedule is developed according to the needs of a specific discipline and its subjects, and each schedule includes the classification of subjects and forms in the particular area, with instructions. However, there are some general similarities in the structure of the schedules, and several models are used to develop schedules. For example, general forms, such as periodicals, directories, and dictionaries, are at the top of a discipline, followed by special aspects of the discipline, and then subtopics.[18] See below for an example of "Subclass TX: Home Economics."

ARRANGEMENT OF SUBCLASS TX: HOME ECONOMICS

TX1: Periodicals, societies, etc.
TX5: Congresses
TX6.A1–Z: Exhibitions. Museums
TX7–9: Collected works (nonserial)
TX11: Dictionaries and encyclopedias

TX13: Theory. Philosophy
TX15–19: History and antiquities
TX21–127: Special countries
TX139–140: Biography
TX144–149: General works
TX150: Home accidents and their prevention
TX151–162: Pocketbooks, tables, receipts, etc.
TX164: Home economics as a profession
TX165–286: Study and teaching
TX295: Essays, light literature, fiction, etc.
TX298–299: Household apparatus and utensils
TX301–339: The house
TX340: Clothing
TX341–641: Nutrition. Foods and food supply
TX641.2–840: Cooking
TX851–885: Dining-room service
TX901–946.5: Hospitality industry. Hotels, clubs, restaurants, etc. Food service
TX950–953: Taverns, barrooms, saloons
TX955–985: Building operation and housekeeping
TX1100–1107.4: Mobile home living
TX1110: Recreational vehicle living

The discipline "Home Economics" lists forms at top (e.g., TX1–TX11), then special aspects of the subject (e.g., TX13–TX140), and then subtopics (e.g., TX144–TX1110). However, this is a very general arrangement and does not necessarily apply to each schedule. Each schedule is developed to best represent a discipline and its subjects.

Hierarchy

LCC is a hierarchical scheme that goes from very general categories to very specific categories. Each main class is broken down into subclasses, which are then broken down into different subdivisions. For example, see below for the subclasses in "Class G: Geography. Anthropology. Recreation."

CLASS G: GEOGRAPHY. ANTHROPOLOGY. RECREATION

Subclass G: Geography (General). Atlases. Globes. Maps
Subclass GA: Mathematical geography. Cartography
Subclass GB: Physical geography
Subclass GC: Oceanography
Subclass GE: Environmental sciences
Subclass GF: Human ecology. Anthropogeography
Subclass GN: Anthropology
Subclass GR: Folklore
Subclass GT: Manners and customs (General)
Subclass GV: Recreation. Leisure

The subclasses are further divided into subjects and forms. For example, here is how subclass "GE: Environmental sciences" breaks down hierarchically:

SUBCLASS GE: ENVIRONMENTAL SCIENCES

GE1: Periodicals. Societies. Serials
GE5: Congresses
GE10: Dictionaries. Encyclopedias
GE15: Terminology. Abbreviations. Notation
GE20: Directories
GE25–35: Communication in environmental sciences
GE40–45: Philosophy. Relation to other topics. Methodology
GE50: History
GE55–56: Biography
GE60: Vocational guidance
GE70–90: Environmental education. Study and teaching. Research
GE95–100: Museums. Exhibitions
GE105: General works
GE110: Popular works
GE115: Juvenile works
GE120: Pictorial works
GE123: Handbooks, manuals, etc.
GE125: Public opinion
GE140–160: Environmental conditions. Environmental quality.
          Environmental indicators. Environmental degradation
GE170–190: Environmental policy
GE195–199: Environmentalism. Green movement
GE220–240: Environmental justice
GE300–350: Environmental management

Subject areas are broken down again into separate subtopics with classification numbers that represent specific subjects in that area. For example, here are the classification numbers for "GE195–199: Environmentalism. Green movement":

GE195–199: ENVIRONMENTALISM. GREEN MOVEMENT

GE195: General works
 GE195.5: Juvenile works
 GE195.7: Environmental responsibility
 GE195.9: Women in the environmental movement
GE196: Sustainability. Sustainable living

GE197–199: By region or country
 GE197–198: United States
  GE197: General works
  GE198.A–Z: By region or state, A–Z
 GE199.A–Z: Other regions or countries, A–Z

A children's book about environmentalism with the LC subject heading "Environmentalism—Juvenile literature" would be assigned the classification number GE195.5. A book about sustainable living with the LC subject heading "Sustainable living" would be assigned the classification number GE196.

Notations

LCC notations include both letters and numbers, and sometimes cutter numbers. There can be a single letter or multiple letters (e.g., K, KB, KBM), and numbers are placed after the letters to represent topics. Numbers run from 1–9999, and additional numbers may be added after a decimal point. This allows for much specialization within each discipline and allows for many subjects to be represented. Some classification numbers also include a cutter number that represents specific aspects such as titles, names, geographic areas, languages, and so on. Sometimes catalogers are instructed to add a cutter number from an internal or external table. Together, the combination of letters and numbers, and sometimes also cutter numbers, form a classification number that represents each subject, concept, or form in the scheme. Here are examples of LCC classification numbers.

AM8	Children's museums
E872	General works about Carter's Administration, 1977–1981
GV1469.62.D84	Dungeons and Dragons (the game)
HM1111	Social interaction
KJV112	Encyclopedias about law of France
NK9585	Weather vanes
TR262	Miniature cameras
Z665.2.U6	Library Science in the United States

Enumerative

LCC is a very enumerative scheme. It assigns a classification number to every subject needed in the scheme. It is a large classification scheme that has one classification number per subject, and unlike *Dewey*, catalogers rarely build numbers, and there are no options to classify broadly or closely. Because it is a large scheme, LCC allows for more specialization than DDC. There are more classification numbers and subjects are broken down into more categories. It is more granular; subjects are cut in more ways in LCC than in DDC.

Tables

Tables are used in LCC, but because it is an enumerative scheme, it does not use as many tables as *Dewey*. Each schedule in LCC has external and internal tables that supplement it for certain classification numbers and are used to bring out certain aspects of subjects, such as geographic areas (e.g., countries, states, regions). Instructions about when to use a table are in each schedule, and they are allowed only in certain numbers. Listing every possible number in the schedules would make the classification, already big, unmanageable. LCC uses tables to add specificity to a classification number. In some internal tables, a process called table math is used to configure a number. Classification Web's Enhanced Classification Browser feature has expanded table numbers, so table math is not often needed.

The most common tables are external tables used to add cutter numbers for geographic areas such as countries, states, and regions. There are places in LCC that allow catalogers to specify "By region or country, A–Z" or "By state or region, A–Z." This is usually done when there is a geographic subdivision in an LC subject heading. The cataloger will look at the Regions and Countries Table or the U.S. States and Canadian Provinces Table to assign a cutter number from that table.

For example, imagine cataloging a book about environmentalism in Maine, and the LC subject heading is "Environmentalism—Maine." Looking back at the example "GE195–199: Environmentalism. Green movement" classification, "GE198.A–Z: By region or state, A–Z" fits the book because Maine is a state. The first part of the classification number would be GE198, and then the cataloger is instructed to add a cutter number "By region or state, A–Z," which means finding the table number for Maine on the U.S. States and Canadian Provinces Table. It is .M2. Put them together and the classification number is: GE198.M2.

Here is another example: Imagine cataloging a book about environmentalism in Japan, and the LC subject heading is "Environmentalism—Japan." Looking at the classification example again, "GE199.A–Z: Other regions or countries, A–Z" fits the book because Japan is a country. The first part of the classification number would be GE199, and then the cataloger is instructed to add a number for "Other regions or countries, A–Z." This means regions or countries other than the United States or Canada. Because Japan is outside of the United States, the cataloger would use the Regions and Countries Table. Japan is .J3. Put them together and the classification number is: GE199.J3.

Literary Warrant

Like the *Library of Congress Subject Headings* and *Dewey*, LCC is based on literary warrant. A classification number does not exist until something has been published

s always used literary warrant. It was created to organize the collec-
, of Congress. It was not meant to organize all knowledge, so it relies
...ary warrant for changes. It reflects published knowledge collected in libraries.

Assigning LCC Classification Numbers

Only one LCC number can be assigned to an item, and LCC numbers almost always represent the first subject heading assigned to the item (there are some exceptions,
such as biography). The first subject heading represents the predominant subject. LCC
works with the *Library of Congress Subject Headings*, so an LCC classification number
can be found for most LC subject headings. In the classification process, a cataloger
looks up the first subject heading assigned to the bibliographic record and finds a corresponding LCC number. However, LCC captions do not always match LC subject
headings. LCC uses its own language and its own naming system that is different
from LCSH. See table 5.6 for examples. Notice that the captions are different from
the subject headings. What LCSH calls "Fishing," for example, LCC calls "Angling."

There are times when a cataloger has to choose between numbers depending on
the focus of the book, as shown in the "Yoga" example in table 5.6. Also, there is no
option for broad or close classification like there is in DDC. In DDC, a cataloger can
decide how broadly or closely to classify something. In LCC, a cataloger has to assign
the one number, and there is a classification number for almost every LC subject

Table 5.6. Examples of LCSH and LCC

LC Subject Heading: Fishing—Minnesota	*LC Subject Heading: Laundry*
LCC number: SH511 LCC caption: Angling in special countries—America—United States—Minnesota	LCC number: TT985 LCC caption: Laundry work—General and domestic
LC Subject Heading: Identity (Philosophical concept)	*LC Subject heading: Hatha yoga*
LCC number: BD236 LCC caption: Epistemology. Theory of knowledge—Comparison. Resemblance. Identity	LCC number: BL1238.56.H38 LCC caption: Hatha Yoga (as a religious and spiritual discipline) *OR* LCC number: B132.Y6 LCC caption: Yoga (under philosophy) *OR* LCC number: RA781.7 LCC caption: Hatha yoga (for health purposes) *OR* LCC number: RM727.Y64 LCC caption: Yoga (for therapeutic purposes)

heading. In addition, some classification numbers include cutter numbers that represent subjects, geographic areas, titles, and so on, such as in the "Yoga" example above.

Classification and Shelflisting Manual

There are several instructions that help catalogers assign appropriate LCC numbers. There are notes and information within each schedule that help catalogers know when to assign a number, and sometimes catalogers are conferred to different numbers. There also is a manual called the *Classification and Shelflisting Manual* (CSM) that instructs catalogers how to classify using LCC. The manual includes information about general classification principles as well as how to classify certain subject areas and forms such as biography, literary authors, juvenile materials, comic books and graphic novels, and so on. It is a helpful resource that must be consulted to assign LCC numbers correctly.[19] Each schedule also has an index that describes subjects in that particular schedule. Indexing terms refer to LCC captions, not to LC subject headings. However, Classification Web has a helpful feature called "Bibliographic Correlations" that maps LC classification numbers to LC subject headings, *Dewey* numbers, and *NLM Classification* numbers.

LCC Call Numbers (Shelflisting)

There are three parts to an LCC call number. First, a classification number is found in the LCC scheme. Then, a separate cutter number is added that represents the primary access point on the bibliographic record (author or title). Then, the year of publication is added. An LCC call number looks like this:

1. Classification number +
2. Cutter number +
3. Year of publication

Classification numbers come from the LCC scheme. They match LC subject headings for the most part, and sometimes a classification number includes a cutter number that represents a subject, geographic area, language, title, or name. Those types of cutter numbers are included as part of the classification number.

To create an LCC call number, an additional cutter number is added to differentiate items at the same classification number. These cutter numbers consist of one letter and usually two or more numbers, and they are unique identifiers (e.g., H43). They are added to distinguish items at the same classification number and to put them in alphabetical order. The cutter is always based on the primary access point on the bibliographic record, usually the author's last name or, if there is no author, the title. LCC uses its own cutter tables. There is a general LCC cutter table that is used throughout the classification scheme. There also are cutter tables used in special subject areas such as biography and literature. Instructions about shelflisting are included in the manual.[20] Cutter numbers are expandable, so if there is a classification number with many books, numbers are added to make each book fit alphabetically. After the cutter number, the year of publication is added. Table 5.7 shows some examples.

Table 5.7. Examples of LCC Call Numbers

Author	Title	First LC Subject Heading	LCC Call Number	LCC Call Number Breakdown
Steven Pinker	Enlightenment Now: The Case for Reason, Science, Humanism, and Progress	Progress	HM891 .P56 2018	HM891 = LCC classification number (Progress) .P56 = Cutter for Pinker 2018 = Year of publication
Amy Shojai	Complete Kitten Care	Kittens	SF447 .S476 2002	SF447 = LCC classification number (Cats — Culture and care) .S476 = Cutter for Shojai 2002 = Year of publication
Richard E. Rubin	Foundations of Library and Information Science	Library science— United States	Z665.2.U6 R83 2016	Z665.2 = LCC classification number (Library science by region or country) .U6 = Table number for United States R83 = Cutter for Rubin 2016 = Year of publication
Daniel Shumski	Will It Skillet?: 53 Irresistible and Unexpected Recipes to Make in a Cast-Iron Skillet	Skillet cooking	TX840.S55 S54 2017	TX840.S55 = LCC classification number (Skillet cooking) S54 = Cutter for Shumski 2017 = Year of publication

Advantages and Disadvantages

There are many advantages to LCC. First, it is an excellent classification for general research collections, which is why it is used in most academic libraries in the United States. Because it is a large, enumerative classification scheme, LCC classifies subjects in more depth and better reflects subjects in academic and research library collections. Specificity is built into the LCC scheme. A number is assigned for each subject, and there is no option to classify broadly or closely. This is different from DDC, in which specificity is added on by adding more numbers at the end of classification numbers. This makes LCC numbers easier to read and understand than long DDC numbers. For example, take the "Forest products industry—United States" example from the *Dewey Decimal Classification* section of this chapter. The LC subject heading is "Forest products industry—United States." The most specific DDC number is 338.174980973, a twelve-digit number built using tables. In LCC, the number is HD9755. The LCC number is much shorter and much easier to read. It is easier to classify complicated and intricate subjects in LCC than in DDC.

In addition, LCC is a hospitable classification scheme. By using a combination of letters and numbers, LCC has more room for growth than DDC, which is limited to ten main numbers and has to fit all subjects into a thousand sections. Knowledge changes constantly, so DDC numbers have to be reused, and the meaning of numbers can change. A *Dewey* library has to reclassify its collection or collocation is lost. LCC handles changes in a much better way. LCC is based on twenty-one letters (with five empty letters), and numbers are used to expand the classification scheme. There is much more room for growth. LCC is a much larger scheme and can easily absorb new knowledge. It does not need to reuse classification numbers. If reclassification needs to happen, LCC closes the old classification number, which may never be used again, and a new classification number is added elsewhere. Libraries do not necessarily have to reclassify their collections when numbers change. Libraries can keep the old number, reclassifying as time allows, or simply direct users to the new classification number. Another advantage is that LCC works with the *Library of Congress Subject Headings*. Almost every LC subject heading has a corresponding LCC number. The cataloger just has to find the appropriate classification number for the first subject heading.

There are disadvantages to LCC as well. One disadvantage is that it is a general classification scheme that covers all subjects. It works well for academic and research libraries that cover multiple subjects, but it does not go deeply into some subject areas. For example, although LCC covers medicine in Class R, the National Library of Medicine has created its own classification scheme, the *NLM Classification*, because LCC is not specific enough to describe all subjects in medicine. Another disadvantage is that LCC is a hierarchical scheme based on academic disciplines, so subjects may be split up within the system. For example, yoga from a philosophical viewpoint and yoga from a health viewpoint are classified in different areas. LCC also does not show relationships well, and it is sometimes difficult to bring out multiple aspects of a subject with one classification number.

Literary warrant can be a disadvantage of LCC as well. When cataloging a book on a brand-new subject, a cataloger may have to wait until the Library of Congress creates a subject heading and a classification number. A cataloger could assign a local subject heading, but it may or may not match the official subject heading the Library of Congress will create. Subjects can exist in the world without being in LCC. Also, like LCSH, LCC can be very slow to change. LCC is a very large classification scheme, and changes may take a long time. LC classification numbers follow LC subject headings, so LC classification numbers may be added or changed after LC subject headings change. They are tied together at the Library of Congress.

Like other standards used in subject analysis, LCC is a general classification scheme, so it is prone to certain biases and it can marginalize subjects, concepts, and people that do not fit into the classification system. When it was developed, it reflected late nineteenth-century and early twentieth-century structures of knowledge, and although it has been modified over the years, it still reflects practices and policies of previous years.

NATIONAL LIBRARY OF MEDICINE CLASSIFICATION

The *National Library of Medicine Classification* (*NLM Classification*) is a specific classification scheme focused on medicine and associated subjects. It is maintained by the National Library of Medicine and used by medical libraries. The scheme was created between 1944 and 1948 by a committee at the National Library of Medicine to organize the library's collection. The committee based *NLM Classification* on the *Library of Congress Classification*, and *NLM Classification* uses areas of LCC that are permanently excluded (subclasses QS–QZ and class W). *NLM Classification* can be thought of as an extension of LCC specifically for medicine and associated subjects. Although LCC's Class R is devoted to medicine, it does not go deeply enough to cover subjects in medical library collections. The first edition of the *NLM Classification* was published in 1951 under the title *Army Medical Library Classification*. The title was changed to *National Library of Medicine Classification* with the publication of the second edition in 1956. *NLM Classification* is available online in a searchable database and also in PDF format. It is updated twice a year by the *NLM Classification* editorial team at the National Library of Medicine to reflect changes in the *Medical Subject Headings*.[21]

NLM Classification Structure and Characteristics

The *NLM Classification* is focused solely on medicine and associated subjects. It is a very detailed and focused classification scheme for those areas. It is much more specific and finely grained than LCC, but *NLM Classification* is based on LCC and follows its structure and use of class numbers. *NLM Classification* uses parts of LCC that will never be developed. Broadly, *NLM Classification* covers preclinical sciences in subclasses QS–QZ, and medicine and related subjects in Class W. It also has a separate "19th Century Schedule" that is used to classify materials published between 1801 and 1913. The subclasses are shown below.

NLM CLASSIFICATION OUTLINE

Preclinical Sciences

QS	Human Anatomy
QT	Physiology
QU	Biochemistry. Cell Biology and Genetics
QV	Pharmacology
QW	Microbiology and Immunology
QX	Parasitology
QY	Clinical Laboratory Pathology
QZ	Pathology

Medicine and Related Subjects

W	General Medicine. Health Professions
WA	Public Health
WB	Practice of Medicine
WC	Communicable Diseases
WD	Disorders of Systemic, Metabolic or Environmental Origin, etc.
WE	Musculoskeletal System
WF	Respiratory System
WG	Cardiovascular System
WH	Hemic and Lymphatic Systems
WI	Digestive System
WJ	Urogenital System
WK	Endocrine System
WL	Nervous System
WM	Psychiatry
WN	Radiology. Diagnostic Imaging
WO	Surgery
WP	Gynecology
WQ	Obstetrics
WR	Dermatology
WS	Pediatrics
WT	Geriatrics. Chronic Disease
WU	Dentistry. Oral Surgery
WV	Otolaryngology
WW	Ophthalmology
WX	Hospitals and Other Health Facilities
WY	Nursing
WZ	History of Medicine. Medical Miscellany

Each class in the *NLM Classification* outline is referred to as a schedule, but unlike LCC, each class is not developed separately. The classes share some common structural elements: Reference works are at the top of each class, then general works are listed, then specific topics.

Hierarchy

NLM Classification is a hierarchical scheme that begins with larger categories that are broken down into more specific subjects until the last category is reached. For example, see below for "Subclass WE: Musculoskeletal System."

WE MUSCULOSKELETAL SYSTEM

WE 1–141: Reference Works. General Works
WE 168–190: Orthopedic Procedures
WE 200–259: Bones
WE 300–400: Joint and Connective Tissues
WE 500–600: Muscles and Tendons
WE 700–708: Head and Neck
WE 710–760: Torso
WE 800–886: Extremities

  WE 800: General Extremities
  WE 805–835: Upper Extremity
  WE 850–886: Lower Extremity

WE 890 Podiatry

Subclass WE is divided into several categories that represent specific forms or subtopics. Each category is then subdivided into more categories until the end of the category is reached. See below for specific subjects in the "WE 805–835: Upper Extremity" subject area.

UPPER EXTREMITY

WE 805   Upper extremity
WE 810   Shoulder. Upper arm
WE 812   Axilla
WE 820   Elbow. Forearm
WE 830   Wrist. Hand
WE 832   Hand infections. Hand injuries
WE 833   Hand deformities
WE 835   Fingers

The upper extremity subject area has been broken down into specific subtopics, and notations are used to represent those subtopics.

Notations

NLM Classification uses alphanumeric notations that are similar to LCC. One or two letters represent a subject area in medicine, then numbers are added that represent subtopics or forms in that particular area. If needed, a cutter number is added to bring out geographic areas such as countries, states, and sometimes cities. Table 5.8 includes two examples that show how the notations work.

Table 5.8.   Examples of *NLM Classification* Notations

NLM number: WV 440	NLM number: WG 620

WV = Otolaryngology
    WV 400–440 = Pharyngeal Region
    WV 440 = Cleft lip. Cleft palate
	WG = Cardiovascular System
	    WG 600–700 = Veins. Capillaries
	    WG 620 = Varicose veins

Enumerative

NLM Classification is a very enumerative classification scheme, meaning that it adds a notation for every subject needed in the system. Unlike other classification systems, it uses one table only, called Table G, which is used to add geographic cutters that bring out specific countries, states, and sometimes cities. Table G is used when an item focuses on a particular geographic area.

Used with the Library of Congress Classification

NLM Classification should be used with LCC. *NLM Classification* replaces parts of LCC, such as LCC's Class R (Medicine) and subclasses QM (Human anatomy) and QR (Microbiology). Libraries that use the *NLM Classification* should never use LCC for those particular subjects. However, medical libraries collect materials in other subject areas outside of medicine, such as psychology, veterinary science, anthropology, and sociology. If a particular subject does not fit within the *NLM Classification*, a cataloger should classify the items using LCC because those subjects are outside of the scope of *NLM Classification*. For example, veterinary medicine is classified in LCC at SF, sociological materials at HM–HX, and anthropology at GN.

Assigning NLM Classification Numbers

It takes some time and experience to assign appropriate NLM classification numbers. NLM classification numbers represent medical subjects, and *NLM Classification* matches the *Medical Subject Headings*. Most NLM classification numbers have a corresponding MeSH heading. However, MeSH includes many more subject headings than *NLM Classification* has classification numbers. This is because MeSH is used to index journal articles and other serial publications, so it includes very specific subjects reflected in the biomedical sciences literature. Although *NLM Classification* and MeSH match, the NLM captions and MeSH subject headings are not an exact match. A cataloger can look up subject headings in the index to find the corresponding classification numbers.

To help catalogers, *NLM Classification* has introductory material that explains the classification scheme and includes instructions for assigning classification numbers. There is also an index of MeSH headings mapped to NLM classification numbers, which can help catalogers assign appropriate classification numbers.

Assigning NLM Call Numbers

There are two parts to an NLM call number:

1. Classification number
2. Identifier

Like other classification schemes, an NLM call number is composed of a classification number that represents a subject, taken from the *NLM Classification*, with a number from Table G added, if needed. The NLM classification number represents the subject of the item being cataloged. Then an identifier is added that distinguishes the items at a particular classification number. This ensures that no two items have the same call number. Identifiers can be cutter numbers and/or numerical designations in the case of series/serials. The year of publication is added at the end of the call number. For books, cutter numbers are created that represent the primary access point. This will be the author or, if there is no author, the title. For series, a cutter number represents a series title. The cutter is created using the *Cutter-Sanborn Three-Figure Author Table*, and a work mark for the title is added to differentiate items by the same author within a particular classification. For serials, the particular enumeration will be added depending on the serial: a volume or issue number, year of publication, a supplement number, and/or year of supplement. This will follow the serial designation. Table 5.9 shows two examples of NLM call numbers.

NLM Classification Advantages and Disadvantages

There are some advantages and disadvantages of *NLM Classification*. The biggest advantage is for medical libraries that need to provide subject access to very detailed medical topics. *NLM Classification* matches MeSH well, and they work together to provide finely grained subject access to medical library collections. Because *NLM Classification* is more detailed than LCC, it can give medical library users better access to biomedical information. In addition, because the classification scheme is relatively small, with only one table, assigning classification numbers is fairly straightforward. The index is an advantage as well because it helps catalogers find NLM classification numbers for MeSH headings.

In addition, because the classification is small, there is still a lot of room available for new topics and new numbers. *NLM Classification* is a very hospitable scheme. It was designed with room for growth. New subject headings and concepts

Table 5.9. NLM Call Number Examples

Author	Title	MeSH Subject Heading	Series	NLM Call Number	NLM Call Number Breakdown
J.L. Burton	Essentials of dermatology	Skin Diseases		WR 140 B974e 1990	WR = Dermatology 140 = Skin Diseases (General) B974e = Cutter for Burton (B974) with work mark (e) added for first word of title (Essentials) 1990 = Year of publication
None	The heuristic potential of models of citizenship and immigrant integration reviewed		Journal of immigrant & refugee studies, v. 10, no. 3	W1 JO676CN v.10 no.3 2012	W = General Medicine. Health Professions 1 = Serials. Periodicals JO676CN = Cutter for serial/series title (Journal of immigrant & refugee studies) with a work mark (CN) added to alphabetize title in catalog v.10 no.3 = Serial/Series numbering 2012 = Year of publication

can easily slide into the scheme because lots of room has been added between numbers and there is often room for growth at the end of each class. Although some shifting may be required in some classes, most new concepts can be fitted into the classification scheme easily.

A disadvantage is that since 1994, the National Library of Medicine does not add NLM classification numbers to its books. The responsibility is on individual catalogers in each medical library to add classification numbers when cataloging. In addition, it can be confusing for libraries who have a main collection classified using LCC and a separate medical collection classified using *NLM Classification*. Because medical libraries can classify nonmedical topics, libraries will have to take extra precautions so users understand where items are shelved.

SUPERINTENDENT OF DOCUMENTS CLASSIFICATION

Another classification scheme used in libraries is the *Superintendent of Documents Classification* (SuDocs). The SuDocs classification scheme is used to classify United States government publications, also called government documents or government information, distributed by the Federal Depository Library Program (FDLP). FDLP is a federally mandated program that sends US government publications to participating libraries for free. Although it was mandated in 1968, a version of FDLP has been around since 1813.[22] Currently, about 1,250 public, academic, and special libraries participate in the program, and each library chooses which government publications it would like to receive. Some libraries receive a few publications and some libraries receive many. At least one library in every state is designated a regional depository library, which has the responsibility of keeping almost everything supplied by FDLP. Libraries receive these materials for free, but they are not the property of the library. They remain the property of the US government, and there are many rules and guidelines for acquisition, processing, and withdrawal. Today, many US government publications are being disseminated online, so fewer physical publications are being sent to depository libraries.

The US government is one of the largest publishers in the world, and it produces many publications.[23] The purpose of SuDocs classification is to manage and organize US government publications, and it has a long history. Adelaide R. Hasse created the SuDocs classification in the 1890s to organize the government documents collection at the Los Angeles Public Library. She then took a job in the Public Documents Library at the Government Printing Office in Washington, DC. There was an explosion of materials at the Government Printing Office in the late nineteenth century, and Hasse allowed the Government Printing Office to use her classification scheme to organize the large volume of materials being produced. Hasse's scheme was first published in 1896 in a publication called *List of Publications of the U.S. Department of Agriculture from 1841 to June 30, 1895, Inclusive*. William Leander Post, superintendent of documents from 1906 to 1909, is credited with further development and implementation of SuDocs classification.[24] It was then adopted by libraries around the United States.

SuDocs classification is used by FDLP to classify government publications, both for organizing government document collections and for identification of titles offered through the FDLP program. SuDocs classification has been adopted by many depository libraries around the United States, especially libraries with large collections of physical government documents. However, use of SuDocs classification is optional for most libraries in FDLP. Using SuDocs classification results in a separate government documents collection in a library, so some depository libraries choose to classify government publications using the *Dewey Decimal Classification* or the *Library of Congress Classification* and shelve them in the main collection.

SuDocs Structure and Characteristics

Unlike most library classification schemes, SuDocs classification is not based on disciplines or subjects. Instead, it is based on US government agency. Each department in the executive, legislative, and judicial branches is represented by one or more letters. Each one is considered a parent agency and together they form the main classes of the classification scheme. There are fifty-six main classes in the scheme that represent current US government agencies, shown below.[25]

SUDOCS CLASSES	
A	Agriculture
AE	National Archives and Records Administration
B	Broadcasting Board of Governors
C	Commerce Department
CC	Federal Communications Commission
CR	Civil Rights Commission
D	Defense Department
E	Energy Department
ED	Education Department
EP	Environmental Protection Agency
FA	Fine Arts Commission
FCA	Farm Credit Administration
FHF	Federal Housing Financing Board
FM	Federal Mediation and Conciliation Service
FMC	Federal Maritime Commission
FR	Federal Reserve System Board of Governors
FT	Federal Trade Commission
FTZ	Foreign-Trade Zones Board
GA	Government Accountability Office
GP	Government Printing Office
GS	General Services Administration

HE	Health and Human Services Department
HH	Housing and Urban Development Department
HS	Homeland Security
I	Interior Department
IC	Interstate Commerce Commission
ID	US Agency for International Development
ITC	International Trade Commission
J	Justice Department
JU	Judiciary
L	Labor Department
LC	Library of Congress
LR	National Labor Relations Board
MS	Merit Systems Protection Board
NAS	National Aeronautics and Space Administration
NC	National Capital Planning Commission
NCU	National Credit Union Administration
NF	National Foundation on the Arts and the Humanities
NMB	National Mediation Board
NS	National Science Foundation
OP	Overseas Private Investment Corporation
P	United States Postal Service
PE	Peace Corps
PM	Personnel Management Office
PR	President of the United States
PREX	Executive Office of the President
PRVP	Vice President of the United States
RR	Railroad Retirement Board
S	State Department
SBA	Small Business Administration
SE	Securities and Exchange Commission
SI	Smithsonian Institution
SSA	Social Security Administration
T	Treasury Department
TD	Transportation Department
TDA	US Trade and Development Agency
VA	Veterans Affairs Department
X	Congress
Y	Congress

Structuring the classification scheme by agency is beneficial for government publications because they are usually serial publications, such as periodicals, annual reports, numbered series, handbooks, bulletins, and so on. Government publications are not necessarily credited to an individual author who created the document; instead, they are issued by the government agencies that are responsible for their creation.

Although individual people work on government documents, government agencies issue them and are given credit for them. This makes government publications unique and challenging to catalog and classify.

Hierarchy and Notation

SuDocs classification is a hierarchical system that uses alphanumeric notations to represent current government agencies and their subordinate bodies. Each main class uses one or more letters to represent a parent agency. Then, each main class is subdivided hierarchically by subordinate bodies, such as bureaus, offices, and so on. Usually there are just two levels of hierarchy (parent agency and subordinate body), but some classes, like the Department of Defense, are divided into three or four levels of hierarchy. Subordinate bodies are represented by whole numbers. The number 1 or 2 is always assigned to the parent agency, and subordinate bodies are assigned a whole number after that. For an example, see the chart below, which shows the Smithsonian Institution and its subordinate bodies as of 2015.

SUBORDINATE BODIES OF THE SMITHSONIAN INSTITUTION

SI 1	Smithsonian Institution
SI 3	National Museum of American History/National Museum of Natural History
SI 6	National Museum of American Art
SI 7	Freer Gallery of Art
SI 8	National Gallery of Art
SI 9	National Air and Space Museum
SI 11	National Portrait Gallery
SI 13	Hirshhorn Museum and Sculpture Garden
SI 14	National Museum of African Art
SI 15	National Museum of the American Indian

Notice that the parent agency, Smithsonian Institution, is assigned SI 1 and then each of its subordinate bodies is assigned a separate number after it. For example, SI 8 is the classification number for the National Gallery of Art.

Then, each parent agency and subordinate body is broken down by publication form or title. Publications issued by each parent body and each subordinate body are assigned a number that represents the form or title of publication. A period (not a decimal) is added between the agency designation number and the publication number. Sometimes slashes and additional numbers are added to expand publication numbers in order to fit in more publications. Combined, the letters and numbers represent parent agencies and subordinate bodies, and the numbers that represent publications are called class stems. For example, here are the class stems for the National Gallery of Art:

SI 8: NATIONAL GALLERY OF ART

SI 8.2:	General Publications
SI 8.8:	Handbooks, Manuals, Guides
SI 8.10:	Posters
SI 8.11:	Film Calendar
SI 8.11/2:	Calendar
SI 8.15:	NGA Classroom: for Teachers and Students
SI 8.16:	NGA Loan Materials Finder

For example, look at class stem SI 8.11. SI 8 represents the Smithsonian Institution's National Gallery of Art. The number 11 represents the Film Calendar. Each Film Calendar published by the National Gallery of Art is assigned the class stem of SI 8.11.

The structure is fairly consistent across the classes. Each parent agency and subordinate body has different publications, so numbers are added that represent each publication form or title that is needed for each particular area. See table 5.10 for more examples of class stems from SuDocs classification. Each parent agency is represented by one or more letters, then a whole number is added that represents a subordinate body, a period is added, and then each publication is represented by a number, with or without a slash. For example, look at A 17.1 in the top left corner of table 5.10. The Agriculture Department is represented by A; A 17 is the National Agricultural Library of the Agriculture Department; A 17.1 is used for annual reports from the National Agricultural Library of the Agriculture Department.

Table 5.10. SuDocs Class Stem Examples

A 17.1	*L 2.121/54*

A = Agriculture Department
    17 = National Agricultural Library
        .1 = Annual Report
	L = Labor Department
	    2 = Labor Statistics Bureau
	        .121/54 = Area Wage Surveys Selected
	                    Metropolitan Areas

L 2.71	*TD 2.19*

L = Labor Department
    2 = Labor Statistics Bureau
        .71 = BLS Reports
	TD = Transportation Department
	    2 = Federal Highway Administration
	        .19 = Public Roads (serial)

Common Forms

Some numbers have been assigned to common publication forms and titles that are used across the scheme, such as annual reports, circulars, handbooks, posters, and so on. See table 5.11 for common forms. For example, whenever .1 is in a class stem, it refers to an annual report of the agency or body. When a .3 is in a class stem, it means bulletins from that agency or body. For example:

P 1.1: Annual report of the United States Postal Service
LC 14.1: Annual report of the Congressional Research Service of the Library
   of Congress
GS 1.1: Annual accountability report of the General Services Administration

It is worth noting that there are exceptions across the scheme, and some numbers are
more consistent than others.

Table 5.11.   Common Forms and Their SuDocs Numbers

SuDocs Common Numbers: Used Often	*SuDocs Common Numbers: Used as Needed*
.1 Annual reports	.5 Laws
.2 General publications	.6 Regulations, rules, and instructions
.3 Bulletins	.7 Press releases
.4 Circulars	.8 Handbooks, manuals, and guides
	.9 Bibliographies and lists of publications
	.10 Directories
	.11 Maps and charts
	.12 Posters
	.13 Forms
	.14 Addresses

SuDocs Call Numbers

There are two parts to a SuDocs call number that work together to bring together
all of the publications from an agency and also to differentiate each item within class
stems. They are:

Class stem: Suffix

They are also called: First figure: Second figure. The class stem is taken from the
SuDocs classification scheme. The class stem represents publication forms and titles
issued by US government departments, agencies, bureaus, and divisions. Using a
consistent class stem ensures that all publication forms and titles issued by a parent
agency or subordinate body are classified together. After the class stem, a suffix, also
called a book number, is added that represents a particular item. A suffix differentiates all items in a given class stem. A colon is added after the class stem to separate
the class stem from the suffix.

Suffixes can be many things depending on the publication. For serial publications,
the suffix reflects the numbering system of the publication. If a serial publication is
published annually, then the year will be used as the suffix. If a serial publication

Table 5.12. SuDocs Suffix Examples

A 17.1: 1998	L 2.121/54: 1990

A = Agriculture Department
    17 = National Agricultural Library
        .1 = Annual Report
            1998 = 1998 Annual Report
	L = Labor Department
	    2 = Labor Statistics Bureau
	        .121/54 = Area Wage Surveys Selected
	            Metropolitan Areas
	                1990 = 1990 Survey

L 2.71: 999	**TD 2.19: 64/3**

L = Labor Department
    2 = Labor Statistics Bureau
        .71 = BLS Reports
            999 = Report no. 999
	TD = Transportation Department
	    2 = Federal Highway Administration
	        .19 = Public Roads (serial)
	            64/3 = Vol. 64, no. 3

has volume and issue numbers, then volume and issue numbers will be used as the suffix. If a serial publication has numbers only, then only a number will be used as the suffix. SuDocs suffixes use whatever designation the serial publication uses. This allows each serial publication to be shelved in order of publication. See the examples in table 5.12. In these examples, the class stem is listed before the colon, and the suffix is listed after the colon. Each suffix represents a serial designation, such as a year, report number, or volume and issue number.

If a publication is a monograph published one time, like a book or other item, then a cutter number is added as the suffix. Cutter numbers are commonly added for suffixes, especially for general publications. The cutter number is created using Cutter's *Two-Figure Author Table* or the *Cutter-Sanborn Three-Figure Author Table*. However, instead of representing the last name of the author or the first word of the title, a SuDocs cutter number represents the first significant word in the title. This word may be a subject, geographic location, state, or the like. It is up to the interpretation of the cataloger. See examples in table 5.13. In these examples, each cutter number has been created based on the first significant word in the title.

Table 5.13. Cutter Numbers Added as Suffixes in SuDocs Call Numbers

LC 1. 2:W 55	SI 13.2:R 27

LC = Library of Congress
    1 = Library of Congress (parent)
        .2 = General Publications
            W 55 = And God Created Great **Whales**:
                Whales and Whaling in the
                Manuscript Collections of the
                Library of Congress by John J.
                McDonough
	SI = Smithsonian Institution
	    13 = Hirshhorn Museum and
	        Sculpture Garden
	            .2 = General Publications
	                R 27 = **Relief** Sculpture:
	                    Selections from the
	                    Museum's Collection

SuDocs Advantages and Disadvantages

There many advantages and disadvantages to using SuDocs classification. One advantage is that it brings together publications from US government agencies. Library users often look for specific publications from particular agencies, and using the SuDocs classification means that the publications are gathered together for users. SuDocs classification is also easy to learn and to understand. SuDocs is based on agency, not subject, so it does not have any issues related to subject analysis. Catalogers do not have to perform complicated subject analysis to assign SuDocs classification numbers. There are no problems with language use, determining subjects, or bias. In fact, there is little to no subjectivity when assigning SuDocs classification numbers. The classification is based simply on agency and publication forms and titles.

Another advantage is that it helps organize and maintain physical government publications collections. The US government is one of the largest publishers in the world, so a depository library can get many publications. SuDocs classification enables libraries to easily organize government publications collections for use. SuDocs also helps with the maintenance and preservation of a physical government publications collection. Government publications include many formats not typically collected by libraries, such as pamphlets, posters, and notices, and government publications are rarely sent to libraries with a hard cover or other sort of binding. Libraries can keep all items together without having to bind them individually or perform preservation to keep them from being destroyed on the shelves. Using the SuDocs classification keeps the collection separate and helps government publications staff maintain it.

SuDocs classification is not beneficial only for physical collections. Many government publications are going online, and fewer print materials are being sent to depository libraries. Yet libraries still add bibliographic records in their catalog for electronic materials, and SuDocs class stems (no suffix) are still being applied to electronic government publications. Including SuDocs class stems is helpful so collections are organized and users can find particular publications. Using the SuDocs classification ensures that both the paper version and the electronic version of a title are brought together in the library catalog.

There are disadvantages, too. One disadvantage of using SuDocs classification is that it is not based on subject. There is no intellectual work that goes into creating a classification number; it is based simply on agency and publication forms and titles. Another disadvantage is that using SuDocs classification creates a separate government publications collection that is shelved separately from library materials classified by subject. Library items are not brought together on library shelves, and subjects are split up in the library. If a user is looking for information about climate change, for example, he or she will have to look in two places: the library's main collection and the government publications collection. Splitting the collection means that users may not find everything on a subject. It is important for a library to advertise the SuDocs collection and make sure users know to check both collections. However, with government publications becoming increasingly available online only, this may become less of an issue for some libraries.

OTHER LIBRARY CLASSIFICATION SCHEMES

Most libraries in the United States use at least one formal library classification scheme, such as the *Dewey Decimal Classification* or the *Library of Congress Classification*. However, there are other library classification schemes used in libraries. A few examples will be discussed.

Universal Decimal Classification

Created in 1895 in Belgium by Paul Otlet and Henri LaFontaine, the *Universal Decimal Classification* is a general classification scheme that seeks to cover all knowledge. It is not used in many libraries in the United States, but it is a popular classification scheme around the world, used in more than 130 countries. It is based on DDC, and similarly divides main disciplines hierarchically using numbers. Yet it is also a faceted classification scheme that uses symbols, punctuation marks, and letters to make notations describe subjects more expressively. It is maintained by the Universal Decimal Consortium.[26]

US State Depository Classification Schemes

Some US states have created their own classification schemes to organize state government publications. State classification schemes are usually used in state depository programs, which send state publications to libraries in a state. The SuDocs classification serves as a model for these classification schemes, and they are structured in a similar way. Classifications are based on state agencies and represent publications from each state agency. There may be differences in formatting of the class stem and suffix. For example, the state of Oregon offers the Oregon Documents Depository Program, run by the Oregon State Library, that sends Oregon state publications to seven academic and public libraries in the state. It has its own classification scheme called the Oregon Documents Classification System (OrDocs).[27] Other states have similar state classification schemes, such as the Texas Documents Classification Scheme (TXDOC),[28] and the California State Agency Classification System (CALDOC).[29]

Subject-Specific Classification Schemes

There are many specialized library collections that utilize very specific classification schemes developed for particular collections. For example, the *Brian Deer Classification System* was developed in the 1970s by Brian Deer for the library of the National Indian Brotherhood (now called Assembly of First Nations). It is a system that uses letters to represent indigenous knowledge and subjects. Modified versions of the scheme are used in several First Nations libraries and indigenous culture libraries in Canada, such as the *X̱wi7x̱wa Classification System*, used at the X̱wi7x̱wa Library at the University of British Columbia.[30]

Another example comes from theological libraries. Some theological libraries use LCC, but some theological libraries may use special classification schemes. For example, some theological libraries may still use the *Classification of the Library of Union Theological Seminary*, developed by Julia Pettee in the early twentieth century.[31] The *Marianist Library Classification* is used in Marianist libraries, which have collections about the Catholic Society of Mary.[32] Judaica libraries can use the *Weine Classification Scheme and Relative Index*.[33]

ALTERNATIVE LIBRARY CLASSIFICATION

While most libraries use a formal classification scheme, like the *Dewey Decimal Classification* or the *Library of Congress Classification*, to classify a library's main collection, many libraries classify parts of their collections in alternative ways outside of these formal library classification schemes. Most libraries use alternatives to formal library classification to help users, to organize collections, to maximize space, to control for theft, and to help maintain collections. Alternatives are usually used to organize physical library collections, but they also can be utilized for electronic collections. There are numerous types of alternative classification used in libraries, too many to cover in one chapter. A few examples will be discussed, but it is important to understand that each library determines its own alternative classification systems.

Accession Numbers

The first alternative is accession numbers. Accession numbers are simply numbers assigned to library materials in the order they are received. They are added to bibliographic records in the library catalog and also used as call numbers; for example: 82, 83, 84, 85. An accession number may include a year, format, location, or any sort of designation that is meaningful to a library. There are numerous ways that accession numbers can be formatted. Please see table 5.14 for some examples.

Accession numbers are helpful to use in certain circumstances. For example, some libraries use them for items in closed stacks, collections that users cannot access on their own. Because users cannot browse closed stacks, library items do not need to be grouped by subject. Accession numbers are also helpful for collections of media, such as audio recordings and video, that are shelved in separate areas. A library could assign accession numbers to CDs or DVDs, for example. Accession numbers also

Table 5.14.   Examples of Accession Numbers

Accession Number	Accession Number with Year	Accession Number with Location	Accession Number with Format
82	2019-60078	RARE A0273	DVD-BLU 223
83	2019-60079	RARE A0274	DVD-BLU 224
84	2019-60080	RARE A0275	DVD-BLU 225
85	2019-60081	RARE A0276	DVD-BLU 226

are helpful for unique items that are not easily classified using a formal classification scheme, such as collections of kitchen items, musical instruments, computer equipment, and so on. Using accession numbers can provide an easy way to locate these materials. The disadvantage of using accession numbers is that items are not arranged by subject or genre, so items are not collocated with other items in the library.

Homegrown Schemes

Some libraries have created homegrown classification schemes. Created by a library, a homegrown scheme can be a more formal classification scheme that organizes a collection in a deliberate way using notations, or it can be more "informal" in nature, using dates, cutters, locations, and/or whole words. Many libraries use homegrown classification schemes to classify various formats, genres, forms, special collections, and children's collections. Homegrown schemes are helpful when a formal library classification scheme does not work well. For example, theses and dissertations written by students at a university are usually assigned a homegrown classification number. Each university does this differently. An example is using a publication year and a cutter number for the last name, such as: 2019 F34.

Fiction in Public and School Libraries

Instead of classifying fiction using *Dewey*, most public and school libraries shelve their fiction in alphabetical order by last name of the author and/or by genre (e.g., mystery, romance). This includes books, large-print books, and audiobooks. These are homegrown schemes; shown below are many examples of homegrown classifications of Gillian Flynn's novel *Gone Girl*. They would be printed on the spine of the book and included in the library catalog.

HOMEGROWN CLASSIFICATIONS OF GONE GIRL

F FLYNN	F FLY	FIC FLYNN
FICTION FLYNN	FICTION FLYNN G	FICTION FLYNN GILLIAN
SUSPENSE FLYNN	MYSTERY FLYNN	FICTION FLYNN
LGE-TYPE FIC FLYNN	LP FICTION FLYNN	LP MYSTERY FLYNN
CD FLYNN	CDBK FLYNN	AUDIO FLYNN G
BKSCD FICTION FLYNN G	CD BOOK FICTION FLYNN, GILLIAN	

The classifications are all variations on a theme, but each library has its own system. This type of classification works well in school and public libraries because it is easier for users to understand and use this system. In Dewey, fiction is classified by language, then genre, and then the time period when it was originally published.

Gone Girl would be classified at: 813.6, for American fiction in English from the year 2000 to the present, and then cuttered for author's last name. Users do not necessarily think in those categories. Formal library classification can be confusing for users who want to quickly find books and other items.

Some public and school libraries "genrefy" their fiction collections by arranging fiction into genre categories created by librarians, then shelving books within each genre alphabetically by author.[34] Because users ask for genres, this is a helpful way to organize fiction collections. There are some issues, however, because although books often fit into multiple genres, only one call number can be printed on a book. A librarian has to decide which genre to choose. Also, some authors write in multiple genres, so their books would be split up on the shelves instead of sitting together in alphabetical order by their last name.

Bookstore Models

Some public libraries are incorporating bookstore models to improve the user experience, especially when browsing nonfiction collections. Some libraries have stopped classifying their nonfiction collections using DDC and instead arrange books using a bookstore model with broad subject categories. In this model, library spaces are designed with low shelving, comfortable seating, and other improvements to the browsing experience, like a bookstore. This is referred to as going "Dewey-less."[35] Think of a bookstore model as extending a public library's homegrown fiction classification to its nonfiction collection. Libraries can create their own homegrown categories to classify the collection, but a popular way is using the *BISAC Subject Headings*, which was mentioned in chapter 4.[36] This is a list of subject headings and codes used in the book industry to exchange subject information about books; for example: "HEALTH & FITNESS / Children's Health"; "PETS / Fish & Aquariums"; "TRAVEL / Mexico." There are fifty-three broad BISAC categories, shown below.

BISAC CATEGORIES

ANTIQUES & COLLECTIBLES	LAW
ARCHITECTURE	LITERARY COLLECTIONS
ART	LITERARY CRITICISM
BIBLES	MATHEMATICS
BIOGRAPHY & AUTOBIOGRAPHY	MEDICAL
BODY, MIND & SPIRIT	MUSIC
BUSINESS & ECONOMICS	NATURE
COMICS & GRAPHIC NOVELS	PERFORMING ARTS
COMPUTERS	PETS
COOKING	PHILOSOPHY
CRAFTS & HOBBIES	PHOTOGRAPHY

DESIGN	POETRY
DRAMA	POLITICAL SCIENCE
EDUCATION	PSYCHOLOGY
FAMILY & RELATIONSHIPS	REFERENCE
FICTION	RELIGION
FOREIGN LANGUAGE STUDY	SCIENCE
GAMES & ACTIVITIES	SELF-HELP
GARDENING	SOCIAL SCIENCE
HEALTH & FITNESS	SPORTS & RECREATION
HISTORY	STUDY AIDS
HOUSE & HOME	TECHNOLOGY & ENGINEERING
HUMOR	TRANSPORTATION
JUVENILE FICTION	TRAVEL
JUVENILE NONFICTION	TRUE CRIME
LANGUAGE ARTS & DISCIPLINES	YOUNG ADULT FICTION
	YOUNG ADULT NONFICTION

When BISAC categories are used as call numbers, whole words are used, and many libraries modify BISAC category names. For example, a book about knitting could be assigned the call number "CRAFT TEXTILES." A book about dog training could be assigned the call number "PETS DOG." A children's book about baseball could be assigned the call number "SPORTS BASEBALL JUVENILE." Every book on a particular subject will have the same call number. All books about cats as pets, for example, will have a call number like "PETS CAT." No attempt is made to add cutter numbers that differentiate each book within a particular subject.

In 2007 the Perry Branch Library of the Maricopa County Library District in Arizona was the first library to switch to a modified BISAC. Several other libraries have since followed suit, including the Frankfort Public Library District in Illinois, which switched from Dewey to a homegrown scheme based on the Maricopa County scheme and BISAC codes.[37] An advantage of using BISAC categories is that it helps users browse library collections and find books on topics, and libraries using it report that circulation numbers have gone up. Using words as call numbers may make it easier for users to find materials. Dewey numbers can be long and confusing, and may scare off users, especially those users who want to find materials on their own. A disadvantage, however, is that BISAC categories use English words, which may be a barrier for non-English speakers. In addition, it may be difficult for users to search for specific titles, especially in large collections with many books at the same classification number. A bookstore model may work better for smaller collections in which users browse fewer items. For larger collections, users may get lost in a sea of books with the same call number. In addition, the *BISAC Subject Headings* was created for the book industry to sell and market books, not to help library users find materials. It is not a classification system based on the intellectual work of dividing the world of knowledge into categories and subcategories. DDC, for example, is a very powerful classification scheme, and libraries that move away from it lose that power.

Yet not all libraries who adopt a bookstore model use BISAC categories. Some libraries keep DDC numbers but group their nonfiction collection into broad categories called neighborhoods, glades, or collections. In DDC, subjects can be dispersed in different areas, for example costume jewelry is at 745.5942 (art perspective: crafting jewelry) or 688.2 (technology perspective: manufacturing costume jewelry). Arranging the nonfiction collection into neighborhoods brings together all books on a subject no matter the DDC number. In surveying their users, these libraries found that some users feel DDC is confusing and intimidating. They argue that using a bookstore model improves circulation and helps users find library materials in familiar ways, like going to their local bookstore.[38] This system can be beneficial because it blends a bookstore model and library classification, providing the benefits of both.

Moving Images

Moving images—such as movies, television programs, documentaries, filmed events, educational programs, and so on—are routinely classified in alternative ways in all types of libraries. For example, there are DDC classification numbers at 791.43 for movies and 791.45 for television programs. A library could choose to use these numbers and cutter them for the title of the movie or program. However, many libraries use a homegrown scheme, very similar to those for fiction, that include a title or part of the title and/or the format. The system depends on the library and the needs of its users. See examples in table 5.15.

Table 5.15.   Classification of the Movie *Gone Girl*

Public Libraries	Academic Libraries
DVD GONE GI	DVD 2561
DVD GONE	DVD 15954
DVD GONE GIRL	DVD GONE GIRL
BLURAY GONE GI	PN1997.2 .G66 2015
GONEGIRL	PS3606.L935 G66 2015
BLURAY GONE GIRL	
BLU GONE	
DVD 791.43 G525W	

The examples in the left-hand column show a variety of ways that public libraries have classified *Gone Girl*, including homegrown schemes or DDC numbers. Each library has its own system. The examples in the right-hand column show that academic libraries use various methods, such as homegrown schemes, accession numbers, or formal LC classification numbers. It depends on the library. Accession numbers and homegrown schemes are useful, especially for large video collections. It may be difficult to manage and shelve collections using formal classification numbers. Using accession numbers or a homegrown scheme may be easier to understand and use.

Audio Recordings

Audio recordings include music, spoken-word recordings, sounds, audiobooks, and the like, and they are usually classified in alternative ways in libraries. Some libraries assign formal classification numbers to music, but most often alternative classification is used. Audio recording collections in libraries can be very large so using a formal classification number can be confusing for users, time consuming for catalogers to assign, and difficult to shelve. In public libraries, audiobooks are usually classified following each library's homegrown scheme for fiction. For music, public libraries may be classifying their collections in the *Dewey* 780s for musical form, instruments, voices, and the like. More often than not, music is classified using homegrown schemes that may include genre, name of artist, title or partial title of album, cutter number, or year. For examples, see table 5.16.

Table 5.16.   Classification of Beyoncé's *Lemonade* Album

Public Libraries	Academic Libraries
ROCK & POPULAR / BEYONCE / LEMONADE	COMPACT DISC MU 54797
POP/ROCK BEYONCÉ	BEYO
CD/R&B BEYONC 2016	LPCD 153,376-153,377
CD R&B B5735L	CDA 30020
CD 782.62 BEYONCE	M1630.18.B49 L46 2016

The left-hand column of table 5.16 shows how some public libraries have classified Beyoncé's *Lemonade* album. Each public library has a different system. Examples of how academic libraries have classified Beyoncé's *Lemonade* album are in the right-hand column. Audio recordings of music can be classified using LCC Class M (Music) following the numbers for scores, and some academic libraries classify their music using formal LCC numbers. Many academic libraries use homegrown schemes for large music collections, which may or may not be accessible directly to users. Instead, some academic libraries use accession numbers or a homegrown classification scheme. Publisher's numbers also may be used. Each academic library has a different system.

Children's Collections

Children's collections are organized in many ways in libraries. Some academic libraries have children's collections, usually in support of higher education programs in education, library and information science, and reading. Academic libraries tend to classify children's fiction in LCC Class PZ (Fiction and Juvenile Belles Lettres) and children's nonfiction in other classes by subject.

The organization of children's collections in elementary school libraries and public libraries, however, can vary quite a bit. Children's ages and reading levels are very important for children's collections in these libraries. Children need to read books at an appropriate reading level, grade level, or age level. Elementary school libraries and public libraries do many things to help children, parents, and teachers find appropriate books. For children's fiction, many libraries shelve their children's books by title or series, and some libraries use stickers or colored dots to indicate genre, age range, reading level, and so on. Many libraries label some books as "E" books, which stands for "Everybody" or the outdated term "Easy." This is a designation for children's fiction intended for children age eight and younger, or in grade 3 and lower. In some libraries, the "E" designation applies to nonfiction as well, such as alphabet books.

For children's nonfiction, many school and public libraries use DDC, but some libraries are going "Dewey-less" and using a bookstore model to organize their children's nonfiction collections into specific subject categories just for kids. As previously discussed with adult fiction, some libraries organize their nonfiction children's collections by broad subject categories, such as BISAC, a modified BISAC, or a homegrown scheme. Some libraries keep the *Dewey* numbers, but arrange the classification numbers into broad neighborhoods for kids. Some libraries are genrefying their nonfiction children's collections using kid-friendly categories instead of *Dewey*.[39] Other libraries organize by reading level—such as *Accelerated Reader* or *Reading Counts!*—instead of *Dewey*.[40] There are many ways to classify children's collections, and each library has its own system.

An alternative classification scheme for elementary school libraries is the *Metis Library Classification for Children*.[41] It is a more formal classification scheme developed in 2011 by school librarians at the Ethical Culture School in New York City. They wanted to help kids search for library materials in a way kids understand. *Metis* uses twenty-six categories based on letters in the alphabet. Each category is then broken down into specific subtopics, shown below.

METIS CLASSIFICATION

A.	Facts/Concepts	O.	Traditions
B.	Machines	P.	Tales
C.	Science	Q.	Verse
D.	Nature	R.	Humor
E.	Animals	S.	Mystery
F.	Pets	T.	Adventure
G.	MakingStuff	U.	Scary
H.	Arts	V.	Graphic Novel
I.	Sports	W.	Memoir
J.	Ourselves	X.	Fiction/Picture stories
K.	Community	Y.	Beginning fiction
L.	USA (Then & Now)	Z.	Middle level fiction
M.	Countries (Then & Now)		
N.	Languages		

Categories are then broken down into specific subjects. Most categories have two sets of subcategories: one set for the Lower Library, or students in prekindergarten through grade 2, and one set for the Upper Library, or students in grades 3–5. For example, here are the *Metis* codes for science in the Upper Library.

METIS UPPER LIBRARY *C SCIENCE

Discoveries:	*C SCIENCE DISCOVERIES
Diseases:	*C SCIENCE DISEASES
Experiments:	*C SCIENCE EXPERIMENTS
Math:	*C SCIENCE MATH
Measurement:	*C SCIENCE MEASUREMENT
Medicine:	*C SCIENCE MEDICINE
Microscope:	*C SCIENCE MICROSCOPE
Nuclear:	*C SCIENCE NUCLEAR
Space:	*C SCIENCE SPACE
Space Travel:	*C SCIENCE SPACE TRAVEL
Time:	*C SCIENCE TIME

Codes are printed as call numbers and added to bibliographic records. This scheme is beneficial because it breaks down the collection into subject/genre categories, but also uses a notation with whole words.[42] This scheme is just for kids, so it arranges the collection in subjects that are meaningful to kids. Its use of English words, however, may be a barrier for non-English-speaking students and parents.

SUMMARY

This chapter discussed library classification, including classification in everyday life, how libraries classify their materials, and construction issues and application issues common to all classification schemes. It discussed specific formal classification schemes used in libraries in the United States, such as the *Dewey Decimal Classification* and the *Library of Congress Classification*. It also discussed alternatives to formal library classification that are used in libraries, such as bookstore models and home-grown schemes. This chapter is the last chapter that focuses specifically on cataloging and metadata theory. Chapter 6 will begin the discussion of how library collections are organized in practice.

DISCUSSION QUESTIONS

1. What are the characteristics, advantages, and disadvantages of library classification? Why is classification important?
2. Compare and contrast the *Dewey Decimal Classification* and the *Library of Congress Classification*. How are they similar? How do they differ? What are the characteristics, advantages, and disadvantages of each one?

3. Some libraries use alternative classification to classify all or some of their collections. What are the advantages and disadvantages of using alternative classification over more formal library classification schemes? Give an example of alternative classification you have seen in libraries.

CLASS ACTIVITIES

1. *Categorization Activity.* With your classmates, sort and categorize something, like a bag of candy. Everyone should categorize the candy according to what makes sense to them. Optionally, the class also could create a notational scheme to represent the candy. Then the class should share their categories/notations in small groups to illustrate how each person thinks differently. Each small group should report a short summary of their group's categories/notations to the class.
2. *Group Presentation.* This assignment will help the class better understand classification schemes used in libraries. Groups of two to four students will present information about one formal classification scheme used in libraries and/or alternative classification schemes. Groups should research the classification scheme and create a presentation. Presentations should define and describe the classification scheme (with examples), discusssing its history, uses, and current research. Each group should create a bibliography and a handout for the class as well.
3. *Classification Assignment.* If this book is used in a cataloging course, then you should assign classification numbers to bibliographic records for books. Classification numbers should be based on the first subject heading assigned to the bibliographic record, when possible. You should use the *Dewey Decimal Classification* (WebDewey or paper) and/or the *Library of Congress Classification* (ClassWeb or PDF files), depending on the classification scheme(s) used in the course. Practice tests in which you find classification numbers for LC subject headings also are very helpful.

NOTES

1. Geoffrey C. Bowker and Susan Leigh Star, *Sorting Things Out: Classification and its Consequences* (Cambridge, MA: MIT Press, 1999), 1.
2. Ibid.
3. "Classifications," World Health Organization, accessed January 11, 2019, https://www.who.int/classifications/icd/en.
4. World International Property Organization. *International Patent Classification* (Geneva: World International Property Organization, 2018), https://www.wipo.int/classifications/ipc/en.
5. Charles A. Cutter, "Rules for a Printed Dictionary Catalog," as *Public Libraries in the United States of America: Their History, Condition, and Management: Special Report, Part II* (Washington, DC: US Government Printing Office, 1876), 10.

6. International Federation of Library Associations and Institutions, *Statement of International Cataloguing Principles (ICP)*, 2016 ed., with minor revisions (The Hague: IFLA, 2017), 10.

7. S. R. Ranganathan, *The Five Laws of Library Science* (Madras: The Madras Library Association; London: Goldston, 1931).

8. S. R. Ranganathan, *Colon Classification* (Madras: The Madras Library Association; London: Goldston, 1933).

9. Daniel N. Joudrey and Arlene G. Taylor, *The Organization of Information*, 4th ed. (Santa Barbara, CA: Libraries Unlimited, 2018), 558–60.

10. See, e.g., the work of Hope Olson, which will be discussed in chapter 10.

11. OCLC Dewey Services, "Dewey Decimal Classification (DDC) Summaries: A Brief Introduction to the Dewey Decimal Classification System," accessed January 11, 2019, https://www.oclc.org/en/dewey/features/summaries.html.

12. Library of Congress, "History: The Dewey Program at the Library of Congress," accessed January 11, 2019, https://www.loc.gov/aba/dewey/history.html.

13. Ibid.

14. OCLC, "Dewey Services: Ordering," accessed January 11, 2019, https://www.oclc.org/en/dewey/ordering.html.

15. OCLC, "Introduction to the Dewey Decimal Classification," in *Dewey Decimal Classification*, 23rd ed. (Dublin, OH: OCLC, 2011), 4.

16. For more history, see, e.g., Lois Mai Chan, Sheila S. Intner, and Jean Weihs, *Guide to the Library of Congress Classification*, 6th ed. (Santa Barbara, CA: Libraries Unlimited, 2016); Library of Congress, "Historical Notes," in *Classification and Shelflisting Manual*, last updated July 2013, accessed January 11, 2019, https://www.loc.gov/aba/publications/FreeCSM/freecsm.html; Library of Congress, "History of the Library of Congress," accessed January 11, 2019, https://www.loc.gov/about/history-of-the-library.

17. Library of Congress, "Library of Congress Classification PDF Files: K-KZ," *Library of Congress Classification*, last updated March 30, 2018, accessed January 11, 2019, https://www.loc.gov/aba/publications/FreeLCC/freelcc.html.

18. Library of Congress, "Subarrangement within Disciplines: F195," in *Classification and Shelflisting Manual*, last updated July 2013, accessed January 11, 2019, https://www.loc.gov/aba/publications/FreeCSM/F195.pdf.

19. Library of Congress, *Classification and Shelflisting Manual*, last updated July 2013, accessed January 11, 2019, https://www.loc.gov/aba/publications/FreeCSM/freecsm.html.

20. Ibid.

21. National Library of Medicine, "Introductory Material," in *NLM Classification*, 2018 Summer ed., accessed January 11, 2019, https://www.nlm.nih.gov/class/classintro.pdf.

22. Federal Depository Library Program, "FDLP Basics," last updated December 18, 2014, accessed January 11, 2019, https://www.fdlp.gov/fdlp-basics.

23. Ibid.

24. Federal Depository Library Program, "The Classification System: A Brief History," in *Superintendent of Documents (SuDocs) Classification Guidelines*, last updated August 14, 2018, accessed January 11, 2019, https://www.fdlp.gov/classification-guidelines/the-classification-system-a-brief-history; Federal Depository Library Program, *GPO Classification Manual* (Washington, DC: FDLP, 1993), accessed January 11, 2019, https://www.fdlp.gov/file-repository/gpo-cataloging/1172-gpo-classification-manual.

25. Federal Depository Library Program, *Superintendent of Documents (SuDocs) Classification Guidelines*.

26. UDC Consortium, accessed January 11, 2019, http://udcc.org.

27. State Library of Oregon, "State Government Publications: Oregon Documents Depository Program," accessed January 11, 2019, https://www.oregon.gov/Library/collections/Pages/State-Government-Publications.aspx.

28. Texas State Library and Archives Commission, "Texas State Publications Depository Program," last updated May 30, 2018, accessed January 11, 2019, https://www.tsl.texas.gov/statepubs/index.html.

29. California State Library, "California State Documents Collection and Depository Library Program Information," accessed January 11, 2019, http://www.library.ca.gov/government-publications/state-document-depository-program.

30. University of British Columbia Library, "Indigenous Knowledge Organization," accessed January 11, 2019, https://xwi7xwa.library.ubc.ca/collections/indigenous-knowledge-organization.

31. Julia Pettee, *Classification of the Library of Union Theological Seminary, New York* (New York: Union Theological Seminary, 1924).

32. North American Center for Marianist Studies, "Marianist Library Classification," accessed January 11, 2019, https://www.nacms.org/library/marianist-library-classification.

33. *Weine Classification Scheme and Relative Index for Judaica Libraries*, 9th ed. (Teaneck, N.J.: Association of Jewish Libraries, 2013).

34. Stephanie Sweeney, "Genrefy Your Library: Improve Readers' Advisory and Data-Driven Decision Making," *Young Adult Library Services* 11, no. 4 (2013): 41–45; Holli Buchter, "Dewey vs Genre Throwdown," *Knowledge Quest* 42, no. 2 (2013): 48–55.

35. See, e.g., Nanci Milone Hill, "Dewey or Don't We?" *Public Libraries* 49, no. 4 (2010): 14–20; Barbara Fister, "The Dewey Dilemma," *Library Journal* 134, no. 16 (2009): 22–25.

36. Book Industry Study Group, *Complete BISAC Subject Headings*, 2018 ed. https://bisg.org/page/bisacedition.

37. Melissa Rice and Joanna Kolendo, "Transition & Reflection: Frankfort Public Library District's Decision to Go Dewey Free," *ILA Reporter* 27, no. 3 (2009): 12–15.

38. Hill, "Dewey or Don't We?" and Fister, "The Dewey Dilemma."

39. Marjorie Gibson, "Innovative 21st Century Classification Schemes for Elementary School Libraries," *Feliciter* 57, no. 2 (2011): 48–61.

40. Cynthia R. Houston, "The Use of Reading Levels as Alternative Classification in School Libraries." *Cataloging & Classification Quarterly* 45, no. 4 (2008): 65–80.

41. METIS Library Classification for Children, accessed January 11, 2019, https://sites.google.com/site/metisinnovations/home; see also Tali Balas Kaplan, Andrea K. Dolloff, Sue Giffard, and Jennifer Still-Schiff, "Are Dewey's Days Numbered?" *School Library Journal* 58, no. 10 (2012): 24–28.

42. METIS Schedules, accessed January 11, 2019, https://sites.google.com/site/metisinnovations/home/metis-schedules.

SELECTED BIBLIOGRAPHY AND ADDITIONAL READING

Book Industry Study Group. *Complete BISAC Subject Headings List*. 2018 Edition. https://bisg.org/page/bisacedition.

Bowker, Geoffrey C., and Susan Leigh Star. *Sorting Things Out: Classification and its Consequences.* Cambridge, MA: MIT Press, 1999.

Bowman, J. H. *Essential Dewey.* New York: Neal-Schuman, 2005.

Broughton, Vanda. *Essential Classification.* Second Edition. London: Facet, 2015.

Buchter, Holli. "Dewey vs Genre Throwdown." *Knowledge Quest* 42, no. 2 (2013): 48–55.

Chan, Lois Mai, Sheila S. Intner, and Jean Weihs. *Guide to the Library of Congress Classification.* Sixth Edition. Santa Barbara, CA: Libraries Unlimited, 2016.

Cutter, Charles A. "Rules for a Printed Dictionary Catalogue." Published as *Public Libraries in the United States of America: Their History, Condition, and Management: Special Report, Part II.* Washington, DC: US Government Printing Office, 1876.

Dewey, Melvil. *A Classification and Subject Index for Cataloguing and Arranging the Books and Pamphlets of a Library.* Amherst, MA: N.p., 1876.

Federal Depository Library Program. *Superintendent of Documents (SuDocs) Classification Guidelines.* 2018. https://www.fdlp.gov/classification-guidelines/the-classification-system-a-brief-history.

———. *GPO Classification Manual.* Washington, DC: FDLP, 1993. https://www.fdlp.gov/file-repository/gpo-cataloging/1172-gpo-classification-manual.

Fister, Barbara. "The Dewey Dilemma." *Library Journal* 134, no. 16 (2009): 22–25.

Freeborn, Robert B. "Planning, Implementing, and Assessing a CD Reclassification Project." *Cataloging & Classification Quarterly* 55, no. 7/8 (2017): 578–87.

Gibson, Marjorie. "Innovative 21st Century Classification Schemes for Elementary School Libraries." *Feliciter* 57, no. 2 (2011): 48–61.

Hill, Nanci Milone. "Dewey or Don't We?" *Public Libraries* 49, no. 4 (2010): 14–20.

Houston, Cynthia R. "The Use of Reading Levels as Alternative Classification in School Libraries." *Cataloging & Classification Quarterly* 45, no. 4 (2008): 65–80.

International Federation of Library Associations and Institutions. *Statement of International Cataloguing Principles (ICP).* 2016 Edition, with minor revisions. The Hague: IFLA, 2017. https://www.ifla.org/publications/node/11015.

Joudrey, Daniel N., and Arlene G. Taylor. *The Organization of Information.* Fourth Edition. Santa Barbara, CA: Libraries Unlimited, 2018.

Kaplan, Tali Balas, Andrea K. Dolloff, Sue Giffard, and Jennifer Still-Schiff. "Are Dewey's Days Numbered?" *School Library Journal* 58, no. 10 (2012): 24–28.

Library of Congress. *Classification and Shelflisting Manual.* Accessed January 11, 2019. https://www.loc.gov/aba/publications/FreeCSM/freecsm.html.

———. *Library of Congress Classification.* Accessed January 11, 2019. https://www.loc.gov/aba/publications/FreeLCC/freelcc.html.

Martínez-Ávila, Daniel, Rosa San Segundo, and Hope A. Olson. "The Use of BISAC in Libraries as New Cases of Reader-Interest Classifications." *Cataloging & Classification Quarterly* 52, no. 2 (2014): 137–55.

National Library of Medicine. *NLM Classification.* 2018 Summer Edition. https://www.nlm.nih.gov/class.

OCLC. "Introduction to the Dewey Decimal Classification." In *Dewey Decimal Classification.* Twenty-third Edition. Dublin, OH: OCLC, 2011. https://www.oclc.org/en/dewey/features.html.

Olson, Hope A., and John J. Boll. *Subject Analysis in Online Catalogs.* Second Edition. Englewood, CO: Libraries Unlimited, 2001.

Pettee, Julia. *Classification of the Library of Union Theological Seminary, New York.* New York: Union Theological Seminary, 1924.

Ranganathan, S. R. *Colon Classification.* Madras: The Madras Library Association; London: Goldston, 1933.

———. *The Five Laws of Library Science.* Madras: The Madras Library Association; London: Goldston, 1931.

Rice, Melissa, and Joanna Kolendo. "Transition & Reflection: Frankfort Public Library District's Decision to Go Dewey Free." *ILA Reporter* 27, no. 3 (2009): 12–15.

Steele, Thomas D., and Jody Bales Foote. "Reclassification in Academic Research Libraries: Is it Still Relevant in an E-book World?" *Cataloging & Classification Quarterly* 49, no. 1 (2011): 14–32.

Sweeney, Stephanie. "Genrefy Your Library: Improve Readers' Advisory and Data-Driven Decision Making." *Young Adult Library Services* 11, no. 4 (2013): 41–45.

Weine Classification Scheme and Relative Index for Judaica Libraries. Ninth Edition. Teaneck, NJ: Association of Jewish Libraries, 2013.

Wiegand, Wayne A. "The 'Amherst Method': The Origins of the Dewey Decimal Classification Scheme." *Libraries & Culture* 33 (1998): 175–94.

Part II

PRACTICE OF ORGANIZING LIBRARY COLLECTIONS

6

Organizing Library Collections: Standards and Policy Development

The first half of this book discussed the theory of organizing library collections. It explained why libraries organize their collections, and it discussed metadata, descriptive metadata, controlled and uncontrolled vocabularies, and classification. The second half of the book will focus on how library collections are organized in practice. This chapter starts the discussion by focusing on standardization and the system of standards, the system that develops cataloging and metadata standards and policies, and influences how libraries organize their collections. It will discuss how standards and policies are developed, the levels of decision making, and which organizations are influential in creating and shaping policies. It will then show how this system influences work in individual libraries. While reading this chapter, keep in mind that the level of standardization differs between cataloging practice and metadata practice. This chapter will primarily discuss library cataloging because it is highly standardized across libraries and has been developed for more than 150 years. Metadata practice uses standards, too, but metadata work is much newer (around 25 years of development), and it is much less standardized across libraries.

STANDARDIZATION

There are many standards, policies, guidelines, and best practices used to organize library collections. They are developed by professional library associations, libraries, organizations, and programs that make decisions about how libraries should provide access to collections. Standardization is so important that "consistency and standardization" is considered a general principle of cataloging in the *Statement of International Cataloguing Principles*: "Descriptions and construction of access points should be standardized as far as possible to enable consistency."[1] Standardization is essential, and cataloging practice in libraries is guided by many standards that have been discussed in this book, such as *Resource Description and Access* for descriptive cataloging, the *Library of Congress Subject Headings*, *Dewey Decimal Classification*, and *Library of Congress Classification* for subject analysis, and the MARC 21 formats for creating bibliographic and authority records. "Standards are the backbone of bibliographic control," as Sally McCallum says,[2] because standards ensure the consistent organization of information within a library catalog and between library catalogs. Standardization helps users understand bibliographic records and allows them to use different library catalogs in predictable ways.

Using standards also allows libraries to share bibliographic records with one another. Libraries tend to collect similar mass-published materials, so working together to catalog library materials benefits all libraries. Sharing bibliographic records reduces duplicate effort across libraries and speeds up the cataloging process. It makes library materials available to users quickly and saves libraries time, labor, and money. As the history of cataloging shows, libraries and library associations have always worked together to organize library collections, and the results of these decisions are realized in standards and policies. Although individual libraries have the power to organize their collections in any way that meets their needs, libraries tend to follow standard practices and procedures that are developed outside of individual libraries. It is cheaper and more efficient for a library to follow cataloging and metadata standards than to create all bibliographic records from scratch following their own procedures. There can be a tension, however, between standard practice and local cataloging policies in individual libraries. Standards do not necessarily meet the needs of all libraries or of all users, and libraries must sometimes live with cataloging decisions that are not necessarily made with their needs in mind.

THE SYSTEM OF STANDARDS

Cataloging and metadata standards and policies in the United States are developed at many levels: (1) international, (2) national, (3) state and regional, and (4) local. These levels work together to create a system, a "unified whole" that determines the best ways to organize library collections.[3] There are several groups at each level that make decisions about cataloging standards and policies. See figure 6.1 for an illustration of this system.

As the figure shows, standards and policies are developed at four levels, and each level influences and is influenced by other levels. Decisions made at the international level influence and are influenced by those made at the national level, decisions made at the national level influence and are influenced by those made at the state and regional level, and decisions made at the local library level influence are influenced by all other levels. Cataloging and metadata policy is not created in a vacuum, however. The entire system is influenced by society, culture, laws, and regulations, and the cataloging and metadata field responds to changes in the wider world.

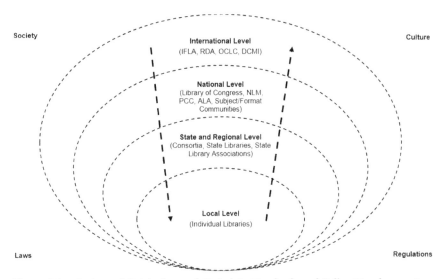

Figure 6.1.   System of Cataloging and Metadata Standards and Policy Development

STANDARDS AND POLICY DEVELOPMENT
AT THE INTERNATIONAL LEVEL

Decisions made at the international level shape standards and policy development at the national level. Libraries from around the world work together to make decisions that benefit all libraries, and standards are increasingly being developed at the international level for libraries around the world. At the international level, there are a variety of groups that make decisions about standards, including the International Federation of Library Associations and Institutions, the RDA Steering Committee, and the Dublin Core Metadata Initiative. In addition, OCLC, a library cooperative, has much power and influence.

International Federation of Library Associations and Institutions

The International Federation of Library Associations and Institutions (IFLA) is the international body that represents libraries at the international level. IFLA defines itself as "the global voice of the library and information profession,"[4] and it creates international standards and provides guidance for many aspects of librarianship. There are several IFLA sections that work on issues involving the organization of library collections, including Cataloguing, Subject Analysis and Access, Bibliography, Information Technology, Serials and Other Continuing Resources, and Rare Books and Special Collections, among others. Each section has a standing committee whose members are elected. Sections have various working groups and review groups that work to develop models and standards. Representatives who work on these committees and groups tend to come from national libraries, academic libraries, and library organizations from around the world.

IFLA sections create standards, models, principles, guidelines, and best practices that guide how library collections are organized around the world. The sections do not make decisions on cataloging policies in any one country or library. One section that guides cataloging is IFLA's Cataloguing Section, which has created important standards, models, and guidelines that are incorporated into cataloging and metadata standards around the world. They include the *Statement of International Cataloguing Principles*, the *IFLA Library Reference Model*, and the *International Standard Bibliographic Description* (IBSD).[5] IFLA is a powerful organization that leads cataloging and metadata standards development around the world, primarily at a theoretical level. When IFLA creates or updates a standard, model, or list of principles, library standards around the world are changed to incorporate the new information. For example, RDA is currently being revised to incorporate the *IFLA Library Reference Model* and the 2016 *Statement of International Cataloguing Principles*. IFLA has power; its decisions are important and influence how cataloging and metadata work is performed in libraries around the world.

RDA Steering Committee

As discussed in chapter 3, *Resource Description and Access* (RDA) is a set of instructions that guides descriptive cataloging in libraries. It is a revision of the *Anglo-American Cataloguing Rules*, second edition, revised and was originally developed by representatives from national libraries and library associations in the United States, Canada, the United Kingdom, Australia, and Germany. However, RDA is fast becoming an international standard, and since 2015 RDA has been maintained by the RDA Steering Committee, with representation from six geographic regions: Africa, Asia, Europe, Latin America and the Caribbean, North America, and Oceania. Each region is represented by a committee or interest group with several members from countries in each region. The United States belongs to the North American RDA Committee (NARDAC), with representatives from the Library of Congress, the Canadian Committee on Cataloging, and the American Library Association.[6] Because RDA is an international standard used by many libraries around the world, decisions made by the RDA Steering Committee affect how library collections are organized around the world.

Dublin Core Metadata Initiative

The *Dublin Core* metadata schema is maintained by the Dublin Core Metadata Initiative (DCMI), a project of the Association for Information Science & Technology (ASIST). Because *Dublin Core* is used by many metadata communities (not just libraries), DCMI takes a much broader focus. It is governed by professionals from around the world who work in various fields, including information technology, librarianship, and education. Decisions made by DCMI affect how *Dublin Core* is used by libraries and other organizations. DCMI maintains the *Dublin Core* metadata schema, but it does not direct how metadata work is performed in libraries. To maintain the metadata schema, DCMI supports metadata work in libraries and other fields by providing professional development opportunities (e.g., webinars, conferences, tutorials) that focus on metadata, metadata projects, and best practices.[7]

OCLC

OCLC (formerly called the Online Computer Library Center) calls itself a "global library cooperative" and has the ominous motto, "Because what is known must be shared."[8] OCLC began in 1967 as a cooperative library organization for Ohio libraries, and since then has expanded to the United States and the world. Today, OCLC has almost 18,000 member libraries in more than 120 countries.[9] It offers a wide variety of products and services in areas such as cataloging and metadata, content management, interlibrary loan, reference, and digital collections; libraries that choose to participate in OCLC pay a membership fee for specific services. OCLC is a nonprofit organization governed by an executive team, a board of trustees, and three regional councils—Americas; Europe, Middle East and Africa; and Asia Pacific—that represent libraries around the world. Each region elects members to serve on the OCLC Global Council, which is a part of OCLC's governance structure.[10]

OCLC has played an important part in library cataloging for more than forty years. Arguably one of its most important contributions is its bibliographic utility, a database of bibliographic records that allows subscribing libraries to create and share bibliographic records. The public interface of OCLC's bibliographic utility is called WorldCat. The cataloging side is currently called Connexion, but it may be phased out eventually to be replaced by OCLC's WorldShare Record Manager. Connexion is used by thousands of libraries around the world for cataloging. In addition to its bibliographic utility, OCLC is responsible for many cataloging and metadata products used in libraries, including those listed in table 6.1.

OCLC has much power and influence over libraries. It is a major player in the organization of library collections because it offers so many products and services used by libraries around the world. It supports research and development, and it has a vested interest in developing cataloging and metadata standards and policies. OCLC's many products and services are beneficial and help libraries organize and manage their collections, but there is a price to pay. OCLC's reach into the global library community expands continually. It consolidates power by routinely buying out competitors, both inside and outside of the United States. For example, since its merger with the Western Library Network in 1999 and the Research Libraries Group in 2006, OCLC offers the only large bibliographic utility left in the United States.[11] In addition, libraries must pay good money to use Connexion and other

Table 6.1. OCLC Products Used to Organize Library Collections

OCLC Product	Description
Connexion/WorldShare Record Manager	Largest bibliographic utility in the world; used for library cataloging and to record library holdings
Dewey Decimal Classification	Published by OCLC through its *WebDewey* database, although editorial control also lies with the Library of Congress
Faceted Application of Subject Terminology	Simplified *Library of Congress Subject Headings*
CatExpress	Tool for copy cataloging
CONTENTdm	Database used to house and manage digital collections
WorldShare Collection Manager	Used to manage electronic and print collections
WorldCat Discovery	Discovery product used by many libraries
Virtual International Authority File	Gathers together authorized forms of names and titles from national authority files around the world; hosted by OCLC
Contract cataloging	Libraries can contract with OCLC to perform cataloging projects
Cataloging for publishers	OCLC partners with some publishers to catalog new materials and send bibliographic records to libraries
Linked data	OCLC is working on various linked data projects, such as adding linked open data to bibliographic records on WorldCat
And much more	

products, and it sometimes seems as if libraries are willing to give up local control of their collections to OCLC in order to realize the benefits of these products. One wonders if perhaps someday there will be no local library catalogs, cataloging, collection development, or acquisitions, because every library will use OCLC's products and services.

Other International Organizations

There are other international organizations that play a role in standards development. For example, the International Organization for Standardization (ISO) is devoted to creating standards in all areas of life that are used around the world (e.g., building construction, clothing, food safety, information technology). It has created many standards used in the library profession, and the cataloging and metadata area specifically. For example, ISO 2108 defines the International Standard Book Number (ISBN) and ISO 3297 defines the International Standard Serial Number (ISSN). These are important international standards that identify resources collected by libraries. In turn, the International ISBN Agency[12] and the ISSN International Centre[13] work with international libraries and library associations to create policies and set standards. In addition, the Book Industry Study Group includes libraries as members and works with libraries to share data through its ONIX metadata schema. It also maintains the *BISAC Subject Headings* list, which is used in several libraries.[14]

For metadata specifically, the World Wide Web Consortium (W3C) is a very important organization that maintains many standards used in web development. This includes standards for creating web pages, such as HMTL and CSS; metadata encoding standards, such as XML; and standards used in linked data, such as RDF. W3C has no direct influence on how metadata work is performed in libraries, but it governs several web standards used by libraries for metadata work.[15]

STANDARDS AND POLICY DEVELOPMENT AT THE NATIONAL LEVEL

Cataloging standards and policy decisions made at the international level shape standards and policies at the national level. Most countries in the world have organizations that set national cataloging and metadata policy, including national libraries and national library associations. In the United States, organizations at the national level include the Library of Congress, its Program for Cooperative Cataloging, the American Library Association, and subject and format communities. Other national organizations, libraries, and programs also play a role in cataloging standards development.

Library of Congress

The Library of Congress has been a leader in cataloging and metadata standards and policy development in the United States for well over a century. It maintains several standards widely used in libraries, develops cataloging and metadata policies and guidelines, and is considered the ultimate authority for bibliographic and authority data in the United States. Other libraries in the United States use Library of Congress standards, follow its cataloging and metadata policies, use its authority file, and download its bibliographic records.

The Library of Congress is considered the de facto national library of the United States, but it is not a national library by law. It was created in 1800 to serve the United States Congress, which is its primary user. The United States has never legally created a national library, but the Library of Congress has taken on the role of a national library because of policies such as mandatory deposit, in which publishers must send the Library of Congress books and other materials published in the United States. The Library of Congress also preserves and provides access to materials and collections that are important to US history and culture. Along with the Library of Congress, there are four other national libraries that serve the United States in special subject areas: National Library of Medicine, National Agricultural Library, National Library of Education, and the National Transportation Library.

The Library of Congress's Acquisitions and Bibliographic Access Directorate is responsible for developing cataloging standards and policies in the United States.[16] Its

Network Development and MARC Standards Office is responsible for maintaining the MARC 21 formats as well as developing and maintaining most of the metadata standards used in libraries to create digital collections.[17] The Library of Congress is responsible for several cataloging and metadata standards listed in table 6.2.

The Library of Congress also creates and/or verifies the majority of bibliographic records used in libraries in the United States. Its Cataloging in Publication Program creates bibliographic information for books before they are published, and its Children's and Young Adults' Cataloging Program creates CIP information for children's

Table 6.2. LC Cataloging and Metadata Standards

LC Cataloging Standards	Definition
Library of Congress Subject Headings	Maintains LCSH with weekly updates
Library of Congress Classification	Maintains LCC with weekly updates
Dewey Decimal Classification	Along with OCLC, has editorial control of the DDC
Children's Subject Headings	Maintains the Children's Subject Headings
Library of Congress Genre/Form Terms for Library and Archival Materials	Maintains these thesauri
Library of Congress Medium of Performance Thesaurus for Music	
Library of Congress Demographic Group Terms	
MARC21 formats	Maintains the MARC21 formats for bibliographic data, authority data, holdings data, classification data, and community data
Library of Congress-Program for Cooperative Cataloging Policy Statements	Develops policies for implementing RDA instructions

LC Metadata Standards	Definition
Metadata Object Description Schema	Maintains this metadata schema for bibliographic information
Metadata Authority Description Schema	Maintains this metadata schema for authority information
Bibliographic Framework Initiative	Maintains the BIBFRAME model, used for linked data
MARCXML	Maintains this encoding standard
Metadata Encoding & Transmission Standard	Maintains this structural metadata standard
PREMIS Data Dictionary for Preservation Metadata	Maintains this administrative metadata standard
VRA Core	Partners with the Visual Resources Association to maintain VRA Core
Encoded Archival Description	Partners with the Society of American Archivists to maintain EAD
And many more	

materials. The Library of Congress maintains its National Authority File and its Linked Data Service. It coordinates the *Program for Cooperative Cataloging* and its constituent programs, described below. The Library of Congress also serves on several international and national committees that develop cataloging and metadata standards, models, principles, and policies.

The Library of Congress is considered the cataloging authority in the United States, and it has a lot of power. It is responsible for many cataloging and metadata standards and policies and is the most influential library in the United States, and perhaps the world. Most libraries in the United States follow Library of Congress cataloging standards and policies, and its influence on libraries in the United States is strong. Bibliographic records created by the Library of Congress are considered to be some of best in the cataloging profession (for the most part), so these records are usually downloaded into library catalogs without question. During fiscal year 2017, for example, the Library of Congress created 286,667 bibliographic records that were added to its library catalog, and it created 59,650 bibliographic records as a part of its Electronic Cataloging in Publication Program (ECIP).[18] Library of Congress bibliographic records flow through the cataloging world. If a cataloger finds a record that was created or verified by the Library of Congress, that record will probably be downloaded into a library's catalog as is without any corrections or changes.

The work done by the Library of Congress benefits libraries. Using bibliographic records created by the Library of Congress saves libraries time, labor, and money. It ensures quality, accuracy, and consistency across library catalogs in the United States. A Library of Congress bibliographic record in a library catalog in New York will be practically identical to one in Texas or California. Users will know what to expect. However, overreliance on Library of Congress cataloging can have negative consequences. Many libraries follow Library of Congress cataloging policies without question, but the Library of Congress creates cataloging policies that meet its needs, not necessarily the needs of all libraries. Although the Library of Congress has several standards and policies that serve public and school libraries, especially for children's materials, its primary responsibility is to serve the United States Congress. This makes the Library of Congress's purpose similar to academic and research libraries, so cataloging and metadata policies can be slanted toward academic and research libraries. The decisions made at the Library of Congress have wide-reaching effects on what libraries can do in practice.

Program for Cooperative Cataloging

The Program for Cooperative Cataloging (PCC), created in 1994, is coordinated by the Library of Congress, but is an influential program worth discussing on its own. It describes itself this way: "The Program for Cooperative Cataloging (PCC) is an international cooperative effort aimed at expanding access to library collections by providing useful, timely, and cost-effective cataloging that meets mutually-accepted standards of libraries around the world."[19] The PCC consists of member libraries around the world, but primarily in the United States. Most members are academic and research libraries, but some public libraries, special libraries, government agencies, and vendors participate as well. The PCC consists of four cooperative cataloging programs in which participants create policies, create bibliographic and authority records, and perform other work in specific areas of cataloging. The four programs and their descriptions are:

1. *Monographic Bibliographic Record Cooperative Program (BIBCO):* Participants create bibliographic records for monographs following the BIBCO Standard Record model.
2. *Cooperative Online Serials Program (CONSER):* Participants create policies, procedures, and bibliographic records for serial publications. The *CONSER Cataloging Manual* and the *CONSER Editing Guide* detail the policies and procedures that participants follow. CONSER is the leader in developing serials cataloging policies.
3. *Name Authority Cooperative Program (NACO):* Participants contribute names, preferred titles, and series titles to the Library of Congress National Authority File. In addition to the Library of Congress, NACO libraries are the only libraries allowed to add authority records to the Library of Congress National Authority File.
4. *Subject Authority Cooperative Program (SACO):* Participants can submit proposals to add or change Library of Congress controlled vocabularies and classification schemes. This includes the *Library of Congress Classification*, the *Library of Congress Subject Headings*, the *Library of Congress Medium of Performance Thesaurus for Music* (LCMPT), the *Library of Congress Genre/Form Terms for Library and Archival Materials* (LCGFT), and the *Library of Congress Demographic Group Terms* (LCDGT).

Member libraries of the PCC may be involved in one or more of these programs. It is important to note that *libraries*, not individual librarians, are members of the PCC. The cataloging and metadata staff of a library must go through extensive training to participate in these programs. A library also must submit a certain number of bibliographic or authority records per year to be involved in each program. Libraries that cannot meet the record requirements can be members of a funnel, which is a group of libraries in a specialized subject area or location, or involved in a consortium. For example, there is a BIBCO funnel for Hebraica materials, a CONSER funnel for University of California libraries, and a NACO funnel that focuses on Chinese, Japanese, and Korean names and titles.

PCC programs play an important role in cataloging policy development in the United States. Only PCC member libraries are obligated to follow requirements and policies of these programs, but their policies still influence cataloging in individual libraries. Bibliographic and authority records that are created by these institutions are considered quality records, and they are copied and downloaded into library catalogs around the United States. In fiscal year 2017, PCC libraries created more than 76,000 new bibliographic records and more than 200,000 new authority records.[20] PCC programs are important because libraries cooperate with each other at the national (and international) level. Through membership in PCC programs, libraries can shape cataloging policies at the national level. Another benefit is that libraries can add their local names and subjects into the National Authority File. This gives more access to people and subjects from local communities.

There are many benefits to PCC membership, but libraries must have the resources to be involved in these programs, including qualified staff with the time to perform this work. Being a member of one of these programs requires a time and work commitment on the part of participating libraries. There is much training, and catalogers must create specific records using national policies and procedures, not local library policies. Work for the PCC may take away from work done for the home library. Larger libraries with bigger budgets, particularly academic and research libraries, tend to be involved in these programs. Few public libraries and no school libraries are involved in PCC programs, so the cataloging needs of public and school libraries may be unintentionally overlooked. Bibliographic records and authority records created by academic and research libraries are usually not for items in public and school libraries. Academic and research collections are different, so the beneficial work being performed by PCC libraries does not always benefit public and school libraries.

American Library Association

Founded in 1876, the American Library Association (ALA) has a vested interest in cataloging and metadata in libraries. ALA and its divisions work to develop cataloging and metadata standards and policies that fit the needs of all libraries. Since its founding, ALA has played a major role in developing cataloging standards and policies. For example, in 1877, ALA appointed a committee to prepare cataloging rules for an author and title catalog. The result, *Condensed Rules for an Author and Title Catalog*, was submitted at the ALA's Buffalo conference in 1883.[21] Another example is ALA's agreement with the Library of Congress that the Library of Congress issue printed cards to libraries. ALA wanted uniformity in bibliographic data in libraries, and the Library of Congress started the program in 1901.[22] ALA also published the first standardized subject headings list. Today, ALA is responsible for publishing *Resource Description and Access* in the United States, and its online tool the *RDA Toolkit*. ALA also publishes various secondary materials such as monographs, textbooks, workbooks, and handbooks that can assist catalogers in their work.

ALA continues to shape cataloging and metadata policy in libraries today. There are several divisions, sections, committees, working groups, round tables, and interest groups that set cataloging and metadata policy. On the cataloging side, the Cataloging and Metadata Management Section (CaMMS) of ALA's Association for Library Collections & Technical Services (ALCTS) division, is the primary section that works on cataloging policy.[23] Originally called the Catalog Section, it was created in 1900 and has changed names several times since that time.[24] CaMMS has several committees that work on cataloging policies and issues. For example, its Committee on Cataloging: Description and Access proposes and reviews changes to RDA and gives recommendations and opinions concerning descriptive cataloging issues. There is representation from the RDA Steering Committee, the Library of Congress, OCLC, and many others.[25] Another CaMMS committee is the Subject Analysis Committee. It has a similar charge, but focuses on issues surrounding controlled vocabularies and classification schemes. It includes representation from the Dewey Program, Library of Congress, and the International Federation of Library Associations and Institutions, among many others.[26] There are other committees that work on cataloging issues for specific formats and audiences. CaMMS's Cataloging of Children's Materials Committee focuses on the cataloging of children's materials.[27] The Continuing Resources Cataloging Committee of ALCTS's Continuing Resources Section (CRS) focuses on serials cataloging issues.[28] There are many other roundtables and interest groups as well.

For metadata practice, the Library and Information Technology Association (LITA) is the ALA division that works with issues surrounding MARC and other encoding standards, and metadata work in libraries. Its LITA/ALCTS Metadata Standards Committee studies issues and makes recommendations surrounding metadata, including MARC.[29] There are also several interest groups that focus on metadata issues.

Subject and Format Communities

There are several subject and format communities outside of ALA that work on cataloging issues and provide guidance to libraries. For example, the Music Library Association is actively involved in developing cataloging policies for music, including scores and audio recordings. It creates best practices documents and provides input about music cataloging to those involved in standards development. Online Audiovisual Catalogers (OLAC) is a group that is involved in best practices for cataloging nonprint items, such as film and video, streaming media, video games, and internet resources. It publishes best practices and is involved in standards development for nonprint formats.[30] The American Association of Law Libraries has a Metadata Management Standing Committee concerned with the cataloging and management of legal information and has several best practices documents.[31] The Art Libraries Society of North America (ARLIS) has a Cataloging Advisory Committee that focuses on cataloging issues in art libraries and issues best practices.[32] The North American Serials Interest Group (NASIG) provides guidance about cataloging and managing serials publications.[33] There are many other subject and format communities that work on cataloging issues as well.

Subject and format communities play an important role in cataloging policy because they provide expert guidance about how to catalog specific subjects and formats. Their guidance is helpful because most catalogers are generalists and do not always have subject or format expertise. Although there is some guidance from standards, such as RDA and LCSH's *Subject Headings Manual*, guidance is scattered, and catalogers have to hunt to find relevant instructions. Best practices documents from subject and format communities pull it all together for catalogers, guiding catalogers in the creation of bibliographic records. When cataloging music, for example, following the best practices from the Music Library Association means catalogers create bibliographic records following guidelines developed by music librarians who understand music and know what users need from bibliographic records.

Other National Organizations

There are several other national organizations, libraries, and programs involved in cataloging and metadata standards and policy development. Large academic and public libraries like Harvard, Stanford, and the New York Public Library influence the development of cataloging policies at the national level. The National Information Standards Organization (NISO) also is influential. Like the International Organization for Standardization, NISO develops standards and recommended practices for cataloging and metadata, information sharing, and the publishing industry. NISO has developed many standards that guide librarianship, especially in the cataloging and metadata area. For example, its Z39.50 standard enables libraries to share bibliographic records, and its Z39.85 standard defines the *Dublin Core* metadata set. NISO standards enable libraries and other communities to share information and use a common set of tools.[34]

The National Library of Medicine (NLM) is responsible for specific cataloging and metadata policy for the biomedical sciences and for medical libraries that use its standards. It is considered the authority for cataloging biomedical materials. NLM maintains the *Medical Subject Headings* and the *National Library of Medicine Classification*, which are used primarily by medical libraries and academic/research libraries with medical collections. NLM also is responsible for indexing journal articles in the biomedical sciences that it makes available in its PubMed database.[35]

Another important program is the Federal Depository Library Program, a federally mandated program that sends US government materials to libraries free of charge. All government agencies are required to make their publications available, except administrative information, classified information for national security, and cooperative publications that must be sold to be self-sustaining (e.g., some National Archives and Library of Congress materials). FDLP collects and distributes government publications (print and/or electronic) to libraries free of charge, but these publications remain the property of the US government. FDLP sets policies for the FDLP program and libraries in the program. It also is responsible for maintaining the *Superintendent of Documents Classification*.[36]

Finally, although not technically national organizations, library catalog vendors play a role in cataloging and metadata practice, especially at the local level. Although vendors do not necessarily develop cataloging and metadata standards and policies, they can influence whether standards and policies are actually implemented in practice. For example, innovative decisions may be made at the international or national levels, but nothing will change in libraries unless library catalogs are updated to reflect these innovations.

STANDARDS AND POLICY DEVELOPMENT AT THE STATE AND REGIONAL LEVEL

Decisions made at the international and national levels influence cataloging and metadata policies in libraries across the United States. These policies and standards filter down to the state and regional level, which includes consortia, state libraries, and state and regional library associations. However, the influence and power of this level varies across the United States. Some consortia, state libraries, and state library associations may have more power and influence than others over cataloging and metadata policies in individual libraries.

Library Consortia

Many libraries are involved in library consortia, also called library networks, library systems, or library cooperatives, in which two or more libraries agree to cooperate. Library consortia offer various services to its member libraries, such as sharing resources, acquiring shared databases, providing education and training, or sharing a library catalog. The purpose is to help member libraries by providing access to resources and services that an individual library could not afford alone. Consortia can be big or small and may serve one state, a part of a state, or a region. There are many consortia in the United States that serve different purposes. For example, Minitex is a program that serves libraries in Minnesota, North Dakota, and South Dakota. It offers contract cataloging services and provides cataloging tools and lists of best practices.[37] Amigos Library Services serves libraries in many states and provides cataloging and metadata education and training, discounts to the *RDA Toolkit*, and more.[38] Lyrasis serves public and academic libraries in the United States and offers education and training, consulting services, and hosting services for digital collections.[39] Some consortia provide shared resources, like databases, and some consortia provide a shared library catalog for participants to use. Libraries may share catalogs across states, like the Orbis Cascade Alliance, which includes a group of academic libraries in Oregon, Washington, and Idaho. Users can search its Summit catalog to see the holdings of libraries in those states.[40] Consortia can be at the state level as well, such as the Online Dakota Information Network (ODIN), which hosts a shared catalog for most public, school, and academic libraries in North Dakota.[41] Consortia also can serve a region within a state; for example, the Harrington Library Consortium serves a group of public, school, and academic libraries in the Texas Panhandle.[42] Consortia that provide a shared library catalog may exert influence over cataloging and metadata policies in individual libraries. Cataloging decisions made for the shared catalog must be followed by individual libraries, and participating libraries must agree on cataloging policies. This can be a source of frustration because libraries have different needs, and a consortium's cataloging policies may not meet the needs of all libraries. Larger libraries in a consortium may unintentionally influence policies because they have bigger collections and more resources, and smaller libraries may feel their needs are not being met.

State Libraries; State and Regional Library Associations

State libraries in each state and territory have an interest in cataloging and metadata issues that concern libraries in the state. The missions of state libraries vary and depend on the state, but most have a mission to preserve state documents, and they tend to provide support for public libraries and school libraries in a state. State libraries may provide services such as continuing education, shared databases, and assistance to libraries that need extra help with their cataloging. They also may be involved in maintaining state documents programs and classification schemes.

State and regional library associations also play a role in cataloging and metadata issues, especially continuing education. All fifty states, the District of Columbia, and the US territories have state library associations with membership from libraries and librarians from around the state or territory. Regional library associations serve members in several states, such as the Mountain Plains Library Association, which serves libraries and librarians in twelve states.[43] State and regional library associations may not necessarily be involved in creating cataloging policies for each state or region, but they are concerned with supporting cataloging and metadata work in each state. Most of them have committees, roundtables, or interest groups in cataloging, metadata, or technical services. They may offer various professional development opportunities and may provide continuing education and resources for libraries.

CATALOGING POLICY DEVELOPMENT AT THE LOCAL LEVEL

Individual libraries at the local level do not operate in a vacuum, but rather in a standards and policy environment that has been created and shaped by decisions made at other levels. Cataloging and metadata practice in individual libraries is guided by standards, policies, and guidelines developed above them. If a library uses standard cataloging and metadata practices, then it must follow the standards. Although an individual library could operate alone and create its own organizational system, classification scheme, subject headings, and cataloging policies, it is expensive, labor intensive, and time consuming to deviate from standard practice. There is much work involved in keeping up a homegrown system. A library that goes on its own is not taking advantage of the benefits of standardization, even though it may be doing what is right for its users.

Local Cataloging and Metadata Policy Development

Individual libraries follow standard cataloging practices and create standard bibliographic records. However, libraries do not have to follow standards blindly. Local libraries have the power to determine what works best for them and to create policies that help their users. Although it is cheaper and easier just to accept and follow standard cataloging and metadata practices, individual libraries develop policies that meet the needs of their users. All libraries organize materials differently and have different processes for cataloging and metadata practice. For example, although all libraries use similar standards for descriptive cataloging, they can choose which subject headings lists, thesauri, and classification schemes to use. These choices depend on the type of library, its users, the size of its collection, and the diversity of subjects and formats in its collection.

Libraries also can customize standard bibliographic records. Records can be customized to meet the needs of individual libraries and their users, adding or changing things that will help local users. There are several ways that libraries customize records. The LCSH *Subject Headings Manual* has an instruction sheet about how many subject headings should be added to a bibliographic record.[44] Some libraries go beyond the standard and add more subject headings than required. Some libraries create local subject headings that are not already in the controlled vocabulary used in the library, perhaps for a special collection, reading program, curriculum standard, or a subject that is important to the community. Catalogers also can provide more access to names on bibliographic records, especially for people affiliated with the library's school, university, or community. Adding additional notes is another way to customize records. This can give users more information about items. Classification numbers are not set in stone, either. Libraries do not have to use classification numbers assigned by the Library of Congress or PCC libraries. A library can change classification numbers to meet its needs, and libraries also can use alternative shelving and classification, like genres, BISAC codes, or a homegrown scheme. However, customization is never free. Every time a standard bibliographic record is touched, a library spends time and money, so libraries are judicious in their customization decisions. It makes much time, labor, and money for libraries to keep up a local organizational system, and documentation must be maintained.

How the System of Standards Affects Libraries

Standardization is fundamental to the organization of library collections. The system of standards helps libraries, yet standards are just that: standard. They do not always meet the needs of all libraries. Decisions made at the international and national levels may be skewed toward academic and research libraries, but not deliberately so. Librarians on these committees work hard to make the best decisions for all libraries, but the decision makers tend to come from larger research and academic libraries because those libraries have bigger budgets and can afford to send representatives. In addition, although all libraries have the power to create local cataloging policies that meet their needs, libraries may be limited in their ability to do so. Customizing bibliographic records is always possible, but libraries may lack the time, staff, and money to customize records. Customization can be expensive, and libraries may choose to just accept bibliographic records as is rather than adding things that would help local users.

SUMMARY

This chapter explored the system of standards that influences how cataloging and metadata standards and policies are developed in the United States. It showed four levels at which decisions are made: international, national, state and regional, and local. It discussed important organizations at all levels that develop standards and shape policy including IFLA, OCLC, the Library of Congress, ALA, and library consortia. Libraries work together to share the workload and ensure quality cataloging and consistent access to library materials. However, individual libraries operate in a standards and policy environment created at levels above them. Although all libraries can create local cataloging and metadata policies and can customize bibliographic records to meet local needs, libraries may lack the resources to do so. Libraries may need to use cataloging standards that do not always meet the needs of their users.

DISCUSSION QUESTIONS

1. What is standardization and why is it important in cataloging and metadata practice?
2. What is the "system of standards" and how does it affect cataloging and metadata policy in individual libraries?
3. Discuss OCLC and the many cataloging and metadata services it provides to libraries. How does OCLC help libraries and what are the downsides of using their services?
4. Discuss the Library of Congress and its cataloging and metadata standards and policies. How does the Library of Congress help libraries, and what are the downsides of relying on the Library of Congress?

CLASS ACTIVITY

Professional Development. This assignment will help you understand the professional organizations responsible for cataloging and metadata practice in your interest area. Research and pick organizations you would join to further your professional development in cataloging and metadata. Choose an area of interest, such as children's materials, film and video, art and architecture materials, serial publications, digital collections, archives, and the like. Perform research to determine the organizations, committees, roundtables, or interest groups at any level (international, national, state/regional) responsible for developing cataloging and metadata standards and policies in your area. Pick at least five groups to join, but do not rely solely on the groups discussed in this chapter. There are many more groups at all levels that develop standards and policies. Then write a short essay that discusses which groups you would join, what each group does, and why you want to join it.

NOTES

1. International Federation of Library Associations and Institutions, *Statement of International Cataloguing Principles (ICP)*, 2016 ed., with minor revisions (The Hague: IFLA, 2017), 5.

2. Sally McCallum, "What Makes a Standard?" *Cataloging & Classification Quarterly*, 21, no. 3/4 (1996): 5.

3. Merriam-Webster Online, "System," accessed January 13, 2019, https://www.merriam-webster.com/dictionary/system.

4. International Federation of Library Associations and Institutions, "About IFLA," last updated January 11, 2019, accessed January 13, 2019, https://www.ifla.org/about.

5. International Federation of Library Associations and Institutions, "Current IFLA Standards," last updated December 10, 2018, accessed January 13, 2019, https://www.ifla.org/node/8750.

6. RDA Steering Committee, "North America," accessed January 13, 2019, http://www.rda-rsc.org/northamerica.

7. Dublin Core Metadata Initiative, "About the Dublin Core Metadata Initiative," accessed January 13, 2019, http://dublincore.org/about.

8. OCLC, accessed January 13, 2019, https://www.oclc.org/en/home.html.

9. OCLC, "About OCLC," accessed January 13, 2019, https://www.oclc.org/en/about.html.

10. OCLC, "Leadership," https://www.oclc.org/en/about/leadership.html.

11. OCLC, "Finance: Mergers & Acquisitions," accessed January 13, 2019, https://www.oclc.org/en/about/finance/mergers.html.

12. International ISBN Agency, accessed January 13, 2019, https://www.isbn-international.org.

13. ISSN International Centre, accessed January 13, 2019, https://www.issn.org.

14. Book Industry Study Group, accessed January 13, 2019, https://bisg.org.

15. World Wide Web Consortium, accessed January 13, 2019, https://www.w3.org.

16. Library of Congress, Acquisitions and Bibliographic Access Directorate, accessed January 13, 2019, https://www.loc.gov/aba.

17. Library of Congress, Network Development and MARC Standards Office, accessed January 13, 2019, https://www.loc.gov/librarians/standards.

18. Library of Congress, Acquisitions and Bibliographic Access Directorate, *Annual Report, Fiscal 2017*, https://www.loc.gov/aba/publications/docs/aba-annualreport-fy17.pdf.

19. Library of Congress, Program for Cooperative Cataloging, "About the PCC," accessed January 13, 2019, http://www.loc.gov/aba/pcc/about.

20. Library of Congress, Program for Cooperative Cataloging, *Annual Compilation, FY 2017*, http://www.loc.gov/aba/pcc/stats/SummaryStatisticsAnnual.pdf.

21. American Library Association, Cooperation Committee, "Condensed Rules for an Author and Title Catalog," *Library Journal* 8, no. 9–10 (September–October 1883): 251–54.

22. American Library Association, Cooperation Committee, *Condensed Rules for an Author and Title Catalog*, 1902 rev. (Washington, DC: US Government Printing Office, 1904), 3.

23. Please note that ALCTS may no longer exist as a separate ALA division. As of the writing of this book, it is looking into merging with the Library Information Technology Association (LITA) and the Library Leadership & Management Association (LLAMA) to form a new division.

24. American Library Association, Cataloging and Metadata Management Section, "Origin and History," accessed January 13, 2019, http://www.ala.org/alcts/mgrps/camms.

25. American Library Association, "Committee on Cataloging: Description & Access (CC:DA)," accessed January 13, 2019, http://www.ala.org/alcts/mgrps/camms/cmtes/ats-ccscat.

26. American Library Association, "CaMMS Subject Analysis Committee," accessed January 13, 2019, http://www.ala.org/alcts/mgrps/camms/cmtes/ats-ccssac.

27. American Library Association, "CaMMS Cataloging of Children's Materials Committee," accessed January 13, 2019, http://www.ala.org/alcts/mgrps/camms/cmtes/ats-ccsccm.

28. American Library Association, "CaMMS Continuing Resources (CRS)," accessed January 13, 2019, http://www.ala.org/alcts/mgrps/crs.

29. American Library Association, "LITA/ALCTS Metadata Standards Committee," accessed January 13, 2019, http://www.ala.org/lita/about/committees/jnt-meta.

30. OLAC Cataloger's Network, accessed January 13, 2019, https://www.olacinc.org.

31. American Association for Law Libraries, "Metadata Management Standing Committee," accessed January 13, 2019, https://www.aallnet.org/tssis/about-us/committees/metadata-committee.

32. Art Libraries Society of North America, "Cataloging Advisory Committee," accessed January 13, 2019, https://arlisna.org/organization/committees/76-cataloging-advisory-committee.

33. NASIG, accessed January 13, 2019, http://www.nasig.org.

34. National Information Standards Organization, accessed January 13, 2019, https://www.niso.org.

35. National Library of Medicine, accessed January 13, 2019, https://www.nlm.nih.gov.

36. Federal Depository Library Program, accessed January 13, 2019, https://www.fdlp.gov.

37. Minitex, accessed January 13, 2019, https://www.minitex.umn.edu.

38. Amigos Library Services, accessed January 13, 2019, https://www.amigos.org.

39. Lyrasis, accessed January 13, 2019, https://www.lyrasis.org/Pages/Main.aspx.

40. Orbis Cascade Alliance, accessed January 13, 2019, https://www.orbiscascade.org.

41. Online Dakota Information Network, accessed January 13, 2019, https://www.odin.nodak.edu.

42. Harrington Library Consortium, accessed January 13, 2019, https://harringtonlc.org.

43. Mountain Plains Library Association, accessed January 13, 2019, https://www.mpla.us.

44. Library of Congress, "Assigning and Constructing Subject Headings: H180," in *Subject Headings Manual*, last updated February 2016, accessed January 13, 2019, https://www.loc.gov/aba/publications/FreeSHM/H0180.pdf.

SELECTED BIBLIOGRAPHY AND ADDITIONAL READING

American Library Association, Cooperation Committee. "Condensed Rules for an Author and Title Catalog." *Library Journal* 8, no. 9–10 (September–October 1883): 251–54.

———. *Condensed Rules for an Author and Title Catalog.* 1902 Revision. Washington, DC: Government Printing Office, 1904.

Charbonneau, Mechael D. "Program for Cooperative Cataloging: The Indiana Experience." *Cataloging & Classification Quarterly* 48, no. 2/3 (2010): 113–25.

Cronin, Christopher, Mary S. Laskowski, Ellen K. W. Mueller, and Beth E. Snyder. "Strength in Numbers: Building a Consortial Cooperative Cataloging Partnership." *Library Resources & Technical Services* 61, no. 2 (2017): 102–16.

International Federation of Library Associations and Institutions. *Statement of International Cataloguing Principles (ICP).* 2016 Edition, with minor revisions. The Hague: IFLA, 2017. https://www.ifla.org/publications/node/11015.

Jansen, Lloyd. "The Craft of Local Practice: How Catalogers are Gaining Efficiency but Losing Control." *OLA Quarterly* 9, no. 1 (2003): 5–8.

Knowlton, Steven A. "Power and Change in the U.S. Cataloging Community." *Library Resources & Technical Services* 58, no. 2 (2014): 111–26.

Li, Xiaoli, and Michael Colby. "From Vision to Action: One Campus's Experience with the UC CONSER Funnel." *Cataloging & Classification Quarterly* 56, no. 2/3 (2018): 214–23.

Library of Congress. 2016. *Subject Headings Manual.* 2016. https://www.loc.gov/aba/publications/FreeSHM/freeshm.html.

Library of Congress, Acquisitions and Bibliographic Access Directorate. *Annual Report, Fiscal 2017.* https://www.loc.gov/aba/publications/docs/aba-annualreport-fy17.pdf.

Library of Congress, Program for Cooperative Cataloging. *Annual Compilation, FY 2017.* http://www.loc.gov/aba/pcc/stats/SummaryStatisticsAnnual.pdf.

McCallum, Sally. "What Makes a Standard?" *Cataloging & Classification Quarterly,* 21, no. 3/4 (1996): 5–15.

Song, Liping. "The Road to CONSER: Taken by the Health Sciences Library System, University of Pittsburgh." *Cataloging & Classification Quarterly* 48, no. 2/3 (2010): 143–52.

Sotelo, Aislinn, Rebecca Culbertson, and Shi Deng. "Cataloging for Consortial Collections: A Survey." *Cataloging & Classification Quarterly* 56, no. 2/3 (2018): 171–87.

Van Kleeck, David Gerald Langford, Jimmie Lundgren, Hikaru Nakano, Allison Jai O'Dell, and Trey Shelton. "Managing Bibliographic Data Quality in a Consortial Academic Library: A Case Study." *Cataloging & Classification Quarterly* 54, no. 7 (2016): 452–67.

7

How Libraries Organize Their Collections

The last chapter began a discussion about cataloging and metadata practice. It focused on standardization and introduced the system of standards. Standardization is important because it allows libraries to share bibliographic records and makes the cataloging process quick and efficient. There are many organizations at the international, national, state, and regional levels that develop cataloging standards and influence how individual libraries perform cataloging and metadata work at the local level. Because standards are developed at higher levels, they do not always meet the needs of every library. Individual libraries have the power to create their own local policies, customize bibliographic records, and organize their collections as they see fit. Yet in order to take advantage of the financial benefits of standardization, libraries may forgo customization and local practices that meet the needs of their users. This chapter will focus on cataloging and metadata practice in general and will discuss aspects of the work that is common to all libraries as a whole. It will discuss cataloging and authorities work, how different formats are organized in libraries, and metadata practice. It also will take a look at various issues facing cataloging and metadata practice. This chapter takes a broad and general look at cataloging and metadata practice. A more detailed discussion of specific organizational practices in different library types can be found in chapter 8.

CATALOGING PRACTICE

Cataloging pushes continually toward more efficient practices, but it is important to remember that no matter what type of library or size of collection, cataloging happens in every library. It does not matter if a library purchases all bibliographic records from vendors or creates all bibliographic records in-house. *Cataloging happens in every library*. Although each library has different cataloging procedures and workflows, there are some parts of the cataloging process common to all libraries.

Types of Cataloging

There are two types of cataloging: copy cataloging and original cataloging. Copy cataloging is when a cataloger copies, or downloads, existing bibliographic records into a library's catalog. Copy cataloging is performed primarily for a library's main collection. There are two main ways copy cataloging is performed. One way is when an in-house cataloger finds a bibliographic record that exists in a database of bibliographic records or in another library's catalog. If needed, the cataloger fixes errors and customizes the bibliographic record, following local library policies. Then the record is downloaded into the library's catalog. Another way to copy catalog is getting files of bibliographic records from library vendors and downloading the bibliographic records into the catalog. Copy cataloging is usually performed by paraprofessional catalogers (e.g., copy catalogers, library technicians), and in some libraries can be performed by student workers or even volunteers. Most of the cataloging performed in libraries is copy cataloging, and most libraries have at least one copy cataloger on staff.

Original cataloging is when a cataloger creates a bibliographic record from scratch. Original cataloging is usually performed for unique and complex items or formats, some foreign-language materials, or anything else that has not been cataloged before. Original cataloging is usually performed by professional catalogers with a master's degree in library science and/or information science, but it can be performed by skilled paraprofessionals as well. Library vendors and contract catalogers also create original bibliographic records. Original cataloging does not happen as often as copy cataloging. However, almost every library must perform some original cataloging. Not everything in a library has bibliographic records available in cataloging databases or other library catalogs: for example, local press items, vanity press items, book fair items, gift items, equipment, or items in special collections. A library should have a professional cataloger who can perform this complex work, but some libraries may not have a professional cataloger on staff.

Each library has at least one person responsible for cataloging, even if that person just downloads files of bibliographic records purchased from vendors. A small library may have one librarian who is responsible for all the work in the library, including cataloging. A large library may have a large cataloging unit with many professional and paraprofessional catalogers. Most libraries have in-house catalogers who perform cataloging. There is usually a mix of paraprofessional and professional catalogers who do this work, but some libraries may have paraprofessional catalogers only. Catalogers may work inside a library or in a central processing center, which is a centralized location where cataloging occurs. This is more common for school districts, public library systems, and academic libraries with lots of branches. Professional and paraprofessional catalogers work at a central processing center, and materials are sent to branch libraries or schools after they are cataloged.

Cataloging units can be a complex work environment, and sometimes there is a rigid line between "professional" and "nonprofessional" work. Professional catalogers perform the professional work, which is complex and nonroutine, requiring much professional judgment. This includes creation of original bibliographic records, performing subject analysis, solving difficult cataloging problems, performing complex copy cataloging, and managing the paraprofessionals. Professional cataloger positions usually require a master's degree in library science and/or information science. Paraprofessional catalogers perform the nonprofessional work, which is routine and requires little judgment, such as copy cataloging. Paraprofessional positions do not require a master's degree, although some paraprofessional catalogers may have earned one. The line between professional and paraprofessional work is constantly shifting to meet the needs of libraries, and libraries all assign work differently.

Sources of Bibliographic Records

Catalogers are responsible for creating bibliographic records that describe and provide access to a library's collection. However, a cataloger does not have to create a bibliographic record from scratch for every resource in a library. Standardization allows libraries to share bibliographic records in a process called shared cataloging or cooperative cataloging. Libraries use bibliographic records created at other libraries or by vendors, which saves time, labor, and money. Every library has a different cataloging process and uses different sources to obtain bibliographic records. Although catalogers could create each bibliographic record from scratch, most libraries obtain their bibliographic records from other sources. Original cataloging is performed only when needed. Sources for bibliographic records include OCLC's bibliographic utility Connexion (which may be replaced eventually by WorldShare Record Manager), other cataloging databases, other libraries' catalogs, library vendors, and outsourcing to contract catalogers. Libraries can get bibliographic records from all five sources.

OCLC Connexion

OCLC Connexion is the biggest bibliographic utility in the world, and it is the most widely used database for cataloging. The public interface is called WorldCat. It is a database of bibliographic records, and it includes bibliographic records for all materials and formats collected in libraries. As of September 2018, it contains more than 430 million bibliographic records in almost 500 languages, and OCLC estimates that a new bibliographic record is added every second.[1] To use Connexion, a library must become a member of OCLC and pay a subscription fee. This contractually obligates the library to perform all original cataloging on the utility. Bibliographic records are created and maintained by OCLC member libraries. Catalogers around the world share their work by creating original records on Connexion and correcting or enhancing other records. Many libraries, vendors, and other organizations use Connexion. The Library of Congress and libraries in the Program for Cooperative Cataloging are responsible for creating and verifying many of the bibliographic records on the database. Other products libraries can use are the CatExpress program, which is a copy cataloging product for smaller libraries that catalog fewer than 7,000 titles a year,[2] and the WorldCat knowledge base, which contains records for collections of electronic materials in libraries.[3]

Libraries work together to create bibliographic records. There is supposed to be one bibliographic record for each edition or manifestation of a work, and OCLC has specific guidelines about when to create a new bibliographic record.[4] This one bibliographic record is referred to as the master record. A cataloger at a library creates the master record in Connexion, and then other catalogers at other libraries can correct/update/enhance the record. In this way, cataloging work is shared, which makes cataloging cheaper and more efficient. Catalogers around the world work together to create the best records possible for users, and catalogers and users benefit from the expertise of other catalogers. For example, if a cataloger is unfamiliar with a subject—for example, law or medicine—then the cataloger can wait for catalogers with subject expertise to create the master record on Connexion.

However, a cataloger may have to wait a long time before a master record is created in Connexion. This can create cataloging backlogs, and users may not have timely access to library materials. There also are many duplicate records on Connexion, which can make it difficult for catalogers to know which master record to use. Although Connexion is a shared database in which catalogers work together, not all libraries have the power to change all things on all bibliographic records. There is a hierarchy of libraries, and only certain libraries have the authority to make certain changes. The hierarchy favors the Library of Congress, libraries that belong to the Program for Cooperative Cataloging, and large academic and public libraries. In addition, cataloging on Connexion can be complicated. There are separate cataloging guidelines called *OCLC Bibliographic Formats and Standards*, which guide the creation of bibliographic records on the utility.[5] This means that a cataloger must know general cataloging standards, local cataloging policies, *and* the OCLC guidelines. This creates two types of cataloging in a library that uses Connexion. One type of cataloging is done on Connexion; this is very formal and follows cataloging standards and OCLC guidelines. The other type of cataloging is done for a local library following local cataloging policies. A cataloger may need to create a record on Connexion, then go back and update the bibliographic record for the local library catalog. In addition, bibliographic records can vary in quality. There may be errors, incomplete information, or missing access points, subject headings, and classification numbers. Sometimes many changes need to be made to a bibliographic record before it can be downloaded into a library catalog. It can take a lot of time to fix a bad record, so some catalogers never make changes to master records on Connexion; instead, they simply make changes for their local catalog and download records without updating the master record.

Cataloging Databases

OCLC Connexion is not the only way libraries obtain bibliographic records. Libraries can get bibliographic records from commercial cataloging databases as well. For example, Mitinet has a suite of products used primarily in school libraries and public libraries. Its BestMARC product is used for cataloging. It is not necessarily a shared database like Connexion. Catalogers can add bibliographic records and take bibliographic records, but they cannot edit bibliographic records.[6] ITS.MARC from the Library Corporation is another database that has bibliographic records. Again, it is not a shared database like Connexion; catalogers can take bibliographic records only. It is used by all types of libraries.[7]

Library Catalogs (Z39.50)

In addition to commercial databases of bibliographic records, libraries can copy bibliographic records from other library catalogs. This is done through Z39.50, a NISO standard for searching and retrieving information from databases.[8] It is useful for cataloging because a library can use Z39.50 to go to another library's catalog and download bibliographic records. This is usually done through an integrated library system (e.g., Destiny from Follett) that allows a cataloger to copy bibliographic records. For example, a cataloger working in a small art library could use Z39.50 to download bibliographic records from the library at the Metropolitan Museum of Art. Getting bibliographic records from other libraries is beneficial because the bibliographic records are free. Libraries also can get bibliographic records from libraries with similar collections and whose bibliographic records they trust.

Library Vendors

Library vendors also provide bibliographic records. Libraries can purchase bibliographic records when they purchase library materials, and the records are just downloaded into the catalog. Vendors sell records primarily for shelf-ready physical materials and for large packages of electronic resources. For physical materials, libraries can purchase shelf-ready materials with spine labels and barcodes, and the librarian or cataloger just downloads the bibliographic records into the library catalog. This is a very common practice, and many libraries purchase at least some (if not most) bibliographic records from vendors. Instead of the lag time that exists between an item's being received by acquisitions and being cataloged—which can be a few days to a few months or more—library materials are available to users immediately. For electronic materials, vendors provide bibliographic records for large packages of electronic books and electronic serials. These records are downloaded into library catalogs so users can access the electronic resources.

Purchasing bibliographic records from vendors is common because it is supposed to save time, labor, and money by not having cataloging staff do the work. However, it can be quite expensive, especially if a library needs more than just basic bibliographic information. If a library wants to customize bibliographic records, perhaps adding subject headings for a reading program or other types of customization, the library will have to pay extra for those services. The quality of vendor records can vary as well, and records need to be checked regularly for accuracy. Vendors may offer different levels of bibliographic records, from very basic bibliographic records with limited information to full bibliographic records with lots of information. A library gets what it pays for, and a vendor simply follows the contract with the library. Libraries need to get the best bibliographic records they can afford, pick good vendors, and always check those bibliographic records. Also, some vendors do not necessarily create their own bibliographic records from scratch; they may be selling bibliographic records created by the Library of Congress or other libraries. Libraries could obtain the bibliographic records for free if they hired catalogers to do the work. Perhaps a better viewpoint is that library vendors sell *time*, not records. It is easier for some libraries to buy records from vendors than to download free records one by one. Yet library cataloging today, especially electronic resources, would not be manageable without obtaining bibliographic records from vendors. There are too many electronic resources for in-house catalogers to handle alone.

Outsourcing to Contract Catalogers

Libraries also can hire contract catalogers or outsourcers to perform cataloging. Outsourcing is when a library sends its materials to an individual or a company to catalog. It is different from a library vendor that sells bibliographic records along with library materials. Contract catalogers can be individual freelance catalogers, a private cataloging company, or a large organization such as OCLC. Outsourcing is usually done when no one on staff has the cataloging knowledge or language expertise to catalog something. Perhaps the items are in a foreign language no one on staff can read, or in a format that requires specialized knowledge, such as music scores. Outsourcing also can be performed for special collections or special projects, and the work can be a one-time project or a regular assignment. Contract cataloging can be beneficial because it gives users access to items that would not otherwise be cataloged. Instead of sitting in a backlog, items are cataloged and made available to users. However, contract cataloging can be expensive and the quality can vary depending on how much a library is willing to pay. As with purchasing bibliographic records from vendors, libraries will need to pay more for full, customized bibliographic records.

Authorities Work

Authorities work is a part of cataloging practice. As discussed in chapter 3, catalogers add authorized access points to bibliographic records for names, preferred titles, series titles, and subjects in a process called authority control. Authorized access points are located in authority records in the authority file, a collection of authority records that contain authorized access points. There are two types of authority files: the Library of Congress National Authority File and a local authority file. The National Authority File is maintained by the Library of Congress. It is the source of authorized access points in the United States, and libraries involved in the NACO and SACO programs, or a funnel, add names, titles, and subject headings to it. A local authority file is an authority file just for use with a particular library catalog. It does not contain every authority record in the Library of Congress National Authority File, just authority records for access points used in a library catalog. A library does not want authority records for items not in the collection, because that may mislead users into thinking that the library owns things it does not own. In library catalogs, the local authority file is a separate file housed away from the bibliographic records. Users cannot access the authority file, and they never see authority records. Only catalogers and library staff can access the authority file.

Authorities work refers to the process of actually setting up authorized access points and creating authority records for the authority file, both for the national file and a local file. Authority records are different from bibliographic records, and they are created following *Resources and Description Access* instructions, local policies, and the *MARC 21 Format for Authority Data*. Catalogers do a lot of work to determine the correct authorized name to use, the correct preferred title, the correct series title, and the correct subject heading. For the Library of Congress National Authority File, catalogers at the Library of Congress, catalogers at NACO and SACO libraries, and catalogers whose libraries are involved in a funnel project are allowed to add and update names, subject headings, and titles.

A library is responsible for updating its own local authority file. Authorities work in an individual library has two parts: updating the local authority file and updating bibliographic records. Access points are constantly changing, so libraries must update their local authority files with any changes made in the National Authority File. Corresponding bibliographic records also must be updated to reflect changes. A library may also need to create local authority records for access points not in the National Authority File. Libraries can perform this work in several ways depending on the size of the collection. Authorities work can be performed in-house by one or more people who are responsible for authorities. In some larger libraries, there may be a separate authorities unit with catalogers who perform only authorities work. A library also can hire a vendor to perform authorities work. Usually authority records and bibliographic records are updated using what is called a global update, which is like a giant find-and-replace process. Anything not changed in a global update may need to be updated by hand.

Authorities work can be expensive and time consuming for libraries, so there are some libraries that do not use an authority file at all. Other libraries have stopped updating their authority file. Although authority control is arguably the most important part of cataloging, libraries may not have the money to keep up a local authority file. This could result in a library catalog that does not work well, includes old and misleading information, and does not bring together library materials with the same name, title, or subject. Users may have a hard time finding what they need.

MONOGRAPHS, SERIALS, AND ELECTRONIC RESOURCES

Cataloging practice in libraries may seem straightforward. Copy cataloging is usually performed by paraprofessional catalogers, original cataloging is usually performed by professional catalogers, bibliographic records are obtained from various sources, and authority files are kept up-to-date. However, the discussion has just gotten started. Different formats collected in libraries tend to drive cataloging practices. To provide better access to various formats, each format is cataloged and managed differently. This section will focus on the basic differences between monographs and serials, how electronic resources have changed cataloging practice, and how different formats are organized in libraries.

Monographs and Serials

Historically, library materials have been divided into two primary material types: monographs and serials. They are cataloged differently and handled differently, and technical services departments usually have a separate serials unit and a cataloging unit with catalogers and other staff devoted to each format. The division between monographs and serials originates with descriptive cataloging rules, although definitions have changed as descriptive cataloging rules have changed. Definitions continue to evolve as *Resource Description and Access* is updated to reflect the *IFLA Library Reference Model*. However, it is helpful to understand the basic terms *monographs* and *serials* to better understand how and why these two broad formats are handled differently in practice. Just keep in mind that these definitions come from Original RDA. They will change if Revised RDA is adopted.

Original RDA defines four types of resources cataloged in libraries, called mode of issuance:[9]

1. *Single unit:* A mode of issuance of a manifestation that is issued either as a single physical unit or, in the case of an intangible manifestation, as a single logical unit. A single volume, a file available online, etc., are included.
2. *Multipart monograph:* A mode of issuance of a manifestation issued in two or more parts, either simultaneously or successively, that is complete or intended to be completed within a finite number of parts. A dictionary in two volumes, three audiocassettes issued as a set, etc., are included.
3. *Serial:* A mode of issuance of a manifestation issued in successive parts, usually bearing numbering, that has no predetermined conclusion. A serial includes a periodical, monographic series, newspaper, etc. Reproductions of serials and resources that exhibit characteristics of serials, such as successive issues, numbering, and frequency, but whose duration is limited, such as newsletters of events, are also included.
4. *Integrating resource:* A mode of issuance of a manifestation that is added to or changed by means of updates that do not remain discrete but are integrated into the whole. A loose-leaf manual that is updated by means of replacement pages, a website that is updated continuously, etc., are included.

Monographs

Single-unit resources and multipart monographs are both considered monographs, even though Original RDA does not explicitly say that. A monograph is defined in the RDA glossary as "a resource that is complete in one part or intended to be completed within a finite number of parts."[10] A monograph can be in one part (a single unit, like a book) or in a finite number of parts (a multipart monograph, like an encyclopedia). A single-unit resource, like a book, is not intended to be published forever. It is published one time, or a particular edition is published one time. Multipart monographs are published in multiple volumes either at one time or over a definite time span. Multipart monographs are still considered monographs because they are not intended to be published forever. After all parts are published, the work is complete.

Monographs can be in any format, physical or electronic. A book, a music album, a map, a hat, a PDF file, and the like are all examples of single-unit resources. A book published in three volumes or a twenty-six-volume encyclopedia are examples of multipart monographs. See figure 7.1 for examples.

A book

A video

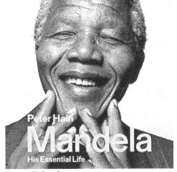
An audiobook

A game

Figure 7.1.   Examples of Monographs

Serials

Serials are completely different from monographs. Instead of being published one time, serials are ongoing; they are continually published. In RDA, a serial publication is "issued in successive parts, usually bearing numbering, that has no predetermined conclusion."[11] Breaking down that definition, serials are "issued in successive parts," which means they are published in separate issues, one after the other. Each serial title is published on a specified frequency, such as daily, weekly, biweekly, monthly, bimonthly, quarterly, annually, and even irregularly. For example, the April 2, 2020, issue of a daily newspaper will be published the day after the April 1, 2020, issue. Volume 31, number 2 (summer 2020) of a quarterly journal will be published as a separate issue after volume 31, number 1 (spring 2020). The 2020 edition of an annual handbook is published a year after the 2019 edition.

Serial parts are "usually bearing numbers," which means that issues usually have some sort of numbering on them. Numbering can include anything, such as volumes, issues, numbers, seasons, years, months, quarters, or a combination. Examples include volume 15, number 1 (January 2021); issue 405; no. 4387; 2019; 3rd quarter 2020; and January 31, 2020. Issues of serials usually have the same title printed on each issue, and the only way to distinguish them is through the numbering. Separate issues may collectively make up one volume.

Serial publications also have "no predetermined conclusion." They are intended to be published indefinitely, which means that a serial title is published until the publisher decides to stop publishing it. There is usually a statement of intent that explains how often a serial title is published. For example, the statement of intent from the magazine *American Libraries* reads, "American Libraries (ISSN 0002–9769) is published 6 times yearly with occasional supplements by the American Library Association (ALA)."[12] Intentionality is important with serials; there can be no indication that a publication intends to end. If a publication has a set end date, then it may be a monograph. Just remember that if a resource is published in successive parts, it has some sort of numbering, and it is intended to continue forever, then it is a serial.

There are many types of serial publications, such as journals, magazines, newsletters, yearbooks, bulletins, annual reports, certain handbooks and manuals, and so on. Serials can be on any format, print or electronic, and there are even serial maps and serial media. Figure 7.2 shows some examples of serials.

Integrating Resources

Integrating resources are different from monographs and serials. They are published in one or more volumes, like a monograph, but the contents are continually changed by updates. An integrating resource is intended to continue forever, like a serial, but it is not published in successive parts and it does not have numbering. Basically, the whole remains the same, but the insides change. For example, the *Anglo-American Cataloguing Rules*, second edition, revised was published in 2002 in a three-ring binder. From 2003 until 2005 there were updates, with new pages that

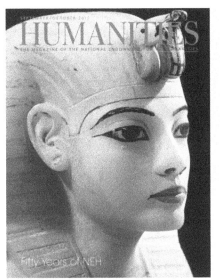

A Magazine

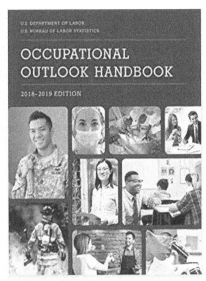

A Yearly Handbook

An Annual Report

Spring 2017

A Bulletin (Online)

Figure 7.2. Examples of Serials

replaced old pages in the binder. Old pages were taken out of the binder and new pages were put in the binder. They kept AACR2 up to date with the latest cataloging information.[13] That is why integrating resources are called integrating: new information is integrated with old information. Legal publishers publish many integrating resources to keep up with constant changes in the law. It is impractical to republish an entire title when information changes on only a few pages. Websites and databases are also considered integrating resources because the website or database is intended to continue indefinitely, but it is updated as needed.

Division of Work

Monographs and serials are each handled differently in cataloging practice. Many libraries have separate cataloging units that catalog monographs, and separate serials units that catalog and manage serials. For an illustration, see figure 7.3. It shows how cataloging work is typically divided between monographs and serials. The vertical dashed line shows the division. The box for "Monographs" was added because although it is not one of the modes of issuance in Original RDA, it is an important part of cataloging practice, and monographs are handled by a cataloging unit. Integrating resources are a separate category but may be cataloged by either unit. Be aware, too, that even though the definitions of a monograph and serial will change when RDA is revised, the structure of the work will remain the same. Monographs and serials will continue to be treated and handled differently in practice. The definitions may change, but the work remains the same.

The division between monographs and serials is important to understand. Each one is acquired and cataloged differently, and cataloging practice has historically been divided into monographs cataloging and serials cataloging, each with a different cataloging philosophy. After a monograph is ordered and received, it goes to

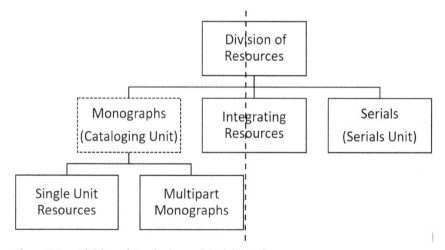

Figure 7.3. Division of Cataloging and Serials Work

cataloging. In monographs cataloging, catalogers handle a finite number of parts, so they focus only on the resource in front of them. A cataloger can apply cataloging standards to make a bibliographic record that perfectly describes and provides access to a monograph. The cataloging philosophy is to catalog it once and move on. The monograph is then processed and shelved. Monographs cataloging and acquisitions work together, but the processes are separate and the work is performed by separate people in a technical services department. In a very small library, one person may be in charge of cataloging and providing access to both monographs and serials, and in a very large library there could be separate cataloging and serials units, each with many employees.

Serials are acquired, cataloged, and handled differently than monographs because they are ongoing; they are active and alive. Serial publications have lives. They grow and change, and can die. Serials can change often, so a cataloger has to update bibliographic records over and over again. The cataloging philosophy is much different for serials. Catalogers embrace change and accept that bibliographic records will need to be updated. Bibliographic records are not perfect and are not set in stone. A bibliographic record needs to reflect events in the life (and death) of a serial publication, not just one part of it. Bibliographic records must be both broad enough to cover everything about a serial publication and specific enough to account for any idiosyncrasies (e.g., a combined issue, an issue not published). The bibliographic record for a serial publication changes and grows as the serial publication changes and grows. Serials work in libraries is more complex than monographs cataloging because acquiring, cataloging, and providing access to serials are closely related and may be performed by one person or several people. Serials catalogers work very closely with serials acquisitions staff, who may order serials titles and/or check in print issues to catch changes that need to be made to bibliographic records. Much work also is performed for electronic serials and keeping access to serial publications in databases. Serials catalogers, often called Electronic Resources Librarians, may work with library systems staff or technology staff to make sure users have continual access to electronic serials in databases.

Physical and Electronic Resources

Monographs and serials have historically divided technical services work because each format requires special knowledge, cataloging, and management. Another dividing line is between physical resources and electronic resources (also called digital resources). Libraries have historically had collections of physical materials, primarily books, serials, and media. For the past twenty-five years or so, library collections have been changing to include many electronic resources, and the proliferation of electronic resources has significantly altered technical services work. The creation of the World Wide Web changed everything. It led to new digital formats and more information being made available online. There has been an explosion of digital content available through many content providers and platforms, and electronic resources have changed library collections significantly. No longer do libraries just have a collection of physical items they own and lend to users. Today, libraries provide access to many electronic resources they do not necessarily own, such as e-books, e-serials, streaming audio and video, audiobooks, digital art and images, digital maps, and so on. A library's collection may provide access to physical and electronic resources, published and unpublished resources, purchased and open source resources available freely online.

Digital resources are rich with information. There are many formats to meet users' needs. Digital materials can enhance a print collection, there are no physical space issues, and access is continual. Patrons do not have to go to a library during library hours to get materials. Yet the explosion of digital materials has been overwhelming for some libraries. The cataloging and management of them can be quite complex. Although they are online, digital resources do not make cataloging and serials work easier. More staff, resources, money, and work are needed to manage and provide access to electronic resources. Professional librarian positions are changing to accommodate electronic resources. Librarians with new job titles such as Electronic Resources Librarian or Digital Resources Librarian are tasked with managing digital resources. Some technical services departments have had to significantly rearrange their organizational structure and staffing to keep up with the workload generated by digital resources. As Joelen Pastva, Gwen Gregory, and Violet Fox say, "Management of electronic resources is now a free-for-all."[14] This work is relatively new in libraries. Electronic content as well as content providers and platforms continue to grow and change, and libraries are trying to figure out the best methods for cataloging and managing them.

Libraries today still hold significant physical collections, but they are collecting more electronic materials. The trend is to purchase more electronic resources, and there is a good chance that in the future, most of a library's circulating collection may be electronic. However, libraries are not fully electronic yet; they still provide access to physical materials. It is important to understand how both physical resources and electronic resources are managed in a library and the work that goes into providing continual access to materials in both formats.

ORGANIZING BOOKS

Library cataloging practice can be quite complex. There is a broad division between monographs and serials in most technical services departments, and electronic resources are changing the workflow and organization of monographs and serials. Taking a deeper look at formats collected in libraries will show how formats drive organizational decisions.

Physical Books

Historically, books are the most common format found in library collections. There are books about everything for every person, from board books for babies to very detailed monographs for researchers. There are countless genres of fiction, nonfiction about every subject, and books for every group, audience, and age, in every language. Books can be a part of numbered or unnumbered series. Books can consist of collections of works, such as an edited book with chapters by different people, a collection of works by a single author or multiple authors, or a collection of short stories, essays, speeches, or poems. Books are selected following a library's collection development policy. Books are acquired through many avenues, such as library vendors, publishers, bookstores, and book dealers, and they can be acquired through gifts and donations, too.

After a book is received in a library, it must be cataloged and processed. Books are considered monographs. Bibliographic records that describe and provide access to books must be downloaded into the library's catalog. As discussed previously, there are multiple sources of bibliographic records, including in-house copy cataloging from cataloging databases and downloading files of bibliographic records from vendors. If no bibliographic record exists, then a cataloger creates a bibliographic record from scratch. After cataloging, a print book must be processed. If a book does not already have a hard binding, then it is usually bound or treated in some way to allow for wear and tear from multiple checkouts (e.g., taping the spine). Barcodes and item records are added for checkout and inventory purposes. If a library has a security system, security strips may be added. Books may be stamped with a library stamp and marked with a call number label. Then the books are ready to shelve. If a library purchases materials shelf-ready from a vendor, all of the processing work can be done by the vendor.

Electronic Books

Electronic books, or e-books, are popular in libraries today and are in high demand. Most libraries provide access to some e-books, and libraries are increasing their e-book collections all the time. The content of e-books is the same as print books. They include all subjects and formats, fiction and nonfiction, for all audiences. It is the format and the way users access them and use them that have changed. Libraries acquire e-books directly through publishers or vendors, and libraries provide access to e-books on various platforms. Some libraries provide online access to e-books through e-book content providers such as EBSCO, OverDrive, or ProQuest, among others. Users can access e-books from a library's catalog and read them on a computer or personal device. Some e-books are available preloaded on an e-book reader or other device that a user can check out from a library. There also are some free options available, mostly for older books already in the public domain.

Another way that libraries acquire e-books is through demand-driven acquisitions, also called patron-driven or user-driven acquisitions. In these programs, instead of purchasing a specific e-book and adding it to the collection, a library downloads bibliographic records for a large group of e-books into the library catalog. When users open an e-book a certain number of times, the library automatically purchases the e-book. A library does not pay for e-books upfront, instead negotiating with the vendor on the terms of the contract (e.g., how many uses trigger the purchase). The program is helpful because it allows a library to purchase only those e-books users actually read rather than purchasing books that may never be read. However, although users may open an e-book enough times to trigger a purchase, they may not have liked the book or found it helpful. Libraries still may end up with e-books users do not want. Bibliographic records for e-books not purchased must be removed from the catalog after a certain amount of time.

Bibliographic records for e-book collections primarily come in large files. They are downloaded into a library catalog using a method called batch loading or batch processing, which downloads the bibliographic records in one big batch. The batch of bibliographic records can be manipulated or changed before the records go into the library catalog, if needed, by removing or adding information to all the records. One popular program that is used to perform this work is MarcEdit, created by Terry Reese.[15] It allows catalogers to manipulate files of bibliographic records easily and get them ready for downloading into the library catalog.

One may be tempted to think that the organizing of e-books is much simpler than print books. There is no physical processing, binding, or shelving with electronic books. However, there are many complications with organizing e-book collections in libraries. The rise of electronic books has changed the cataloging process in libraries, especially for libraries that receive large sets of bibliographic records for e-books. If a library receives a handful of e-books, then catalogers will be able to catalog them. However, a library may receive large packages of e-books with hundreds of bibliographic records that need to be downloaded into the library catalog. It would be impossible for catalogers to handle this amount of work in a reasonable timeframe. Instead of cataloging, fixing errors, and customizing bibliographic records before they are made available to users (cataloging on the front end), bibliographic records are downloaded pretty much as is into a library catalog. Then database maintenance is performed afterward to fix any problems (cataloging on the back end).

There are other issues surrounding e-books. Libraries may collect books in multiple print and/or electronic formats and may use multiple e-book platforms. Bibliographic records must explain clearly to users the format of each item and how to access it. In addition, the library does not necessarily own e-books. Libraries are just licensing them, paying for the privilege of accessing them. Complex contracts must be negotiated with vendors or publishers, and there can be many access issues and troubleshooting problems.

ORGANIZING SERIALS

Another important format collected in libraries is serials. Serials provide current information, news, research, statistics, trends, and gossip. Monographs are beneficial for delving deeply into one topic or for an artistic expression, but they are frozen in time. A book published in 2010, for example, will have information current as of 2010. A musical work recorded in 1989 may have been reissued multiple times by multiple music publishers, but the work remains the same. The meaning and interpretation may change, but not necessarily the recording itself. However, a serial publication is ongoing; it is continually publishing new, current information.

Most, if not all, libraries collect serials. However, they are collected most in academic and research libraries because serials are an important vehicle for publishing research in academic fields. Yet serials are more important in some academic fields than in others. In the sciences, serial publications are the most important vehicle for publishing new research, and books are secondary. This is different from other fields, such as in the humanities, in which books are an important vehicle for publishing research and a source for research. For example, an edition of *Pride and Prejudice* published in 1911 is just as important for research as an edition of *Pride and Prejudice* published in 2019. Serials are important in the humanities, but are secondary.

Libraries may collect serials in print and/or electronic formats, depending on the needs of the library and budget considerations. Some serials titles offer print or electronic versions, and some titles are available electronically only. Serial prices can vary wildly. Some serials are inexpensive and some can be incredibly expensive. Libraries must pay a separate institutional rate, which is higher than the personal subscription rate, for some serial titles. For example, an elementary school library may want a print subscription to *Highlights* magazine for ages 6–12, which is around $50.00 or less a year.[16] A chemistry research library may want the electronic version of *Molecular and Cellular Biochemistry*, which is around $13,000 a year.[17] No, that is not a typo. That serial title is around $13,000 a year—more than most people's first car.

Managing Print Serials

Providing access to serials is quite a bit of work. In serials cataloging, the goal is to describe the overall run of a serials title. The bibliographic record is broad enough to cover the entire run of the journal, yet specific enough to describe changes in publisher, numbering, and title. Libraries do not index individual articles in journals, magazines, newspapers, or other similar serials; electronic databases and indexes do that work. On a library catalog, users should understand which serials a library owns and the holdings (the exact volumes, issues, and/or years).

Serials work does not end with cataloging, as it does with books and other formats. Serials are ongoing, so print serials titles require more management than books and other items. A library can subscribe to serials such as magazines, journals, and newspapers, which are generally published more than once a year. A library can have standing orders for serials such as handbooks, yearbooks, series, and the like, which are published annually or at irregular intervals. After serials have been cataloged, they must be received. This is a very special part of print serials management, called check-in. Issues of print serials are checked into the library, meaning that a certain volume/issue is marked as "received," and it is usually stamped with the library's date stamp. Check-in used to be done by hand, putting check marks on cards, but now check-in is done using an integrated library system, an electronic resources manager, or another tool. Checking in serials is helpful so librarians and users know when new issues have arrived in the library. However, not all libraries check in their serials. Instead, the issues are processed and placed on the shelves.

Another important step in serials management is claiming. If an issue of a print serial has not been received, then it should be claimed. A claim is a note to the publisher or vendor that tells them an issue was not received, and the publisher will resend it. Another important aspect of print serials management is binding. Loose issues of a serial are sent to a commercial bindery to be bound together in one volume, usually in a material called buckram. When a complete volume and/or year of a journal has been received in a library, those issues are gathered together and sent to a bindery. However, with the proliferation of electronic serials, libraries are not binding their journals as much as in the past; instead, they often withdraw the issues when the electronic version is made available. In addition, withdrawing of superseded serials is an important part of print serials management. When a new edition is received for serials such as handbooks, manuals, and directories, the old edition is withdrawn. Some academic and research libraries keep older editions for research purposes.

Electronic Serials and Databases

Although most libraries collect print serials, the bulk of serial publications in libraries are electronic serials available online through a computer. They fit the definition of a serial in that they are issued in successive parts, have numbering, and are intended to continue forever; the only difference is the electronic format. Every type of library provides access to electronic serials, whether it is an academic library that purchases a large database, a group of school libraries that have access to databases through a school district, or a public librariy that has access to databases through a consortium. Electronic serials are available directly through a publisher's website or are available through large subscription databases or aggregators. Some serials are open source, meaning there is free and open access to the title online. Most electronic serials, however, are not free; libraries pay a lot of money to access them through databases, and subscription prices rise every year. More than half of some academic libraries' budgets may be dedicated to electronic serials and databases. Some publishers do not make current issues available online, so libraries must pay for both the print and electronic versions so users can read current issues. However, many libraries are increasingly moving to electronic-only versions of some serials, with no corresponding print version. There are more electronic-only serials than print serials available in libraries today.

The most common electronic serials are journals, magazines, and newspapers available in large databases called aggregators. Aggregators are databases that provide packages of electronic serials and index each article in each serial title. They also may include other resources, such as reports, reference material, book chapters, and so on.

Examples include *Academic Search Complete*, *JSTOR*, and *Project Muse*. Many aggregators focus on a particular subject area or format, providing access to multiple serial titles from multiple publishers. For example, EBSCO's *Political Science Complete* database provides access to serials and other materials about political science, and its *Music Index* provides access to serials and other materials about music.

Aggregators provide much-needed access to articles in electronic serials, yet aggregators also pump up their packages with materials a library may not want. A library may be forced to accept everything in a package even if some titles do not interest its users. This means that a library provides access to many more titles than it would have received on print. In addition, libraries usually license more than one aggregator, and journals can be duplicated across aggregators. Unlike print serials, in which a library subscribes to one or two copies of a title, libraries must manage multiple electronic subscriptions to the same title. They also need to convey this information to users in a clear way so users can find the serials. This has made electronic serials holdings explode in libraries, and managing them is difficult. Even the smallest of libraries may have access to thousands of electronic serials through databases. For example, Texas Woman's University is a medium-sized academic library but it has access to *American Libraries* in twelve different databases, each with varying coverage.[18] This duplicate coverage is overkill, but the library has to provide multiple access because *American Libraries* is in many aggregator packages the library needs. A library does not necessarily have the option of picking and choosing which electronic serials it wants.

Aggregators also have varying coverage and varying access to full-text issues. For example, a database may not provide any full-text articles, instead providing abstracts only. Some databases may provide full-text coverage for all issues and articles of a serial title, and other databases may provide full-text access to more recent issues and articles. An aggregator could have full-text issues from 2004 forward, but not have any articles before that. Coverage varies from aggregator to aggregator. It is important for libraries not only to tell users which journal titles they have access to, but the overall coverage and full-text coverage as well. Some aggregators and databases have moving walls or embargoes. This means they will not provide the most recent issues of journals. For instance, *JSTOR* has a moving wall of two to five years for each journal title. The wall of access moves forward as new issues are published.[19] Libraries may be forced to purchase print subscriptions so that users can access the most current issues.

Aggregators can be very expensive and often have different pricing. Some may charge a flat rate, some may charge the library per use, and some may have tiered pricing, in which a library with more users pays a higher rate. Licensing is also a huge issue. A license is a contract between a library and a publisher or vendor. There are many issues surrounding licensing, such as negotiating how many users can use a database at one time, whether a library can interlibrary loan articles from the database, copyright restrictions, and cancelation parameters. Archiving is another issue. Print serials can be kept permanently. Electronic journals, however, may not be permanent. Libraries do not own electronic serials. They pay for the privilege of accessing them, and they may lose access. To address this issue, some libraries participate in the Lots of Copies Keep Stuff Safe (LOCKSS) program, which is committed to archiving electronic information.[20] There also may be collection agreements among libraries in which each library commits to keeping certain print titles.

Managing Electronic Serials and Databases

There is much work involved in managing electronic serials. Libraries must tell users which electronic serials the library owns and the coverage in the databases. Like e-books, database vendors provide libraries with large files of bibliographic records that libraries download into their library catalogs through batch processing. In addition, libraries can provide an A–Z alphabetical list of electronic serials and database holdings that can be searched separately from the library catalog. Some libraries use a link resolver function that allows users searching a database to find full-text articles in other databases. In addition to bibliographic records and other tools, libraries must provide continual access to electronic serials. Electronic serials are not housed on a library's server but are located on servers around the world. There could be problems with a publisher's, vendor's, or library's server that affect access. Publishers, vendors, and websites change links, so libraries have to check links often to keep them current. Troubleshooting access problems is a big part of the work in electronic serials management. Managing electronic serials and databases is a lot of work, and this work can be done in-house with or without the use of an electronic resources manager (ERM). ERMs can provide bibliographic records, keep links current, and fix problems.

ORGANIZING MEDIA AND OTHER FORMATS

Media, also known by the older term audiovisual materials (AV), are an important part of a library's collection. Media includes formats one can listen to, look at, play, and manipulate, such as film and video, music, audiobooks, software, games, slides and images, kits, objects, apps, and on and on. In the past, media was not a big part of library collections. Today, media is extremely popular and is becoming a much bigger part of library collections.

Physical Media and Other Formats

Libraries collect much physical media, such as music on CD, films on VHS or DVD, software on CD or DVD, game cartridges, and so on. They also collect other physical formats, such as board games, kits, and objects (e.g., puppets, toys, baking supplies). These materials may be cataloged through the regular cataloging process by in-house catalogers, or bibliographic records can be obtained from vendors, if available. After cataloging, they must be processed, which includes putting them in containers or boxes, adding security devices, and adding call numbers. They are usually shelved in dedicated bins, cabinets, display racks, or library shelves.

An important issue with media is obsolescence. As technology progresses, old media formats become obsolete as they are replaced by new formats. For example, music was once available only on LP records, then it was available on 8-track tapes, then cassette tapes, then CDs, and now it can be streamed online. A library has to plan for obsolescence and may have to purchase replacements. Unfortunately, libraries do not always have the right to migrate data to a new format, and publishers often do not allow libraries to do this. Libraries may have to pay for the new format unless, perhaps, material is no longer available on any other format. With each new format, a new bibliographic record must be created. There are many issues associated with collecting physical media formats. With obsolete formats come legacy media collections. Some libraries have collections of media on older and obsolete formats, such as floppy disks, beta tapes, or laserdiscs. There might even be some 8-track tapes lying around somewhere. Libraries keep legacy media for scholarly purposes and to preserve culture. However, legacy media may be difficult to manage and circulate because a library no longer has the equipment needed to play the items and they may be hidden in a back room. A library may want to migrate the content to a digital format, but it may not have the money or equipment to digitally reproduce the items.

Digital Media

Media materials are increasingly going digital, and e-media content is being created constantly. People can listen to songs through iTunes. People can watch movies, television shows, and other content through Netflix, Hulu, or television network apps. People can listen to audiobooks through Audible. There is also much user-generated content available on various sites, such as YouTube, and people can play games or watch and listen to content on their personal devices. Everything is becoming seamless; there is easy access to media if a person has the money to pay for it.

Libraries are increasingly collecting digital media, such as streaming audio, streaming video, audiobooks, and much more. There are several programs, such as Playaway, Hoopla, and OverDrive that provide access to e-media. Just like with e-books and e-serials, vendors provide large files of bibliographic records that are downloaded into library catalogs through the batch processing process. Libraries also can use the information from the e-content platform instead of downloading bibliographic records. Users can access the e-media through bibliographic records, or libraries may have databases that provide access to e-media, such as the Naxos Music Library. There also are many free media materials available online through digital libraries and digital collections, such as the Library of Congress's digital collections. Yet there are several issues with e-media. Like with other electronic resources, libraries do not own e-media, so they have no control over preservation or access.

GOVERNMENT PUBLICATIONS

Government publications are an important part of a library's collection, and all libraries collect government publications to a certain extent. Governments produce a lot of information, and the United States government is one of the largest publishers in the world. It publishes many important publications, such as the *World Factbook*, *Occupational Outlook Handbook*, census materials, tax forms, maps, and on and on. Even the *Library of Congress Classification* and the *Library of Congress Subject Headings* are government publications. Subjects run the gamut from very technical, scientific publications to the most basic health and consumer information. Government publications also include items not typically collected by libraries, such as brochures, coloring books, and posters. Government publications are published in all formats and many languages, including braille, and many government publications are serials published in large, numbered series. Although many government publications are available in print, most of them are also—or only—available online. This has implications for access and archiving, because it can be difficult for libraries to ensure free and open access to government information since there is no guarantee an online government publication will remain available in the future.

Government publications are produced at the international, national, regional, state, county, and city levels. A library may collect publications at any level and may receive publications on any format. A library may receive them for free from a government agency, purchase them through a vendor or a government bookstore, or receive them for free through a state, federal, or international depository program that distributes government publications, such as the Federal Depository Library Program.

Federal Depository Library Program

As discussed in chapter 5, the Federal Depository Library Program (FDLP) is a government program that librarians can join to acquire free US government publications. The public has a right to free access to these publications because they were created at the public's expense, using funding from taxes. FDLP is open to any library that wants US government publications, and there are currently around 1,250 libraries that participate in the program.[21] At least one library in every state is designated a regional depository library. The regional depository library has the responsibility of keeping almost everything supplied by FDLP. It is considered the library of last resort for US government publications in each state.

FDLP takes the burden of collecting and distributing government publications off each individual library. However, these materials remain the property of the US government; they do not belong to libraries. In addition, participating libraries must make these materials available to the public. A library in the program is obligated to provide free and open access to the public during regular working hours. Libraries also must go through a Public Access Assessment, which is an inspection about every five years. There also are certain requirements about withdrawing government publications from the collection. Participating libraries are not obligated to keep everything, but there are guidelines that libraries must follow to determine whether something can be withdrawn.

Government publications obtained through FDLP are managed in many ways in libraries. First, a library chooses the publications it wants from the list of classes. There is a minimum amount that must be selected. A library will periodically receive boxes of physical items. To facilitate the processing of physical materials, most libraries receive bibliographic records, barcodes, and labels through a vendor. This makes processing print government publications very quick. Bibliographic records are downloaded into the library's catalog, and physical items are stamped with a depository stamp to indicate they are part of FDLP and belong to the US government. For online materials, bibliographic records are downloaded into the catalog.[22]

Libraries do not have to use a vendor to process government publications. Items may be cataloged in-house in a cataloging unit. It depends on where the publications are housed. Libraries with large collections of government publications will most likely shelve them in a separate *Superintendent of Documents Classification* collection, and likely use a vendor for processing. As discussed in chapter 5, the SuDocs Classification system is a classification scheme just for federal government publications based on a federal government agency. A library with a smaller government publications collection may shelve them in the main collection using the library's regular classification scheme, and cataloging may be handled in-house by the cataloging unit. There are other possible combinations, too. Some libraries shelve government documents in multiple areas, so high-traffic items are classified in the main collection and low-traffic items are kept in the SuDocs collection.

METADATA PRACTICE

Metadata practice includes all work done to create and manage institutional repositories and digital collections. Not all libraries do this work; it is done primarily by academic libraries and larger public libraries. Yet it is becoming an important part of cataloging and metadata practice. Unlike cataloging work, which has been refined over the last 150 years and is standardized across libraries, metadata work is not standardized across libraries. Libraries have been performing this work only for the past 25 years or so, and although there are best practices concerning metadata, each library has, for the most part, created its own policies and practices. This is because metadata work deals with items that are unique, rare, or special, and are part of special collections and archives. These are not mass-produced items. It is difficult to standardize the cataloging and organization of these items because they are not duplicated across libraries. These items are unique, and describing and providing access to them can change depending on the needs of a particular collection. How a library describes and provides access to a local government archives in a small town in Illinois, for example, can be different from how a library describes and provides access to a local govern-ment archives in a small town in Florida. In addition, this work is often performed in-house and is usually not outsourced to contract catalogers because of cost. The unique, sometimes fragile nature of these materials means that digitization and cata-loging may be complex; it is often more cost-effective to perform the work in-house.

There are two types of materials in digital collections: items that are born digital and items that are digitized. Materials that are born digital were created using a computer and stored digitally. Examples are digital photos and videos, Word docu-ments, PowerPoint presentations, and the like. A library may or may not own the file or house the resource on its server. Materials that are digitized means that a resource started its life as something physical, like a diary, photograph, or a book, and was scanned and made into a digital file. The library owns the physical item and the file, which is housed on the library's server or the parent organization's server.

There are two primary types of metadata work performed in libraries: (1) creat-ing and managing an institutional repository and (2) creating and managing digital collections. For institutional repository work, metadata specialists gather materials created by faculty and staff at a college or university. Materials can include anything related to the institution, such as PowerPoint presentations given at conferences, prepublication copies of articles, published articles that are openly available, videos, and so on. It also can include work by students: theses and dissertations, photo ar-chives, and the like. Anything related to the institution is fair game. Newer items are usually born digital, so digital files are already available to load into the institutional repository. However, libraries may want to digitize older items created by people at the university. Items in an institutional repository are made available in a separate database using content management products such as DSpace.[23]

For digital collections work, metadata specialists make digital copies of physical items. Digitization is performed for special collections and archives, and is usually performed for a particular collection, for example, the archives of a local family, the personal archives of a scholar, or a collection of photos from an old newspaper. These special collections are digitized and gathered together into digital collections. A library may have multiple digital collections housed in a separate database using content management products like CONTENTdm.[24]

For items in institutional repositories and digital collections, a metadata record that describes each item is created using a metadata schema, such as *Dublin Core*. Unlike library cataloging, in which standard records are created across libraries, metadata records are not standardized across libraries. They reflect the needs of one library and its collection. *Dublin Core*, for example, can be modified to fit a library's needs, and how information is entered into the record is determined by the library. Libraries also may or may not choose to add subjects from a controlled vocabulary. There is no standardized practice across libraries about how things should be de-scribed. Each library can decide on its own. These projects can be time and labor intensive, especially with digitized materials. Each item must be digitized first, and then a metadata record is created for each item in a digital collection.

However, creating metadata records can be easier than creating bibliographic records. Both types of work involve creating descriptive metadata, but metadata schemas are much more flexible than cataloging standards. A library can choose which metadata schema it would like to use, and it can modify the elements to meet the needs of the collection. There are no strict rules about how information is entered into metadata records. A library can determine its own policies and procedures, and description can be as simple or as detailed as the library wants. This gives libraries a lot of flexibility and control over the organization of their digital collections.

Yet, although creating descriptive metadata may be easier in metadata work, libraries with digital collections must deal with administrative and structural data, too. Libraries are creating digital files of their collections housed on the library's server or a parent organization's server. Lots of metadata are required so that users can open and read the files, and libraries can manage and preserve the files. Technical metadata is important to give information about the files, and structural metadata is important to show where files are located and how they fit together.

Because metadata work includes different types of metadata, the organization of this work happens in many ways in libraries. There may be one or two people working on metadata projects in a small library, or there may be hundreds of people working on metadata projects in a large library. Staffing depends on the library and the size of its digital collections. Metadata work also may be performed in different areas of the library, and possibly even outside the library. It may be a separate unit in a technical services department, included as part of a cataloging and metadata unit, or located in a special collections unit. The work also may be performed partly by staff in systems or informational technology. Metadata work often requires the expertise of several departments to make sure digital collections are available to users.

ISSUES IN CATALOGING AND METADATA PRACTICE

Cataloging and metadata practice is complex. Much work is involved in cataloging and managing physical collections, electronic resource collections, and digital collections. The unbridled growth of electronic resources, especially, has changed how cataloging is performed in libraries. Although there are still libraries that perform all cataloging in-house, most libraries have had to change their practices to accommodate dwindling budgets, receiving fewer print materials, and receiving many electronic materials. Cataloging work and metadata work have experienced much change over the years, and there are several trends and issues that have affected how cataloging and metadata work is performed in libraries today.

Technological Change

One issue that cataloging and metadata practice continually face is keeping up with new technology. New technologies continually drive change in cataloging and metadata practice. With more sophisticated technologies come new and more technologically complicated ways to access, store, and retrieve information. Change through technology has been a constant factor in libraries and cataloging work since the beginning of the profession. The use of typewriters in libraries meant that catalog cards could be typed and not written in library hand, which led to quicker cataloging. The development of the MARC format and bibliographic records led to shared cataloging in libraries, and the creation of the World Wide Web led to the proliferation of electronic resources and batch processing, the creation of digital collections, and metadata work. The development of the Semantic Web and RDF technologies has led libraries to perform linked data projects, which has the potential to change how cataloging is performed in libraries. (For more on this, see chapter 10.) It can be difficult to keep up with technological change, to know how to incorporate and use new technologies, or even to know how to prepare for change.

Less Traditional Cataloging and More Database Maintenance

Another issue in cataloging and metadata practice is that less traditional cataloging is being performed. Traditional cataloging is cataloging on the front end of the catalog. A cataloger fixes up and customizes bibliographic records *before* they go into the library catalog. Catalogers have control over the catalog and can ensure that bibliographic records in the catalog are correct and appropriate. However, shelf-ready books and the growth of electronic resources in libraries have changed cataloging practice. Vendors provide files of bibliographic records that can be downloaded at once using batch processing. The batch of records can be modified and changed if necessary, and then any errors can be fixed *after* the bibliographic records are in the catalog. This makes cataloging quicker and more efficient and makes library materials available to users much faster. Yet this changes the cataloging process. Instead of cataloging on the front end and creating the bibliographic record before library resources are available to users, bibliographic records are downloaded into the library catalog and then errors are fixed on the back end, after the records go into the catalog. This may be problematic because record quality can vary among vendors, and libraries may have to perform lots of database maintenance to fix problems. A library catalog may not help users and may not be fulfilling the IFLA user tasks discussed in chapter 1: find, identify, select, obtain, and explore. Even the smallest of spelling errors or MARC formatting errors on a bibliographic record can negatively affect searching, and incorrect access points can prevent users from fulfilling the IFLA user tasks. It also means that to a certain extent, catalogers have had to give up control of library catalogs. Catalogers have to accept mistakes on bibliographic records and have to be okay with "good enough" cataloging. This is a difficult transition for many catalogers. "Good enough" cataloging may not be "good enough" for users or for discovery on library catalogs,[25] and users may not find what they need.

Fewer Catalogers and More Metadata Librarians

Another issue is change in cataloging jobs. Before computers, there were many professional and paraprofessional catalogers who performed cataloging. The development of the MARC format, bibliographic records, and shared cataloging through bibliographic utilities changed the cataloging process. Professional catalogers were not needed to perform push-button copy cataloging, so more paraprofessional catalogers were hired to do this work. Cataloging work has been passed from professional catalogers to paraprofessional catalogers, while the professional catalogers have become supervisors, perform original cataloging, and focus on cataloging complex items. Libraries have been affected by budget cuts, and as professional catalogers retired, those professional jobs have been downgraded or eliminated in many libraries. There is still a need for professional catalogers, and many cataloging units are short on staff today, yet many professional positions have been eliminated. This has caused some to claim that cataloging has been "deprofessionalized."[26]

The cataloging workforce was deprofessionalized by technology starting in the 1970s and continuing through the 1990s and beyond. There are far fewer professional catalogers working today than in the past. The next change in the cataloging workforce was the elimination of many paraprofessional cataloger positions due to increased purchasing of bibliographic records from vendors. Because bibliographic records from vendors are simply batch processed into library catalogs, paraprofessionals are not needed to perform as much copy cataloging as in the past. Libraries also are receiving fewer print books than they have in the past and are still affected by budget constraints. Therefore, many paraprofessional cataloger positions have been eliminated or reassigned, too.

However, there has been job growth in metadata work, both for professional and paraprofessional positions. In a 2006 survey of academic libraries, for example, 76 percent of the libraries surveyed created jobs dedicated to metadata work, especially work with digital collections.[27] Many technical services departments in academic libraries and larger public libraries are restructuring to accommodate metadata work. Instead of a traditional technical services department, some libraries have created new departments with names such as Collections, Delivery and Access, or Access Services. There are also new librarian and paraprofessional positions that work in this area, with job titles such as Digital Collections Librarian, Metadata Librarian, or Electronic Resources Librarian.[28]

Showing Value

A final issue that affects cataloging and metadata practice is the importance of showing value to libraries and organizations. The value of cataloging and metadata is often questioned when administrators are faced with budget cuts, because the work can be expensive. Catalogers and metadata specialists know that cataloging and metadata work is vital to support the mission of libraries and to help users find what they need. However, getting the message out can be difficult, and it is very important for catalogers and metadata specialists to advocate continually for the important work they do to help users. Performing regular assessment of cataloging and metadata services is essential to help a cataloging or metadata unit show how it contributes to a library and helps meet its mission.

SUMMARY

This chapter discussed cataloging and metadata practice in general. It talked about cataloging work, serials work, and metadata work. It discussed the differences between monographs and serials and how this historical difference is reflected in cataloging practice today. Cataloging units catalog monographs in all formats, while serials units catalog and manage serial publications. Different formats have different organizational needs. In addition, this chapter discussed many issues that affect cataloging and metadata practice in most libraries, such as keeping up with technological change, less traditional cataloging, fewer cataloging jobs, and showing value. This chapter looked at all libraries in general. Chapter 8 will discuss how library collections are organized in academic, public, school, and special libraries.

DISCUSSION QUESTIONS

1. What are the differences between monographs and serials, and how is each type of publication organized in libraries?
2. What are the issues surrounding batch processing of bibliographic records (e-books and e-serials)? What are its advantages and disadvantages, and how has it changed cataloging work?
3. Talk about the issues facing cataloging and metadata practice. Are the changes good for libraries? Good for users?

CLASS ACTIVITIES

1. *Evaluate a Library's Physical Organization.* Visit a library, any library you choose. Describe and evaluate the organization of the library. How is the library organized? What types of materials are in the library and where are they housed (e.g., books, serials, music, film, children's materials)? What formal classification scheme(s) is used (DDC, LCC, etc.)? How are the materials arranged in the library? Is the library's organization easy to understand/intuitive? Is it clear where materials are located? Is it easy to find things? What do you think could make the organization better? Then write an essay that describes the organization of items in the library and evaluates the library's organization.

2. *Evaluate a Library's Electronic Organization.* Perform the same assignment as above, except focusing on electronic resources available in the library. Explore the library's website and its electronic collections. What electronic resources and collections are available in the library? How are they organized? Is it easy to find and access the materials? Is there anything done to help users navigate the electronic collection? Then write an essay that describes the organization of electronic resources in the library and evaluates the organization of electronic resources.

3. *Evaluate a Library's Digital Collection.* Perform the same assignment as above, except focusing on a digital collection available in a library. This may be a different library from the one you initially visited. Explore the library's digital collections. What is in the collection? What types of materials? How are they organized? Is it easy to find and access the digital resources? Is there anything done to help users navigate the digital collection? Then write an essay that describes the organization of the digital collection and evaluates the organization of the digital collection.

NOTES

1. OCLC, "Inside WorldCat," accessed January 13, 2019, https://www.oclc.org/en/worldcat/inside-worldcat.html.

2. OCLC, "CatExpress," accessed January 13, 2019, https://www.oclc.org/en/catexpress/ordering.html.

3. OCLC, "Inside WorldCat."

4. OCLC, "When to Input a New Record," in *Bibliographic Formats and Standards*, 4th ed., 2018, accessed January 13, 2019, https://www.oclc.org/bibformats/en/input.html.

5. OCLC, *Bibliographic Formats and Standards*, 4th ed., 2018, accessed January 13, 2019, https://www.oclc.org/bibformats/en.html.

6. Mitinet Library Services, accessed January 13, 2019, https://www.mitinet.com.

7. The Library Corporation, accessed January 13, 2019, https://tlcdelivers.com.

8. National Information Standards Organization, *Z39.50: A Primer on the Protocol* (Bethesda, MD: NISO Press, 2001), accessed January 13, 2019, https://www.niso.org/publications/z3950-primer-protocol.

9. RDA Toolkit, "RDA 1.1.3: Mode of Issuance," accessed January 13, 2019, https://access.rdatoolkit.org.

10. RDA Toolkit, "RDA Glossary: Monograph," accessed January 13, 2019, https://access.rdatoolkit.org.

11. RDA Toolkit, "RDA 1.1.3: Mode of Issuance."

12. *American Libraries* (May 2018): 3.

13. *Anglo-American Cataloguing Rules*, 2nd ed., rev. (Chicago: American Library Association, 2002).

14. Joelen Pastva, Gwen Gregory, and Violet Fox, "Keep Calm and Carry On: The New Technical Services," in *Rethinking Technical Services: New Frameworks, New Skill Sets, New Tools, New Roles*, ed. Bradford Lee Eden (Lanham, MD: Rowman & Littlefield, 2016), 29–40.

15. MarcEdit: Your Complete Free MARC Editing Utility, accessed January 13, 2019, https://marcedit.reeset.net.

16. *Highlights* Magazines for Kids, accessed January 13, 2019, https://www.highlights.com/store/highlights-magazines-for-kids.

17. Springer Nature, "2019 Springer Nature Journals Price List," accessed January 13, 2019, https://www.springernature.com/gp/librarians/licensing/journals-price-list.

18. Texas Woman's University, "Libraries," accessed January 13, 2009, https://twu.edu/library.

19. JSTOR, "Journals," accessed January 13, 2019, https://about.jstor.org/whats-in-jstor/journals.

20. Stanford University, "LOCKSS: Lots of Copies Keep Stuff Safe," accessed January 13, 2019, https://www.lockss.org.

21. Federal Depository Library Program, "Federal Depository Libraries," accessed January 13, 2019, https://www.fdlp.gov/about-the-fdlp/federal-depository-libraries.

22. Federal Depository Library Program, accessed January 13, 2019, https://www.fdlp.gov.

23. DSpace, accessed January 13, 2019, https://duraspace.org/dspace/about.

24. OCLC, "CONTENTdm," accessed January 13, 2019, https://www.oclc.org/en/contentdm.html.

25. See, e.g., Mary S. Laskowski, "When Good Enough Is Not Good Enough: Resolving Cataloging Issues for High Density Storage," *Cataloging & Classification Quarterly* 54, no. 3 (2016): 147–58.

26. Roma Harris, *Librarianship: The Erosion of a Woman's Profession* (Norwood, NJ: Ablex, 1992); Ling Hwey Jeng, "Knowledge, Technology, and Research in Cataloging," *Cataloging & Classification Quarterly* 24, no. 1 (1997): 113–27.

27. Michael Boock and Ruth Vondracek, "Organizing for Digitization: A Survey." *Portal: Libraries and the Academy* 6 (2006): 197–217.

28. Myung-Ja Han and Patricia Hswe, "The Evolving Role of the Metadata Librarian: Competencies Found in Job Descriptions," *Library Resources & Technical Services* 53 (2010): 129–41.

SELECTED BIBLIOGRAPHY AND ADDITIONAL READING

Acedo, Shannon, and Cathy Leverkus. "Updates on Ebooks: Challenges & Changes." *Knowledge Quest* 43 no. 1 (2014): 44–52.

Anglo-American Cataloguing Rules. Second Edition, Revised. Chicago: American Library Association, 2002.

Ayers, Leighann, Beth Picknally Camden, Lisa German, Peggy Johnson, Caroline Miller, and Karen Smith-Yoshimura. *What We've Learned from the RLG Partners Metadata Creation Workflows Survey*. Dublin, OH: OCLC Research, 2009. https://www.oclc.org/content/dam/research/publications/library/2009/2009-04.pdf.

Bade, David. "Rapid Cataloging: Three Models for Addressing Timeliness as an Issue of Quality in Library Catalogs." *Cataloging & Classification Quarterly* 45, no. 1 (2007): 87–123.

Banush, David. "Stepping Out: The Expanding Role of Catalogers in Academic Libraries and Academic Institutions." *Cataloging & Classification Quarterly* 45, no. 3 (2008): 81–90.

Boock, Michael, and Ruth Vondracek. "Organizing for Digitization: A Survey." *Portal: Libraries and the Academy* 6 (2006): 197–217.

Borie, Juliya, Kate MacDonald, and Elisa Sze. "Asserting Catalogers' Place in the 'Value of Libraries' Conversation." *Cataloging & Classification Quarterly* 53, no. 3–4 (2015): 352–67.

Boydston, Jeanne M. K., and Joan M. Leysen. "ARL Cataloger Librarian Roles and Responsibilities Now and in the Future." *Cataloging & Classification Quarterly* 52, no. 2 (2014): 229–50.

———. "Observations on the Catalogers' Role in Descriptive Metadata Creation in Academic Libraries." *Cataloging & Classification Quarterly* 43, no. 2 (2006): 3–17.

Cerbo, Michael A. "Is There a Future for Library Catalogers?" *Cataloging & Classification Quarterly* 49, no. 4 (2011): 323–27.

Chapman, John W. "The Roles of the Metadata Librarian in a Research Library." *Library Resources & Technical Services* 51, no. 4 (2007): 279–85.

Clair, Kevin. "Creative Disorder: The Work of Metadata Librarians in the 21st Century." In *The Expert Library: Staffing, Sustaining, and Advancing the Academic Library in the 21st Century*, edited by Scott Walter and Karen Williams, 270–91. Chicago: Association of College and Research Libraries, 2010.

Crosetto, Alice. "The Management of Electronic Resources." In *Rethinking Library Technical Services: Redefining our Professional for the Future*, edited by Mary Beth Weber, 73–84. Lanham, MD: Rowman & Littlefield, 2015.

Davis Jeehyun Yun. "Transforming Technical Services: Evolving Functions in Large Research University Libraries." *Library Resources & Technical Services* 60 (2016): 52–65.

Dieckman, Christopher S. "Qualifications for Serials Catalogers in the 21st Century: A Content Analysis of Job Advertisements." *Cataloging & Classification Quarterly* 56, no. 5–6 (2018): 487–506.

Doran, Claire, and Cheryl Martin. "Measuring Success in Outsourced Cataloging: A Data-Driven Investigation." *Cataloging & Classification Quarterly* 55, no. 5 (2017): 307–17.

Eden, Bradford Lee, ed. *Rethinking Technical Services: New Frameworks, New Skill Sets, New Tools, New Roles*. Lanham, MD: Rowman & Littlefield, 2016.

Giesecke, Joan. "Institutional Repositories: Keys to Success." *Journal of Library Administration*, 51, no. 5–6 (2011): 529–42.

Hall-Ellis, Sylvia D. "Metadata Competencies for Entry-Level Positions: What Employers Expect as Reflected in Position Descriptions, 2000–2013." *Journal of Library Metadata* 15, no. 2 (2015): 102–34.

Han, Myung-Ja, and Patricia Hswe. "The Evolving Role of the Metadata Librarian: Competencies Found in Job Descriptions." *Library Resources & Technical Services* 53 (2010): 129–41.

Harris, Roma. *Librarianship: The Erosion of a Woman's Profession*. Norwood, NJ: Ablex, 1992.

Jeng, Ling Hwey. "Knowledge, Technology, and Research in Cataloging." *Cataloging & Classification Quarterly* 24, no. 1 (1997): 113–27.

Johnson, Peggy. *Developing and Managing Electronic Collections: The Essentials*. Chicago: ALA Editions, 2013.

———. *Fundamentals of Collection Development and Management*. Fourth Edition. Chicago: ALA Editions, 2018.

Kelsey, Marie. *Cataloging for School Librarians*. Lanham, MD: Rowman & Littlefield, 2014.

Khurshid, Zahiruddin. "The Impact of Information Technology on Job Requirements and Qualifications for Catalogers." *Information Technology & Libraries* 22, no. 1 (2003): 18–21.

Laskowski, Mary S. "When Good Enough Is Not Good Enough: Resolving Cataloging Issues for High Density Storage." *Cataloging & Classification Quarterly* 54, no. 3 (2016): 147–58.

Lopatin, Laurie. "Metadata Practices in Academic and Non-Academic Libraries for Digital Projects: A Survey." *Cataloging & Classification Quarterly* 48, no. 8 (2010): 716–42.

Mitchell, Anne M., J. Michael Thompson, and Annie Wu. "Agile Cataloging: Staffing and Skills for a Bibliographic Future." *Cataloging & Classification Quarterly* 48, no. 6–7 (2010): 506–24.

National Information Standards Organization. *Z39.50: A Primer on the Protocol*. Bethesda, MD: NISO Press, 2001. https://www.niso.org/publications/z3950-primer-protocol.

OCLC. *Bibliographic Formats and Standards*. Fourth Edition. 2018. https://www.oclc.org/bibformats/en.html.

Pastva, Joelen, Gwen Gregory, and Violet Fox. "Keep Calm and Carry On: The New Technical Services. In *Rethinking Technical Services: New Frameworks, New Skill Sets, New Tools, New Roles*, ed. Bradford Lee Eden, 29–40. Lanham, MD: Rowman & Littlefield, 2016.

Payant, Andrea, Becky Skeen, and Liz Woolcott. "Initiating Cultural Shifts in Perceptions of Cataloging Units through Interaction Assessment." *Cataloging & Classification Quarterly* 55, no. 7–8 (2017): 467–92.

Sellberg, Roxanne. "Cooperative Cataloging in a Post-OPAC World." *Cataloging & Classification Quarterly* 48, no. 2–3 (2010): 237–46.

Simpson, Betsy. "Collection Define Cataloging's Future." *Journal of Academic Librarianship* 33, no. 4 (2007): 507–11.

The Survey of Academic Library Cataloging Practices. New York: Primary Research Group, 2013.

Steinhagen, Elizabeth N., Mary Ellen Hanson, and Sharon A. Moynahan. "Quo Vadis, Cataloging?" *Cataloging & Classification Quarterly* 44, no. 3–4 (2007): 271–80.

Valentino, Maura L. "Integrating Metadata Creation into Catalog Workflow." *Cataloging & Classification Quarterly* 48, no. 6–7 (2010): 541–50.

Veve, Marielle, and Melanie Feltner-Reichert. "Integrating Non-MARC Metadata Duties into the Workflow of Traditional Catalogers: A Survey of Trends and Perceptions among Catalogers in Four Discussion Lists." *Technical Services Quarterly* 27, no. 2 (2010): 194–213.

Walters, William H. "E-books in Academic Libraries: Challenges for Sharing and Use." *Journal of Librarianship and Information Science* 46, no. 2 (2014): 85–95.

Weber, Mary Beth. 2015. "Introduction: What Is Technical Services?" In *Rethinking Library Technical Services: Redefining our Professional for the Future*, ed. Mary Beth Weber, ix–xviii. Lanham, MD: Rowman & Littlefield, 2015.

West, Wendy L., Heather S. Miller, and Kristen Wilson. "Electronic Journals: Cataloging and Management Practices in Academic Libraries." *Serials Review* 37, no. 44 (2011): 267–74.

8

Organizing Collections in Academic, Public, School, and Special Libraries

The last chapter focused on organizing library collections in general. It discussed aspects of cataloging and metadata practice common to all types of libraries as well as some issues facing the cataloging and metadata field as a whole. This chapter extends that discussion by exploring how library collections are organized in academic, public, school, and special libraries. Each type of library organizes collections differently depending on its mission and the community it serves. Yet, although there are similarities among each library type, each individual library has its own policies and procedures. There are around 117,000 libraries in the United States,[1] and it would be impossible to discuss all ways libraries organize their collections. This chapter will discuss how academic, public, school, and special libraries are typically organized and the factors that drive organizational decisions.

SIMILARITIES AND DIFFERENCES ACROSS LIBRARIES

There are many similarities and differences in how library collections are organized across libraries. As discussed throughout this book, all libraries organize their collections. Libraries catalog their main collections to help users find and use library materials. Libraries create standard bibliographic records that describe and provide access to a library's collection, which are housed in online public access catalogs. Libraries use the same descriptive cataloging standard, add subject headings and/ or thesaurus descriptors to bibliographic records, and use classification schemes to organize their collections. Libraries perform copy and original cataloging; deal with monographs, serials, media, and electronic resources; and obtain most of their bibliographic records from outside sources.

Despite these similarities, there are many differences. Each type of library has different missions, users, and needs, which drive how library collections are organized. They use different standards for subject analysis, perform cataloging and metadata work differently, and have different issues and challenges. Libraries can choose from a wide variety of subject headings lists and thesauri that meet their needs, such as the *Library of Congress Subject Headings* or the *Sears List of Subject Headings*. Libraries classify their collections in many ways, using the *Dewey Decimal Classification*, *Library of Congress Classification*, and/or alternative classification.

Cataloging and metadata practice also can differ among libraries. There is no one standard way that cataloging and metadata work should be performed in libraries. Each library can determine how its collections are organized, and its own policies, procedures, and workflows. These policies and procedures depend on several factors that were discussed in chapter 1, such as mission and users, size, complexity, format, and budget/institutional concerns. These factors drive organizational decisions in libraries. A library's mission is an important factor because a library's purpose and who it serves determine the nature of a library's collection and how it is organized. For example, a research library serving a technology company will have a very specialized collection to serve the research needs of the company. Materials will be organized to facilitate quick retrieval. This is different from an elementary school library serving students in kindergarten through grade 6. It will have a less complicated collection, but it will need to organize its collection to encourage reading and support learning.

The size of a library's collection is another factor that can determine cataloging and metadata practice. A bigger collection means that a library collects more materials and formats, and more bibliographic records are added to the library catalog on a regular basis. Size can determine how bibliographic records are obtained for a library, whether cataloging is performed by in-house catalogers or purchased from a vendor, and how many catalogers are needed to perform the work. Different types of libraries can share similarities based on size of collection. Cataloging work in a large academic library can be similar to a large public library, and cataloging work in a small public library can be similar to a school library.

Complexity and format are other factors. Complex subjects (e.g., physics, nuclear engineering) and formats (e.g., archival materials, music scores) can be difficult to catalog and often require specialized subject knowledge and cataloging knowledge. A library may need a more specialized cataloging or metadata staff. Budget/institutional concerns may be the most important factor that affects cataloging practice. The budget determines what is possible, how many catalogers are employed, how many bibliographic records are purchased from a vendor, whether a library can customize bibliographic records, if metadata work can be performed, and on and on. Most libraries are affected by continually decreasing budgets and continually higher prices for materials. Determining how much of the budget to devote to cataloging and metadata work is difficult, and libraries may not be able to spend much of the budget on cataloging or metadata work. As a consequence, many cataloging units have too much work to do and too few staff to do it. The budget can impact greatly how cataloging and metadata work is performed in a library.

ACADEMIC LIBRARIES

According to the National Center for Education Statistics, "[A]n academic library is the library associated with a degree-granting institution of higher education. Academic libraries are identified by the post-secondary institution of which they are a part."[2] Academic libraries serve any postsecondary higher education institution that grants degrees, such as colleges, universities, and community colleges. An academic library does not serve elementary, middle, or high schools. According to the American Library Association, there are around 3,100 academic libraries in the United States.[3] The first academic library in the United States was at Harvard College, which was founded in 1636. In 1638 John Harvard passed away and gifted the college his library of around 400 volumes. As discussed in chapter 1, academic libraries grew as colleges and universities were founded across the United States.[4]

Each academic library serves students, faculty, staff, and administrators at the college or university and supports the programs and mission of the college or university. A college or university can be large or small, public or private, religious or secular, nonprofit or for-profit, fully online or not, and can offer different types of degrees (e.g., bachelor's degrees, master's degrees, doctoral degrees, certificates) in different academic programs (e.g., biology, engineering, history, art). Academic libraries also serve community colleges, which are primarily public institutions that offer associate's degrees and certificates in vocational programs and also offer programs that prepare students to transfer to a college or university. Academic libraries may serve specialized institutions, such as art and design schools or nursing colleges. Colleges and universities are defined by their level of research activity. Some colleges and universities are more research intensive than other universities, and their faculty are required to perform research, apply for grants, and publish.[5,6]

In addition, some academic libraries, particularly community college libraries in small towns, may be combined with public libraries. They are called joint-use libraries, which means that the library serves both a college and the general community. Instead of just serving academic programs, students, and faculty, these libraries need to serve the general public of all ages.

Nature of Academic Library Collections

There are far fewer academic libraries than any other type of library. However, as a whole, they have larger collections and keep more of those collections permanently. Each college or university has its own mission, degree programs, and curricula, so it is important for academic libraries to understand the institution it serves. This will determine the types of materials collected in the library and the types of organization that are needed. Collections in academic libraries can be large or small, depending on the university and library. Academic libraries serving research institutions that offer many doctoral programs with high research activity will have larger collections to meet those research needs. For example, Cornell University is a private university in New York State with 23,600 students[7] and several doctoral programs; it is classified as "Doctoral Universities: Very High Research Activity."[8] Cornell has a large library collection to meet these needs. It has several libraries holding more than 8 million print volumes, more than a million e-books, access to 120,000 electronic serials, and special collections and other materials to support programs and research.[9] Compare this to Lincoln University in Pennsylvania, which has almost 2,400 students[10] but offers only undergraduate and master's degrees. It is classified as "Master's Colleges & Universities: Medium Programs."[11] Lincoln University has a smaller library collection to meet these needs. Its Langston Hughes Memorial Library has 185,000 volumes, access to 30,000 electronic serials, and special collections and other materials to serve its programs.[12] Its student body is smaller, it offers fewer programs, and it is not research intensive, so its library's collection is smaller.

An academic library's collections include resources needed to support research, teaching, and learning at its parent institution. The complexity and depth of a collection will depend on the programs offered at the institution. For example, a college that offers undergraduate, master's, and PhD programs in dance will have a larger and deeper collection that supports teaching and learning on the subject at the undergraduate, graduate, and doctoral levels. This is different from a college that offers only one undergraduate degree in dance. Although there may be some higher-level items that support faculty research, most of the collection will be at an undergraduate level to support that program. Larger universities with more programs have larger libraries because more materials are needed to support each program.

Academic libraries collect materials in any format needed to support teaching and research. This can include books, serials, film and video, music, scores, maps, slides, objects, and many electronic resources and digital collections. The bulk of an academic library collection consists of books and serials, both print and electronic. Although academic libraries are still getting books and serials in print, academic libraries are increasingly purchasing more e-books, e-serials, and other electronic resources. Although e-books can be purchased separately, they are often purchased in large packages and made available through a library's catalog. E-serials are located primarily in research databases (aggregators) that offer packages of electronic serials, and academic libraries subscribe to multiple databases depending on their budget and their needs. Databases are often the most expensive part of an academic library collection, and a library must negotiate a license for each database.

Unlike public and school libraries, academic libraries do not collect popular fiction or genres. Instead, academic libraries collect literature used for teaching and research. Some academic libraries, however, provide popular fiction collections for their students, called leisure reading collections, and they are usually located in a separate area away from the main collection. Leisure reading collections can be licensed through leasing programs like McNaughton, which provide books and bibliographic records for popular fiction. The library keeps the books for a set amount of time and then gets new fiction on a rotating basis. Some academic libraries have children's collections to support education, reading, and library and information science programs.

Some academic libraries receive government publications through the Federal Depository Library Program, and some academic libraries are considered regional depository libraries for a state. A library may have a separate collection of federal and/or state government publications, and there may be a separate government publications unit that handles the cataloging and maintenance of them. Academic libraries also provide access to master's theses and doctoral dissertations. Theses and dissertations may be available in print in a library, but they are increasingly being made available online only, housed in a university's institutional repository or other digital collection.

Many academic libraries have special collections, which are collections of old, rare, or unique materials. Unlike the main collection, which consists mostly of mass-published materials, special collections are unique to a particular library and may contain manuscripts, rare books, rare materials, archival collections, and so on. Some academic libraries also oversee a university or college's archives, which contain items produced by the university or college, such as fact books, budgets, newsletters, yearbooks, directories, and so on. Special collections set apart each academic library. Each one has different collections and special materials. The collections may be housed in a special collections department, rare books room, or something similar. Patrons do not have direct access to special collections or archives and often must request materials.

Many academic libraries make their special collections and archival materials available in digital collections. Materials are digitized and made available in content management databases. Many academic libraries are in charge of a university's institutional repository that includes materials from students, faculty, and staff of a particular university. Institutional repositories are digital collections, although some libraries may have historical preprint collections of faculty publications. In addition, some academic libraries perform linked data projects.

Academic library collections are more permanent than collections in other types of libraries. Deselection (weeding) happens, but more materials are kept for research and preservation purposes, depending on the nature of each university and its collection. A very large research library supporting many doctoral programs will keep more of its collection than a smaller academic library supporting undergraduate programs. Collection agreements and other types of sharing among academic libraries allow them to work together to ensure that library resources are preserved.

How Academic Library Collections Are Organized

Academic libraries tend to have two broad types of collections: a main collection and special collections. Main collections tend to be organized in similar ways across academic libraries, but there can be variations when it comes to special collections.

Main Collection

An academic library's main collection consists primarily of mass-published books, serials, film and video, music, and the like, and can consist of physical or electronic resources. The main collection does not include resources in special collections or archives. Bibliographic records are created for each item in a library's main collection located in the library's online catalog. There are many library catalogs for academic libraries to choose from, depending on the size of the library, but common catalogs are Innovative, Ex Libris, and SirsiDynix. Academic libraries also use discovery products with features that enhance users' searching experiences, such as the ability to search all library collections at once. Academic libraries also may be part of a consortium that shares a library catalog with other libraries.

Academic libraries catalog their collections using national cataloging standards, policies, and guidelines. Most academic libraries use *Resource Description and Access* for descriptive cataloging, although smaller academic libraries may not have made the switch from the old *Anglo-American Cataloguing Rules*, second edition, revised, to RDA yet. Academic libraries also tend to follow the Library of Congress-Program for Cooperative Cataloging Policy Statements for RDA, because the Library of Congress's policies tend to fit the needs of academic libraries well. Customization can differ among academic libraries. Some academic libraries do not customize records at all, instead accepting bibliographic records as is. Other academic libraries customize bibliographic records to meet users' needs, such as adding access points for people affiliated with the university or college.

For subject analysis, academic libraries use various standard controlled vocabularies. Most academic libraries use the *Library of Congress Subject Headings* as their preferred subject headings list. LCSH covers all academic disciplines, and it uses technical terms appropriate for each discipline. Academic libraries with medical collections also may use the *Medical Subject Headings*, and some medical schools and nursing colleges use MeSH alone. OCLC's *Faceted Application of Subject Terminology* subject headings are starting to be used by academic libraries because *FAST* subject headings have been added to bibliographic records in Connexion. Many academic libraries also use specialized thesauri, such as the *Art & Architecture Thesaurus*, to provide subject access to specialized collections.

Classification in academic libraries can vary. The most widely used classification scheme in academic libraries is the *Library of Congress Classification*. The classification scheme covers all academic disciplines and matches subject headings in LCSH as well. There is an LCC number for almost every Library of Congress subject heading. LCC meets the needs of academic libraries. However, although LCC is a better fit for most academic library collections, not all academic libraries use it. Some smaller academic libraries use the *Dewey Decimal Classification* because historically, it was adopted first by many academic libraries. Although most academic libraries have reclassified their collections to LCC, there are some smaller academic libraries that still use *Dewey*.

In addition to LCC, academic libraries with medical collections, medical schools, and nursing colleges may use the *National Library of Medicine Classification*, which is used with MeSH to provide subject access to medical collections. Some academic libraries may have a separate government publications section classified by *Superintendent of Documents Classification* and/or a state documents classification scheme. Academic libraries may also use homegrown schemes or other types of classification for particular formats or collections, such as music, video, or objects. Theses and dissertations are usually assigned a homegrown classification number.

Special Collections

In addition to a main collection, many academic libraries have special collections. Special collections can include specific collections of materials, unique or significant items, and/or rare books and manuscripts. Some academic libraries also are responsible for a university's archives or have other archival collections. These materials may be in print, and some academic libraries digitize these materials and make them available in digital collections. Print items may be cataloged following cataloging standards and policies for the library's main collection. However, some items in special collections do not fit traditional cataloging standards well and can be quite difficult to catalog, such as archival materials. Therefore, a library may use other standards, such as *Describing Archives: A Content Standard* to create finding aids to describe archival collections. Subject analysis for special collections can vary widely among academic libraries. A library could use LCSH, a thesaurus that fits the content in a special collection, or assign nothing at all. A library could choose to shelve its special collections by Library of Congress classification number, a homegrown scheme, an accession number, or another type of collection number. It really depends on the needs of the special collection and the items in the collection.

Digital collections are handled differently from physical special collections. Digital collections include special collections that have been digitized and a university's institutional repository or archives. Metadata records are created that describe each digital item in a collection using a metadata schema, such as *Dublin Core*. They are usually available in a separate content management system. A library creates its own policies for describing its digital collections. Also, any subject headings list or thesaurus can be used, or a library could choose to assign no controlled vocabulary terms at all. Metadata work is much more flexible than cataloging, but at the same time, special collections items are complex and can be quite difficult to describe, even with flexible guidelines.

Cataloging and Metadata Process in Academic Libraries

In the past, academic libraries tended to perform cataloging in similar ways, with a cataloging unit full of professional and paraprofessional catalogers performing cataloging in-house. There are still some academic libraries with this structure. However, the growth of electronic resources and the push to perform metadata work have changed how cataloging is performed in academic libraries. There is now a wide variety of ways that cataloging and metadata work can be performed, depending on the size of the collection and the types of work performed. Many academic libraries perform both cataloging work for the main collection and metadata work for digital collections, and the work may be performed in one dedicated cataloging and metadata unit or split among several units. To make room for metadata work, some academic libraries have restructured their cataloging units or technical services departments. Professional catalogers and paraprofessional catalogers handle work for the main collection, and metadata specialists and staff handle the digital collections.

The number of employees depends on the size of the library. A large research university can have many catalogers and metadata specialists working on various projects, while a small college may have one person working on cataloging only.

Academic libraries perform original cataloging and copy cataloging, and the proportions of each one can differ depending on the library. Because of the nature of academic library collections, a library with complex subjects or formats may perform quite a bit of original cataloging, especially for complex items, gifts, local items, vanity press materials, foreign-language items, items from special collections and archives, and so on. As a result, there may be backlogs of uncataloged materials in some academic libraries. Smaller academic libraries may perform little original cataloging and instead perform mostly copy cataloging. Academic libraries use various tools to perform cataloging. OCLC Connexion is by far the most widely used tool for copy and original cataloging. However, smaller academic libraries may not use it, preferring to use Z39.50 to obtain bibliographic records from other library catalogs or to use cataloging databases. Academic libraries of all sizes are increasingly purchasing bibliographic records from vendors that are batch loaded into library catalogs for shelf-ready books and e-books.

Academic libraries collect many serial publications, so serials cataloging and management is usually handled by a separate serials unit. A serials unit handles serials cataloging, the checking-in of print serials, as well as managing electronic serials and other electronic resources in databases. Bibliographic records for e-serials are usually batch loaded into the library catalog. Libraries do not index individual articles in serial issues. Instead, serials catalogers explain the overall holdings of each serials title. There is much work performed to maintain serials collections, including database maintenance to fix errors in the library catalog, negotiating licenses, and troubleshooting access problems.

Authorities work is important for academic libraries. Most academic libraries have a local authority file that includes access points for names, titles, and subject headings on bibliographic records in the library's catalog. The local authority file and any corresponding bibliographic records need to be updated regularly to reflect changes made in the National Authority File. Authorities work in academic libraries is handled either in-house or through a vendor. If handled in-house, cataloging staff update the local authority file and bibliographic records. If handled through a vendor, then the vendor does this work, and any problems that the vendor encounters are handled in-house.

In addition, some academic libraries are involved in the Program for Cooperative Cataloging, and some libraries are in a funnel program to add local names and subjects into the National Authority File. There are extra requirements for academic libraries who participate in these programs.

Issues and Challenges for Academic Libraries

All libraries have issues and challenges when organizing their collections, such as the lack of time, the lack of staff, and the lack of money. These are challenges faced by many academic libraries. However, academic library collections tend to be more complex than other collections, and there are some special issues and challenges involved in organizing academic library collections.

Managing Electronic Resources

Although all types of libraries provide access to electronic resources, the fast growth of e-resources has affected academic libraries greatly because they collect many more electronic resources and e-serials than other types of libraries. It would be impossible for individual catalogers to catalog each e-title in a large package, so libraries simply batch load bibliographic records from vendors into the catalog. Little customization is performed for these records, and they are often added to the library catalog as is, errors and all. Errors are fixed later, if they are found. This has changed the cataloging process in academic libraries. Libraries have had to shift their work processes to accommodate electronic resources, accept mistakes on bibliographic records, and perform more database maintenance to fix errors after the records have been loaded into the catalog.

More Metadata Work

Another challenge is moving from cataloging to metadata work. Academic libraries are not collecting as many print materials as in the past, instead focusing more on managing e-book and e-serial collections and performing metadata projects. Paraprofessional catalogers may not perform as much cataloging as in the past, so they may be reassigned from cataloging to metadata projects, or cataloging positions may be eliminated. Metadata work is not standardized across libraries, so it is the responsibility of the library to determine policies and procedures, which can be time and labor intensive. Libraries may not have the resources to perform metadata work, and collections may be left undigitized or uncataloged.

Backlogs

Some academic libraries have backlogs of uncataloged items waiting to be cataloged. Backlogs can include many things such as gifts, older materials, special or unique items, foreign-language materials, and so on. These materials tend to be complex and time consuming, requiring original cataloging, and libraries may not have the resources to catalog them. This means either that materials are unavailable to users or that there is a brief bibliographic record in the catalog with minimal information.

Table 8.1 shows a summary of how academic library collections are organized.

Table 8.1. How Academic Library Collections Are Organized

	Academic Libraries
Parent Organization	Institutions of higher education: colleges, universities, community colleges
Primary Users	Students, faculty, staff, administrators
Collections	Main collection with all formats, special collections, digital collections (institutional repositories, digitized special collections, digital archives)
Types of Work	Cataloging for the main collection and physical special collections; metadata work for digital collections
Sources for Records	Bibliographic records are purchased from vendors, copy and original cataloging on Connexion, other cataloging databases, or Z39.50 Metadata records are usually created in-house
Controlled Vocabularies	Primary: *Library of Congress Subject Headings*; Secondary: FAST headings, thesauri, genre terms
Classification Scheme(s)	*Library of Congress Classification*, homegrown schemes; some small academic libraries use the *Dewey Decimal Classification*
Issues	Managing electronic resources, metadata work, backlogs

PUBLIC LIBRARIES

Public libraries are libraries used by the general public, usually supported by public funds in the form of taxes. Public libraries were created to uphold democracy by educating the public and disseminating knowledge. A democracy functions only when "well-informed" people have the knowledge needed to make decisions.[13] The precursor to public libraries in the United States was the Library Company of Philadelphia, which was a subscription library founded in 1731 by Benjamin Franklin and others. The first tax-funded library was the Peterborough Town Library in New Hampshire, opened in 1833. The first large public library was the Boston Public Library, which opened in 1854. Since then, public libraries have expanded across the United States and its territories. Most people in the United States have access to a public library. According to the ALA, there are more than 9,000 public library systems in the United States, with more than 16,000 separate library buildings.[14] In addition, there are many tribal libraries that serve Native American tribes in the United States.

A public library could be one building in a town, or it could be a large library system with several branch libraries located throughout a city. Some public library systems may have floating collections, which means that item locations move as they are checked in and out of various branch libraries. Some public libraries also have bookmobiles or mobile libraries that bring library materials to people who live in rural areas or otherwise cannot access a library. Some public libraries are joint-use libraries, in which public libraries are combined with other types of libraries. A public library may combine with a school library to serve elementary, middle, or high school students and teachers, or a public library may combine with an academic library to support a local community college or university. These public libraries may need to collect educational or research material that would not necessarily be collected by public libraries. Public libraries are funded primarily by taxes and are part of town, city, or county governments.

Public libraries serve communities in every state, usually at the town, city, or county level in a particular geographic area. Public libraries in less-populated areas can serve several state counties, while public libraries in a densely populated city may serve only one area within the city. Public libraries serve diverse communities. Every public library serves a different community made up of different people with different needs. It includes people of all ages, genders, ethnicities, religions, backgrounds, abilities, and socioeconomic statuses. It includes citizens and noncitizens, and native English speakers and nonnative English speakers, too. The public library serves everyone, acting as an anchor for a community, and can play an important role in serving a community's needs. A public library needs to be constantly aware of its users and the shifting demographics in its community so it can develop collections, services, and programs that meet the needs of its community.[15]

Nature of Public Library Collections

Public libraries serve the general public, everyone in a community from babies to older people. Public library collections tend to be more general in nature to meet the needs of its community, who use the library for information, entertainment, general education, and so on. Public libraries have collections for adults and collections for children. Children's materials are a large part of a public library's collection. Public libraries collect fiction, general nonfiction on all topics, music, video, general reference information, and much more. A collection can have fiction to serve the leisure-reading needs of the community, picture books to help children learn how to read, and lots of general nonfiction to help its citizens learn things (e.g., history, cooking, gardening, auto repair) or help them do things (e.g., applying for a job, paying taxes, starting a business). Public library collections also can have makerspaces and objects that people can check out of the library. For example, libraries may have collections of cooking equipment, toys, or musical instruments. A public library's collection reflects the needs of its community.

Public libraries collect lots of physical resources, especially books and media. They collect lots of electronic resources, too, such as e-books, and use particular platforms like OverDrive or Playaway. They also collect general databases that are of interest to the community. Public libraries collect serials, too, but these are not as large a part of the collection as in academic libraries. Public libraries collect serials such as newspapers, general interest magazines, and reference works. Public libraries also may provide access to electronic serials through its databases. Some public libraries receive government publications through the FDLP.

Unlike academic library collections, public library collections tend to be current and are—or should be—weeded often. Public libraries should give users the latest, most current information. For example, the latest research says babies should sleep on their backs, so public libraries should withdraw books that suggest babies should sleep on their stomachs. Older guidelines would be of value in academic research collections, but public libraries cannot give users wrong or misleading information. The collection needs to stay current and relevant to users.[16]

Public libraries do not usually have permanent research collections, but there are exceptions. The very largest public libraries, such as the New York Public Library, have significant research collections. Many public libraries, however, have special collections or archives that are permanent, such as local history or genealogy collections. Some public libraries partner with genealogical associations or local history societies to preserve and provide local history materials to users. In addition, many public libraries have various uncataloged collections that may or may not be available to users. These collections are good candidates for digitization into digital collections, but a public library may not have the resources to perform metadata projects.

How Public Library Collections Are Organized

Public library collections reflect a community and its needs, and can be vastly different from one another. How library collections are organized in public libraries can differ widely. There are exceptions to everything when it comes to organizing public library collections. All public libraries catalog their materials, but public libraries, as a whole, do not perform much metadata work. Yet larger public libraries may perform much metadata work to create digital collections for their local materials. For the most part, public libraries catalog their materials using bibliographic records housed in an online public access catalog. Popular integrated library systems and catalog products used in public libraries include SirsiDynix, Polaris, and BiblioCommons, and there are open source options such as Koha and Evergreen. There also are options for smaller libraries. Some public libraries offer a kids' catalog, which is a subset of the regular catalog that children can search. Public libraries may be part of a consortium that shares a library catalog. However, some smaller, rural public libraries may still use a card catalog.

Public libraries tend to use similar cataloging standards, but there can be some variation. For example, public libraries should use RDA as the descriptive cataloging standard. Yet some public libraries have not made the switch to RDA and may still use AACR2, and some public libraries may use a hybrid of RDA and AACR2. Public libraries vary in their level of customization as well. Some libraries customize records a lot and some libraries do not customize at all. Authority control can vary among public libraries, too. On one end of the spectrum, some public libraries have a local authority file that is updated regularly, either in-house or by a vendor. Larger public libraries may be involved in PCC programs, such as the Name Authority Cooperative Program or the Subject Authority Cooperative Program, or a funnel, and add local names and subject headings into the National Authority File. On the other end of the spectrum, some public libraries may not use a local authority file at all.

For subject analysis, public libraries use a wide variety of subject headings lists and classification schemes. It really depends on the size of the library and its needs. Because public libraries serve all ages, they can use a variety of subject heading lists geared toward adults or children. For example, the *Library of Congress Subject Headings* is used most often in public libraries, but it is geared toward adults. Public libraries that use LCSH also can use the Library of Congress's *Children's Subject Headings*. Some smaller public libraries may use the *Sears List of Subject Headings*, which can be used for both adult and children's materials. Public libraries also may use BISAC subject headings, and public libraries that serve Spanish-speaking communities may add Spanish subject headings from *Bilindex* to bibliographic records.

Classification can vary widely among public libraries. *Dewey Decimal Classification* is by far the most commonly used classification scheme in public libraries. It is used to classify nonfiction, although it can be used to classify fiction as well. Large public libraries with research collections may classify their entire collection, or parts of it, using the *Library of Congress Classification* because it is a better fit for large research collections. Genealogical collections and other local history collections usually are shelved separately in public libraries, sometimes using a homegrown classification scheme. For fiction and media, most public libraries tend to classify and shelve them by genre, author's or artist's last name, and/or title, but DDC also may be used. Every public library shelves its fiction and media differently. Children's fiction is usually classified by genre or author using a homegrown scheme, but children's nonfiction can be classified using a homegrown scheme, genre, or by Dewey number. A trend in public libraries is to use alternative classification for nonfiction, as discussed in chapter 5. Instead of using DDC, libraries can use bookstore models or homegrown schemes. In the end, public libraries organize their collections to help their users. There is no one right way to organize public library collections. As long as it helps users, it is good.

Cataloging Process in Public Libraries

How cataloging work is performed in public libraries varies widely depending on the size of the library and its funding. Very large libraries with large budgets have formal cataloging processes similar to academic libraries, while small rural libraries with small budgets may have no set cataloging processes at all. Cataloging work may be done in one library or may be performed in a central processing unit, which is especially beneficial for public library systems with many branches. A library system receives multiple copies of the same book, so cataloging can be done in a central place and then books and other materials are sent to the branches. This reduces duplication of effort in the branches.

Cataloging units and staff can differ among public libraries. Some public libraries have a dedicated cataloging unit with professional and paraprofessional catalogers responsible for cataloging all library materials in-house. Some libraries purchase all bibliographic records from vendors and perform no cataloging in-house. Most public libraries fall somewhere in between. Funding, unfortunately, has a way of dictating how cataloging work is performed. Some public libraries cannot afford to have a professional cataloger on staff, so they just employ paraprofessional catalogers. Some public libraries may not have anyone on staff with cataloging knowledge, and they do what they can to make materials available to users. In addition, some public libraries find themselves in a feast-or-famine situation every year: When the budget comes in, materials are ordered and there is too much cataloging to do; after the budget is spent, there is little cataloging to do.

Public libraries receive their bibliographic records from many places. Most public libraries purchase bibliographic records from vendors. For physical materials, most public library materials arrive shelf-ready, and bibliographic records are downloaded into the library catalog. For public libraries with electronic resources, large files of bibliographic records from vendors can be batch loaded into a library catalog, or they can use the information from the e-content provider.

However, there is still some copy cataloging and original cataloging to perform in public libraries for genealogical collections, local history collections, gift items, items obtained at book fairs and conferences, and the like. For items not received through vendors, public libraries can use OCLC Connexion or other cataloging databases, or they can copy bibliographic records from other library catalogs using Z39.50. It depends on the library and its needs.

Issues and Challenges for Public Libraries

Lack of time, lack of staff, and lack of money are challenges for most public libraries. They affect how collections are organized and what is possible. Yet there are some special issues and challenges that affect the organization of collections in public libraries.

Special Collections

Some public libraries have special collections of genealogical materials, local history materials, or other materials of interest to the community. Some public libraries work with a local history center, museum, or archive to provide access to these materials. Larger public libraries perform metadata work to make these items available in digital collections, but this work is not performed in all public libraries. Materials in special collections can be complex and require special cataloging and processing, and a public library may not have the staff or the budget to do the work. In addition, public library catalogers may not have the knowledge or the time to catalog special collections. This means that special collections may or may not be cataloged and available in some public libraries.

Foreign-Language Materials

Public libraries serve their communities, which can include people who speak and read many languages and dialects. Public libraries often collect resources in foreign languages to help users. Cataloging foreign-language materials can be challenging for public libraries that do not have language expertise on staff. If bibliographic records for these materials cannot be purchased from a vendor or copy cataloged, then the materials may end up sitting in a backlog waiting to be cataloged and not made available to users.

Lack of Cataloging Knowledge

Another consideration for public libraries is that not all public libraries employ catalogers or people with cataloging knowledge. Some public libraries have no professional cataloger on staff at all. This can hinder libraries' efforts to use standard cataloging practices and provide quick access to library materials. In addition, even when public libraries have catalogers on staff, those catalogers may have a hard time keeping up with professional development and cataloging trends. Public libraries may not keep up with the latest developments in the field. Not all public libraries have the funding to support conference travel or professional development activities, so the responsibility is left to individual catalogers to keep up their cataloging and technology skills. This can be especially difficult for librarians in small rural libraries, who may not have access to professional development resources.

Table 8.2 shows a summary of how public library collections are organized.

Table 8.2.   How Public Library Collections Are Organized

	Public Libraries
Parent Organization	Towns, cities, counties, and other municipalities
Primary Users	People in local communities
Collections	Main collection with all formats; some libraries have genealogy collections, local history collections, and/or digital collections
Types of Work	Cataloging for the main collection; some larger libraries may perform metadata work for digital collections
Sources for Bibliographic Records	Purchases bibliographic records from vendors, copy and original cataloging through cataloging databases, Z39.50, or Connexion
Subject Headings List(s)	*Library of Congress Subject Headings, Children's Subject Headings, Sears List of Subject Headings,* or *BISAC Subject Headings*
Classification Scheme(s)	*Dewey Decimal Classification;* BISAC codes, homegrown schemes; some large public libraries use the *Library of Congress Classification*
Issues	Special collections, foreign-language materials, lack of cataloging knowledge

SCHOOL LIBRARIES

A school library supports primary and secondary education of students from kindergarten through grade 12, and sometimes prekindergarten. School libraries are located in elementary or grade schools, middle or junior high schools, and high schools, and support students, teachers, administrators, and staff at each school. There are more school libraries in the United States than all other types of libraries combined. According to the ALA, there are more than 98,000 school libraries in the United States.[17] This number includes more than 81,000 libraries in public schools, more than 17,000 libraries in private schools, and around 160 school libraries on Native American reservations. Each state is divided into school districts based on geographical area that include various combinations of elementary, middle, and high schools. Some districts also offer magnet schools that focus on a particular subject area, such as the performing arts or science. The number of schools within a school district can vary. A school district in a rural area with a small population may have one school that educates all students from pre-kindergarten through grade 12. A school district in an urban area within a city may have hundreds of schools, and some very large school districts (such as the Los Angeles Unified School District) have more than a thousand schools. School districts are controlled by the states, and each state has an education department that sets curriculum standards, rules, and policies for the state. Private schools are not controlled by the states; they are organized and run privately by an organization or board of directors that sets educational curriculum and policy in each school. There also are charter schools, which are schools funded by the state but run privately outside of state education departments.

Each school library is usually managed by one school librarian who is responsible for running the entire library, including working with students and teachers, collection development, and cataloging and maintaining the collection. School librarians may be assisted by volunteers or aides. School librarians are responsible for all aspects of library management, but they are not prepared equally across the United States. Education requirements of school librarians vary by state. Some states, like Ohio, have many requirements for school librarians; they must have a teaching license and a library media license, which includes earning a master's degree (master of library or information science or another master's degree) and graduate-level school librarian certification.[18] Other states, such as Idaho, simply require a teaching license and a library media endorsement.[19] Alaska does not require a teaching certification or a master's degree at all.[20] Differing educational requirements means that some school librarians have had coursework in cataloging and some have not. Although school librarians are dedicated teachers and librarians, some of them may not have the cataloging knowledge needed to organize their collections.[21]

Nature of School Library Collections

Collections in school libraries tend to include mass-produced materials that support teaching and learning. Collections differ, however, depending on the type of school the library serves. For example, as of 2012, the average number of books in school library collections was around 13,000 physical volumes, but libraries can have smaller or larger collections depending on funding and the number of students in the school.[22] The type of school and the state curriculum standards drive what is in the collection. Elementary school library collections contain children's books, both fiction and nonfiction, print and electronic. This includes board books, picture books, chapter books, and lots of books that are included in series. They also will have materials that support teachers. Some children's books are designated as "E" books, which stands for "Everybody" or the outdated term "Easy," and some of them are included in reading programs used at the school, such as *Accelerated Reader* and *Reading Counts!* Collections become more advanced in subject and reading level as students move into middle and high school, as collections move from supporting the education of children to supporting the education of young adults. Libraries in high schools, for example, have lots of fiction, including genres and books in series, but also classic literature to support English classes. They include nonfiction on all subjects to support subjects taught at the high school. A high school collection can include materials outside of the curriculum, such as college and career materials, as well as general interest materials.

School libraries of all types collect print books, but they also collect e-books, e-serials, apps, databases, e-media, and other e-content. They collect nonbook items such as kits, manipulatives, music, video, puppets, and anything else needed to support teaching and learning. Serial publications are not a large part of school library collections, and libraries primarily collect current magazines and newspapers. Some school libraries provide access to objects, such as toys, games, sports equipment, technology, and the like. Some school libraries are responsible for cataloging all technology checked out to students in the school (e.g., laptops, tablets), including power cords and replacement parts. This can be a challenge in large districts with thousands of students.

School library collections should be weeded regularly to ensure a relatively current collection. Unlike academic libraries, school libraries do not intend to keep their materials forever, and collection turnover can be high in school libraries because of outdated materials, wear and tear on the collection, and missing items. Although school library collections should be kept up to date, other factors affect weeding, such as school library funding.

How School Library Collections Are Organized

School library collections tend to hold similar materials and tend to be organized in similar ways, although there is some variation. As in all libraries, bibliographic records that describe and provide access to each item in the school library are housed in OPACs. The most popular system is Follett's Destiny product, but other systems may be used, such TLC's Library Solution for Schools. School libraries tend to share library catalogs. All the school libraries in a particular school district may share a library catalog, or a school library may be a member of a consortium that shares a library catalog. Although beneficial, sharing a catalog can be difficult because school libraries may organize their collections differently and may disagree about cataloging policy.

School libraries mainly perform cataloging. There are very few metadata projects in school libraries because they do not necessarily have special collections (although they could). Most school libraries include the same mass-published materials, so school libraries follow cataloging standards when cataloging their collections. Bibliographic records are created using RDA and MARC 21. However, some school libraries have not yet made the switch to RDA and are still using AACR2. Unlike the descriptive cataloging guidelines, school libraries can choose which subject headings list and classification scheme to use, but in some school districts, these choices are set at the district level. It depends on the type of library and the ages of the students it serves. For subject headings, elementary school libraries may use the *Children's Subject Headings* or the *Sears List of Subject Headings*. Middle school libraries and high school libraries may use the *Children's Subject Headings* and LCSH, or just the *Sears List of Subject Headings*. Classification also depends on the type of library. School libraries tend to use DDC for nonfiction and a homegrown scheme for fiction and media. Some school libraries use alternatives to DDC. They may genrefy their collections so the entire collection is organized by broad, child-friendly categories instead of DDC number. They also can use alternative classification schemes, such as *Metis Library Classification for Children*, which was developed just for elementary school libraries. Again, it depends on the size of the collection, the type of materials, and what the students need from the collection.

Authority control is handled differently in school libraries than in academic and public libraries. Most school libraries do not have a local authority file, although larger districts may have one. Although an authority file function exists on catalogs, it is not always utilized. Instead, librarians rely on access points to match up in the catalog. This can be problematic because there are no authority records that link names, subject headings, and titles in the library catalog. If a name or subject heading changes, then newer bibliographic records will be added to the catalog with the new access point, while the old, outdated access point still exists on bibliographic records. Collocation is lost in the catalog and users searching the catalog may not receive everything in the search results. Not using a local authority file may not be as problematic in school libraries as in public and academic libraries, however, because of turnover in school library collections. As older materials and their bibliographic records are removed from the library, authority control issues on the library catalog may work themselves out.

Cataloging Process in School Libraries

Unlike other types of libraries, school libraries tend to share a similar cataloging process. There are two primary ways cataloging work is performed in school libraries: in a central processing unit or by individual school librarians. Cataloging done at the district level in a central processing unit is a common arrangement for districts with many schools. There may be one or more professional and/or paraprofessional catalogers who perform cataloging for an entire school district. This arrangement is beneficial because cataloging is performed by people with cataloging knowledge, and it takes the cataloging responsibility off busy school librarians who do not have time to perform cataloging. However, there never seems to be enough cataloging staff at central processing units. A few people may be responsible for a large amount of cataloging performed for a school district that can have hundreds of schools. There may not be enough catalogers to get the work done in a timely manner. There also may be issues with items that need original cataloging, such as gift items or items obtained at book fairs. These may need to be sent to the central processing unit for cataloging, which can take time.

Some districts do not utilize a central processing unit; instead, each school librarian is responsible for cataloging in their library. One school librarian may be considered the point person for cataloging in the district. This arrangement is beneficial because materials can get to the shelves quickly and there is no middle person performing cataloging at a central processing unit. However, school librarians are busy and may not have the time, knowledge, or inclination to perform cataloging. It may be something that falls by the wayside.

The cataloging process is fairly streamlined in school libraries. Bibliographic records are usually purchased through library vendors such as Follett. When librarians make purchases, they purchase the bibliographic records along with the materials, and the bibliographic records are downloaded into the library catalog after the books are received in the library. Books arrive shelf-ready and librarians can just shelve the books. This makes cataloging quick and efficient, and materials are available to students and teachers quickly. School libraries can customize bibliographic records, and common customizations are alternative classification, adding subject headings for reading programs and curriculum standards, and adding notes for intended grade, age, and/or reading level. If a school library or district has the funding to pay for customization, a vendor will do it. For library items not received through vendors, such as gift items, items obtained at conferences or book fairs, and objects, there are many options. A school librarian may use the cataloging system available through the library catalog to create an original record for the item. A librarian also may use a program such as Z39.50 to copy bibliographic records from another library's catalog.

Issues and Challenges for School Libraries

There are several issues and challenges for school libraries that affect how collections are organized and cataloging is performed. Dwindling budgets may directly or indirectly cause these issues.

Lack of Time

One challenge is lack of time. Although all libraries are challenged by lack of time, it is especially an issue for school librarians who are responsible for all cataloging in a school library. A school librarian is a solo librarian who not only works closely with students and teachers but also does everything else needed to manage the library. There is often little time to devote solely to cataloging. Most materials purchased for school libraries come with bibliographic records, so a school librarian may download bibliographic records into the library catalog without checking them. This is problematic because vendors make mistakes, and some vendors make a lot of mistakes. The catalog may have errors and other issues that are never fixed. One small error on a bibliographic record can render an item unfindable—and thus unretrievable—in the library catalog.

Lack of Staff

Lack of staff is a challenge for most libraries, but it is a big issue for central processing units at the school district level. Central processing units tend to be greatly understaffed for the amount of cataloging work performed in each district. These units can be in charge of cataloging at hundreds of schools, and even though bibliographic records are purchased primarily from vendors, there is still much work done to make them ready for libraries. In addition, each school in a district may have special cataloging needs and use different classification methods, so records and materials may need to be customized accordingly. Also, because bibliographic records are downloaded into catalogs, there can be quite a bit of database maintenance required to fix errors. If a district uses a local authority file, then the authority file and bibliographic records need to be updated with new and modified names, titles, and subjects. It is a lot of work to manage the cataloging in a district, but there never seems to be enough staff to do it all.

Lack of Cataloging Knowledge

Another issue is school librarians who do not know how to catalog or who do not keep up with professional development in cataloging. Because school librarian education requirements vary widely by state, some school librarians may not have learned library cataloging as part of their certification programs. This is a problem because some school librarians may not understand why cataloging is important or the basics of bibliographic records and MARC 21. They may not even know the subject headings list used in the library. These librarians rely on library vendors to take care of cataloging, but vendors do not know the individual school or its students and teachers. A vendor cannot know what a school needs, so it is important for each school librarian to understand the basics of library cataloging to create a catalog that helps students and teachers. School librarians also need to keep up with professional development in cataloging. State and national library organizations provide online learning opportunities, and there are many resources available online for beginning catalogers. Cataloging changes constantly, as does technology, so it is important for school librarians to keep up on the latest developments.

Original Cataloging

Original cataloging is also a challenge, and it is related directly to the challenge of lack of cataloging knowledge. Although not much original cataloging is performed in school libraries, it must be done periodically for gift items and items obtained at book fairs and conferences, as well as for technology and equipment. School librarians who do not know how to catalog have a difficult time performing original cataloging, and students and teachers may not find what they need. Original cataloging is also a challenge for school districts with central processing units, because it can take some time for busy catalogers to create an original bibliographic record and send the item back to the school library. Library materials may not be made available to users in a timely manner.

Table 8.3 shows a summary of how school library collections are organized.

Table 8.3.   How School Library Collections Are Organized

	School Libraries
Parent Organization	School districts in each state
Primary Users	Students, teachers, staff, administrators
Collections	Main collection with all formats, primarily children's and young adult materials, and materials to support teachers and the curriculum
Types of Work	Cataloging for the main collection; can be done in each library by a school librarian or by catalogers in a school district's central processing unit
Sources for Bibliographic Records	Purchases bibliographic records from vendors; copy and original cataloging using Z39.50 as needed
Subject Headings List(s)	*Library of Congress Subject Headings, Children's Subject Headings,* or *Sears List of Subject Headings*
Classification Scheme(s)	*Dewey Decimal Classification* for nonfiction, homegrown schemes for fiction; some school libraries genrefy their collections or use alternative classification
Issues	Lack of time for school librarians, lack of staff for central processing units, lack of cataloging knowledge

SPECIAL LIBRARIES

Every library that is not an academic, public, or school library is considered a special library. A special library is a library that provides specific information and resources to a specialized clientele. Special libraries are located in many places, such as law firms, government agencies, corporations, organizations, hospitals, museums, prisons, and so on. According to the ALA, there are more than 6,000 special libraries, including government libraries and military libraries, in the United States.[23] The mission of a special library can vary widely depending on who it serves. A corporate library may provide a very focused, specialized collection, such as legal resources for a law firm or research materials for a chemical manufacturer. Time is of the essence in a corporate library, so special library collections must be organized well to facilitate quick and efficient retrieval of information. Special libraries also can serve more general populations, such as a military library that supports military members and their families. The collection in these libraries is more general in nature and includes materials for adults and children, and must be organized well so users can find what they need. It should be noted that some special librarians do not manage a collection at all, and instead work as embedded librarians on teams.[24]

Nature of Collections

Special library collections contain a wide variety of materials. Collections can be small or large, broad or specialized, depending on the parent organization and its needs. Some special library collections are very specialized, such as corporate libraries and medical libraries, and include anything needed to support a business, hospital, or other organization. Collections can include physical and/or digital materials, and may include published and unpublished information. Special libraries tend to collect more gray literature than other types of libraries. Gray literature contains materials published by governments, businesses, and other organizations, such as technical reports, newsletters, technical manuals, white papers, datasheets, design handbooks, and the like. These materials are not published by commercial publishers and are not typically collected by academic or public libraries. They are in a gray area. However, gray literature is of vital interest to some special libraries. For example, a business may collect technical reports, newsletters, and design manuals. A nonprofit environmental organization may collect everything disseminated by state environmental protection agencies. A law firm library may collect specialized legal resources in a specific type of law.[25]

Some special libraries may have broader collections. For example, military library collections can include general interest materials and children's materials in all formats to serve military families. Special libraries may also have digital collections of e-books, e-serials, databases, and online resources; anything to support the parent organization. Libraries may also create digital collections to provide online access to an organization's resources.

How Special Library Collections Are Organized

Special libraries must have systems of organization that support quick and efficient work, but not all of them follow standard library cataloging practices. Organization in a special library may be formal or informal, depending on the size of the collection and the nature of the items in the collection. A special library may use cataloging standards or do its own thing. Yet many special libraries use standard cataloging tools: for example, creating bibliographic records using RDA and the MARC21 format. Special libraries may or may not have a local authority file.

Subject analysis is important in special libraries, and libraries can choose from a wide variety of subject headings lists and thesauri to meet their needs. LCSH is used in many special libraries, medical libraries use MeSH, and art libraries may use the *Art & Architecture Thesaurus*. Special libraries with specialized collections, such as those in business and industry, may use ontologies and thesauri to provide specialized subject access to their collections. Every industry is different, so using a thesaurus for a particular industry provides subject access to a collection. A special library for an oil and gas company, for example, needs to provide access to subjects using the language of the oil and gas industry. A special librarian may even need to create an index of materials in the library to provide subject access to very specialized items in the collection.

Special libraries may or may not use a classification scheme, depending on the size of the collection and the items in the collection. A military library with a general collection may use DDC, a medical library may use the *NLM Classification*, and a library in a government agency may use SuDocs or a state government classification. A special library may use a homegrown classification scheme or no classification scheme at all.

Cataloging and Metadata Process in Special Libraries

The cataloging process in special libraries can differ widely depending on the size of the library, the subject matter, and its parent organization. A large special library in a government agency may mirror cataloging processes in academic libraries. There may be a large cataloging unit with many professional and paraprofessional catalogers who catalog the collection and perform metadata work. A military library may mirror a small public library in that one or two people are responsible for cataloging. A corporate library may mirror a school library in that there is one person responsible for managing the entire library, including providing information services, managing the library, and cataloging.

Special libraries that create bibliographic records can perform all work in-house using OCLC Connexion or other cataloging databases, or they may get bibliographic records from other libraries' catalogs using Z39.50. Special libraries may purchase bibliographic records from vendors. Some special libraries do not use these tools at all. Using standard bibliographic records from other sources is much quicker and cheaper, but due to the nature of the items in special collections, bibliographic records may not be available. A collection may have very specialized gray materials, which are not always available in OCLC Connexion or other cataloging sources, so a special librarian may need to perform original cataloging for these items using cataloging standards or the library's own cataloging system. A special library with its own cataloging system will need to do more work to maintain the system. A special library may also perform metadata work to digitize and provide access to library collections. The purpose of a special library is to serve its parent organization, so a special library does what is needed to support work in the organization.

Issues and Challenges for Special Libraries

There are some challenges and issues that special libraries face when organizing their collections. The wide range of special libraries means that each library has unique challenges, and they dovetail with challenges faced by other types of libraries. A military library may have similar challenges to a public library, and a government agency library may have similar challenges to an academic library.

Specialized Collections

One issue for special libraries is the specialized nature of the materials in their collections. Some special libraries collect much gray material, and bibliographic records are not always available for this material. In addition, cataloging is not always standardized across special libraries. Special libraries need to be quick and nimble, and they need to develop organizational processes that will support quick and efficient work. Standard cataloging tools may not be helpful when cataloging specialized collections, and special librarians may need to create indexes, ontologies, or thesauri that support the work of the parent organization. For example, a library that serves a pharmaceutical company will have specialized pharmaceutical resources. The items in the collection can be incredibly specialized and may not be mass-produced or available in other libraries. The subjects in LCSH are not as deep as needed for this subject area or industry. A special librarian may need to perform original cataloging to provide access to the collection, and may need to create a thesaurus to provide subject access to specialized information in the collection.

Analytical Descriptions

Analytical descriptions are a particular challenge for special libraries. Although most libraries collect whole items, such as a whole book or a whole run of a serials title, special libraries—particularly government and corporate libraries—often collect parts of items. Parts can be things like one chapter in an edited book, one article in one issue of a serials title, one conference paper published in a proceedings, and so on. To provide access to these parts, special libraries create what are called analytical descriptions, also referred to as in-analytics. The cataloging of these items can be tricky because it is important to tell users in a clear way that the item is just one part of a whole.

Lack of Time

Another challenge for special libraries is lack of time. Like school librarians, special librarians tend to be solo librarians responsible for all aspects of library management. They may not have much time to devote to cataloging, and they may be under pressure to assist the parent organization in other ways.

Table 8.4 shows a summary of how special library collections are organized.

Table 8.4.   How Special Library Collections Are Organized

	Special Libraries
Parent Organization	Corporations, law firms, the military, government agencies, hospitals, etc.
Primary Users	Specialized clientele of parent organization
Collections	Main collection with needed formats, digital collections; collections can be very specialized depending on the special library
Types of Work	Cataloging and/or metadata work
Sources for Bibliographic Records	Copy and original cataloging using Connexion, other cataloging databases, or Z39.50 as needed; some special libraries purchase bibliographic records from vendors
Controlled Vocabularies	*Library of Congress Subject Headings*, *Medical Subject Headings*, thesauri, ontologies, indexes, etc.
Classification Scheme(s)	Depends on the special library: *Library of Congress Classification*, *Dewey Decimal Classification*, *SuDocs Classification*, homegrown schemes, etc.
Issues	Specialized collections, analytical descriptions, lack of time

SUMMARY

This chapter discussed how library collections are organized in academic, public, school, and special libraries. It discussed each type of library, the nature of collections, how collections are organized, and the issues and challenges facing cataloging and metadata practice in each type of library. Although there are many similarities across all libraries, each type of library has a different mission and serves a different community. These needs drive what is collected and how collections are organized.

DISCUSSION QUESTIONS

1. How do the mission and users of each type of library determine how collections are organized?
2. How are collections organized in each type of library? What are the similarities and differences across library types?
3. Discuss the issues and challenges facing each library type. Why is each one a challenge?

CLASS ACTIVITY

Interview. In this assignment, you will explore how cataloging and metadata work is performed in practice. Interview a cataloging or metadata librarian, or a school librarian who is responsible for cataloging. To make the interview more meaningful for you, consider interviewing a cataloging/metadata librarian in your interest area (school, public, academic, special). Please address six areas during the interview:

1. *Description of library:* Describe the library (e.g., type of library, size, users).
2. *Cataloging/metadata unit:* Give specific information about the cataloging/metadata unit (e.g., number of catalogers, paraprofessionals).
3. *Collection:* Describe the materials collected in the library.
4. *Cataloging/metadata process:* Fully explain how books and other materials are cataloged in the library and made available to users. Address things like how bibliographic records are obtained for the library, the amount of copy cataloging and original cataloging done in the library, the subject headings list(s) and classification scheme(s) used in the library, authority control/local authority file maintenance, customization done in the library, metadata work performed in the library, etc.
5. *Two challenges:* Discuss at least two challenges facing the cataloging/metadata unit, and why/how each one is a challenge.
6. *What you learned:* Explain what you learned about cataloging/metadata work from the interview. Be specific.

After the interview, write a paper that addresses all six areas. Do not name the librarian or the library in the paper.

NOTES

1. American Library Association, "Number of Libraries in the United States: Home," accessed January 14, 2019, https://libguides.ala.org/numberoflibraries.

2. National Center for Education Statistics, "Academic Libraries," accessed January 14, 2019, https://nces.ed.gov/surveys/libraries/academic.asp.

3. ALA, "Number of Libraries in the United States: Home."

4. G. Edward Evans and Stacey Greenwell, *Academic Librarianship*, 2nd ed. (Chicago: ALA Neal-Schuman: 2018).

5. Carnegie Classification of Institutions of Higher Education, "Basic Classification Description," accessed January 14, 2019, http://carnegieclassifications.iu.edu/classification_descriptions/basic.php.

6. For more information about academic librarianship in general, see, e.g., Evans and Greenwell, *Academic Librarianship*; Todd Gilman, ed., *Academic Librarianship Today* (Lanham, MD: Rowman & Littlefield, 2017).

7. Cornell University, "University Facts," accessed January 14, 2019, https://www.cornell .edu/about/facts.cfm.

8. "The Carnegie Classification of Institutions of Higher Education," accessed January 14, 2019, http://carnegieclassifications.iu.edu/index.php.

9. Cornell University Library, "Collections," accessed January 14, 2019, https://www .library.cornell.edu/about/collections.

10. Lincoln University, "University Facts," accessed January 14, 2019, https://www.lin coln.edu/about/university-facts.

11. "The Carnegie Classification of Institutions of Higher Education," accessed January 14, 2019, http://carnegieclassifications.iu.edu/index.php.

12. Lincoln University, "Langston Hughes Memorial Library," accessed January 14, 2019, https://www.lincoln.edu/departments/langston-hughes-memorial-library.

13. See, e.g., Thomas Jefferson, "Extract from Thomas Jefferson to Richard Price," January 8, 1789, accessed January 14, 2019, http://tjrs.monticello.org/letter/118; Kathleen De la Peña McCook and Jenny S. Bossaller, *Introduction to Public Librarianship*, 3rd ed. (Chicago: ALA Neal-Schuman, 2018).

14. ALA, "Number of Libraries in the United States: Home."

15. For more information about public librarianship, see, e.g., De la Peña McCook and Bossaller, *Introduction to Public Librarianship*; Ann E. Prentice, *Public Libraries in the 21st Century* (Santa Barbara, CA: Libraries Unlimited, 2011).

16. Jeanette Larson, *CREW: A Weeding Manual for Modern Libraries*, rev. and updated (Austin: Texas State Library and Archives Commission, 2012), https://www.tsl.state.tx.us/ld/ pubs/crew/index.html.

17. ALA, "Number of Libraries in the United States: Home."

18. Ohio Department of Education, "Educator Licenses," accessed January 14, 2019, http://education.ohio.gov/Topics/Teaching/Licensure.

19. Idaho State Department of Education, accessed January 14, 2019, https://www.sde .idaho.gov.

20. Alaska Department of Education and Early Development, "Teacher Certification," accessed January 14, 2019, https://education.alaska.gov/TeacherCertification.

21. For more information about school librarianship, see, e.g., Blanche Woolls and Sharon Coatney, *The School Library Manager: Surviving and Thriving* (Santa Barbara, CA: Libraries Unlimited, 2018); Blanche Woolls and David V. Loertscher, eds., *The Whole School Library Handbook 2* (Chicago: American Library Association, 2013).

22. American Association of School Librarians, *School Libraries Count! National Longitudinal Survey of School Library Programs* (Chicago: American library Association, 2012).

23. ALA, "Number of Libraries in the United States: Home."

24. For more information about special librarianship, see, e.g., Ellis Mount and Renée Massoud, *Special Libraries and Information Centers: An Introductory Text*, 4th ed. (Washington, DC: Special Libraries Association, 1999); Sigrid E. Kelsey and Marjorie J. Porter, eds., *Best Practices for Corporate Libraries* (Santa Barbara, CA: Libraries Unlimited, 2011).

25. For more information about gray literature, see, e.g., Joachim Schöpfel and Dominic Farace, *Grey Literature in Library and Information Studies* (Berlin: De Gruyter Saur, 2010); Grey Literature Network Service, accessed January 14, 2019, http://www.greynet.org.

SELECTED BIBLIOGRAPHY AND ADDITIONAL READING

American Association of School Librarians. *School Libraries Count! National Longitudinal Survey of School Library Programs*. Chicago: American library Association, 2012.

Austin, Richard J., and Diane Austin. "Technology in Public Libraries: An Overview of the Past, Present, and Future." In *Introduction to Public Librarianship*, third edition, edited by Kathleen De la Peña McCook and Jenny S. Bossaller. Chicago: ALA Neal-Schuman, 2018.

De la Peña McCook, Kathleen, and Jenny S. Bossaller. *Introduction to Public Librarianship*. Third Edition. Chicago: ALA Neal-Schuman, 2018.

Evans, G. Edward, and Stacey Greenwell. *Academic Librarianship*. Second Edition. Chicago: ALA Neal-Schuman, 2018.

Gilman, Todd, ed. *Academic Librarianship Today*. Lanham, MD: Rowman & Littlefield, 2017.

Intner, Sheila S., Joanna F. Fountain, and Jean Weihs, eds. *Cataloging Correctly for Kids: An Introduction to the Tools*. Fifth Edition. Chicago: American Library Association, 2011.

Intner, Sheila S., and Weihs, Jean. *Special Libraries: A Cataloging Guide*. Englewood, CO: Librarian Unlimited, 1998.

Jefferson, Thomas. "Extract from Thomas Jefferson to Richard Price." January 8, 1789. http://tjrs.monticello.org/letter/118.

Jurkowski, Odin L. *Technology and the School Library: A Comprehensive Guide for Media Specialists and Other Educators*. Third Edition. Lanham, MD: Rowman & Littlefield, 2017.

Kelsey, Marie. *Cataloging for School Librarians*. Lanham, MD: Rowman & Littlefield, 2014.

Kelsey, Sigrid E., and Marjorie J. Porter, eds. *Best Practices for Corporate Libraries*. Santa Barbara, CA: Libraries Unlimited, 2011.

Larson, Jeanette. *CREW: A Weeding Manual for Modern Libraries*. 2012. Revised and Updated. Austin: Texas State Library and Archives Commission. https://www.tsl.state.tx.us/ld/pubs/crew/index.html.

Mount, Ellis, and Renée Massoud. *Special Libraries and Information Centers: An Introductory Text*. Fourth Edition. Washington, DC: Special Libraries Association, 1999.

Prentice, Ann E. *Public Libraries in the 21st Century*. Santa Barbara, CA: Libraries Unlimited, 2011.

Schöpfel, Joachim, and Dominic Farace. *Grey Literature in Library and Information Studies*. Berlin: De Gruyter Saur, 2010.

Woolls, Blanche, and Sharon Coatney. *The School Library Manager: Surviving and Thriving*. Santa Barbara, CA: Libraries Unlimited, 2018.

Woolls, Blanche, and David V. Loertscher, eds. *The Whole School Library Handbook 2*. Chicago: American Library Association, 2013.

9

Ethical Issues in Organizing Library Collections

This book has discussed the theory and practice of organizing library collections, including why it is done, the professional standards used to organize collections, and how cataloging and metadata work is performed. This chapter reflects on the material presented in the book. It focuses on professional ethics and explores some ethical issues in organizing library collections. It will discuss obligations directed by the American Library Association's Code of Ethics and ethical guidelines from the Association for Library Collections and Technical Services. It will examine the role of the user, and it will explore ethical issues surrounding standards for subject access. Finally, it will address ethical decision making by individual catalogers and metadata specialists.

NEUTRALITY AND POWER

It might be tempting to think there are few ethical issues to consider when organizing library collections. It may seem as if catalogers and metadata specialists are just neutral players who link users to library materials: Cataloging and metadata standards have been developed based on an understanding of users and their needs, so catalogers and metadata specialists just objectively follow standards to meet the needs of users. Unfortunately, organizing library collections is not this ethically straightforward. There are ethical considerations in any type of professional work, and the cataloging and metadata field is no exception. Although there are many cataloging and metadata instructions, guidelines, and policies that direct cataloging and metadata work, in the end, cataloging and metadata work can be highly subjective. "Cataloging is not a neutral act," as a familiar quote says.[1] Nothing about cataloging and metadata theory and practice is neutral. Cataloging and metadata standards are not neutral. Choices are made about how to describe and provide access to library materials, and those choices may not always be the right ones for every type of library. Library collections and local cataloging policies are not neutral. Choices are made about what goes into the library collection and how to best provide access to library materials. Libraries can choose subject headings lists, classification schemes, and specific cataloging and metadata policies that may or may not enhance access to a library's collection. Catalogers and metadata specialists are not neutral. They make choices about how to apply cataloging and metadata standards and to what extent they will provide access to materials.

There is lot of power in cataloging and metadata theory and practice. Patrick Wilson explains: "Bibliographic control is a form of power, and if knowledge itself is a form of power, as the familiar slogan claims, bibliographical control is in a certain sense power over power, power to obtain the knowledge recorded in written form."[2] Bibliographic control, including cataloging, indexing, and metadata work, is power over knowledge, power over power. There is power in how library materials are organized. Organizations involved in the system of standards discussed in chapter 6 have a lot of power to determine how library collections are organized and how users access them. Their decisions affect users and can provide access or hinder access. The International Federation of Library Associations and Institutions, for example, has the power to develop standards and policies that affect library users around the world. The Library of Congress and other national organizations develop standards and set cataloging policies that affect library users in the United States. Cataloging units have the power to create local cataloging policies that affect local library users. Catalogers and metadata specialists have the power to give access or take away access. They have the power to determine how library materials are described and how they are accessed. If library materials are not organized well, then users will not find what they need.

ETHICS AND VALUES STATEMENTS

Professional ethics are "the justified moral values that should govern the work of professionals."[3] A code of ethics lists the principles of conduct and the professional obligations of individuals in a profession. It serves as a guide to professional behavior and decision making.

ALA Code of Ethics

The profession of librarianship, which includes the cataloging and metadata field, is governed by the ALA Code of Ethics, eight "ethical principles that guide the work of librarians." It covers these areas: (1) providing equitable service and access to resources, (2) supporting intellectual freedom, (3) protecting privacy and confidentiality, (4) respecting intellectual property rights, (5) treating coworkers and employees with respect, (6) avoiding conflicts of interest, (7) striving for neutrality, and (8) engaging in professional development.[4] Librarians are professionally obligated to follow these principles in their work, and they also apply to the library profession and to libraries. See the following ALA Code of Ethics.

CODE OF ETHICS OF THE AMERICAN LIBRARY ASSOCIATION

As members of the American Library Association, we recognize the importance of codifying and making known to the profession and to the general public the ethical principles that guide the work of librarians, other professionals providing information services, library trustees and library staffs.

Ethical dilemmas occur when values are in conflict. The American Library Association Code of Ethics states the values to which we are committed, and embodies the ethical responsibilities of the profession in this changing information environment.

We significantly influence or control the selection, organization, preservation, and dissemination of information. In a political system grounded in an informed citizenry, we are members of a profession explicitly committed to intellectual freedom and the freedom of access to information. We have a special obligation to ensure the free flow of information and ideas to present and future generations.

The principles of this Code are expressed in broad statements to guide ethical decision making. These statements provide a framework; they cannot and do not dictate conduct to cover particular situations.

I.   We provide the highest level of service to all library users through appropriate and usefully organized resources; equitable service policies; equitable access; and accurate, unbiased, and courteous responses to all requests.

II.   We uphold the principles of intellectual freedom and resist all efforts to censor library resources.

III. We protect each library user's right to privacy and confidentiality with respect to information sought or received and resources consulted, borrowed, acquired or transmitted.

IV.   We respect intellectual property rights and advocate balance between the interests of information users and rights holders.

V.   We treat co-workers and other colleagues with respect, fairness, and good faith, and advocate conditions of employment that safeguard the rights and welfare of all employees of our institutions.

VI.   We do not advance private interests at the expense of library users, colleagues, or our employing institutions.

VII. We distinguish between our personal convictions and professional duties and do not allow our personal beliefs to interfere with fair representation of the aims of our institutions or the provision of access to their information resources.

VIII. We strive for excellence in the profession by maintaining and enhancing our own knowledge and skills, by encouraging the professional development of co-workers, and by fostering the aspirations of potential members of the profession.

Adopted at the 1939 Midwinter Meeting by the ALA Council; amended June 30, 1981; June 28, 1995; and January 22, 2008.[5]

Although all principles are important to uphold, the principle that is especially relevant to the cataloging and metadata field is the first principle: "We provide the highest level of service to all library users through appropriate and *usefully organized resources*; equitable service policies; equitable access; and accurate, unbiased, and courteous responses to all requests." The phrase "usefully organized resources" is the professional obligation to organize library collections to help library users. This is an important obligation of librarianship. As discussed throughout this book, if library collections are not organized well, then users will not be able to find, access, and use library materials. Yet these three words are very broad; they do not explain how to actually organize resources. Libraries organize resources in ways deemed best by the profession, but there is little guidance about ethical situations that arise when organizing library collections.

ALCTS Guidelines

In addition to the ALA Code of Ethics, the cataloging and metadata field is guided by ALCTS, the division of the ALA concerned with collection development, cataloging and metadata, serials, acquisitions, and preservation.[6] In 1994 ALCTS developed a supplement to the ALA Code of Ethics with nine ethical guidelines for librarians in technical services areas. See the ALCTS guidelines, below.

GUIDELINES FOR ALCTS MEMBERS TO SUPPLEMENT THE AMERICAN LIBRARY ASSOCIATION CODE OF ETHICS, 1994

The following guidelines are to assist ALCTS members in the interpretation and application of the ALA Code of Ethics as it applies to issues of concern to ALCTS.

Within the context of the institution's missions and programs and the needs of the user populations served by the library an ALCTS member:

1. strives to develop a collection of materials within collection policies and priorities;
2. strives to provide broad and unbiased access to information;
3. strives to preserve and conserve the materials in the library in accordance with established priorities and programs;
4. develops resource sharing programs to extend and enhance the information sources available to library users;
5. promotes the development and application of standards and professional guidelines;
6. establishes a secure and safe environment for staff and users;
7. fosters and promotes fair, ethical and legal trade and business practices;
8. maintains equitable treatment and confidentiality in competitive relations and manuscript and grant reviews;

> 9. supports and abides by any contractual agreements made by the library or
> its home institution in regard to the provision of or access to information
> resources, acquisition of services, and financial arrangements.
>
> Developed by the ALCTS Task Force on Professional Ethics; adopted by the
> ALCTS Board of Directors, Midwinter Meeting, February 7, 1994.[7]

The ALCTS guidelines focus primarily on collection development and acquisitions issues. This makes a certain amount of sense because there are many ethical issues in the development of library collections, such as being balanced and unbiased when selecting materials, and upholding ethical business practices when acquiring library materials. The guidelines are helpful for many technical services librarians, but only two guidelines are relevant to the cataloging and metadata field. They are guideline 2, which states that an ALCTS member "strives to provide broad and unbiased access to information," and guideline 5, which states that an ALCTS member "promotes the development and application of standards and professional guidelines."[8] These guidelines are helpful, but they are rather vague. They do not explain how catalogers and metadata specialists should provide unbiased information or what standards and professional guidelines are needed in cataloging and metadata.

Value of Cataloging Librarians

The ALA Code of Ethics and the ALCTS Guidelines are important, but there are many ethical issues in the cataloging and metadata field not addressed in these statements. However, there is some ethical guidance in a document called "Value of Cataloging Librarians" created by the ALCTS Cataloging & Classification Section in 2006 (today called the Cataloging and Metadata Management Section). The document describes itself as "a tool for describing the critical importance of cataloging librarians," and it can apply to both catalogers and metadata specialists. It provides some ethical guidance as well, but not to the extent that one would expect in an ethics document. See the document, below.

> ### VALUE OF CATALOGING LIBRARIANS
>
> by the Association for Library Collections & Technical Services Cataloging &
> Classification Section Executive Committee, 13 June 2006.
>
> The CCS Executive Committee is charged with encouraging and promoting
> cataloging and classification of library materials in all types of institutions.
> Although not explicitly stated, this support extends to the professionals who

do the work. Cataloging librarians comprise a small but valuable subset of the library profession that provides critical but sometimes hidden services to their libraries.

With this document, the committee hopes to provide catalogers and cataloging managers a tool for describing the critical importance of cataloging librarians.

Cataloging librarianship is, at its heart, about service. Cataloging librarians provide customer service, through their work, to thousands of users who use library catalogs and databases on a daily basis, as well as supporting future library users. They create coherent catalogs, which enable a reliable search experience for users, many of whom use the catalog remotely without access to a librarian who can interpret results or respond to questions.

Further, cataloging librarians:

Lead

- Envision bibliographic control of collections of the world's knowledge and implement this vision to create local, regional, and international catalogs and digital access systems.
- Create standards, such as the Resource Description and Access (RDA), Anglo-American Cataloging Rules (AACR), Machine-Readable Cataloging (MARC) and newer metadata standards, such as Dublin Core (DC) and Cataloging Cultural Objects (CCO), by working with national and international organizations.
- Manage, train and mentor cataloging support staff, creating efficient workflows to catalog and process items added to library collections, thus supporting the information needs of users.

Collaborate

- Work with systems librarians to configure catalogs and databases to provide optimal indexing and display of bibliographic records.
- Work with reference librarians to answer complex searching questions.
- Work with collection development, acquisitions and serials librarians to create effective cross-departmental workflows.
- Work with digital library projects to develop local policies and to create metadata records, following local and international standards.
- Contribute to the creation and ongoing development of international databases, catalogs and authority files.

Create & Improve Access

- Apply standards to cataloging records and metadata so that they can be shared in international databases, saving time and money for thousands of libraries, both now and in the future.

- Create functional catalogs and databases, by providing quality control services, record enrichment and authority control.
- Describe and provide access to items in library collections, including unique items in special formats and foreign languages, and items of local interest. These original cataloging records provide access to local users, as well as being shared in international databases.
- Provide subject analysis for items in library collections, creating subject-based call numbers, which allow shelf browsing by users, and subject headings using standardized terminology and thesauri, which allow for increased retrieval by subject and/or keyword searching. This subject analysis is shared in original cataloging records added to international databases.
- Enhance cataloging provided by other libraries and vendors with additional subject terms, call numbers, search terms, links and other information of local interest, reflecting the needs of local users and increasing retrieval.
- Provide authority control on all types of headings added to records, including authors' names, series titles and subject terms. This provides the basis for reliably consistent search results and collocates the terms, saving the time for users.
- Provide direct user services including rush cataloging in-process items on request, and resolving errors in the catalog.

Develop Professionally

- Educate themselves in new technologies and changing standards and apply those new technologies and standards to local workflows.
- Research issues in cataloging and publish or present the results, so that other libraries can apply them.
- Work collaboratively in local, regional, national and international groups, both in person and online, to solve problems, learn, grow and develop.[9]

The document says that providing service to users is at the "heart" of cataloging. In addition to focusing on users, catalogers and metadata specialists *lead* efforts to organize information, including the creation of professional standards and library cataloging management. Catalogers and metadata specialists *collaborate* by working with other departments in a library and with national and international initiatives. Catalogers and metadata specialists *create and improve access* to library collections by creating catalogs that describe and provide access to resources in a library with appropriate subject analysis and authority control. Catalogers and metadata specialists *develop professionally* to learn about new trends in cataloging, to publish research, and to help the field develop and grow. This statement, however, is not a statement of ethics. Not all catalogers and metadata specialists are able to perform everything on the list, such as contributing to international databases, and individual items may change over time as technology and libraries change. The statement also is missing some important ethical issues, such as being inclusive and avoiding bias. However, the main areas of lead, collaborate, create and improve access, and develop professionally are important and can be used to address ethical issues.

Currently, the Cataloging and Metadata Management Section of ALCTS is working on an ethical document for cataloging and metadata librarians.

THE ROLE OF THE USER

Serving users is an important ethical principle of librarianship, and one that is vital to the effective functioning of a library. "Usefully organizing resources" to help users is the first principle of the ALA Code of Ethics and a primary purpose of cataloging and metadata.[10] The "Value of Cataloging Librarians" document says, "Cataloging librarianship is, at its heart, about service."[11] However, there are important questions underlying the principle: Who are the users? What are their needs? Are libraries organizing collections in ways that are truly useful to users? The user plays a large role in cataloging and metadata principles and practice, but understanding their needs and meeting their needs is very difficult. How can cataloging and metadata really help users?

Principle of Convenience of the User

The fundamental principle in the cataloging and metadata field is to focus on the user. As discussed in chapter 3, the *Statement of International Cataloguing Principles* lists thirteen principles that provide a foundation for cataloging codes: (1) convenience of the user, (2) common usage, (3) representation, (4) accuracy, (5) sufficiency and necessity, (6) significance, (7) economy, (8) consistency and standardization, (9) integration, (10) interoperability, (11) openness, (12) accessibility, and (13) rationality.[12] The principle of convenience of the user, however, is "the most important" principle, according to the *Statement*. The principle says,

> 2.1. Convenience of the user. Convenience means that all efforts should be made to keep all data comprehensible and suitable for the users. The word "user" embraces anyone who searches the catalogue and uses the bibliographic and/or authority data. Decisions taken in the making of descriptions and controlled forms of names for access should be made with the user in mind.[13]

Catalogers are directed to keep their users in mind while cataloging, a library's cataloging policies need to meet the needs of its users, and the library profession needs to develop standards that help users. Users are put above everything else.

This is not a new idea. The principle of convenience of the user has a long history in cataloging. It was first stated by Charles Cutter in 1904:

> The convenience of the public is always to be set before the ease of the cataloger. In most cases they coincide. A plain rule without exceptions is not only easy for us to carry out, but

easy for the public to understand and work by. But strict consistency in a rule and uniformity in its application sometimes lead to practices which clash with the public's habitual way of looking at things. When these habits are general and deeply rooted, it is unwise for the cataloger to ignore them, even if they demand a sacrifice of system and simplicity.[14]

The principle was reinforced in 1951 by David Judson Haykin, who spoke of focusing on users when he outlined the principles underlying the *Library of Congress Subject Headings*. He instructs catalogers that

> the subject catalog clearly points to the fundamental principle that the reader is the focus in all cataloging principles and practice. All other considerations, such as convenience and the desire to arrange entries in some logical order, are secondary to the basic rule that the heading, in wording and structure, should be that which the reader will seek in the catalog, if we know or can presume what the reader will look under.[15]

The principle of convenience of the user is beneficial because it directs catalogers to think of their users. It gives libraries and catalogers the freedom and power to organize library collections in ways that will help their users. Whatever helps users is perfectly fine. Libraries should do what they can to meet their users' needs.

Problems with the Principle

The principle of convenience of the user is important, but it raises many issues and can be difficult to follow in practice. Although the principle of convenience of the user eases the pressure to conform to standards, it does not direct catalogers on how to understand their users' needs or how to adapt standard practices to meet those needs. Libraries are left to figure it out for themselves, and it is difficult for individual catalogers to know exactly what their users need without direction and guidance.

The principle also makes the assumption that users are a homogenized group with similar needs. In a critique of Cutter's statement about user convenience, Hope A. Olson says, "The use of the singular in the phrases 'the convenience of the public,' and 'the public's habitual way of looking at things,' especially of the definite article 'the,' indicates that Cutter envisions a community of library users with a unified perspective and a single way of seeking information."[16] This is problematic because there is not one generic "user" with the same needs. There are many library users who are a constantly shifting, diverse mix of different perspectives, different groups, different backgrounds, different cultures, and on and on. Every person fulfills different roles in his or her life, and each of these roles has different information needs. A person can simultaneously be an expert in nuclear engineering who needs cutting-edge research (preferably electronic) and also a beginning home cook who needs introductory cookbooks (preferably on paper). It is difficult to create national cataloging and metadata standards that reflect the rich variety of people in the world and their various needs.

At the same time, it is difficult for catalogers to account for a wide variety of different users while working with cataloging standards. Cataloging standards are not necessarily developed based on an understanding of information-searching behavior or what users need from library systems.[17] Developers of the standards have good intentions. They make decisions with users in mind and want to help users; they are librarians, after all. The focus in standards development seems to be on modeling bibliographic and authority data, including how best to model resources collected in libraries, how to show relationships between them, and so on. That work is incredibly important, no doubt, and it is done in the service of users. It is just that standards' developers do not seem to study users, and there have been many calls over the years to study users and incorporate research into the standards.[18] Karen Snow, for example, suggests a design-thinking approach that would understand users first, and then create systems of cataloging and metadata that meet their needs.[19]

The principle of convenience of the user also is problematic because it is often at odds with the economic realities of libraries and other principles of cataloging, especially the principle of consistency and standardization and the principle of economy. The principle of consistency and standardization says, "Descriptions and construction of access points should be standardized as far as possible to enable consistency."[20] Standardization is essential to cataloging because it ensures the consistent organization of information. Users can search library catalogs in predictable ways and find similarly created bibliographic records, not only in one library's catalog but across all library catalogs. Library users can use different library catalogs and find similar information. Standards also allow for the sharing of bibliographic data across libraries, which reduces duplicate work among libraries, speeds up the cataloging process, and gets library materials to users more quickly. Standards save libraries time, labor, and money. The principle of economy says, "When alternative ways exist to achieve a goal, preference should be given to the way that best furthers overall expediency and practicality (i.e., the least cost or the simplest approach)."[21]

Both principles are important to cataloging, but they can be at odds with what users need. What users need may go against standardized practice and may be expensive. A library may not have the time, labor, or money to modify standard practice to meet its users' needs. For instance, imagine local users at a public library would like the library to reclassify science materials (normally in the *Dewey* 500s) so they are shelved with the art materials (normally in the *Dewey* 700s). Should the library meet their users' needs and make the change? This is not an easy decision. The change would make their users happy, but the library may not have the time, staff, or money to make the change. Does the library have catalogers on staff who are trained to make these classification number changes? Do catalogers on staff have the time to perform this work? Does the library have enough money to pay library vendors to do it? Helping users is the fundamental principle in cataloging, but decisions to help users are not always easy to make in practice.

LESS CUSTOMIZATION

How can libraries and their catalogers work with the standards and also account for their users' needs? Libraries have always been encouraged to customize bibliographic records to meet the needs of local users. Customization happens when catalogers modify standard bibliographic records to meet the needs of local library users. A cataloger could make a fuller record by adding extra subject headings, adding more access points for names, assigning a local classification number, or adding helpful notes and detailed contents—adding or changing anything that would help library users. Yet, as discussed in chapters 7 and 8, there is a wide variety of cataloging and metadata practices and procedures in libraries. It runs the gamut from small libraries with one librarian who performs all library work, including cataloging (e.g., school libraries, special libraries, and small public and academic libraries), to very large libraries with complex cataloging and metadata units with many employees and complicated procedures (e.g., large public and academic libraries). Local cataloging policies are developed to meet the needs of each library and its users, but these policies can vary widely from no local policies to very complicated and detailed instructions for catalogers to follow. Developing policies may be difficult because cataloging units may not know what users need from cataloging, and implementing local policies may be difficult because of money, labor, and time constraints.

There can be a tension between the mandate to meet users' needs and the economic reality of libraries. As discussed throughout this book, cataloging today is very standardized. Cataloging work is shared among libraries, and most libraries purchase bibliographic records from library vendors. Standardization has improved the cataloging process because shared cataloging saves time, labor, and money, and makes library materials available to users quickly. Bibliographic records no longer need to be created from scratch for most items, and work has been passed down from professional catalogers with the knowledge of cataloging standards to paraprofessional staff and library vendors who may not have a complete understanding of cataloging standards and practices. Yet for libraries to benefit financially from shared cataloging, it is cheaper and more cost efficient to accept bibliographic records as is instead of customizing them to meet local users' needs. To be cost-effective, libraries and their catalogers should use standard bibliographic records and avoid local customization. Accepting standard bibliographic records is also a necessity for many libraries who are struggling to keep up with their electronic resources cataloging. The proliferation of electronic resources means that libraries are batch processing large packages of bibliographic records into library catalogs, with very little done to those records. Performing no customization may be necessary for libraries that cannot handle the large amount of bibliographic records received in libraries today.

The batch processing of large files of bibliographic records into the catalog has changed the cataloging process. Instead of customizing bibliographic records and fixing errors before bibliographic records are downloaded into the library catalog, database maintenance is performed after bibliographic records have already been loaded into the catalog. No customization is performed, and errors are fixed later, if they are found. In addition, almost all libraries purchase bibliographic records from library vendors, but library vendors work to contract. A library can ask a vendor to customize standard bibliographic records, but customization is not free. Libraries must pay for anything extra that vendors add to bibliographic records, which can discourage customization. Also, the quality of bibliographic records from library vendors can vary widely. There may be poor-quality bibliographic records going into the library catalog. Essentially, some have argued that because of the financial benefits of using standard bibliographic records, catalogers have given up control of their library catalogs.[22]

Today, there is less customization of bibliographic records performed to meet local users' needs. Many libraries customize their records to help users, but customization is performed less and less all the time. How does this affect library users? If the ALA Code of Ethics obligates libraries and their catalogers to provide "usefully organized resources," then a library should do everything possible to meet the needs of its users. But what prevents local customization from happening today? Absolutely nothing. Local customization is always possible, but three main factors can prevent it from happening in practice: time, labor, and money. Customization takes time, and there is precious little of it in libraries today. Customization also requires catalogers who know how to meet users' needs, and it can be difficult to know exactly how to customize bibliographic records to meet local users' needs. Cataloging and metadata units do not typically perform user research, so they do not necessarily know what local users want. If even they did know, there may not be enough professional catalogers with the knowledge and training to customize bibliographic records. In addition, libraries may not have the money to customize bibliographic records. It is more cost effective to accept bibliographic records as is rather than customize them for users. As Elaine Svenonius says, "Different cultures and subcultures classify differently, use different retrieval languages, and subscribe to different naming conventions. The technical problem to be solved is how to provide for local variation without abrogating the standards that facilitate bibliographical control."[23] This is not an easy problem to solve.

BIAS AND MARGINALIZATION IN SUBJECT STANDARDS

There are many ethical issues surrounding the standards for subject access, such as the *Library of Congress Subject Headings*, the *Library of Congress Classification*, and the *Dewey Decimal Classification*. The standards for subject access have been criticized strongly for having an American, white, male, East Coast, Christian, heterosexual bias, and for focusing on the majority user while excluding other subjects, concepts, and groups that do not fit into that majority. Many argue for standards that are a more accurate and culturally sensitive reflection of subjects, concepts, and groups of people in society. To a certain extent, these criticisms may be warranted. Standards for subject access were first developed in the late nineteenth and early twentieth centuries by white, Christian men living on the East Coast of the United States, and the standards were structured to reflect knowledge, societal norms, and values of that time. For example, Melvil Dewey attended Amherst College in Massachusetts in the 1800s. Although he wanted to objectively organize all knowledge, the structure of his *Dewey Decimal Classification* is based on a specific worldview, specifically that of the curriculum of Amherst College.[24] James C. M. Hanson and Charles Martel created the *Library of Congress Classification* to represent subjects in the Library of Congress's collection, but the structure represents the worldview of certain people in the United States in the late nineteenth century.[25]

Today, subject headings and classification numbers are based on literary warrant, which means subject headings and classification numbers are not created or changed until something is published on a particular subject. This means that published knowledge is favored over unpublished knowledge, and the language and ideas of those who are published are preferred over those who are not published. For example, "Computers" did not exist as a subject heading with a classification number until a book was published about computers. Yet literary warrant makes practical sense. The Library of Congress cannot create subject headings and classification numbers for all knowledge existing in the world. It would be a waste of time, labor, and money for the Library of Congress to create subject headings and classification numbers that may never be assigned, and they might mislead users into thinking libraries own materials on those subjects. However, it is important to keep in mind that literary warrant means that users will not find subject headings or classification numbers for everything in the world.

Criticisms of standards of subject access began to be published in the 1970s, with Sanford Berman's *Prejudices and Antipathies: A Tract on the LC Subject Heads Concerning People* (1971),[26] Steve Wolf's "Sex and the Single Cataloger" (1972),[27] Joan K. Marshall's "LC Labeling: An Indictment" (1972)[28] and her *On Equal Terms: A Thesaurus for Nonsexist Indexing and Cataloging* (1977).[29] Berman, former head cataloger at Hennepin County Library in Minneapolis, Minnesota, is probably the most well-known and prolific critic of cataloging and metadata standards, particularly the *Library of Congress Subject Headings*. Berman was one of the first people to argue that LCSH is offensive and biased, especially in its treatment of people, and he has submitted hundreds of suggestions for changes to LCSH.[30] For example, Berman identified the subject heading "God" as problematic in 1971 because it referred to the Christian God only. Subject headings for the concept of God in all other religions were established with a qualifier in parentheses, such as "God (Judaism)," "God (Hinduism)," "God (Islam)," and so on. This privileged the Christian God and made other religions exceptions to it. The Library of Congress did not change the subject heading to "God (Christianity)" until thirty-five years later, in 2006. Another example is Berman's 1971 suggestion to change "Vietnamese Conflict" to "Vietnam War." This was a controversial suggestion because, although it is known colloquially as the "Vietnam War," the United States Congress never officially declared war on Vietnam. The subject heading was not changed to "Vietnam War, 1961–1975" until 2006. Berman has been incredibly influential and has succeeded in changing many subject headings in LCSH. By 2005 it was estimated that more than 64 percent of Berman's suggestions had been changed or partially changed.[31]

Hope Olson has been another strong critic of standards for subject access. She argues that the focus on a universal language in standards for subject access can marginalize and exclude subjects, concepts, and groups of people that do not fit into the system.[32] The developers of the standards want to make good subject heading and classification number decisions, but they come from certain backgrounds and hold certain views of knowledge, which can unknowingly influence the standards. As Olson and Rose Schlegl say, "These standards tend to represent the mainstream well and the margins poorly in spite of their sincere intentions toward objectivity of representation and user friendliness."[33] Standards tend to represent subjects, concepts, and people that reflect the dominant culture and majority viewpoints.

In addition, Olson points out that majority viewpoints tend to win out over minority viewpoints. Subjects, concepts, and people that do not fit into the system are treated as exceptions. For example, there are Library of Congress subject headings for "Nurses" and "Male nurses" but not for "Female nurses." The assumption is that nurses are women and that male nurses are the exception to the norm. Another example is "Executives." There are subject headings for "Executives" and "Women executives," but not for "Male executives," which assumes that executives are men and that women executives are the exception to the norm. There are many examples like this throughout the standards. To a certain extent, subject headings follow the publishing industry, literary warrant, and the Library of Congress's attempts to be as neutral and objective as possible. There are particular books written about male nurses and women executives, so the subject headings and corresponding classification numbers objectively make sense. However, as Olson points out, the standards "actually hide their exclusions under the guise of neutrality."[34]

Olson also argues that not only do librarians represent subjects when naming subjects, concepts, and people, they are actually constructing knowledge.[35] During the process of creating subject headings and classification numbers, librarians decide what to include and to exclude in the standards, and what to name subjects, concepts, and people. These decisions can reflect biases or what she calls "subtle, insidious marginalizations."[36] Olson argues that the standards should find ways to become more "permeable" to include marginalized concepts, such as using nonhierarchical relationships.[37] She says, "Individual libraries, as well as the institutions that govern our standards, must be held accountable for poor and biased access to information."[38]

In addition to the work of Berman and Olson, there have been many studies about how standards treat groups of people and subjects. Many studies over the years have looked at how standards for subject access treat various groups, such as the Spanish-speaking population;[39] lesbian, gay, bisexual, transgender, queer (LGBTQ) people and subjects;[40] Indigenous knowledge;[41] people with disabilities;[42] and many others topics.

Practical and Political Considerations

Changing offensive and outdated subject headings and classification numbers is important to avoid bias, to better represent subjects, to serve all user groups, and to provide better access to library collections. Yet decisions to change subject headings and classification numbers are not always easily made. The Library of Congress can take a long time to change subject headings and classification numbers, so standards do not always reflect current usage, current knowledge, or the most culturally sensitive terms and phrases. It takes a lot of work to keep pace with knowledge and societal views toward certain topics. The Library of Congress seems to be more open to suggestions today than in the past, and catalogers are encouraged to submit suggestions to change subject headings and classification numbers. Yet these decisions are not made lightly. Whenever subject headings change, for example, authority and bibliographic records must be changed as well, and every library that uses LCSH must make these changes. This was a huge task when libraries used card catalogs. Whenever a subject heading changed, every library would have to update cards, sometimes manually, so subject heading changes were not made as frequently as today. For a large library like the Library of Congress, it was an immense undertaking whenever a subject heading changed. In today's online catalogs, it is much easier to make changes to bibliographic and authority records, but it still takes time, labor, and money. For an example of how subject headings change, see the case study "From Cookery to Cooking," below.

FROM COOKERY TO COOKING

In June 2010, the Library of Congress changed the Library of Congress subject heading "Cookery" to "Cooking." This was a momentous change.

"Cookery" has been the subject heading used to describe the subject of cooking and cookbooks since 1909, when the first edition of LCSH was published. For many years, librarians and users in the United States, particularly in public libraries, criticized the subject heading because the word "Cookery" is not used in the United States. However, it is used in other English-speaking countries. Users in the United States prefer the word "Cooking" as the subject, and they had a hard time finding cookbooks in libraries.

"Cookery," however, reflects LCSH's use of technical terms. Technically, "Cookery" is the word that refers to the subject of cooking. "Cooking" is the process of preparing food. Also, "Cookbooks" is the form. A book *is* a cookbook, but it is *about* cookery.

After many years, the Library of Congress changed its mind in 2010. It changed the subject heading "Cookery" to "Cooking." This was a welcome change for users around the United States.

Although the change was beneficial for users, it meant quite a bit of work for libraries. The Library of Congress changed more than 800 LC subject headings and children's subject headings in the Library of Congress National

Authority File from "Cookery" to "Cooking," and thousands of bibliographic records as well.

This change meant that every library using LCSH had to update every authority record in its local authority file that had the word "Cookery," including authorized headings and cross-references. Libraries had to change their bibliographic records as well. Every bibliographic record that included the word "Cookery" in a subject heading had to be changed to "Cooking." Consequently, this was a large project for many libraries. Despite the work involved, this change improved access to cookbooks and other materials on cooking.[43]

Changing the subject heading "Cookery" to "Cooking" was a good change for users in the United States. However, it was a lot of work for libraries that had to change hundreds of authority records and thousands of bibliographic records to reflect this change. In the end, however, it helped users in the United States by improving access to cookbooks in libraries.

Changes to subject headings are not always easy to make. There are many sides and different views about subject headings and what to call them. Subject heading development can get political. For an example, see the case study "Efforts to Change Illegal Aliens," below.

EFFORTS TO CHANGE ILLEGAL ALIENS

The Library of Congress subject heading "Illegal aliens" has been very controversial. A student group at Dartmouth College in New Hampshire objected to the subject heading and found it offensive, arguing that people are not illegal or alien. In 2014 the student group worked with the Dartmouth library to submit a proposal to the Library of Congress to change the subject heading. This proposal was supported by an American Library Association resolution in January 2016. The Library of Congress agreed, and in 2016 the Library of Congress canceled the subject heading "Illegal aliens" in favor of two subject headings: "Noncitizens" and "Unauthorized immigration."

This change was controversial. Some representatives in Congress were upset by this change. They argued that "Illegal aliens" is the phrase used by Congress in the laws of the United States.

The representatives sent a letter to the Librarian of Congress, and US Representative Diane Black (6th District, Tenn.) introduced a bill in April 2016 to the House of Representatives called the "Stopping Partisan Policy at the Library of Congress Act" (H. R. 4926). The text of the bill says, "The Librarian of Congress shall retain the headings 'Aliens' and 'Illegal Aliens,' as well as related headings, in the Library of Congress Subject Headings in the same manner as the headings were in effect during 2015."

The House voted in favor of the bill. The Library of Congress was ordered on June 10, 2016, to keep using the subject heading "Illegal aliens." This was the first time Congress has stepped in on cataloging matters at the Library of Congress.[44]

As this case study shows, updating subject headings is not a straightforward process. Subject headings can be political and naming subject headings can be very controversial. Cataloging is far from neutral.

ETHICAL OBLIGATIONS OF CATALOGERS AND METADATA SPECIALISTS

What are the professional ethical obligations of catalogers and metadata specialists in their individual jobs? What is the appropriate professional conduct? Catalogers and metadata specialists are ethically obligated to provide "usefully organized resources" (ALA Code of Ethics)[45] and to provide "broad and unbiased access to information" (ALCTS Guidelines).[46] They put service to users at the heart of the work they do. They lead, collaborate, create and improve access, and develop professionally (Value of Cataloging Librarians).[47] Yet there are many cataloging and metadata policy decisions made above individual catalogers and metadata specialists, who do not necessarily have the power to circumvent established guidelines and policies. However, catalogers and metadata specialists still have power over the bibliographic and metadata records they create. Although catalogers—and to a certain extent, metadata specialists—follow standards in the creation of bibliographic records, there is still quite a bit of judgment involved in the process. Individual catalogers and metadata specialists have the power to provide access to library materials, or not. They can add the best subject headings, or not. They can classify appropriately, or not. They can add authorized access points, or not. Although there are quite a few safeguards at the national level when contributing to shared databases like OCLC Connexion, catalogers and metadata specialists have power when organizing local library collections.

Catalogers and metadata specialists often confront ethical situations and make ethical decisions in their jobs. Catalogers and metadata specialists may have to catalog items that anger or offend them. They may have to catalog items in a language they cannot read, in a subject they know nothing about, or in a format they have never cataloged before. They may be asked to speed up production and create lesser-quality bibliographic or metadata records. There are many sticky situations.

Yet there exists a tension between the right thing to do and the economic realities of libraries. Often decisions are affected by economic restraints such as lack of money, lack of staff, or lack of time to perform cataloging and metadata work. For example, one could argue that libraries with a backlog are acting unethically because library materials are not cataloged and made available to users. However, backlogs tend to include the most difficult items to catalog, which may require special cataloging knowledge. Would it be unethical to catalog items with incorrect subject headings just to get them out of the backlog? Libraries, especially those in remote areas, may not be able to hire professional catalogers or even staff with cataloging knowledge, and may not have the funds for professional development or training. Is it more ethical to keep books in the back until a person is hired with cataloging training (which may be never), or is it more ethical to make something available to users even if the record is substandard? What should catalogers and metadata specialists do?

Handling Ethical Situations

Consider this situation: A cataloger objects to a book's content and does not think library users should read it. The cataloger assigns inappropriate subject headings and a bad classification number so the book is never found again. This is a clear violation of the ALA Code of Ethics, especially principle 7, "We distinguish between our personal convictions and professional duties and do not allow our personal beliefs to interfere with fair representation of the aims of our institutions or the provision of access to their information resources."[48] The cataloger is acting unethically by denying users access to the book. However, there are very few clear-cut ethical situations like this one in cataloging and metadata work. Ethical situations are not always easy to recognize or to navigate. Catalogers and metadata specialists may have to choose between competing interests, and libraries may need to make tough economic decisions that unintentionally affect access to collections. For example, should catalogers who are required to catalog a certain number of items a day take the time to add extra subject headings they know would help users? Should a public library undergoing budget cuts eliminate a cataloging position in its overworked cataloging unit or cancel its summer reading program? These questions are never easy to answer. There are many shades of gray when performing cataloging and metadata work, and answers to ethical situations are not always clear.

Consider the following situations. What is the "right" thing to do?

- A cataloger does not know anything about the subject he or she is cataloging. He or she was hired to catalog all subjects and has a daily cataloging quota.
- A cataloger does not know how to catalog a nonbook format. He or she was trained only to catalog books and the library has no money for professional development.
- A cataloger does not know the language of a book he or she is cataloging, and a user has requested the book. The cataloger reads English only, and there are no staff members who read the language.
- A cataloger has too much work and too little time. In his or her haste to make library materials available to users, he or she makes mistakes and misspells words on bibliographic records.
- A cataloger does not want to catalog a video that goes against his or her political beliefs. The cataloger believes that the other side of the political spectrum is immoral and cannot stomach the video's content. The cataloger does not want the video removed from the library; he or she just does not want to catalog it.
- A cataloger does not want to catalog a young adult book for religious reasons. The cataloger does not want the book removed from the library; he or she just does not want to catalog it.

- A metadata specialist does not want to digitize/catalog a personal diary about dealing with cancer because that topic is a trigger for his or her grief. The metadata specialist's brother passed away from cancer. The metadata specialist does not want the diary removed from the library; he or she just does not want to catalog it.
- A metadata specialist does not want to digitize a photograph with nudity. The photo shows a man running naked down a crowded street during a famous political march. The metadata specialist does not want the photograph removed from the library; he or she just does not want to digitize or catalog it.
- A library has a large backlog of uncataloged items. It does not have enough staff to perform cataloging work. The library routinely takes open positions in cataloging and moves them to other departments.
- A library receives a large donation of important genealogical materials from a famous researcher. It includes books, manuscripts, research data, photographs, diaries, maps, oral history recordings, and more. It is an impressive collection that would add a lot to the library's genealogical collection. The researcher wants the library to have the collection digitized and made available in two months or the collection will be given to another library. The library wants the collection but does not have the staff with the knowledge to appropriately handle this collection, or the time or money to digitize and catalog this collection. The donor gives the library a sizable donation each year that partly pays the salaries of librarians in the genealogy department.

These are difficult ethical situations with few clear-cut answers. Instead of one "right" answer, there are many possible ways to tackle each situation. What is needed is ethical guidance, and there is guidance from the ALA Code of Ethics, ALCTS Guidelines, and the "Value of Cataloging Librarians" documents. These documents can be used to frame ethical issues and help catalogers and metadata specialists with difficult situations. There are often no perfect solutions to ethical dilemmas, but guidance from these documents may be able to help prepare catalogers and metadata specialists.

Focus on Service to Users

To make ethical decisions, catalogers and metadata specialists can focus on serving users. Are cataloging and metadata decisions serving users? What would serve users the most? Are catalogers and metadata specialists putting their needs above users or access? Is the library putting its needs above users? Every cataloging policy and decision should be made to serve users. Libraries should assess their users' needs, and cataloging can use the results to improve cataloging and metadata services.

Focus on Access

Catalogers and metadata specialists also can focus on access. Are cataloging and metadata decisions facilitating access? What would provide the most access to the collection? Catalogers and metadata specialists should look for ways to provide access to library materials. Catalogers and metadata specialists must not restrict or block access.

Focus on Leading

A focus on leading can also help make ethical decisions. Are catalogers and metadata specialists serving the cataloging and metadata field? Are they serving librarianship? Is the cataloging and metadata unit setting trends or just following? Catalogers, metadata specialists, and libraries should lead from wherever they are and whenever they can. They can advocate for users and help create standards that meet their needs. They can join associations and serve on roundtables, interest groups, and committees. They can take an active part in the field and profession.

Focus on Collaboration

Catalogers and metadata specialists also can focus on collaboration. Does the cataloging or metadata unit work with other units in the library? Are the catalogers and metadata specialists flexible and work with colleagues to improve cataloging and metadata services? Cataloging and metadata specialists should never automatically say no to an honest request. They should consider what is possible, even if it may differ from what the person requested. In addition, they should ask for help. Cataloging and metadata work is complex. There are too many formats, too many subjects, and too many standards and guidelines; it is impossible to know what to do in all situations. Catalogers and metadata specialists should confer with colleagues to make the best decisions.

Focus on Professional Development

Finally, catalogers and metadata specialists can focus on professional development. Catalogers and metadata specialists need regular professional development to keep up with changes in standards and technology and to learn about trends and issues in the field. Libraries need to support professional development of their staff. Catalogers and metadata specialists can attend conferences, workshops, trainings, webinars, and e-forums—and many of these opportunities are available online. Catalogers and metadata specialists also need to keep up with professional reading, join listservs, and get involved professionally. They should join national and state library associations, including roundtables, interest groups, and committees. This is a way for catalogers and metadata specialists to shape policy, network, and get new ideas for their libraries.

SUMMARY

This chapter discussed ethical issues involved in cataloging and metadata practice. Cataloging and metadata practice is not neutral. It has a lot of power to provide or limit access to library collections. There are several ethical issues surrounding the organization of library collections, including the role of the user when developing cataloging and metadata standards and policies, the lack of customization being performed to help meet users' needs, and the loss of control of the library catalog. The chapter also discussed ethical issues surrounding standards for subject access, including bias and marginalization. Ethical situations are difficult, and the answers are never clear. However, ethical statements can be used to frame ethical decision making. There are no "right" answers, but having an ethical framework can help catalogers and metadata specialists make better decisions.

DISCUSSION QUESTIONS

1. What are the ethical issues surrounding users in cataloging and metadata practice? Why is it difficult for cataloging and metadata practice to meet users' needs?
2. Can catalogers and metadata specialists be neutral? Why or why not?
3. Discuss the ethical issues surrounding the standards for subject analysis. Why have they been criticized?
4. How can the ALA Code of Ethics, the ALCTS Guidelines, and the "Value of Cataloging Librarians" statement help a cataloger or metadata specialist make ethical decisions?

CLASS ACTIVITIES

1. *Ethical Situation Discussion.* In small groups, pick two or three of the ethical situations listed on pages 318–319 and discuss them. What are the ethical issues involved in each situation? What should the cataloger, metadata specialist, or library do in each situation? Then discuss each situation as a group.
2. *Personal Ethics Essay.* Write a short essay that explains the importance of the ALA Code of Ethics and what you will do to uphold its principles. You can focus on any type of librarianship for this assignment; you do not need to focus on the organization of library collections. If you intend to go into cataloging or metadata work, also address how the ALCTS Guidelines and the "Value of Cataloging Librarians" statement will help you make ethical decisions in your work.

NOTES

1. I have seen this quote in various places, such as the American Library Association Conference. I am not entirely sure who said it first, but I credit that person, whomever they are.

2. Patrick Wilson, *Two Kinds of Power: An Essay on Bibliographical Control* (Berkeley: University of California Press, 1968).

3. Robert Audi, ed., *The Cambridge Dictionary of Philosophy*, 2nd ed. (Cambridge: Cambridge University Press, 1999), 749.

4. American Library Association, "Code of Ethics of the American Library Association," American Library Association" (1939, amended 1981, 1995, 2008), accessed January 14, 2019, http://www.ala.org/tools/ethics.

5. Ibid.

6. Please note that ALCTS may no longer exist as a separate ALA division. As of the writing of this book, it is looking into merging with the Library Information Technology Association (LITA) and the Library Leadership & Management Association (LLAMA) to form a new division.

7. Association for Library Collections & Technical Services, "Guidelines for ALCTS Members to Supplement the American Library Association Code of Ethics, 1994," February 7, 1994, accessed January 14, 2019, http://www.ala.org/alcts/resources/alaethics.

8. Ibid.

9. Association for Library Collections & Technical Services, Cataloging and Classification Section Executive Committee, "Value of Cataloging Librarians," June 13, 2006, accessed January 14, 2019, http://www.ala.org/alcts/resources/org/cat/catlibvalue.

10. ALA, "ALA Code of Ethics."

11. ALCTS, "Value of Cataloging Librarians."

12. International Federation of Library Associations and Institutions, *Statement of International Cataloguing Principles (ICP)*, 2016 ed., with minor revisions (The Hague: IFLA, 2017), https://www.ifla.org/publications/node/11015, 5–6.

13. Ibid., 5.

14. Charles A. Cutter, *Rules for a Dictionary Catalog*, 4th ed. (Washington, DC: US Government Printing Office, 1904), 6.

15. David Judson Haykin, *Subject Headings: A Practical Guide* (Washington, DC: Government Printing Office, 1951), 7.

16. Hope A. Olson, "The Power to Name: Representation in Library Cataloging," *Signs: Journal of Women in Culture and Society* 26 (2001): 642.

17. See, e.g., Gretchen L. Hoffman, "Meeting Users' Needs in Cataloging: What Is the Right Thing to Do?" *Cataloging & Classification Quarterly* 47, no. 7 (2009): 631–41.

18. See, e.g., Allyson Carlyle, "User Categorization of Works: Toward Improved Organization of Online Catalogue Displays," *Journal of Documentation* 55 (1999): 184–208; Hoffman, "Meeting Users' Needs in Cataloging"; Ling Hwey Jeng, "Knowledge, Technology, and Research in Cataloging," *Cataloging & Classification Quarterly*, 24, no. 1–2 (1997): 113–40.

19. Karen Snow, "Defining, Assessing, and Rethinking Quality Cataloging," *Cataloging & Classification Quarterly* 55, no. 7–8 (2017): 438–55.

20. IFLA, *Statement of International Cataloguing Principles*, 5.

21. Ibid.

22. Lloyd Jansen, "The Craft of Local Practice: How Catalogers Are Gaining Efficiency but Losing Control," *OLA Quarterly* 9, no. 1 (2003): 5–8.

23. Elaine Svenonius, *The Intellectual Foundation of Information Organization* (Cambridge, MA: MIT Press, 2000), 13.

24. Wayne A. Wiegand, "The 'Amherst Method': The Origins of the Dewey Decimal Classification Scheme," *Libraries & Culture* 33, no. 2 (1998): 175–94.

25. Colin Higgins, "Library of Congress Classification: Teddy Roosevelt's World in Numbers?" *Cataloging & Classification Quarterly* 50, no. 4 (2012): 249–62.

26. Sanford Berman, *Prejudices and Antipathies: A Tract on the LC Subject Heads Concerning People* (Metuchen, NJ: Scarecrow Press, 1971).

27. Steve Wolf, "Sex and the Single Cataloger," in *Revolting Librarians*, ed. Celeste West, Elizabeth Katz, et al. (San Francisco: Booklegger Press, 1972).

28. Joan K. Marshall, "LC Labeling: An Indictment." in *Revolting Librarians* ed. Celeste West, Elizabeth Katz, et al. (San Francisco: Booklegger Press, 1972).

29. Joan K. Marshall, *On Equal Terms: A Thesaurus for Nonsexist Indexing and Cataloging* (New York: Neal-Schuman, 1977).

30. See, e.g., Berman, *Prejudices and Antipathies*; Sanford Berman, *The Joy of Cataloging: Essays, Letters, and Other Explosions* (Phoenix: Oryx Press, 1981); Sanford Berman, "Jackdaws Strut in Peacock's Feathers: The Sham of 'Standard' Cataloging," *Librarians at Liberty* 5, no. 2 and 6, no. 1/2 (1998): 3–21; Sanford Berman, "Finding Material on 'Those People' (and Their Concerns) in Library Catalogs," *MultiCultural Review* (June 2000): 26–28, 48–52.

31. Steven A. Knowlton, "Three Decades Since Prejudices and Antipathies: A Study of Changes in the Library of Congress Subject Headings," *Cataloging & Classification Quarterly* 40, no. 2 (2005): 123–45.

32. See, e.g., Hope A. Olson, "Difference, Culture, and Change: The Untapped Potential of LCSH," *Cataloging & Classification Quarterly* 29 (2000): 53–71; Hope A. Olson, "Sameness and Difference: A Cultural Foundation of Classification," *Library Resources & Technical Services* 45 (2001): 115–22; Olson, "The Power to Name"; Hope A. Olson, "The Ubiquitous Hierarchy: An Army to Overcome the Threat of a Mob," *Library Trends* 52 (2004): 604–16.

33. Hope A. Olson and Rose Schlegl, "Standardization, Objectivity, and User Focus: A Meta-Analysis of Subject Access Critiques," *Cataloging & Classification Quarterly* 32, no. 2 (2001): 61–80.

34. Olson, "The Power to Name," 640.

35. Hope A. Olson, *The Power to Name: Locating the Limits of Subject Representation in Libraries* (Dordrecht: Kluwer Academic, 2002), 6.

36. Ibid.

37. Hope A. Olson, "How We Construct Subjects: A Feminist Analysis," *Library Trends* 56 (2007): 509–41.

38. Olson, "The Power to Name," 663.

39. Marielena Fina, "The Role of Subject Headings in Access to Information: The Experience of One Spanish-Speaking Patron," *Cataloging & Classification Quarterly* 17, no. 1–2 (1993): 267–74.

40. Ben Christensen, "Minoritization vs. Universalization: Lesbianism and Male Homosexuality in LCSH and LCC." *Knowledge Organization* 35, no. 4 (2008): 229–38; Matt Johnson, "Transgender Subject Access: History and Current Practice," *Cataloging & Classification Quarterly* 48, no. 8 (2010): 661–83.

41. Marisa Elena Duarte and Miranda Belarde-Lewis, "Imagining: Creating Spaces for Indigenous Ontologies," *Cataloging & Classification Quarterly* 53, no. 5–6 (2015): 677–702; Deborah Lee, "Indigenous Knowledge Organization: A Study of Concepts, Terminology, Structure and (Mostly) Indigenous Voices," *Partnership: The Canadian Journal of Library & Information Practice & Research* 6, no. 1 (2011): 1–33; Heather Moulaison Sandy and Jenny Bossaller, "Providing Cognitively Just Subject Access to Indigenous Knowledge through Knowledge Organization Systems," *Cataloging & Classification Quarterly* 55, no. 3 (2017): 129–52.

42. Melissa Adler, Jeffrey T. Huber, and A. Tyler Nix, "Stigmatizing Disability: Library Classifications and the Marking and Marginalization of Books about People with Disabilities," *Library Quarterly* 87, no. 2 (2017): 117–35.

43. Library of Congress, "Revision of Headings for Cooking and Cookbooks: Library of Congress Decisions," January 8, 2010, accessed January 14, 2019, https://www.loc.gov/catdir/cpso/cooking3.pdf.

44. Library of Congress, "Library of Congress to Cancel the Subject Heading 'Illegal Aliens,'" March 22, 2016, accessed January 14, 2019, http://www.loc.gov/catdir/cpso/illegal-aliens-decision.pdf; Jasmine Aguilera, "Another Word for 'Illegal Alien' at the Library of Congress: Contentious," *New York Times*, July 22, 2016, accessed January 14, 2019, https://www.nytimes.com/2016/07/23/us/another-word-for-illegal-alien-at-the-library-of-congress-contentious.html.

45. ALA, "ALA Code of Ethics."

46. ALCTS, "Guidelines for ALCTS Members to Supplement the American Library Association Code of Ethics."

47. ALCTS, Cataloging and Classification Section Executive Committee, "Value of Cataloging Librarians."

48. ALA, "ALA Code of Ethics."

SELECTED BIBLIOGRAPHY AND ADDITIONAL READING

Adler, Melissa, Jeffrey T. Huber, and A. Tyler Nix. "Stigmatizing Disability: Library Classifications and the Marking and Marginalization of Books about People with Disabilities." *Library Quarterly* 87, no. 2 (2017): 117–35.

American Library Association. "Code of Ethics of the American Library Association." 1939 (amended 1981, 1995, 2008). http://www.ala.org/tools/ethics.

Association for Library Collections & Technical Services. "Guidelines for ALCTS Members to Supplement the American Library Association Code of Ethics, 1994." http://www.ala.org/alcts/resources/alaethics.

Association for Library Collections & Technical Services, Cataloging and Classification Section Executive Committee. "Value of Cataloging Librarians." 2006. http://www.ala.org/alcts/resources/org/cat/catlibvalue.

Audi, Robert, ed. *The Cambridge Dictionary of Philosophy*. Second Edition. Cambridge: Cambridge University Press, 1999.

Bair, Sheila. "Toward a Code of Ethics for Cataloging." *Technical Services Quarterly* 23 (2005): 13–26.

Beghtol, Clare. "Professional Values and Ethics in Knowledge Organization and Cataloging." *Journal of Information Ethics* 17 (2008): 12–19.

Berman, Sanford. "Finding Material on 'Those People' (and Their Concerns) in Library Catalogs." *MultiCultural Review* (June 2000): 26–28, 48–52.

———. "Jackdaws Strut in Peacock's Feathers: The Sham of 'Standard' Cataloging." *Librarians at Liberty* 5, no. 2; 6, no. 1/2 (1998): 3–21.

———. *The Joy of Cataloging: Essays, Letters, and Other Explosions*. Phoenix: Oryx Press, 1981.

———. *Prejudices and Antipathies: A Tract on the LC Subject Heads Concerning People*. Metuchen, NJ: Scarecrow Press, 1971.

Biswas, Paromita. "Rooted in the Past: Use of 'East Indians' in Library of Congress Subject Headings." *Cataloging & Classification Quarterly* 56, no. 1 (2018): 1–18.

Carlyle, Allyson. "User Categorization of Works: Toward Improved Organization of Online Catalogue Displays." *Journal of Documentation* 55 (1999): 184–208.

Cherry, Alissa, and Keshav Mukunda. "A Case Study in Indigenous Classification: Revisiting and Reviving the Brian Deer Scheme." *Cataloging & Classification Quarterly* 53, no. 5–6 (2015): 548–67.

Christensen, Ben. "Minoritization vs. Universalization: Lesbianism and Male Homosexuality in LCSH and LCC." *Knowledge Organization* 35, no. 4 (2008): 229–38.

Cutter, Charles A. *Rules for a Dictionary Catalog.* Fourth Edition. Washington, DC: US Government Printing Office, 1904.

Drabinski, Emily. "Queering the Catalog: Queer Theory and the Politics of Correction." *Library Quarterly* 83, no. 2 (2013): 94–111.

Duarte, Marisa Elena, and Miranda Belarde-Lewis. "Imagining: Creating Spaces for Indigenous Ontologies." *Cataloging & Classification Quarterly* 53, no. 5–6 (2015): 677–702.

Ferris, Anna M. "The Ethics and Integrity of Cataloging." *Journal of Library Administration* 47 (2008): 173–90.

Fina, Marielena. "The Role of Subject Headings in Access to Information: The Experience of One Spanish-Speaking Patron." *Cataloging & Classification Quarterly* 17, no. 1–2 (1993): 267–74.

Gross, Tina. "Expand, Humanize, Simplify: An Interview with Sandy Berman." *Cataloging & Classification Quarterly* 55, no. 6 (2017): 347–60.

Haykin, David Judson. *Subject Headings: A Practical Guide.* Washington, DC: US Government Printing Office, 1951.

Higgins, Colin. "Library of Congress Classification: Teddy Roosevelt's World in Numbers?" *Cataloging & Classification Quarterly* 50, no. 4 (2012): 249–62.

Hoffman, Gretchen L. "Meeting Users' Needs in Cataloging: What Is the Right Thing to Do?" *Cataloging & Classification Quarterly* 47, no. 7 (2009): 631–41.

Howard, Sara A., and Steven A. Knowlton. "Browsing through Bias: The Library of Congress Classification and Subject Headings for African American Studies and LGBTQIA Studies." *Library Trends* 67, no. 1 (2018): 74–88.

International Federation of Library Associations and Institutions. *Statement of International Cataloguing Principles (ICP).* 2016 Edition, with minor revisions. The Hague: IFLA, 2017. https://www.ifla.org/publications/node/11015.

Jansen, Lloyd. "The Craft of Local Practice: How Catalogers Are Gaining Efficiency but Losing Control." *OLA Quarterly* 9, no. 1 (2003): 5–8.

Jeng, Ling Hwey. "Knowledge, Technology, and Research in Cataloging." *Cataloging & Classification Quarterly* 24, no. 1–2 (1997): 113–40.

Johnson, Matt. "Transgender Subject Access: History and Current Practice." *Cataloging & Classification Quarterly* 48, no. 8 (2010): 661–83.

Knowlton, Steven A. "Three Decades Since Prejudices and Antipathies: A Study of Changes in the Library of Congress Subject Headings." *Cataloging & Classification Quarterly* 40, no. 2 (2005): 123–45.

Kublik, Angela, Virginia Clevette, Dennis Ward, and Hope A. Olson. "Adapting Dominant Classifications to Particular Contexts." *Cataloging & Classification Quarterly* 37, no. 1–2 (2003): 13–31.

McCourry, Maurine W. "Domain Analytic, and Domain Analytic-Like, Studies of Catalog Needs: Addressing the Ethical Dilemma of Catalog Codes Developed with Inadequate Knowledge of User Needs." *Knowledge Organization* 42, no. 5 (2015): 339–45.

Lee, Deborah. "Indigenous Knowledge Organization: A Study of Concepts, Terminology, Structure and (Mostly) Indigenous Voices." *Partnership: The Canadian Journal of Library & Information Practice & Research* 6, no. 1 (2011): 1–33.

Marshall, Joan K. "LC Labeling: An Indictment." In *Revolting Librarians*, edited by Celeste West, Elizabeth Katz, et al. San Francisco: Booklegger Press, 1972.

———. *On Equal Terms: A Thesaurus for Nonsexist Indexing and Cataloging*. New York: Neal-Schuman, 1977.

Moulaison Sandy, Heather, and Jenny Bossaller. "Providing Cognitively Just Subject Access to Indigenous Knowledge through Knowledge Organization Systems." *Cataloging & Classification Quarterly* 55, no. 3 (2017): 129–52.

Olson, Hope A. "Difference, Culture, and Change: The Untapped Potential of LCSH." *Cataloging & Classification Quarterly* 29, no. 1–2 (2000): 53–71.

———. "How We Construct Subjects: A Feminist Analysis." *Library Trends* 56 (2007): 509–41.

———. "The Power to Name: Representation in Library Cataloging." *Signs: Journal of Women in Culture and Society* 26 (2001): 639–68.

———. *The Power to Name: Locating the Limits of Subject Representation in Libraries*. Dordrecht: Kluwer Academic, 2002.

———. "Sameness and Difference: A Cultural Foundation of Classification." *Library Resources & Technical Services* 45 (2001): 115–22.

———. "The Ubiquitous Hierarchy: An Army to Overcome the Threat of a Mob." *Library Trends* 52 (2004): 604–16.

Olson, Hope A., and Rose Schlegl. "Standardization, Objectivity, and User Focus: A Meta-Analysis of Subject Access Critiques." *Cataloging & Classification Quarterly* 32, no. 2 (2001): 61–80.

Shoemaker, Elizabeth. "No One Can Whistle a Symphony: Seeking a Catalogers' Code of Ethics." *Knowledge Organization* 42, no. 5 (2015): 353–57.

Snow, Karen. "Defining, Assessing, and Rethinking Quality Cataloging." *Cataloging & Classification Quarterly* 55, no 7–8 (2017): 438–55.

———. "An Examination of the Practical and Ethical Issues Surrounding False Memoirs in Cataloging Practice." *Cataloging & Classification Quarterly* 53, no. 8 (2015): 927–47.

Švab, Katarina, and Maja Žumer. "The Value of a Library Catalog for Selecting Children's Picture Books." *Cataloging & Classification Quarterly* 53, no. 7 (2015): 717–37.

Svenonius, Elaine. *The Intellectual Foundation of Information Organization*. Cambridge, MA: MIT Press, 2000.

Wiegand, Wayne A. "The 'Amherst Method': The Origins of the Dewey Decimal Classification Scheme." *Libraries & Culture* 33, no. 2 (1998): 175–94.

Wilson, Patrick. *Two Kinds of Power: An Essay on Bibliographical Control*. Berkeley: University of California Press, 1968.

Wolf, Steve. "Sex and the Single Cataloger." In *Revolting Librarians*, edited by Celeste West, Elizabeth Katz, et al. San Francisco: Booklegger Press, 1972.

10

Current Developments in Organizing Library Collections

Everything is becoming more connected and seamless. Technologies such as the World Wide Web, smartphones, smart devices, social media tools, and apps have changed how we interact with each other and how we interact with the world. For libraries, there seem to be endless opportunities to provide access to more electronic resources, give enhanced access to collections, and create more personalized services for users. The organization of library collections is more connected and more seamless as well, and new technologies are changing how library collections are organized. Bibliographic data is busting out of silos, such as library catalogs and digital collections; discovery products are enhancing users' searching experiences; and libraries are creating more digital collections. The cataloging and metadata field seems to be constantly changing. These changes were predicted in a 2008 report by the Library of Congress: "The future of bibliographic control will be collaborative, decentralized, international in scope, and Web-based."[1] These predictions are fast becoming reality.

This book has discussed many new projects and initiatives in the organization of library collections, such as the *IFLA Library Reference Model*, the *3R Project: RDA Toolkit Restructure and Redesign*, OCLC's *Faceted Application of Subject Terminology*, many types of alternative classification, and the move away from traditional cataloging. This chapter builds on those discussions and will focus on several current developments in the organization of library collections: linked open data, the proliferation of electronic resources, providing access to special collections, and discovery products. It also will discuss how cataloging and metadata practice may be affected by these developments.

LINKED OPEN DATA

An important development that may change how libraries organize their collections is linked data, specifically linked *open* data. Libraries are starting to make their data—the bibliographic information about their collections—available openly on the web. Why? There is a lot of data in library catalogs and digital collections. Libraries have spent more than 150 years cataloging their collections, and only around 25 years building digital collections. A lot of time, labor, and money has been put into creating library collections that serve users and help them meet their needs. The problem is that information in library catalogs and digital collections cannot be searched directly using a search engine like Google. Users like to perform Google searches and often use Google first when searching for information. However, Google cannot search library catalogs and other databases, so users do not get library holdings in their results list. Bibliographic records in library catalogs and metadata records in digital collections are in silos that can be searched only through a library catalog or other library databases. People must search library catalogs and databases separately, and many people do not know they need to do that. In addition, materials in library collections are found in many other places, like government databases, Google Scholar, Google Books, iTunes, streaming apps, and many more. No matter where they are housed, materials should be linked together across the web to give users more options. In order to make library bibliographic information available on the web, it needs to be published as linked open data so that it is open and freely available to users during web searches.

Linked data is a part of the broader Semantic Web movement, which is an effort by the World Wide Web Consortium (W3C) to help computers understand the meaning of information. It goes beyond linking *documents* to linking *data*. The web was created to link together websites and web pages, creating a "Web of Documents." Individual pieces of data on those websites cannot be linked together. A search engine simply performs a keyword search to find a list of websites that meet a person's search query. Search engines like Google can improve search results by using sophisticated algorithms, but a person cannot find all places where specific data is located on the web, such as all music by musicians from Ghana, all poems by Maya Angelou, or all movies about cowboys in Texas. However, with linked data, it becomes possible to link specific data across the web, creating a "Web of Data."[2] In 2006 Tim Berners-Lee first used the phrase "linked data" as a part of the Semantic Web. He said, "The Semantic Web isn't just about putting data on the web. It is about making links, so that a person or machine can explore the web of data. With linked data, when you have some of it, you can find other, related, data."[3] Basically, make links so people can find related things on the web. Linked data can do a lot of things; for example, see figure 10.1.

Shown in figure 10.1 are Google knowledge cards.[4] One card is about the country Egypt. It uses linked data to pull together various information about Egypt from Google Maps, *Wikipedia*, Google Flights, and other information. It is pulled together for a user who wants to find more information about Egypt. The other Google knowledge card is about the book *The Complete Collected Poems of Maya Angelou*. It provides brief bibliographical information about the book, a summary, ratings information, recommendations for similar books, and, most importantly for libraries, it includes links to local public libraries that hold the book (the search

Egypt
Country

Egypt, a country linking northeast Africa with the Middle East, dates to the time of the pharaohs. Millennia-old monuments sit along the fertile Nile River Valley, including Giza's colossal Pyramids and Great Sphinx as well as Luxor's hieroglyph-lined Karnak Temple and Valley of the Kings tombs. The capital, Cairo, is home to Ottoman landmarks like Muhammad Ali Mosque and the Egyptian Museum, a trove of antiquities.

Capital: Cairo

Currency: Egyptian pound

Plan a trip

    Egypt travel guide

    15 h 23 min flight

Continent: Africa, Asia

Official languages: Arabic, Modern Standard Arabic

Points of interest
View 15+ more

| Giza Necropolis | Great Sphinx of Giza | Abu Simbel Temples | Egyptian Museum | Valley of the Kings |

People also search for
View 15+ more

| Cairo | Africa | Saudi Arabia | Syria | United Arab Emirates |

Figure 10.1. Google Knowledge Cards

The Complete Collected Poems of Maya Angelou

Book by Maya Angelou

4.4/5	4.1/5
Goodreads	Barnes & Noble

90% liked this book

Google users

The Complete Collected Poems of Maya Angelou is author and poet Maya Angelou's collection of poetry, published by Random House in 1994. It is Angelou's first collection of poetry published after she read her poem "On the Pulse of Morning" at President Bill Clinton's inauguration in 1993. Wikipedia

Originally published: 1986

Author: Maya Angelou

Genre: Poetry

Publisher: Random House

Country: United States of America

Borrow ebook

Available near you

Edit location

Dallas Public Library

Timberglen Branch Library, Park Forest Branch Library... >

Plano Public Library System

Plano Public Library System >

Arlington Public Library

Arlington Northeast Branch Library, Central Express, ... >

People also search for

View 15+ more

And Still I Rise	The Top 500 Poems	Do Not Stand at My Grave...	A Dream Within a Dream	Phenome... Woman: Four Poe...
Maya Angelou		Mary Elizabeth Frye	Edgar Allan Poe	Maya Angelou

Figure 10.1. *Continued*

was performed in Denton, Texas). A user can go to a library catalog to see more information about the book.

Figure 10.2 shows another example of linked data, this time from Wikidata, a site that provides linked data for *Wikipedia* and other Wiki products.[5] The data about Pocahontas is pulled from *Wikipedia*, Wikidata, and other communities' linked data about Pocahontas, including the *American National Biography* and the Library of Congress National Authority File. Many communities across the web have published datasets as linked data, including media, publishing, government agencies, organizations, and libraries, archives, and museums.

The goal of linked data is to link things across the web, and the goal of linked open data is to make linked data open and free to all. Linking data may seem impossible, but it is possible by using structured data. Linked open data is both new and familiar to librarianship. Helping people find related information has been a purpose of libraries and library cataloging since the beginning. The only difference is that the web has facilitated the creation of more formats and the availability of more information,

Figure 10.2. Information about Pocahontas on Wikidata

and it has opened up more ways for libraries to help users. Libraries also have lots of structured data in bibliographic and metadata records. There are billions of bibliographic and metadata records in libraries, but the data is not fully structured, nor is it structured in a way that search engines can search. It is structured for specific tools such as library catalogs and databases, not for use by large search engines like Google. Libraries need to make sure their data is structured so it can be linked to other data across the web. Libraries also need to make sure their data is open and freely available to all users, no matter who they are or whether they can afford access. Library data cannot be hidden behind paywalls, restrictions, or access gates.

How Linked Data Works

Linked data is structured in a specific way. In 2006 Berners-Lee stated four rules for linking data. They are:

1. Use URIs as names for things.
2. Use HTTP URIs so that people can look up those names.
3. When someone looks up a URI, provide useful information, using the standards (RDF, SPARQL).
4. Include links to other URIs so that they can discover more things.[6]

There are several models that can be used to link data, but the *Resource Description Framework* (RDF) is widely used by communities across the web and in library linked data projects. RDF is maintained by the W3C for use with linked data and the Semantic Web. What follows is a very basic explanation.[7] In RDF, things are described in triples. As the name implies, there are three parts to a triple: (1) a subject, (2) a predicate, and (3) an object. Together, the three parts create a statement, as shown below:

$$\text{Subject} \rightarrow \text{Predicate} \rightarrow \text{Object}$$

A subject is an entity or a resource. Subjects represent things, like an e-book, the title of a film, the composer of a symphony, or anything else that can be described. A predicate in RDF terminology is also called a property. Properties are like the elements that have been discussed in this book. They describe something about the resource using a specific content standard or metadata schema, like "title" in RDA or *Dublin Core*, and they show how the subject is related to the object. Properties are very important because they help computers understand how two things are linked. The relationship is made explicit. An object is a value that finishes the statement. It is a thing to which the predicate is referring, such as a particular person who wrote a book, a particular subject a play is about, or a particular title of a magazine.

RDF triples can be created to describe anything. See table 10.1 for an example using the book *Life of Pi* by Yann Martel. *Life of Pi*, the book, is the subject of this RDF triple. "Is authored by" is the predicate or the property. It explains the relationship of the subject to the object. "Yann Martel" is the object or the value. He is the author of the book. Read that as a statement, "*Life of Pi* is authored by Yann Martel."

Table 10.1.   RDF Triple Example

Subject (resource)	Predicate (property)	Object (value)
Life of Pi	Is authored by	Yann Martel

Triples can go the other way, too. See table 10.2. It shows another RDF triple, this time making Yann Martel the subject and *Life of Pi* the object. Notice how the predicate changes so the statement makes sense: "Yann Martel is author of *Life of Pi*." In this way, RDF triples not only provide a description, they also show the relationship of the subject to the object.

Table 10.2.   Another RDF Triple Example

Subject (resource)	Predicate (property)	Object (value)
Yann Martel	Is author of	Life of Pi

RDF triples, or statements, can be made about any aspect of anything: "*Life of Pi* is about shipwreck survival," or "Penguin Random House Canada is publisher of *Life of Pi*." Also, the RDF model is used to describe things as they are. RDF does not care what each community calls a thing. For example, different communities may have different authorized forms of Yann Martel's name, but to RDF it does not matter. Each community can call Yann Martel whatever it wants. Each form of the name will be linked together no matter what each community calls him.

Yet linked data needs more than just triple modeling. The statements are not enough. Uniform Resource Identifiers (URI) must be added for computers to be able to find, use, and link the data. (Internationalized Resource Identifiers [IRI] can also be used). URIs are consistent HTTP links that represent each part of a triple statement. A link points to each part in a triple. Each part of a triple can be assigned a URI, and the URI used depends on the community. A very basic example is shown in table 10.3. Each URI represents each part of a triple. For the subject and object, for example, libraries in the United States could use URIs for title and author from the Library of Congress's Linked Data Service.[8] The predicate can come from any source, like *Resource Description and Access* or a metadata schema. The RDA URI for author is shown in this example, but the URI could come from any standard.

Table 10.3   RDF Triple Example with URIs

Subject (resource)	Predicate (property)	Object (value)
Life of Pi http://id.loc.gov/authorities/ names/noxxxx	Is authored by http://rdaregistry.info/ Elements/u/P60434	Yann Martel http://id.loc.gov/authorities/ names/n94009985

RDF does not work by itself. It requires a markup language to transmit data, and there are several options, such as RDF/XML, Turtle, N-Triples, and others. The most commonly used set of markup vocabularies on the web is Schema.org. It is used by many online communities around the world and is the preference of search engines.[9] It has many schemas that can be used to mark up data about different types of materials, such as movies, books, events, products, offers, and more.[10] Other tools used with RDF are Simple Knowledge Organization System (SKOS), which is used to represent controlled vocabularies in RDF; Web Ontology Language (OWL), which is a language used to create ontologies; and SPARQL Protocol and RDF Query Language (SPARQL), which is used to search and retrieve linked data.

LINKED DATA IN LIBRARIES

In order to make library data searchable on the web, it must be published as linked open data using RDF and URI links, or other similar standards. When data is structured using URIs, then computers can link the data across the web. Libraries are joining the movement toward linked data, and many things have been done to prepare for a linked data future.

Linked Data in Cataloging Models and Standards

Most cataloging standards and models have either incorporated linked data or have been released as linked data. One example is the *IFLA Library Reference Model*, published in 2017. It was "developed very much with semantic web technologies in mind,"[11] and the model can be used to express RDF statements. If the previous *Life of Pi* example was expressed using LRM, it could look something like table 10.4. The LRM statement reads, "*Life of Pi* was created by Martel, Yann." Notice that in this example, the object changes slightly to be the authorized access point for Yann Martel from the Library of Congress National Authority File.

Table 10.4.   RDF Triple Example using *IFLA Library Reference Model*

Subject (resource)	Predicate (property)	Object (value)
Life of Pi (LRM work)	was created by (LRM relationship)	Martel, Yann (LRM Agent; authorized access point)

LRM is important because it is being incorporated into RDA, which itself has been linked data–ready since Original RDA was published in 2010. The RDA Registry website[12] contains "the RDA entities, elements, relationship designators, and vocabulary encoding schemes . . . represented in Resource Description Framework (RDF), the syntax of open linked data and the Semantic Web."[13]

For subject analysis, most controlled vocabularies and classification schemes have been published as linked open data. The Library of Congress has released their cataloging standards and tools as linked open data, available in the LC Linked Data Service website.[14] This includes *Library of Congress Subject Headings, Children's Subject Headings, Library of Congress Classification, Library of Congress Genre/Form Terms for Library and Archival Materials, Library of Congress Medium of Performance Thesaurus for Music, Thesaurus for Graphic Materials*, and the *American Folklore Society Ethnographic Thesaurus*. The National Library of Medicine has made the *Medical Subject Headings* available as linked open data,[15] and OCLC has made the *Dewey Decimal Classification* and *Faceted Application of Subject Terminology* available as linked open data.[16] Figure 10.3 shows an example from LCSH for the subject heading "Cooking (Pecans)."[17] Notice the URIs at the top of the page.

Cooking (Pecans)

URI(s)
> http://id.loc.gov/authorities/subjects/sh85032081
> info:lc/authorities/sh85032081
> http://id.loc.gov/authorities/sh85032081#concept

Instance Of
> MADS/RDF Topic
> MADS/RDF Authority
> SKOS Concept ☑

Scheme Membership(s)
> Library of Congress Subject Headings

Collection Membership(s)
> LCSH Collection - Authorized Headings
> LCSH Collection - General Collection
> LCSH Collection - May Subdivide Geographically

Variants
> Cooking with pecans
> Pecan--Use in cooking

Broader Terms
> Cooking (Nuts)

Earlier Established Forms
> Cookery (Pecans)

LC Classification
> TX814.2.P4

Change Notes
> 1986-02-11: new
> 2017-09-19: revised

Alternate Formats
> RDF/XML (MADS and SKOS)
> N-Triples (MADS and SKOS)
> JSON (MADS/RDF and SKOS/RDF)
> MADS - RDF/XML
> MADS - N-Triples
> MADS/RDF - JSON
> SKOS - RDF/XML
> SKOS - N-Triples
> SKOS - JSON
> MADS/XML
> MARC/XML

Figure 10.3.   Cooking (Pecans) from LC's Linked Data Service

Figure 10.4.   Arundhati Roy from the Virtual International Authority File

The Library of Congress also has made its National Authority File available as linked data (names and titles only),[18] and OCLC has made the Virtual International Authority File (VIAF) available as linked data.[19] VIAF pulls together authority files from different national libraries around the world into one database. Figure 10.4 shows partial VIAF information for the writer Arundhati Roy and many authorized access points for her in national authority files around the world.[20] The linked data URI, called "Permalink," is used to link all forms of her name.

Bibliographic Framework Initiative

RDA, controlled vocabularies, classification schemes, and the Library of Congress National Authority File all have been made available as linked data. Yet there must be a way to mark up library data. Linked data cannot operate fully within the closed confines of bibliographic, authority, or metadata records in library catalogs and databases. Instead, linked data requires something different, and to realize the potential of linked data, libraries need to move past the "record."[21] This is where the *Bibliographic Framework Initiative* (BIBFRAME) comes in. BIBFRAME is being developed to help libraries move their MARC 21 formatted bibliographic and authority data into linked data, moving libraries away from the MARC 21 format. BIBFRAME was originally published in 2012, and BIBFRAME 2.0 was released in 2016. The developers describe BIBFRAME this way: "BIBFRAME (Bibliographic Framework) is an initiative to evolve bibliographic description standards to a linked data model, in order to make bibliographic information more useful both within and outside the library community."[22] Instead of using Schema.org, BIBFRAME is how libraries will structure their data and put their collections on the web. BIBFRAME is important for libraries because libraries deal with much legacy data, including billions of bibliographic records in library catalogs. BIBFRAME will eventually replace the MARC 21 format, but BIBFRAME is also mapped to MARC so that bibliographic and authority records encoded in MARC 21 can be converted to BIBFRAME.[23]

Currently, BIBFRAME is still under development, and it is being tested by the Library of Congress and some academic and research libraries. An important development, however, happened in May 2017, when the Library of Congress converted its entire library catalog—all bibliographic records and some authority records—to BIBFRAME. The data is housed in a separate BIBFRAME database that is not yet publicly available. The Library of Congress is currently testing and refining its BIB-FRAME database.[24] BIBFRAME has the potential to help libraries move to linked data. Yet BIBFRAME is just for libraries and their data. It cannot be used by other communities, most of whom already use Schema.org.

Linked Data in Bibliographic and Authority Records

The Library of Congress's conversion of its library catalog into BIBFRAME is a big step forward in the implementation of linked data in libraries. Yet BIBFRAME is still a long way from replacing MARC and being implemented fully in all librar-ies. The billions of records encoded in MARC will be housed in library catalogs for many years to come. Instead of waiting to be replaced, MARC has incorporated linked data. In 2017 several subfields were added to many fields in the MARC 21 formats to accommodate URIs, including the *MARC 21 Format for Bibliographic Data*[25] and the *MARC 21 Format for Authority Data*.[26] In 2017–2018, OCLC added the MARC subfields for URIs to Connexion, so catalogers can add URIs to bibliographic records. In addition, in 2018 the Program for Cooperative Cataloging provided guidance to PCC libraries about adding URIs.[27] Depending on the library and its library catalog vendor, individual libraries may be able to add URIs to their bibliographic records.

Several libraries have performed linked data projects, primarily at the Library of Congress, the National Library of Medicine, and larger public and academic librar-ies. For example, the Dallas Public Library's "#DPLWhatsNext" Personal Librarian program uses linked data to display recommendations from personal librarians.[28] The North Carolina State University Libraries used linked data in their Organization Name Linked Data project, which focused on the names of acquisitions vendors.[29] OCLC also has been working on many linked data projects.[30] Linked data has been added to bibliographic records in WorldCat, and the linked data includes URIs for all parts of the bibliographic record. For example, see figure 10.5, which shows some linked data embedded in the WorldCat record for Neil Gaiman's book *Coraline*.[31] OCLC's linked data uses Schema.org rather than BIBFRAME, but the linked data is available only on the public side of WorldCat; it is not added to bibliographic records in Connexion.

Linked Data Implementation in Libraries

Linked data has the power to link library data to the rest of the online world, and the cataloging and metadata field is getting ready. National libraries and larger academic libraries are leading the charge, and some libraries have put significant resources into linked data projects. Most cataloging models and standards are linked

Coraline

Author	Neil Gaiman; Dave McKean
Publisher	New York : HarperCollins, ©2002.
Edition/Format	📖 Print book View all editions and formats
Summary	Looking for excitement, Coraline ventures through a mysterious door into a world that is similar, yet disturbingly different from her own, where she must challenge a gruesome entity in order to save herself, her parents, and the souls of three others.
Rating	☆☆☆☆☆ (not yet rated) 📄 0 with reviews - Be the first.
Subjects	Paranormal fiction. Young adult fiction.
More like this	📄 Similar Items

⌐ **Linked Data**

More info about Linked Data

Primary Entity
<http://www.worldcat.org/oclc/989446905>
   a schema:Book, schema:CreativeWork ;
   library:oclcnum "989446905" ;
   library:placeOfPublication <http://dbpedia.org/resource/New_York_City> ;
   library:placeOfPublication <http://id.loc.gov/vocabulary/countries/nyu> ;
   schema:about <http://experiment.worldcat.org/entity/work/data/4921065660#Topic/paranormal_fiction> ;
   schema:about <http://experiment.worldcat.org/entity/work/data/4921065660#Topic/young_adult_fiction> ;
   schema:bookFormat bgn:PrintBook ;
   schema:contributor <http://experiment.worldcat.org/entity/work/data/4921065660#Person/mckean_dave> ;
   schema:copyrightYear "2002" ;
   schema:creator <http://experiment.worldcat.org/entity/work/data/4921065660#Person/gaiman_neil> ;
   schema:datePublished "2002" ;
   schema:description "Looking for excitement, Coraline ventures through a mysterious door into a world that is similar, yet disturbingly different from her own, where she must challenge a gruesome entity in order to save herself, her parents, and the souls of three others."
   ;
   schema:exampleOfWork <http://worldcat.org/entity/work/id/4921065660> ;
   schema:name "Coraline" ;
   schema:productID "989446905" ;
   schema:publication <http://www.worldcat.org/title/-/oclc/989446905#PublicationEvent/new_york_harpercollins_2002> ;
   schema:publisher <http://experiment.worldcat.org/entity/work/data/4921065660#Agent/harpercollins> ;
   schema:workExample <http://worldcat.org/isbn/9780060575915> ;
   wdrs:describedby <http://www.worldcat.org/title/-/oclc/989446905> ;

Figure 10.5.   WorldCat Linked Data for *Coraline*

data ready. BIBFRAME is still under development, but the Library of Congress has converted its library catalog into BIBFRAME. OCLC has added linked data to bibliographic records in WorldCat. Subfields for URIs have been added to MARC 21 formats so that catalogers can add URIs to bibliographic and authority records. Much has been done at the national level, but how will linked data be implemented in individual libraries at the local level?

A current project that may affect linked data's implementation in libraries is the Linked Data for Production: Pathway to Implementation (LD4P2) project. The goal of this project is to determine how linked data can be implemented in libraries, specifically "to begin the implementation phase of the cataloging community's shift to linked data for the creation and manipulation of their metadata."[32] There are seven specific goals of the project:

1. The creation of a continuously fed pool of linked data expressed in BIB-FRAME from a core group of academic libraries;
2. Development of a cloud-based sandbox editing environment in support of an expanded cohort of libraries to create and reuse linked data;
3. The development of policies, techniques, and workflows for the automated enhancement of MARC data with identifiers to make its conversion to linked data as clean as possible;
4. The development of policies, techniques, and workflows for the creation and reuse of linked data and its supporting identifiers as libraries' core metadata;
5. Better integration of library metadata and identifiers with the Web through collaboration with Wikidata;
6. The enhancement of a widely adopted library discovery environment (Blacklight) with linked-data based discovery techniques;
7. The orchestration of continued community collaboration through the development of an organizational framework called LD4, ensuring continued exchange of ideas and techniques across a distributed developing community.[33]

This is a tall order and will require a lot of work. Five large academic and research libraries are partners in the project: Cornell, Harvard, Stanford, the University of Iowa, and the Program for Cooperative Cataloging at the Library of Congress. In addition, in 2018, seventeen more PCC libraries, all larger academic and research libraries, were picked to be a cohort to work on the project.[34] This project, if successful, has the potential to move linked data forward in libraries and to determine how to implement it in libraries. The project may determine the future of how library collections are organized.

Implications of Linked Data

The Linked Data for Production grant has the potential to determine how linked data is implemented in libraries. Cataloging and metadata practice will need to change as well to accommodate linked data. How cataloging and metadata work is performed today may be quite different after linked data is implemented in libraries. Change may not happen in the near future, but it will happen eventually.

Linked data may affect cataloging and metadata practice in libraries and change how libraries provide access to their collections. The purpose of linked data is to link data across the web and to better help users find and use library materials. Focusing on users and their needs is important while libraries transition to linked data, and keeping users in mind can be a touchstone for possible uncertain times ahead. Yet libraries seem to be focused on linked data as a technology, and not necessarily on the potential of linked data to help library users. It is important for libraries to join the rest of the linked data world, but users' needs must be at the heart of the work. Some researchers have questioned whether linked data really will be a disruptive technology in libraries,[35] and others have questioned how it will help users. For example, Ted Fons says, "Narrative descriptions of where libraries want to be relative to the reader's experience of searching on the web are difficult, if not impossible, to find, but detailed descriptions of what some libraries are doing relative to web technologies are abundant. This means that libraries are investing significantly in some of the dimensions of technology, but the community's goal and commitment to the convenience of the reader isn't articulated."[36]

Will linked data really be able to help users find and use library materials in quick, efficient, and meaningful ways? Will linked data be able to understand what users really want from library catalogs or understand their searches? Is linked data simply a model that is good for computers, but not for users? Will linked data really help users with more than just basic information searches? These are important questions that may not be answered until after linked data is adopted in libraries.

IDENTITY MANAGEMENT

In addition to linked data, there have been current developments regarding names. The Library of Congress and the PCC are moving past the term *authority control* because of its close tie to cataloging. The current term is *identity management*, which places the work of identifying names within a wider context of linked data and working with other communities to identify names. As discussed in chapter 3, there are many people, families, and corporate bodies responsible for works and expressions. Cataloging uses one consistent form of a name as an authorized access point on bibliographic records. Authorized forms of names are set up in authority records in the Library of Congress National Authority File and local authority files. Catalogers check the authority file and add authorized names to their bibliographic records. Following developments in linked data, there have been efforts to link authorized forms of names across libraries and across the web. As discussed earlier, the Library of Congress National Authority File and the Virtual International Authority File have been published as linked data, and URIs have been assigned to names in these authority files. These URIs are being linked to names in Wikidata and other websites, so that names are linked across the web.

Another current development in identity management is the International Standard Name Identifier (ISNI). In 2012 the International Organization for Standardization approved ISO 27729, which created the ISNI. Similar to the ISBN for books and the ISSN for serials, the ISNI is a 16-digit number used to identify people, groups, and organizations responsible for creative works. It describes itself this way: "The ISNI system uniquely identifies public identities across multiple fields of creative activity and provides a tool for disambiguating public identities that might otherwise be confused."[37] Identifiers are not like authorized access points for names used in authority records; instead, they are unique numbers that are used no matter the form of the name. Each community can use a different form of the name, but the identifier is consistent and links different forms of a name together.

For example, the ISNI for Arundhati Roy is shown in figure 10.6. It shows her ISNI number, 0000 0001 1071 6772, and many forms of her name used around the

ISNI: 0000 0001 1071 6772

Name: Arundhati Roy
           Arundhati Roy (Indiaas romanschrijfster)
           Arundhati Roy (Indian novelist, essayist)
           Arundhati Roy (indische Schriftstellerin, politische Aktivistin und
           Globalisierungskritikerin)
           Arundhati Roy (scrittrice indiana)
           Aruntati Raȳ
           Raȳ, Aruntati
           Rāȳa, Arundhati
           Roja, Arundhati
           Roy, A.
           Roy, Arundhati
           Roy (Suzanna Arundhati)
           Roy, Suzanne Arundhati
           Rôya, Arundhati
           Rūy, Arūndhātī
           Suzanna Arundhati Roy
           Αρουντάτι Ρόι (Ινδός συγγραφέας)
           Арундати Рой
           Арундаті Рой
           Рой, Арундати
           Արունդհատի Ռոյ
           ארונדהטי רוי
           רוי, ארונדהטי
           ‏أروندائى روي‏،
           أروندائى روى (نويسنده هندى)
           أروندهتى راے
           ‏روي، أروندائى‏،
           ‏روي، أروندهتى‏،
           अरुंधति राय
           अरुन्धति राय
           অরুন্ধতী রায়
           ਅਰੁੰਧਤੀ ਰਾਏ
           அருந்ததி ராய்
           అరుంధతీ రాయ్
           ಅರುಂಧತಿ ರಾಯ್
           അരുന്ധതി റോയ്
           아룬다티 로이
           アルンダティ・ロイ
           ロイ, アルンダティ
           阿蘭達蒂·羅伊

Dates: 1961-

Figure 10.6.   ISNI for Arundhati Roy

world, including the authorized form in the Library of Congress National Authority File, "Roy, Arundhati." ISNI is also linked data ready. A URI for each ISNI can be created by using "http://isni.org/isni/" and then adding the ISNI number, so "http://isni.org/isni/0000000110716772" would be the URI for Arundhati Roy.[38]

The Conference of European National Libraries and OCLC were founding members of ISNI, among other groups across several industries. The Program for Cooperative Cataloging is not a member of ISNI yet, but in 2017–2018, PCC had a pilot project with twelve academic libraries to add existing ISNI identifiers to authority records and to create new identifiers in the ISNI database.[39] Cataloging may be involved in ISNI soon, adding names to the ISNI database and adding ISNI numbers to authority records.

ELECTRONIC RESOURCES

Another current development is managing ever-growing electronic resources collections. Library collections have been changing. Although libraries still hold significant physical collections and will continue to do so, libraries also provide access to more electronic resources. As discussed in chapter 7, electronic resources include many types of electronic content that libraries make available to users, such as e-books, e-serials, databases, e-media, and other online content. Libraries do not own electronic resources, and they are not housed on a library's server. Libraries pay to access these materials, primarily through large reference databases or e-content providers like OverDrive or Hoopla. Instead of picking and choosing specific titles based on collection development selection criteria and cataloging each title individually, libraries receive large packages of bibliographic records from vendors and batch load them into library catalogs. Some libraries have had to rearrange staff to manage the work, and some libraries use electronic resources managers to help.

Libraries receive many electronic resources, and libraries of all types have increased their electronic collections. Even the smallest library has access to thousands of titles that previously would not have been selected for the library. For example, according to the 2014 Public Libraries Survey, public libraries reported an average of 23,543 e-books per library.[40] This is in stark contrast to the 2016 Public Libraries Survey, in which public libraries report an average of 45,768 e-books per library.[41] The number of electronic books available in public libraries has practically doubled in two years, and it will continue to grow. This is not to say that libraries will not have physical collections; they will. Library users still want physical materials, and libraries will collect them as long as users want them and publishers provide them. However, the amount of information available electronically will continue to grow. The proliferation of electronic resources will continue to affect how work is performed in cataloging and serials units, because libraries will always need to quickly and efficiently make these materials available to users. Cataloging and managing the vast amount of electronic resources available in libraries will continue to be a challenge.

METADATA WORK

Yet another development that shows no signs of slowing is performing metadata work to create digital collections. As discussed throughout this book, metadata work involves creating institutional repositories and digitizing and making available materials in special collections and archives. For institutional repositories, the overall purpose is "capturing and preserving the intellectual output of a single or multi-university community."[42] For special collections, the overall purpose is "exposing hidden collections."[43] Unlike electronic resources, libraries are responsible for creating digital collections and housing them on a library's or a parent organization's server. Metadata work is not necessarily a new development. It has been performed in academic and larger public libraries since the late 1990s and early 2000s. Yet it is slowly becoming the focus of work in some academic and public libraries. As discussed in chapter 7, some libraries have added professional metadata librarian positions and moved staff from cataloging to metadata. Some cataloging and technical services departments have changed their names to reflect this change in focus.

However, there are many barriers to performing metadata work. The types of materials in special collections are just that: special. They are rare, unique, special materials not typically collected by libraries. Digitizing and providing access to materials in special collections can be quite difficult and may take specialized knowledge. Unlike books and other mass-produced items in libraries, which can be cataloged using standardized practices, items in special collections are unique to each library, so metadata work resists standardization across libraries. To help each other, librarians publish and share best practices,[44] but each library has figured out its own metadata processes and how to provide access to its special collections. Each library is responsible for creating its own metadata records, determining which standards to use and how to record data in metadata records. This is a significant amount of work, especially because metadata records cannot be shared across libraries like bibliographic records.

In addition, metadata work has only been performed for the past twenty-five years, so there is not necessarily established metadata practice. Metadata work may be treated as a side project, even though it is becoming an essential part of providing access to some library collections. In addition, the American Library Association and its divisions have interest groups devoted to digital collections, but metadata work is not necessarily a focus of any one division or section. Also, some libraries may be working with archives staff to create digital archives, and there may be a blurring of lines between libraries and archives. This can be challenging because libraries and archives do not necessarily speak the same language, and each field has its own practices. It may be difficult for metadata specialists and archivists to communicate, and each side may need to learn about the other to provide access to archival materials.

Although metadata work is currently being performed at academic libraries and some large public libraries, there is a lot of work to do in public libraries and smaller academic libraries. Most public libraries have collections of genealogical materials and/or local history materials, or they partner with local history societies or museums. Making these special materials available online is a benefit to users because it preserves access to a community's culture and history. Even the smallest public library may have a special collection that needs attention, and an academic library may be considering creating an institutional repository. There is a lot of potential for metadata work to provide access to these collections. In addition to all of the barriers previously discussed, public libraries and smaller academic libraries do not necessarily have the budget, staff, or time to perform this work. The work is there, but the resources may not be. This is definitely an area that needs attention in the future.

DISCOVERY PRODUCTS

Another not so very new development is discovery, which describes products, services, and systems that help library users better use and retrieve information on library catalogs. Discovery grew out of developments in integrated library systems and online public access catalogs in the mid- to late 2000s, called "next-generation catalogs."[45] Next-generation catalogs have more sophisticated searching features and better search interfaces than traditional library catalogs, which just provide a list of bibliographic records with linked access points. Next-generation catalogs incorporate social media features and user-generated content, such as links to social networking sites (e.g., Facebook, Twitter), and they give library users the ability to add tags to bibliographic records. They also can include things not typically included in traditional library catalogs, like reviews, recommendations, links to blogs and websites, and cover images. In the early to mid-2010s, the term *discovery* became associated with these catalogs. Discovery products are known by many names, such as discovery systems, discovery tools, discovery interfaces, discovery services, discovery layers, and web-scale discovery services or systems.

Discovery products incorporate all the next-generation features and add a few more, such as web-scale discovery, which searches all library content at once, including a library's catalog, its databases, its digital collections, and its institutional repository. Discovery services also can help libraries manage their websites, give users the ability to borrow e-books, and support smartphones and other mobile devices.[46] There are two primary types of discovery products: discovery interfaces and index-based discovery services. Discovery interfaces fit over the top of an existing integrated library system (ILS) or digital collection and provide an interface for users. All types of libraries use them. Many academic libraries use index-based discovery services (also called web-scale discovery services), which are separate discovery systems with a central index. In a survey of 1,357 academic libraries, around 84 percent of them reported using one of those tools.[47]

Academic and large public libraries primarily use discovery products, but as they become more popular and effective, other libraries will adopt them, too. A search using a discovery product can enhance a user's searching experience and improve discovery. Features like reviews and tagging work with bibliographic information to help users decide whether library materials meet their needs. In addition, using an index-based discovery service means that users can search all library content at once. A user does not have to perform separate searches in the library catalog, the digital collection, and each separate reference database to find information. An index-based discovery service provides a one-stop searching experience that can save users time. Discovery tools have the potential to provide a very powerful searching experience.

Yet there can be problems, especially with index-based discovery services. There is a lack of authority control across library databases. A library's catalog, digital collections, and databases may have different forms of names, titles, and subjects. Users may receive many duplicate records for the same item in a search. Information in a library catalog is created based on cataloging and metadata standards and can be quite consistent, while information in reference databases is not standardized and can be very inconsistent. Making data work together is a huge problem when it comes to harvesting metadata for a discovery service. In addition, users can get too many results. For example, a keyword search for "Elton John" on the Texas Woman's University library catalog retrieves twenty-nine results. Compare this with a search for the keywords "Elton John" in the library's discovery service. There are more than fifty thousand results—too many results for most people to sort through.[48] Users will need to refine or limit searches, or learn how to create better search queries. Additional limiting or more refined search techniques are needed. Searching a discovery system is a much broader search and will give a user many more results than just searching the library catalog. It is very convenient to search everything at one time, but it can be incredibly frustrating to have a huge results list, much of which may be duplicated.

SUMMARY

This chapter discussed some current developments in how library collections are organized. Advances in discovery products, the shift to metadata work, and growing electronic resources collections give users better access to more library materials and change how cataloging and metadata work is performed in libraries. Linked data, however, may be a game changer. It has the potential to change how library collections are made available to users. The cataloging and metadata field is getting ready for a linked data future in which library data is linked across the web. Library data wants to be accessible and useful. It does not want to sit alone in a dusty book, hidden away on a database, or buried in a spreadsheet. Users should not have a hard time finding the data they need. Searching should be intuitive, easy, and seamless. For data to be found, it needs to be open, structured, rich, and connected to other data. A user performing a search should see the relationships and links between data, no matter where the data is housed. However, creating data that is linked openly, that is easily accessible, and that is found in seamless ways takes a lot of work—a lot of *people* work, not just computer work. For libraries and other information agencies to link data, information organization work needs to be decentralized, collaborative, and flexible. Everyone needs to work together to ensure a successful linked data future.

Even in light of all of these developments, it is unknown whether linked data will help all users equally. There seems to be a widening gap between libraries. Academic libraries, on the whole, have bigger budgets and more staff, and are able to perform cutting-edge work such as linked data projects. Their librarians attend conferences and serve on national committees that create cataloging and metadata policy for everyone else. Although they are working in the best interests of every library, the needs of academic libraries may overshadow the needs of public libraries and school libraries. Cataloging and metadata practice may be moving toward a linked data future, but it is unclear how linked data will help users or how it will affect libraries that do not have the resources to perform linked data projects.

Yet despite differences in size or budget, all libraries organize their collections to meet their users' needs, and they always will. New technologies may change how library collections are organized and how cataloging and metadata work is performed, but it always comes down to helping people. The theory and practice of organizing library collections are centered around helping people find what they need. The organization of library collections must always be done in the service of people.

DISCUSSION QUESTIONS

1. Discuss linked open data. What is its purpose and how will it benefit libraries? How will it affect cataloging and metadata practice?
2. How are electronic resources and digital collections changing cataloging and metadata work?
3. Discuss discovery products. How are they changing how users find library materials?
4. What is the future of cataloging and metadata in libraries? What do you see?

CLASS ACTIVITY

Research Paper. The purpose of this assignment is to go deeper into a topic concerning the organization of library collections. It can be a topic discussed in chapter 10 or a topic discussed in the book. Research the topic and write a paper that explains the topic, the current research surrounding the topic, and how the topic affects libraries. Include in-text and reference citations to the literature using an appropriate citation manual. *Alternative research products:* Annotated bibliography or bibliographic essay.

NOTES

1. Library of Congress, "On the Record: Report of the Library of Congress Working Group on the Future of Bibliographic Control," January 9, 2008, accessed January 14, 2019, http://www.loc.gov/bibliographic-future/news/lcwg-ontherecord-jan08-final.pdf, 4.

2. W3C, "Semantic Web," accessed January 14, 2019, https://www.w3.org/standards/semanticweb.

3. Tim Berners-Lee, "Linked Data," July 27, 2006, last updated June 18, 2009, accessed January 14, 2019, https://www.w3.org/DesignIssues/LinkedData.html.

4. Images from a Google search, https://www.google.com.

5. Wikidata, "Pocahontas," accessed January 14, 2019, https://tools.wmflabs.org/reasonator/?&q=193406.

6. Berners-Lee, "Linked data."

7. There are many resources available online if you are interested in learning more about RDF. I used several sources as a guide, including Steven J. Miller, *Metadata for Digital Collections: A How-To-Do-It Manual* (New York: Neal-Schuman, 2011); and Marcia Lei Zeng and Jian Qin, *Metadata*, 2nd ed. (Chicago: Neal-Schuman, 2016).

8. Library of Congress, "ID.LOC.GOV: Linked Data Service," accessed January 14, 2019, https://id.loc.gov.

9. Ted Fons, "Improving Web Visibility: Into the Hands of Readers," *Library Technology Reports* 52, no. 5 (2016).

10. Schema.org, "Organization of Schemas," accessed January 14, 2019, https://schema.org/docs/schemas.html.

11. International Federation of Library Associations and Institutions, *IFLA Library Reference Model: A Conceptual Model for Bibliographic Information* (The Hague: IFLA, 2017), https://www.ifla.org/files/assets/cataloguing/frbr-lrm/ifla-lrm-august-2017_rev201712.pdf, 40.

12. RDA Registry, accessed January 14, 2019, https://www.rdaregistry.info.

13. RDA Steering Committee, "RDA Frequently Asked Questions," last updated July 16, 2018, accessed January 14, 2019, http://www.rda-rsc.org/content/rda_faq#13.

14. Library of Congress, "ID.LOC.GOV."

15. National Library of Medicine, "Medical Subject Headings RDF," accessed January 14, 2019, https://id.nlm.nih.gov/MeSH.

16. OCLC, "OCLC Linked Data," accessed January 14, 2019, https://www.oclc.org/developer/develop/linked-data.en.html.

17. Library of Congress, "ID.LOC.GOV."

18. Ibid.

19. OCLC, "OCLC Linked Data."

20. Virtual International Authority File, "Arundhati Roy," accessed January 14, 2019, https://viaf.org/viaf/76457869/#Roy,_Arundhati.

21. See, e.g., Rachel Ivy Clarke, "Breaking Records: The History of Bibliographic Records and Their Influence in Conceptualizing Bibliographic Data," *Cataloging & Classification Quarterly*, 53, no. 3–4 (2015): 286–302.

22. Library of Congress, "Overview of the BIBFRAME 2.0 Model," April 21, 2016, accessed January 14, 2019, https://www.loc.gov/bibframe/docs/bibframe2-model.html.

23. Library of Congress, "MARC 21 to BIBFRAME 2.0 Conversion Specifications," accessed January 14, 2019, https://www.loc.gov/bibframe/mtbf.

24. Jodi Williamschen, "Creating and Updating a BIBFRAME Database," presentation at the American Library Association Annual Conference, New Orleans, LA, June 24, 2018.

25. Library of Congress, "MARC 21 Format for Bibliographic Data. Format Change List. Update No. 25," December 2017, accessed January 14, 2019, https://www.loc.gov/marc/up25bibliographic/bdapndxg.html.

26. Library of Congress, "MARC 21 Format for Authority Data. Format Change List. Update No. 25," December 2017, accessed January 14, 2019, https://www.loc.gov/marc/up25authority/adapndxf.html.

27. Library of Congress, Program of Cooperative Cataloging URI Task Group on URIs in MARC, "URI FAQs," September 26, 2018, accessed January 14, 2019, https://www.loc.gov/aba/pcc/bibframe/TaskGroups/URI%20FAQs.pdf.

28. Katie Meador, Pauline Stacchini, and Andrew Wright, "#DPLWhatsNext: How Dallas Public Library Engages Readers Using Linked Data," *Medium*, April 20, 2017, accessed January 14, 2019, https://medium.com/library-link-network/dplwhatsnext-how-dallas-public-library-engages-readers-using-linked-data-1ed878e40579.

29. Eric M. Hanson, "A Beginner's Guide to Creating Library Linked Data: Letters from NCSU's Organization Name Linked Data Project," *Serials Review* 40 (2014): 251–58.

30. OCLC, "OCLC Linked Data."

31. WorldCat, https://www.worldcat.org.

32. "LD4P2 Project Background and Goals," *Linked Data for Production: Pathway to Implementation (LD4P2)*, accessed January 14, 2019, https://wiki.duraspace.org/display/LD4P2/LD4P2+Project+Background+and+Goals.

33. Ibid.

34. Stanford University, "Stanford Libraries Announces Linked Data for Production (LD4P) Cohort Members and Subgrant Recipients," November 1, 2018, accessed January 14, 2019, http://library.stanford.edu/node/155851.

35. Heather Lea Moulaison and Anthony J. Million, "The Disruptive Qualities of Linked Data in the Library Environment: Analysis and Recommendations," *Cataloging & Classification Quarterly* 52, no. 4 (2014): 367–87.

36. Fons, "Improving Web Visibility," 20.

37. International Organization for Standardization, "ISO 27729:2012: Information and Documentation; International Standard Name Identifier (ISNI)," accessed January 14, 2019, https://www.iso.org/standard/44292.html.

38. ISNI, "Arundhati Roy," accessed January 14, 2019, http://isni.org/isni/0000000110716772.

39. Library of Congress, Program of Cooperative Cataloging, "PCC Participants' Meeting," PowerPoint presentation at the American Library Association Annual Conference, New Orleans, LA, June 24, 2018; DuraSpace, "PCC ISNI Pilot Home," October 31, 2018, accessed January 14, 2019, https://wiki.duraspace.org/display/PCCISNI/PCC+ISNI+Pilot+Home.

40. Institute of Museum and Library Services, *Public Libraries Survey, Fiscal Year 2014: Supplementary Tables* (Washington, DC: Institute of Museum and Library Services, 2016), https://www.imls.gov/sites/default/files/fy2014_pls_tables.pdf.

41. Institute of Museum and Library Services, *Public Libraries Survey, Fiscal Year 2016: Supplementary Tables* (Washington, DC: Institute of Museum and Library Services, 2018), https://www.imls.gov/sites/default/files/fy2016_pls_tables.pdf.

42. Raym Crow, "The Case for Institutional Repositories: A SPARC Position Paper," *ARL Bimonthly Report* 223 (August 2002): 1.

43. See, e.g., Barbara M. Jones and Judith M. Panitch, "Exposing Hidden Collections: Introduction," *RBM: A Journal of Rare Books, Manuscripts, & Cultural Heritage* 5, no. 2 (2004): 84–87.

44. See, e.g., Jung-ran Park, ed. *Metadata Best Practices and Guidelines: Current Implementation and Future Trends* (London: Routledge, 2012).

45. See, e.g., Marshall Breeding, "Next-Generation Library Catalogs," *Library Technology Reports* 43, no. 4 (2007): 5–14; Jenny Emanuel, "Next Generation Catalogs: What Do They Do and Why Should We Care?" *Reference & User Services Quarterly* 49 (2016): 117–20; Chew Chiat Naun, "Next Generation OPACs: A Cataloging Viewpoint," *Cataloging & Classification Quarterly* 48, no. 4 (2010): 330–42.

46. Marshall Breeding, "Library Resource Discovery Products: Context, Library Perspectives, and Vendor Positions," *Library Technology Reports* 50, no. 1 (2014).

47. Marshall Breeding, "Index-Based Discovery Services: Current Market Positions and Trends," *Library Technology Reports* 54, no. 8 (2018).

48. Texas Woman's University, "Libraries," accessed January 14, 2019, https://twu.edu/library.

SELECTED BIBLIOGRAPHY WITH ADDITIONAL READINGS

Berners-Lee, Tim. "Linked Data," July 27, 2006, last updated June 18, 2009, accessed January 14, 2019, https://www.w3.org/DesignIssues/LinkedData.html.

Borgman, Christine L. "Why Are Online Catalogs Still Hard to Use?" *Journal of the American Society for Information Science* 47 (1996): 493–503.

Bossaller, Jenny S., and Heather Moulaison Sandy. "Documenting the Conversation: A Systematic Review of Library Discovery Layers." *College & Research Libraries* 78, no. 5 (2017): 602–19.

Breeding, Marshall. "Index-Based Discovery Services: Current Market Positions and Trends." *Library Technology Reports* 54, no. 8 (2018).

———. "Library Resource Discovery Products: Context, Library Perspectives, and Vendor Positions." *Library Technology Reports* 50, no. 1 (2014).

———. "Next-Generation Library Catalogs." *Library Technology Reports* 43, no. 4 (2007): 5–14.

Calhoun, Karen. *The Changing Nature of the Catalog and Its Integration with Other Discovery Tools.* Report prepared for the Library of Congress. March 17, 2006. http://www.loc.gov/catdir/calhoun-report-final.pdf.

Clarke, Rachel Ivy. "Breaking Records: The History of Bibliographic Records and Their Influence in Conceptualizing Bibliographic Data." *Cataloging & Classification Quarterly* 53, no. 3–4 (2015): 286–302.

Coyle, Karen. 2010b. "RDA Vocabularies for a Twenty-First-Century Data Environment." *Library Technology Reports* 46, no. 2 (2010).

———. "Understanding the Semantic Web: Bibliographic Data and Metadata." *Library Technology Reports* 46, no. 1 (2010).

Crow, Raym. "The Case for Institutional Repositories: A SPARC Position Paper." *ARL Bimonthly Report* 223 (August 2002): 1.

Davis, Jeehyun Yun. "Transforming Technical Services: Evolving Functions in Large Research University Libraries." *Library Resources & Technical Services* 60 (2016): 52–65.

Emanuel, Jenny. "Next Generation Catalogs: What Do They Do and Why Should We Care?" *Reference & User Services Quarterly* 49 (2016): 117–20.

Fons, Ted. "Improving Web Visibility: Into the Hands of Readers." *Library Technology Reports* 52, no. 5 (2016).

Godby, Carol Jean, and Karen Smith-Yoshimura. "From Records to Things: Managing the Transition from Legacy Library Metadata to Linked Data." *Bulletin of the Association for Information Science and Technology* 43, no. 2 (2017): 18–23.

Hanson, Eric M. "A Beginner's Guide to Creating Library Linked Data: Letters from NCSU's Organization Name Linked Data Project." *Serials Review* 40 (2014): 251–58.

Hastings, Robin. "Linked Data in Libraries: Status and Future Direction." *Computers in Libraries* 35, no. 9 (November 2015): 12–16.

Institute of Museum and Library Services. *Public Libraries Survey, Fiscal Year 2014: Supplementary Tables*. Washington, DC: Institute of Museum and Library Services, 2016. https://www.imls.gov/sites/default/files/fy2014_pls_tables.pdf.

———. *Public Libraries Survey, Fiscal Year 2016: Supplementary Tables*. Washington, DC: Institute of Museum and Library Services, 2018. https://www.imls.gov/sites/default/files/fy2016_pls_tables.pdf.

International Federation of Library Associations and Institutions. *IFLA Library Reference Model: A Conceptual Model for Bibliographic Information*. The Hague: IFLA: 2017.

Jones, Barbara M., and Judith M. Panitch. "Exposing Hidden Collections: Introduction." *RBM: A Journal of Rare Books, Manuscripts, & Cultural Heritage* 5, no. 2 (2004): 84–87.

Jones, Ed, and Michele Seikel, eds. *Linked Data for Cultural Heritage*. Chicago: ALA Editions, 2016.

Library of Congress, Program of Cooperative Cataloging. "PCC Participants' Meeting." PowerPoint presentation at the American Library Association Annual Conference, New Orleans, LA, June 24, 2018.

Library of Congress, Program of Cooperative Cataloging URI Task Group on URIs in MARC. "URI FAQs." September 26, 2018. https://www.loc.gov/aba/pcc/bibframe/Task Groups/URI%20FAQs.pdf.

Library of Congress, Working Group on the Future of Bibliographic Control. *On the Record: Report of the Library of Congress Working Group on the Future of Bibliographic Control.* 2008. https://www.loc.gov/bibliographic-future/news/lcwg-ontherecord-jan08-final.pdf.

MacEwan, Andrew, Anila Angjeli, and Janifer Gatenby. "The International Standard Name Identifier (ISNI): The Evolving Future of Name Authority Control." *Cataloging & Classification Quarterly* 51, no. 1–3 (2013): 55–71.

Miller, Steven J. *Metadata for Digital Collections: A How-To-Do-It Manual*. New York: Neal-Schuman, 2011.

Miller, Steven, and Jody Perkins. "Introduction." *Journal of Library Metadata* 15 (2015): 135–41.

Mitchell, Erik T. "Library Linked Data: Early Activity and Development." *Library Technology Reports* 52, no. 1 (2016).

Moulaison, Heather Lea, and Anthony J. Million. "The Disruptive Qualities of Linked Data in the Library Environment: Analysis and Recommendations." *Cataloging & Classification Quarterly* 52, no. 4 (2014): 367–87.

Naun, Chew Chiat. "Next Generation OPACs: A Cataloging Viewpoint." *Cataloging & Classification Quarterly* 48, no. 4 (2010): 330–42.

Park, Jung-ran, ed. *Metadata Best Practices and Guidelines: Current Implementation and Future Trends*. London: Routledge, 2012.

Purcell, Aaron D. *Digital Library Programs for Libraries and Archives: Developing, Managing, and Sustaining Unique Digital Collections*. Chicago: ALA Neal-Schuman, 2016.

Qiang Jin, Jim Hahn, and Gretchen Croll. "BIBFRAME Transformation for Enhanced Discovery." *Library Resources & Technical Services* 60, no. 4 (2016): 223–35.

Schreur, Philip Evan. "The Academy Unbound: Linked Data as Revolution." *Library Resources & Technical Services* 56 (2012): 227–37.

Seeman, Dean, and Lisa Goddard. "Preparing the Way: Creating Future Compatible Cataloging Data in a Transitional Environment." *Cataloging & Classification Quarterly* 53, no. 3–4 (2015): 331–40.

Southwick, Silvia B., Cory K. Lampert, and Richard Southwick. "Preparing Controlled Vocabularies for Linked Data: Benefits and Challenges." *Journal of Library Metadata* 15 (2015):177–90.

Spiteri, Louise, ed. *Managing Metadata in Web-Scale Discovery Systems*. London: Facet, 2016.

Van Hooland, Seth, and Ruben Verborgh. *Linked Data for Libraries, Archives and Museums: How to Clean, Link Will and Publish Your Metadata*. Chicago: American Library Association, 2014.

Williamschen, Jodi. "Creating and Updating a BIBFRAME Database." Presentation at the American Library Association Annual Conference, New Orleans, LA, June 24, 2018.

Xu, Amanda, Kirk Hess, and Laura Akerman. "From MARC to BIBFRAME 2.0: Crosswalks." *Cataloging & Classification Quarterly* 56, no. 2–3 (2018): 224–50.

Zeng, Marcia Lei, and Jian Qin. *Metadata*. Second Edition. Chicago: Neal-Schuman, 2016.

Glossary

AACR2: *See* Anglo-American Cataloguing Rules, Second Edition.

Access Point: An element used to access a database. For libraries, access points include names, titles, and subject headings. One consistent form of each access point is used to bring together items in a library catalog or other database.

Accession List: A list of items assigned numbers in the order they were received.

Administrative Metadata: Metadata that is used for the management, preservation, and use of digital resources. It records things like acquisitions information, technical information, ownership and rights, legal access, preservation, use, etc.

Anglo-American Cataloguing Rules, Second Edition (AACR2): A set of descriptive cataloging rules used in libraries from 1978 until 2013. It directed catalogers in the creation of bibliographic records that describe and provide access to library materials. It has been replaced by Resource Description and Access (RDA).

Authority Control: In library cataloging, this is the process of ensuring that one consistent form of names, titles, and subject headings is used in bibliographic records. Authority control ensures that items in a library catalog are brought together in a search.

Authority File: A file of authority records that includes one consistent form of authorized names, titles, and subjects used on bibliographic records. The Library of Congress maintains the National Authority File, which includes authorized names, titles, and subjects used in libraries in the United States. Individual libraries may maintain a local authority file, which includes authorized names, titles, and subjects used in one or more library catalogs.

Authority Record: A record that contains information about names, titles, and subject headings, including authorized access points, cross-references, variant forms, broader terms, narrower terms, related terms, and other information.

Batch Loading/Batch Processing: The process of downloading large files of bibliographic records into library catalogs. The files may be manipulated to add or remove information before the records are added to the catalog.

BIBCO: *See* Monographic Bibliographic Record Cooperative Program (BIBCO).

BIBFRAME: *See* Bibliographic Framework Initiative.

Bibliographic Control: Any organizational system existing outside of library materials used to facilitate access to them.

Bibliographic Framework Initiative (BIBFRAME): An initiative from the Library of Congress to develop a new framework that will replace the MARC 21 format. It is used for linked data purposes.

Bibliographic Record: A record that describes and provides access to items in a library collection.

Bilindex: A Spanish-English subject headings list used to provide Spanish-language access to library collections.

BISAC Subject Headings: A list of subject headings created by the publishing industry. Some public libraries use them to arrange library collections using a bookstore model.

Card Catalog: A tool used to provide access to a library's collection. Bibliographic information is transcribed on 3x5 cards that are filed in drawers. There are usually separate files for titles, names, and subjects.

Catalog: *See* Library Catalog.

Catalog Card: A 3x5-inch card that describes and provides access to materials in a library's collection. These are shelved in drawers in a library's physical card catalog. In most libraries, cards have been replaced by bibliographic records located in the online public access catalog.

Cataloging: The process of creating bibliographic records that describe and provide access to library materials.

Children's Subject Headings: Subject headings list maintained by the Library of Congress that is geared toward children. It includes Library of Congress Subject Headings that have been modified for children.

Chronological Subdivision: In subject headings lists, such as the Library of Congress Subject Headings, a chronological subdivision is sometimes added to bring out the time period of the item being cataloged. Example: Art, Modern—19th century.

Classification: The arranging of knowledge/things into categories and building a notational scheme to represent those categories.

CONSER: *See* Cooperative Online Serials Program.

Content Standard: When discussing metadata, a content standard focuses on content and provides guidance about what types of bibliographic information should be described. It does not explain how bibliographic information should be displayed or formatted. For example, Resource Description and Access (RDA) is a content standard used in libraries.

Controlled Vocabulary: A list of approved words and phrases used to represent subjects. A controlled vocabulary can be a list of subject headings, a thesaurus, or any other controlled list of terms.

Cooperative Online Serials Program (CONSER): A program within the Program of Cooperative Cataloging in which participants create policies, procedures, and bibliographic records for serial publications.

Customization: Ways in which libraries tailor cataloging standards and bibliographic records to meet the needs of their users.

Cutter Number: An alphanumeric number added to a call number that represents something, such as a name, title, geographic area, special topic, etc. It is added to arrange items alphabetically at a classification number.

DACS: *See* Describing Archives: A Content Standard.

DC: *See* Dublin Core.

DDC: *See* Dewey Decimal Classification.

Describing Archives: A Content Standard (DACS): A content standard used by the archival community to describe archival materials.

Descriptive Cataloging: The part of the library cataloging process in which an item is described (e.g., title, author, date, publisher) and access points are assigned. It is separate from subject analysis.

Descriptive Metadata: Metadata used to describe and provide access to each resource in a library's collection. It describes elements such as title, creator, publisher, keywords, subject headings, classification, etc. It is the primary type of metadata created in libraries.

Dewey Decimal Classification: A numeric classification scheme developed by Melvil Dewey to represent subjects in library collections. Used primarily in public and school libraries.

Discovery Products: Products used to enhance discovery of library materials. They allow library users to search multiple databases at once, and include features like reviews, recommendations, the ability to lend e-books, and link resolvers. There are several types of products, including discovery interfaces, which add an interface discovery layer on top of library catalogs, and discovery systems, which are separate systems with their own central index.

Dublin Core: A metadata schema used to provide access to digital content. In libraries, it is used to create metadata records for items in digital collections.

EAD: *See* Encoded Archival Description.

Element: The attributes, properties, or characteristics used to describe any type of information resource, such as library materials (e.g., title, author, date, subject). Each standard or schema includes different elements depending on its purpose.

Encoded Archival Description (EAD): A metadata schema used to create finding aids for archival materials.

Enumeration: In serials cataloging, enumeration refers to numbering on a serial publication such as volume, issues, years, etc.

Enumerative: In classification, an enumerative classification scheme is one in which a notation is assigned to every subject, concept, or group needed in the classification scheme.

Exhaustivity: Exhaustivity refers primarily to subject analysis. Exhaustivity is how deeply a cataloger/indexer should index an item. Back-of-the-book indexes are considered high exhaustivity because every page is indexed. Library bibliographic records are considered low exhaustivity because only a few subject headings are assigned.

Extensible Markup Language (XML): A popular markup language used by online data communities around the world that allows for the sharing of structured information. In libraries, XML is used to encode metadata records in digital collections.

Faceted Application of Subject Terminology: *See* FAST Subject Headings.

FAST Subject Headings: Simplified Library of Congress Subject Headings based on facets.

FDLP: *See* Federal Depository Library Program.

Federal Depository Library Program (FDLP): A government program that libraries join to receive selected government publications. At least one library from every state is designated a regional depository library and is considered the library of last resort for federal government publications in the state.

Finding Aid: Used in archives to describe and provides access to archival collections.

Fixed Field: A field in the MARC encoding standard with a predetermined character limit. The fixed field includes codes that represent certain aspects of a bibliographic record, such as language, country, date of publication, etc.

Form Subdivision: In subject headings lists, such as the Library of Congress Subject Headings, a form subdivision is sometimes added to describe the literary form or type of publication, such as periodicals, biography, fiction, poetry, or drama. Example: Nuclear physics—Periodicals.

FRAD: *See* Functional Requirements for Authority Data.

FRBR: *See* Functional Requirements for Bibliographic Records.

FRSAD: *See* Functional Requirements for Subject Authority Data.

Functional Requirements for Authority Data (FRAD): A conceptual model for authority data developed by the IFLA and published in 2009. It showed important entities in authority records, with corresponding attributes and relationships, and tied them to user tasks. It provided a framework for Resource Description and Access (RDA), but has been replaced by the IFLA Library Reference Model (LRM).

Functional Requirements for Bibliographic Records (FRBR): A conceptual model for bibliographic data developed by the IFLA and published in 1998. It showed important entities in bibliographic records, with corresponding attributes and relationships, and tied them to user tasks. Its WEMI model (Work–Expression–Manifestation–Item) has been particularly influential as a framework for Resource Description and Access (RDA). FRBR has been replaced by the IFLA Library Reference Model (LRM).

Functional Requirements for Subject Authority Data (FRSAD): A conceptual model for subject authority data developed by the IFLA and published in 2010. It showed important entities in subject authority records, with corresponding attributes and relationships, and tied them to user tasks. It has been replaced by the IFLA Library Reference Model (LRM).

Genre Heading: *See* Genre Term.

Genre Term: In subject analysis, genre terms are added to describe the form or category of literary works, music, film and television, and so on. Genre terms describe what an item *is* (e.g., dictionary, biography, fiction, drama), not what an item is *about* (the subject).

Geographic Subdivision: In subject headings lists, such as the Library of Congress Subject Headings, a geographic subdivision is sometimes added to describe the geographic area of the item being cataloged. Example: Restaurants—Texas.

Global Update: In cataloging processing and maintenance, global updates are used to make changes to all bibliographic or authority records at one time; a giant find-and-replace process.

Half Title Page: A page at the front of a book that lists the title, but usually no statement of responsibility or publication information. It is usually ignored in library cataloging in favor of the title page.

Heading: An authorized access point on a bibliographic or authority record.

IFLA Library Reference Model (LRM): A conceptual model of bibliographic data developed by the IFLA that consolidates three models: FRBR, FRAD, and FRSAD. It keeps the WEMI entities but includes a new model of bibliographic relationships.

Index: An alphabetical list of words used to provide access to something. An index can provide access to one item (e.g., a back-of-the-book index) or multiple items (e.g., an index to a serial title, discipline, subject, etc.). A computerized index is used in online library catalogs to allow users to search for specific titles, subjects, or names.

Indexing: Usually refers to the process of providing subject access to an item, such as creating a back-of-the-book index or adding subject headings to library bibliographic records. Can also be used in a broad sense to mean cataloging library materials.

International Federation of Library Associations and Institutions (IFLA): The international organization that represents libraries and librarianship around the world. IFLA is responsible for many cataloging and metadata models, standards, and guidelines.

International Standard Bibliographic Description (ISBD): A sort of cataloging standard for cataloging standards, ISBD is an international descriptive cataloging standard developed by the IFLA that directs how library materials should be described. It has been incorporated into descriptive cataloging standards around the world.

International Standard Bibliographic Number (ISBN): A 10- or 13-digit number assigned to books and other nonserial items. Not all items are assigned an ISBN.

International Standard Name Identifier (ISNI): A 16-digit number used to identify people, groups, and organizations responsible for creative works.

International Standard Serial Number (ISSN): An 8-digit number assigned to serial publications. Not all serial publications are assigned an ISSN number.

Keyword: A natural-language word or phrase used to search for information through the use of a computer.

Keyword Searching: A type of search in which people use their own natural-language words and phrases to search for information through the use of a computer. Considered an uncontrolled vocabulary.

LC: *See* Library of Congress.

LCC: *See* Library of Congress Classification.

LCCN: *See* Library of Congress Control Number.

LCSH: *See* Library of Congress Subject Headings.

Library Catalog: A database that contains representations of the contents of a library's collection. Can contain cards in a card catalog or bibliographic records in an online public access catalog.

Library of Congress (LC): The de facto national library of the United States. It is considered the authority for cataloging in the United States, and maintains and develops cataloging and metadata standards and policy.

Library of Congress Card Number (LCCN): *See* Library of Congress Control Number.

Library of Congress Classification (LCC): An alphanumeric classification scheme developed by the Library of Congress to represent subjects in academic and research libraries.

Library of Congress Control Number (LCCN): A set of numbers assigned to a book in the Library of Congress's collection. Previously called Library of Congress Card Number.

Library of Congress National Authority File: Contains authority records for authorized names, titles, and subjects used on bibliographic records.

Library of Congress Subject Headings (LCSH): A controlled vocabulary developed by the Library of Congress. It is a subject headings list used on bibliographic records in all types of libraries to represent subjects, concepts, groups of people, etc.

Library Reference Model (LRM): *See* IFLA Library Reference Model (LRM).

Linked Open Data: A part of the Semantic Web movement to help computers understand the meaning of information. Some libraries are performing linked data projects to make library data available openly on the web.

Literary Warrant: In subject analysis, literary warrant means that subject headings and classification numbers are created for a subject headings list or classification scheme only after something has been published on a subject and the subject heading/classification number is needed for cataloging purposes.

LRM: *See* IFLA Library Reference Model.

Machine-Readable Cataloging (MARC): MARC is an encoding standard that allows a computer to read bibliographic and authority information. The current version is MARC 21.

MADS: *See* Metadata Authority Description Schema.

Main Entry: Phrase used in the old AACR2 cataloging rules that referred to the primary access point on a bibliographic record.

MARC: *See* Machine-Readable Cataloging.

Medical Subject Headings (MeSH): A specialized controlled vocabulary developed by the National Library of Medicine. It is a subject headings list used by medical libraries and the PubMed database to represent subjects and concepts used in the biomedical sciences.

Metadata: Literally, data about data. Metadata is at the heart of information organization and is used to describe and provide access to materials available through libraries. Metadata is located on bibliographic records in a library's catalog and metadata records in digital collections and other databases. There are three broad types: administrative metadata, descriptive metadata, and structural metadata.

Metadata, Administrative: *See* Administrative Metadata.

Metadata Authority Description Schema (MADS): An XML metadata schema used to describe authority data in digital collections.

Metadata, Descriptive: *See* Descriptive Metadata.

Metadata Object Description Schema (MODS): An XML metadata schema used to describe bibliographic data in digital collections.

Metadata, Structural: *See* Structural Metadata.

Metadata Work: Usually refers to work done to provide access to digital collections, including digitization and the creation of metadata records using metadata schemas.

MODS: *See* Metadata Object Description Schema.

Monograph: A type of publication that, according to Resource Description and Access, is "A resource that is complete in one part" (e.g., a book, a map, a DVD) "or intended to be complete in a finite number of parts" (e.g., an encyclopedia, a multivolume title).

Monographic Bibliographic Record Cooperative Program (BIBCO): A program within the Program for Cooperative Cataloging (PCC) in which participants create bibliographic records for monographs following the BIBCO Standard Record model.

Name Authority Cooperative Program (NACO): Program within the Program for Cooperative Cataloging (PCC) in which participants contribute names, preferred titles, and series titles to the Library of Congress National Authority File.

National Authority File: *See* Library of Congress National Authority File.

National Library of Medicine (NLM) Classification: A specialized classification scheme developed by the National Library of Medicine that represents medical subjects.

OCLC: A cooperative library organization that provides multiple products and services to libraries that are members.

OCLC Connexion: A bibliographic utility from OCLC that includes more than 400 million bibliographic records from libraries around the world. OCLC Connexion is used for library cataloging; WorldCat is the public side. OCLC Connexion eventually may be replaced by OCLC WorldShare Record Manager.

Online Public Access Catalog (OPAC): Contains bibliographic records that represent the contents of a library's collection. It is the public side of a library catalog that is searched by library users. *See also* Library Catalog.

OPAC: *See* Online Public Access Catalog.

PCC: *See* Program for Cooperative Cataloging.

Program for Cooperative Cataloging (PCC): An organization coordinated by the Library of Congress made up of four cooperative cataloging programs (BIBCO, CONSER, NACO, SACO) in which participants create policies, create bibliographic and authority records, and perform other work in specific areas of cataloging (monographic bibliographic records, serials, name authorities, and subject authorities).

Provider-Neutral Record: A bibliographic record used to catalog electronic materials (e.g., e-books, e-serials) provided by different vendors.

RDA: *See* Resource Description and Access (RDA).

RDF: *See* Resource Description Framework (RDF).

Relationship Designator: A term or phrase used in cataloging to describe the relationship between entities on a bibliographic record, such as a person to a work. They are added after name and title access points. Examples from Resource Description and Access (RDA) include author, illustrator, artist, composer, writer of introduction, based on (work), and adaptation of (work).

Representation: A fundamental concept in information organization. To help users search a collection, catalogers and metadata specialists create bibliographic and metadata records that represent library collections.

Resource Description and Access (RDA): The current set of descriptive cataloging instructions that guide catalogers in creating bibliographic records. Includes instructions for description and name and title access points only. It does not include instructions for subject analysis or creating access points for subject headings. RDA replaced the Anglo-American Cataloguing Rules, Second Edition (AACR2).

Resource Description Framework (RDF): A model used to link data. "Things" are described in triples (a subject, a predicate, and an object) to form statements.

SACO: *See* Subject Authority Cooperative Program.

Sears List of Subject Headings: A subject headings list that includes broad subject headings for use in a more general library collection. Coordinates well with the Dewey Decimal Classification. Used in some public and school libraries.

Semantic Web: An initiative of the World Wide Web Consortium (W3C) to help computers understand the meaning of information.

Serial: A type of publication that, according to Resource Description and Access, is "issued in successive parts, usually bearing numbering, that has no predetermined conclusion." Examples include journals, magazines, newspapers, and yearbooks.

Series: A set of publications (e.g., books) that are related through a collective title for the set. Series can be numbered or unnumbered, and can originate with authors, organizations, or publishers.

Specificity: In subject analysis, specificity refers to how exact catalogers should be when assigning subject headings. Usually, catalogers are directed to be as specific as possible. For example, a book about roses should be assigned the subject heading "Roses," not "Flowers."

Structural Metadata: Metadata that is concerned with the structural components of digital resources and how files fit together.

Subdivision: In subject headings lists, a subdivision is used to break down a subject heading into more specific detail. Subdivisions can show a particular aspect of a main subject heading, such as topic, geographic area, chronology, or form.

Subfield: In the MARC format, a field is broken down into specific subfields that encode specific aspects of a bibliographic record. For example, the 245 field (title statement) is broken down into several subfields, including subfield a (title), subfield b (remainder of title), and subfield c (statement of responsibility).

Subject Analysis: The process of providing subject access to library materials to explain what they are about. Subject analysis can include assigning subject headings, genre terms, thesaurus terms, classification numbers, etc.

Subject Authority Cooperative Program (SACO): Program within the Program for Cooperative Cataloging (PCC) in which participants submit proposals for Library of Congress controlled vocabularies and classification schemes.

Subject Headings List: A controlled vocabulary that contains subject headings to be used when providing subject access to library materials.

SuDocs: *See* Superintendent of Documents Classification (SuDocs).

Superintendent of Documents Classification (SuDocs): A classification scheme based on agencies in the United States government. Used primarily by libraries that receive United States government documents through the Federal Depository Library Program (FDLP).

Table: In some classification schemes, a table is used to build classification numbers. It usually adds specificity to a classification number, for example, when an item deals with a specific aspect of a topic, time period, geographic area, or form.

Tag: A word or phrase assigned by anyone to describe items online, such as in library catalogs, databases, social media sites, websites, etc.

Tagging: The process of adding natural-language words and phrases to describe items online. Some discovery products provide a tagging feature for library catalogs.

Thesaurus: A controlled vocabulary with a list of authorized words and phrases, called descriptors, used for indexing a specialized subject area or collection. Used in some research databases and library catalogs.

Title Page: A page at the front of a book that lists the title, statement of responsibility, publisher, and sometimes date of publication. It is the preferred source of information used when creating library bibliographic records.

Title Page Verso: The back side of the title page. Usually includes technical information about the book, such as publisher's information, book credits, Cataloging in Publication information, etc.

Topical Subdivision: In subject headings lists, such as the Library of Congress Subject Headings, a topical subdivision is added after a main subject heading to bring out a specific aspect of the subject heading. Example: Dogs—Selection.

Uncontrolled Vocabulary: A natural-language vocabulary that is not controlled by indexers or catalogers. People use their own natural language to search for information or to tag items. Includes keyword searching and tagging.

Uniform Resource Identifier (URI): Part of linked data used to identity a thing.

Uniform Resource Locator (URL): A set of characters used to identify a web address.

URI: *See* Uniform Resource Identifier.

URL: *See* Uniform Resource Locator.

Variable Fields: These are the fields in the MARC encoding standard with no predetermined character limit. Catalogers can add as much bibliographic information as needed.

Vendor: An organization that performs mostly paid services for libraries. Vendors are contracted for various work in libraries such as acquisitions, cataloging, marking, binding, providing an integrated library system, etc.

WEMI Model: WEMI stands for Work–Expression–Manifestation–Item. It is a model from Functional Requirements for Bibliographic Records (FRBR) that shows the relationships between the intellectual and artistic products primarily collected by libraries. It is used as a framework for Resource Description and Access (RDA).

WorldCat: A bibliographic utility operated by OCLC that includes more than 400 million bibliographic records from libraries around the world. WorldCat is the public side that users can search; OCLC Connexion is used for library cataloging.

XML: *See* Extensible Markup Language.

Z39.50: The international standard (ISO 23950) for searching and retrieving on databases. In library cataloging, a library can use Z39.50 to obtain bibliographic records from another library's online catalog.

Index

Page references for figures are italicized.

and Redesign, 82; characteristics, 82–83; elements, 83–85; entities, Revised RDA, 92–93; history, 33, 81–82; implementation, 82; mode of issuance, 248; models, 87–93; principles, 86–87; RDA Steering Committee, 81, 224
Resource Description Framework (RDF). *See* linked open data
retrieval, 48–49
Rules for a Dictionary Catalog. *See* Cutter, Charles

SACO. *See* Subject Authority Cooperative Program
Schema.org. *See* linked open data
school libraries, 287–*93*; bookstore model, 149–51, 208–10, 212; cataloging process, 290–91; children's collections, 211–13; collections, 288–89; fiction, 207–8; genres, 208, 212; issues, 291–293; organization, 289–290. *See also* Metis Library Classification for Children
Sears List of Subject Headings, 142–44; advantages and disadvantages, 144; cross-references, 143–44; examples, *143*; history, 28, 142; structure, 142–44; subdivisions, 143
Sears, Minnie Earl, 142
Semantic Web, 34, 328
serials, 248, 250–*51*, 256–57; cataloging, *252*–53; electronic, 258–60; print, 257–58. *See also* databases
SGML (Standard Generalized Markup Language), 61
shared cataloging, 26, 30–31, 56, 243, 266–67, 311
social tagging. *See* tagging
Soergel, Dagobert, 111
special collections. *See* library collections
special libraries, 293–*97*; cataloging and metadata process, 295–96; collections, 294; gray literature, 294, 296; issues, 296–97; organization, 294–95
specific entry. *See* specificity
specificity, 25, 109, 120, 176, 186, 190;

Standard Generalized Markup Language. *See* SGML
standardization, 221–22, 311–12
standards and policy development, 221–37; international level, 223–27; local level, 235–37; national level, 227–34; state and regional level, 234–35
state and regional library associations, 235
state classification schemes, 205
Statement of International Cataloguing Principles: general principles, 86–87, 221, 308, 310; history, 29, 33; objectives and functions of the catalogue, 13–14, 107, 162
structural metadata, 48
subject access points. *See* access points
subject analysis, 107–13; determining subjects, 108–11; history, 25–33; images and objects, 112–13; language use, 111–12; subjectivity, 108, 110–13, 119–20, 163, 169, 301–2
subject and format communities, 232–33
Subject Authority Cooperative Program (SACO), 129, 182, 284, 230, 247
subject cataloging. *See* subject analysis
subject headings, 114–16; history, 26–27, 29–30, 33. *See also* controlled vocabularies; Library of Congress Subject Headings (LCSH); Medical Subject Headings (MeSH); Sears List of Subject Headings
Superintendent of Documents Classification (SuDocs), 197–204, 263; advantages and disadvantages, 204; call numbers, 202–3; classes, 198–99; examples, 200, *201*, 202, *203*; history, 28, 197–98; structure, 198–202
Svenonius, Elaine, 70, 118, 312
system of standards development, 222–23

tagging, 125–28
Taube, Mortimer, 28, 123
Technical Metadata for Text (TextMD), 54
technical services, 18–19
TEI Guidelines for Electronic Text Encoding and Interchange, 65

About the Author

Gretchen L. Hoffman is an associate professor of library and information studies at Texas Woman's University, in Denton, Texas. Her research and teaching interests center on the organization of information, specifically library cataloging. She focuses on issues surrounding the work of catalogers, the cataloging process, and the administration of cataloging departments, with the broader goal of understanding how work is performed in libraries. She also is interested in the teaching and learning of cataloging. She has published several articles and book chapters and has given numerous presentations in these areas.

Hoffman has had an interest in organizing library collections since 1992, when she was a student worker at her undergraduate university's library, focusing on serials check-in and binding. She continued to work in academic libraries in paraprofessional positions in serials acquisitions and serials cataloging, eventually working as a professional cataloger in both serials and monographs. She especially enjoyed cataloging serials, music scores, and audio recordings. She enjoyed organizing library collections so much that she earned her PhD and started teaching students how to organize library collections. She wants students to understand that organizing library collections is essential to helping users find and use library materials, and that although the work is challenging, it can be a lot of fun, too. She has been teaching in this area since 2004, and has taught fully online courses at Texas Woman's University since 2007.

Hoffman earned a PhD in library and information science from Emporia State University in 2008, a master of library science from Emporia State University in 2000, and a bachelor of arts in music from the University of Nevada, Reno, in 1995. She has won several awards for her teaching. In 2011 she was given the Outstanding Faculty Award for Teacher in Distance Education from TWU's College of Professional Education, and in 2013 she was awarded the TWU Faculty Award for Distinction in Distance Education. In 2018 she was given the Award for Outstanding Academic Mentor/Advisor from TWU's College of Professional Education.

A native of northwestern Minnesota living in Texas, she loves the Texas winters but misses the Minnesota summers.

Milton Keynes UK
Ingram Content Group UK Ltd.
UKHW021856310524
443562UK00002B/2